MAY   2016

Global Rogues and Regional Orders

GLOBAL ROGUES
AND REGIONAL ORDERS

The Multidimensional Challenge
of North Korea and Iran

Il Hyun Cho

6912500296097

OXFORD
UNIVERSITY PRESS

OXFORD
UNIVERSITY PRESS

Oxford University Press is a department of the University of Oxford.
It furthers the University's objective of excellence in research, scholarship,
and education by publishing worldwide.

Oxford   New York
Auckland   Cape Town   Dar es Salaam   Hong Kong   Karachi
Kuala Lumpur   Madrid   Melbourne   Mexico City   Nairobi
New Delhi   Shanghai   Taipei   Toronto

With offices in
Argentina   Austria   Brazil   Chile   Czech Republic   France   Greece
Guatemala   Hungary   Italy   Japan   Poland   Portugal   Singapore
South Korea   Switzerland   Thailand   Turkey   Ukraine   Vietnam

Oxford is a registered trade mark of Oxford University Press
in the UK and certain other countries.

Published in the United States of America by
Oxford University Press
198 Madison Avenue, New York, NY 10016

Library of Congress Cataloging-in-Publication Data
Cho, Il Hyun, author.
 Global rogues and regional orders : the multidimensional challenge of North
Korea and Iran / Il Hyun Cho.
    p.   cm.
 Includes bibliographical references and index.
 ISBN 978–0–19–935547–1 (hardback : acid-free paper)
1. Nuclear nonproliferation—Korea (North) 2. Nuclear nonproliferation—Iran.
3. Nuclear nonproliferation—Middle East. 4. Nuclear nonproliferation—East
Asia. 5. Regionalism. 6. Security, International. 7. United States—Foreign
relations—East Asia. 8. United States—Foreign relations—Middle East. I. Title.
 JZ5675.C455 2015
 327.1'747095193—dc23
                               2015016972

9   8   7   6   5   4   3   2   1

Printed in the United States of America on acid-free paper

CONTENTS

ACKNOWLEDGMENTS

One of the key messages that I wanted to convey in this book is that political actors perceive a seemingly common problem in starkly different ways. In the process of envisioning, conducting, and writing this research, I have benefited enormously from many individuals. Like many political actors discussed in this book, they were often drawn to vastly different aspects of the project. Unlike the diverse and competing political actors examined in this book, however, the people that I have met were invariably helpful. It is their guidance, criticism, and encouragement that helped me navigate the bewildering and at times seemingly never-ending process of completing this book.

This project began as a doctoral dissertation written at Cornell University, where I had the privilege of having Peter Katzenstein as my dissertation supervisor. Peter's scholarly achievements and commitment to students are legendary in the field of International Relations. However, I am still in awe of his uncanny ability to offer the perfect mix of prodding and encouragement, always at the right time. Peter has deeply shaped my thinking on global and regional dynamics and my scholarly endeavors more generally. Even after my Ph.D. studies, Peter has continued to inspire me as scholar and co-author. I will strive to pay back to my students what I learned from him.

Matthew Evangelista was also inspirational in many ways and offered tremendous help with his careful reading of and extensive suggestions on numerous drafts of the dissertation. Matt's insightful comments on domestic politics in particular were crucial to sharpening the book's argument. I am also grateful to Jae-Jung Suh who provided penetrating feedback on numerous occasions, including several times from the other side of the world during his own research trips to Asia. My thanks also go to Allen Carlson who not only offered useful advice on my field research in China but also provided invaluable comments on multiple versions of the dissertation.

Apart from my dissertation committee members, I am grateful to Jonathan Kirshner, Chris Way, Valerie Bunce, Richard Bensel, and Elizabeth Sanders for their advice and encouragement for this project. Prior to my study at Cornell, it was Professor Jung-Hoon Lee, my advisor at the Graduate School of International Studies at Yonsei University in Seoul, who introduced me to the study of International Relations and encouraged me to pursue doctoral studies. I owe a great deal of appreciation to him for sparking my interest in international politics and profoundly shaping my career plans. At Yonsei, Professors Jongryn Mo and Chung Min Lee also provided helpful and timely guidance for which I am deeply grateful.

I wish to acknowledge with gratitude financial support for my research from the following institutions: Cornell University's Graduate School, Mario Einaudi Center for International Studies, Peace Studies Program, the Department of Government, and Harvard University's Belfer Center for Science and International Affairs (BCSIA). The Institute of Social Sciences at the University of Tokyo and the Department of Political Science at Stanford University facilitated my research and writing by granting me visiting and exchange scholar status. I thank in particular Kenji Hirashima of the University of Tokyo and Stephen Krasner, Gi-Wook Shin, and Jessica Weeks of Stanford University. Some of the early findings were presented at various conferences, including the annual meetings of the American Political Science Association and the International Studies Association. I also presented portions of my research at the International Security Program seminar and the Managing the Atom Project seminar at the Belfer Center, where I received helpful feedback from Steven Miller, Sean Lynn-Jones, Richard Rosecrance, Matt Bunn, Jeffrey Lewis, and other participants.

Although I began drafting the book manuscript at Cleveland State University, I have completed most of the revisions for the book at Lafayette College. I would like to thank my former colleagues in the Department of Political Science at Cleveland State, especially Dave Elkins, Rodger Govea, Chuck Hersch, and Jeff Lewis. I am also grateful to my current colleagues in the Government and Law Department and the Asian Studies Program at Lafayette, in particular Paul Barclay, Michael Feola, Ingrid Furniss, Josh Miller, Bruce Murphy, Ilan Peleg, Robin Rinehart, Helena Silverstein, and David Stifel, for their support and encouragement. I would like to thank the Academic Research Committee at Lafayette for providing financial support for indexing. Melanie Furey provided helpful research assistance for the chapter on Iran.

Beyond my home institutions, I owe a great deal of debt to many individuals and institutions. For this research I conducted numerous interviews with government officials and regional experts at various governmental, semi-governmental, and other research institutions in China, Japan, and South Korea. I am grateful for their generous time and candid views. I had many helping hands during my yearlong field research in East Asia. The research for this book would have not been possible without their timely support and guidance. I am particularly grateful to Professor Gong Shaopeng of the Chinese Foreign Affairs University and Professor Tang Shiping of the Chinese Academy of Social Sciences and now at Fudan University. In South Korea, I would like to thank Professors Jung-Hoon Lee and Sukhee Han of Yonsei University, Professor Taeho Kim of Hallym University, Professor Jaewoo Choo of Kyunghee University, and Professor Young Nam Cho of Seoul National University. In Japan, Professor Norihito Kubota of the National Defense Academy and Professors Kenji Hirashima and Gregory Noble of the Institute of Social Sciences at the University of Tokyo were particularly helpful.

For their friendship and moral support, I thank colleagues and friends at Cornell and other institutions: Minhyo Bae, Tom Bielefeld, Munchul Cho, Wooyoung Cho, Hong Duan, Jennifer Erickson, Dev Gupta, Stephanie Hofmann, Hyeran Jo, Jai Kwan Jung, Hyunwook Kim, Junga Kim, You-jin Kim, Tomas Larsson, Gun Lee, Col. Jong Bong Lee, Jay Lyall, Barak Mendelsohn, Jae Jeok Park, Margarita Petrova, Andrew Phillips, Lisa Sansoucy, Scott Siegel, Moeun Sung, Yuriko Takahashi, Israel Waismel-Manor, Steve Watts, Jessica Weeks, Hyunsik Woo, Andrew Yeo, Rong Yu, and Maria Zaitseva.

Special thanks go to Angela Chnapko and her team at Oxford University Press. As a first time author, I was very fortunate to have Angela as my editor, who patiently and skillfully shepherded this project into publication. I would also like to thank Princess Ikatekit, B. Gogulanathan, and Susie Hara for their timely and valuable help in the copyediting and production process. I am deeply grateful to two anonymous reviewers for Oxford University Press, who provided insightful and detailed sets of comments that helped me sharpen this book's central argument and empirical analysis. Needless to say, I am solely responsible for any errors that remain in the book.

My parents, Gyu Yeol Cho and Seok Rye Kim, and parents-in-law, Myung Soo Park and Young Ju Kim, have been enormously supportive throughout my doctoral studies, and they deserve special thanks. They not only provided comfortable places to stay during my field trips in Seoul, their homes also served as invaluable research base camps from which I made subsequent research trips to and from Beijing and Tokyo. Furthermore, they made several visits to the other side of the world to provide care for my infant daughter and son in times of need. For that and more, I am eternally grateful to them. I also wish to thank my sisters, Mi Young and Mi Kyoung, and siblings-in-law, Seo-Jin and Chang-Seo, for their support and smiles.

More than anyone else, Seo-Hyun Park knows what the completion of this book means to me. But she has no idea how much I admire her as a scholar, a parent, and a person. Her intellect, love, and support have sustained me throughout the long and arduous process of completing this book. We have also shared great memories during our peripatetic journey through various places in East Asia and the United States. The best we share, of course, is our children, Emily Yuna and Jason Youngwu. Our deepest sources of joy and pride, they have grown up so much while I was working on this book and have now become avid readers themselves. I hope they keep turning the page for more great stories. I dedicate this book to Emily and Jason and their incredible mom and my irreplaceable companion in life, both academic and otherwise, Seo-Hyun.

Global Rogues and Regional Orders

CHAPTER 1

Nuclear Proliferation and Regional Order

A Framework for Analysis

1.1 INTRODUCTION

The 2010 *U.S. National Security Strategy* singled out nuclear proliferation as one of the gravest threats confronting the United States.[1] In the past decade, no other proliferation challenges have garnered more global attention than the nuclear ambitions of North Korea and Iran, two international pariahs accused of accumulating or seeking nuclear weapons. These "archetypal rogue states" not only violated numerous global nonproliferation rules and UN Security Council resolutions but also engaged in a series of provocative actions, including nuclear or ballistic missile tests. The conventional view about the decade-long nuclear conundrum is thus premised on the presence of what is believed to be the uniquely dangerous and defiant nature of the communist regime in Pyongyang and the clerical regime in Tehran. This is why coercive measures, such as "crippling" sanctions or preemptive strikes, are often deemed to be the most effective solution to the current stalemate over the two global proliferation challenges.

This book contends that this "global" narrative, which is widespread in the United States and other regions of the world, is fundamentally misguided. It tends to downplay the views of North Korea's and Iran's regional neighbors, and, in its fixation on the nuclear question, neglects larger—and arguably more important—regional dynamics surrounding the two states. Contrary to the seemingly unified global concern about the problem of nuclear proliferation, regional perceptions of North Korea and Iran reveal a far more complex picture. For instance, various regional actors have blamed U.S. policy toward North Korea as the main problem, while often challenging the U.S. position even at the risk of jeopardizing strategic ties with the United States. In various regional surveys, Arab respondents in the Middle East, including some of U.S. allies such as Egypt and Jordan, selected Israel and the United States as the greatest threats to their security, while only a fraction cited Iran. In fact, no Persian Gulf state has engaged in civil defense planning in anticipation of an Iranian strike.[2]

What shapes the perceptions and policies of regional actors in the face of the North Korean and Iranian nuclear challenges? Why do some regional actors cooperate with the United States in nuclear diplomacy, while others do not? What are the consequences of such varying responses for regional order and global security? These questions have yet to be addressed in a comprehensive manner in the literatures on nuclear proliferation and regional security. Lacking in the current scholarly debate on proliferation in general and the North Korean and Iranian crises in particular is a realization that global efforts to address the two nuclear challenges have coincided with a shift in the political landscape in the two regions. In the Middle East, the collapse of Iran's two enemies, Saddam Hussein in Iraq and the Taliban in Afghanistan, has led to Tehran's growing regional influence. In East Asia as well, a rising China raises questions about the future of the U.S.-led regional order, prompting the Asia "pivot" strategy of the Obama administration.[3]

This suggests that prior to seeking solutions to each of the nuclear crises, we need to locate these nuclear challenges in specific regional contexts and empirically examine the sources and consequences of the regional understandings of the nuclear proliferation challenge.[4] In this vein, Joseph Cirincione called for greater attention to regional security situations that are often a main driver behind nuclear proliferation.[5] In fact, the origin of Iran's nuclear pursuit was due in large part to considerations of regional order in the Middle East in the 1970s. During the Shah's rule, then U.S. Secretary of State Henry Kissinger pushed for substantial arms sales to Iran and helped Iran launch its own nuclear weapons program. These efforts were made in consideration of Iran's regional strategic role vis-à-vis the Soviet Union.[6] Similarly, North Korea's nuclear pursuit intensified in the early 1990s when the regional strategic landscape surrounding the Korean Peninsula was transformed in the wake of Russia's and China's diplomatic normalization with South Korea.

However, the plea for exploring the regional underpinnings of nuclear crises has not been systematically taken up by the vast literatures on the

North Korean and Iranian nuclear challenges.[7] Instead, analysts have focused almost solely on the question of how best to solve the nuclear situations in North Korea and Iran, with little discussion on how regional countries themselves understand, and grapple with, the North Korean and Iranian challenges. This analytical oversight in turn has complicated both the resolution of nuclear crises and the stable maintenance of regional order in East Asia and the Middle East.

To remedy this analytical shortcoming common in the proliferation and regional security literatures, this book poses two questions: (1) What are the sources of regional understandings of the North Korean and Iranian challenges? and (2) What are the regional consequences of such understandings with respect to alliance politics and regionalism in East Asia and the Middle East? In addressing these questions, this book aims to unpack the interplay between the U.S.-led global nuclear proliferation approach and regional orders surrounding North Korea and Iran. It seeks to provide context and meaning to the seemingly clear-cut global problems as the two countries interact with the domestic politics of regional countries and affect the regional order in East Asia and the Middle East, respectively, in unexpected ways.

1.2 ARGUMENT IN BRIEF

This book contends that the regional role conceptions of North Korea's and Iran's neighbors—the pursuit of new regional roles and status in the changing regional and global environments—shape regional actors' threat perceptions and policy preferences vis-à-vis North Korea and Iran, which in turn affects alliance relations and regionalism in East Asia and the Middle East. Despite the U.S. frame of North Korea and Iran primarily as the global nuclear menace, the two countries present a dual challenge as newly nuclear or nuclear-seeking global rogue states and, at the same time, traditional regional security issues. At the global level, the two countries are the remaining members of what President George W. Bush called the "axis of evil," a band of global rogues bent on disrupting the international nonproliferation regime. Hence, Bush officials contended that the two countries represented one of the two major security challenges against which a widespread global campaign should be pursued.[8]

In East Asia and the Middle East, however, the global rogue frame did not take root. This is because the global narrative is fundamentally at odds with the regional debate centered on multiple understandings of what North Korea and Iran respectively mean for the regional order. Despite North Korea's and Iran's nuclear provocations and latent threats to regional stability, their geostrategic location and importance in each region and their potential to boost the regional roles of their neighbors have been central to the regional narratives about North Korea and Iran. Both civilizational and contemporary political differences notwithstanding, countries in East Asia and the Middle East also share dissatisfaction with the current regional order premised on the dominance of an external superpower, the United States, even after the Cold War's demise. In their efforts to gain greater regional status and foreign policy autonomy in the shifting post–Cold War context, East Asian and Middle Eastern states have been seeking new regional roles.

The regional countries' drive to enhance regional roles in turn led them to recast previous—often precarious—relations with North Korea and Iran. In this context, North Korea and Iran are hardly an unambiguous security threat as depicted at the global level and in the proliferation literature but instead are key moving parts of the shifting regional order, and the nature of their threats is regionally contested.[9] As a result, while some regional actors, such as Israel and Saudi Arabia in the Middle East and conservatives in Japan and South Korea in East Asia, side with the United States, others seek to challenge, or dissociate from, the U.S. position as a means to enhance their countries' regional status and foreign policy autonomy. Such political contestation over North Korea and Iran in turn shapes the regional order by influencing alliance politics and regional cooperation in East Asia and the Middle East.

This distinctive regional pattern is evidenced in contrasting regional responses to what appear to be similar North Korean problems in the past two decades. Although North Korea sparked two nuclear crises, the first in the early 1990s and the second since 2002, regional reactions to the crises are a study in contrast. The first nuclear standoff between North Korea and the United States began in 1993 when North Korea started processing at the Yongbyon nuclear reactor and threatened to withdraw from the Nuclear Nonproliferation Treaty (NPT). The first post–Cold War nuclear crisis, however, was resolved in less than two years in October 1994, when North Korea and the United States signed the Agreed Framework in which North Korea promised to dismantle the Yongbyon reactor in return for a number of U.S. concessions, including provision of heavy-fuel oil and construction of two weapon-resistant light water reactors. During this period, regional countries, including Japan and South Korea, not only supported the bilateral agreement but also provided funding for the construction of the light water reactors pledged by the United States.

Less than a decade after the first crisis, North Korea triggered another nuclear standoff with the United States, or what Michael McDevitt called "an instant replay" of the first crisis, involving similar provocative steps.[10] In response, the Bush administration launched a systematic campaign aimed at pressuring the Kim Jong Il regime through the Six Party process.[11] As documented in this book, however, regional support was conspicuous by its absence this time around. Despite heightened tension arising from North Korea's repeat performance, most regional actors did not share the threat perception of the United States. Instead, East Asian countries were united in their opposition to the Bush administration's efforts to "globalize" the North Korean problem.

Given America's status in East Asia as a de facto hegemon since the end of World War II and the widespread regional support for the United States during the first crisis, the regional resistance to the U.S. approach during the second crisis is particularly puzzling and not fully explained by existing accounts informed by power and material interest considerations. While keeping diplomatic channels open with North Korea, each East Asian country pressed the Bush administration to discard its coercive approach.[12] Regional reactions in the early rounds of the Six Party Talks underscored the breadth of challenge to America's policy on North Korea and regional influence.

After the first Six Party meeting in August 2003, for instance, China's chief delegate Wang Yi declared, "America's policy toward the D.P.R.K., that is the main problem we are facing."[13] South Korean President Roh Moo-hyun also warned that "taking too tough a stance against North Korea could cause friction and disagreement between South Korea and the United States."[14] Despite his close friendship with President Bush, Japanese Prime Minister Koizumi Junichiro also urged Bush to have direct talks with North Korea: "[U]nless you open the negotiation process, there will be no improvement on the issues."[15] The region's collective resistance to the hardline U.S. approach and North Korea's nuclear test eventually led to the February 2007 agreement between the United States and North Korea. In an apparent about-face, the Bush administration discarded its previous position of "comprehensive, verifiable and irreversible dismantling" (CVID) of North Korean nuclear programs and showed greater flexibility toward North Korea.[16]

The regional response had implications for the regional order as well. Following successful resolution by the Clinton administration, the first North Korean nuclear crisis was a catalyst for the renewal and strengthening of U.S. alliances in the region, manifested in the so-called Nye Initiative in 1995 to maintain U.S. force levels in East Asia and the 1997 agreement on a revision of the U.S.-Japan Defense Cooperation Guidelines. Along the way, the U.S. regional influence increased substantially, enabling its crucial role in the Taiwan Strait Crisis of 1995–1996 and the North Korean missile crisis in 1998. During the second North Korean nuclear crisis, however, alliance management and regionalism have faced increasing difficulties, while the U.S. regional role has been in question and its regional influence in decline.[17]

In the Middle East as well, the Iranian challenge has sparked domestic and regional debates, significantly affecting regional dynamics. Israel's depiction of Iran as an "existential threat" has been a key rationale for its aggressive approach, including its repeated calls for a preemptive strike on Iran's nuclear sites.[18] Saudi Arabia and Bahrain also highlighted the specter of Iran's regional ascendancy and suspected ties between Iran and Shia dissidents in their own countries. On the other hand, Turkey and most Gulf states, which are all U.S. allies in the region, expressed little concern about Iran's nuclear pursuit and called for a moderate approach toward Iran. For instance, Oman maintained "balanced relations with Iran and continued to advocate the re-integration of Tehran into both the Gulf and the international community."[19] As a result, alliance relations with the United States became strained and regional relations splintered.

More broadly, the overarching narrative emerging in the two regions suggests that the nuclear question itself is not even the main focus of regional debates. In fact, the regional discourse centers instead on the evolving regional order in East Asia and the Middle East, as well as changing relations with the United States. Hence, examining the relationship between nuclear proliferation and regional order in the two strategically important regions, as this book seeks to do, has the potential to yield valuable lessons for both nuclear diplomacy and regional security. As the North Korean and Iranian nuclear crises have passed the ten-year mark, the time is ripe for a systematic reexamination of both regions. By turning the focus onto regional actors and the regional dimension of nuclear proliferation, this book offers a novel way to analyze global proliferation challenges and provides new insights into the making of regional orders in East Asia and the Middle East.

1.3 EXISTING LITERATURES ON PROLIFERATION AND REGIONAL SECURITY

Global nuclear proliferation and regional orders in East Asia and the Middle East are among the most crucial topics in world politics in the twenty-first century. However, few existing works in both proliferation studies and the vast literatures on East Asian and Middle Eastern security systematically explore the link between them.[20] Students of proliferation have focused on the causes and consequences of nuclear proliferation, examining the motivations of nuclear aspirants and their global and regional effects.[21] Largely absent in this debate is an empirical analysis of how nuclear proliferation is actually perceived and responded to by local actors and with what regional consequences. Studies of regional order in East Asia and the Middle East pay greater attention to local dynamics surrounding North Korea and Iran but tend to neglect the complex interplay between U.S.-led global proliferation efforts and regional approaches that has evolved in the past decade. By examining the relationship between nuclear proliferation and regional order, this book draws on and challenges existing analyses in both the proliferation and regional security literatures.

Realist scholars highlight the importance of strategic interests in responding to proliferation challenges. For instance, Matthew Kroenig offers a valuable analytical framework for understanding varied responses to proliferation.[22] With respect to the North Korean and Iranian challenges, he argues that different strategic implications of nuclear proliferation for a global superpower, the United States, and smaller regional states may explain varied global and regional responses.[23] While helpful in understanding different strategic payoffs behind nuclear proliferation, his book lacks empirically grounded, regionally specific analyses of North Korea and Iran.[24] The assumption of objective strategic logics held by local actors also ignores the subjective and multiple understandings of the nuclear challenges in different regional contexts and is therefore unable to capture regional dynamics that go beyond the issues of immediate strategic benefits and costs.

More sensitive to inter-regional and intra-regional variations is Etel Solingen's analysis, which systematically examines regional proliferation patterns in East Asia and the Middle East.[25] She argues that the different types of dominant domestic coalitions in the two regions have led to opposite regional outcomes on questions of nuclearization. When states are export-driven and internationalizing domestic coalitions prevail, then, according to Solingen, the nuclear option is rejected because it would cause a negative regional externality. In contrast, states with inward-looking, nationalistic domestic coalitions will be prone to nuclear pursuit. While pathbreaking in its analytical rigor and empirical scope, Solingen's analysis unduly privileges domestic consensus centered on a prevailing political coalition and tends to overestimate regional contrasts between

East Asia and the Middle East. Her account is also insufficient to explain divergent responses to the proliferation challenges by different administrations in the same export-seeking, internationally oriented U.S. allies, such as South Korea, Japan, or Turkey. More important, both Kroenig and Solingen uncritically accept the fixed material interests of policymakers or coalitional leaders (i.e., military–strategic or economic interests), while overlooking the ideational sources of national interests (e.g., search for a greater regional role and foreign policy autonomy), which may at times reinforce or counteract the effects of material interests in influencing strategic outcomes.

Another alternative account for the different regional responses to the nuclear challenge concerns threat perception: specifically regional threat perceptions of North Korea and Iran.[26] In fact, all the East Asian countries are, albeit to varying degrees, concerned about the threat coming out of North Korea (e.g., missiles, artillery shells, or refugees). In the Middle East, Iran's threat also comes in many forms (e.g., missiles, support for its political proxies and radical Islamists, nuclear accidents, speedboats, and sea mines that can be used to block the Strait of Hormuz, etc.). Given the East Asian alliance posture that is arrayed to address North Korean contingencies, in this view, North Korean aggressive intentions manifested in its nuclear provocation should serve to strengthen alliance ties between the United States and its Asian allies.[27] However, not only did the East Asian countries resist the U.S. approach, alliance coordination faced mounting difficulties during the second crisis.[28] In the Middle East as well, the increasing U.S. military presence and provision of unprecedented arms transfer to its regional allies did not lead to greater alliance cooperation, and its regional standing has been increasingly damaged throughout the region. Moreover, the fact that South Korea's threat perception of North Korea has been lowered substantially *in spite of* North Korea's increasing nuclear capabilities and aggressive behavior begs an explanation.[29]

Apart from the proliferation studies, the vast literature on North Korea and Iran can be divided into three camps. The first category uncritically assumes the North Korean and Iranian threats and seeks to explain their motivations and global ramifications.[30] Tanya Ogilvie-White, for instance, argues that as the two defiant regimes face greater pressures and criticism from the international society, they tend to resist such pressure even more in an effort to rally domestic and international support.[31] While the defiance of the two regimes is certainly a factor in making the situation more intractable, this explanation fails to appreciate the evolving nature of the North Korean and Iranian challenges.

As detailed in chapter 4, North Korea's current tension with the United States cannot obscure its earlier records of cooperation with the United States in the early 1990s and the late 1990s. Similarly, in 2003 the Mohammed Khatami regime in Tehran offered to cooperate with the United States over terrorism, its role in Iraq and Lebanon, and nuclear programs in return for the end of U.S. sanctions and improved relations with the United States.[32] More importantly, this line of inquiry—while helpful in understanding the inner workings of the two regimes—has little to say about the regional dimension of the North Korean and Iranian nuclear challenges.

A second group of analyses on this subject devotes greater attention to the complex, multi-layered nature of the North Korean and Iranian challenges.[33] These studies stress domestic, political, or historical factors as the main reason for failed diplomacy. Prominent examples include Charles Pritchard's scathing criticism of the ideologically based diplomatic failure of the Bush administration in its approach to North Korea and Trita Parsi's penetrating indictment of both the Obama administration and the Iranian regime's domestic political dynamics as the root cause of the nuclear stalemate. While useful in dissecting the domestic political processes behind the U.S. approaches and informative in their chronicles of the two nuclear crises, these works remain largely descriptive and policy-driven, lacking an analytical framework to illuminate the sources of different national interests and threat perceptions among regional actors and their consequences for regional order.

The third category looks at the regional dimension in a systematic manner. In the East Asian context, Gilbert Rozman and Yoichi Funabashi provide detailed analyses of North Korea's regional neighbors as their national approaches coincided with the U.S. approach to North Korea.[34] In the Middle Eastern context, several recent works provide a welcome regional perspective.[35] With the empirical focus on either one of the two nuclear challenges, however, these books are oblivious to similar regional patterns surrounding proliferation challenges in the two regions, instead highlighting varied national priorities. These analyses echo the proliferation expert Gary Samore's observation that North Korea's neighbors are at times "reluctant to hold their bilateral relations with Pyongyang completely hostage to the nuclear issue."[36] However, the seemingly disparate interests of the regional actors share a common thread centered on regional role and foreign policy autonomy. As a consequence, all the regional actors are concerned far more about what Iran and North Korea respectively mean for the regional order than about how to address the nuclear challenge.

A systematic comparison of the two regions not only offers a fuller account of the regional underpinnings of nuclear proliferation challenges but also provides an invaluable window into the nature and forms of the emerging regional order in East Asia and the Middle East. This book's analysis suggests that the success of future global nonproliferation campaigns hinges less on a coercive approach aimed at the target states than on grasping the complexities of the regional dimension surrounding the proliferators. It also argues that given the salience of North Korea and Iran in the regional visions of their neighbors, the regional actors' understandings of both the nuclear and non-nuclear dimensions of the North Korean and Iranian challenges should be carefully considered. By focusing only on the nuclear aspects, the United States runs the risk of complicating nuclear diplomacy and losing its regional influence in the two vitally important regions.

1.4 REGIONAL ROLE CONCEPTIONS, THREAT PERCEPTIONS, AND REGIONAL ORDER

The regional patterns illustrated above highlight the significance of domestically or regionally contested ideas about threat perceptions and nuclear proliferation. Instead of assuming a priori the shared threat perception of global rogues and a common interest in resolving the nuclear crisis, we need to examine empirically the ways in which regional actors articulate and grapple with the North Korean and Iranian challenges. This analytical move also provides a window into how national interests are forged at the domestic level and affect regional order in East Asia and the Middle East.[37] In this vein, this book is part of a larger effort to bring constructivist insights, especially ideational sources of foreign policymaking, into security and proliferation studies.[38]

Jacques Hymans is among a few exceptions in the proliferation literature, as he explores an ideational factor (i.e., top leaders' national identity conceptions) as a key variable shaping nuclear decision.[39] In this book, I seek to broaden the analytical scope to examine not just proliferators themselves but also their regional neighbors. Specifically, I argue that the East Asian and Middle Eastern responses to the North Korean and Iranian nuclear challenges are shaped by regional role conceptions, defined as a set of ideas held and articulated by domestic political elites about their nation's proper roles and status in a given region. Along with material power and economic considerations, how political actors envision their nation's role on the regional or world stage has important consequences for their threat perception and national interest formation.

In fact, several scholars have explored the pursuit of international status as a key source of the state's foreign policy behavior.[40] Deborah Larson and Alexei Shevchenko, for instance, contend that the search for an "appropriate role in the world" is a primary driver of China and Russia's international behavior.[41] Specifically, they point to China's hosting of the Six Party Talks as a textbook example of China's quest for a "new identity as a responsible great power."[42] Highlighting both the global and regional dimensions of status-seeking behavior, Yong Deng also argues that the Six Party process has served as "a multilateral instrument for Beijing to earn diplomatic capital in and beyond Northeast Asia."[43] What is missing in their analyses, however, is a realization that status seeking is neither confined to emerging great powers nor unproblematically accepted at the domestic level. As Japan, South Korea, Turkey, and Gulf states pursued greater regional status in their respective regions, they have also been debating competing regional roles linked to North Korea and Iran, problematizing the earlier threat perceptions of, and policies toward, Pyongyang and Tehran.

In advancing regional role conceptions as a key variable affecting regional actors' national interest and threat perception, this book builds on the earlier and under-examined literature on role conceptions in the fields of political science and sociology.[44] In his seminal article on role conceptions, K. J. Holsti defined national role conceptions as policymakers' perceived "image" of "the appropriate orientations or functions of their state toward, or in, the external environment."[45] Along the line of role conceptions, international relations scholars have used various concepts, such as national self-image or elite belief systems, as key variables shaping foreign policy behavior.[46]

The focus on individual policymakers, however, raises questions about the generalizability of a particular individual leader's self-image to the national level.[47] Similarly, the earlier literature on role conceptions focused on the "psychological" rather than "social" dimensions of foreign policymaking. Foreign policy, by definition, assumes relationships with other nations, and each nation's social position is inherently intertwined with that of others.[48] Hence, we need to go beyond the earlier focus on the individual and cognitive dimensions of decision-making to capture the social and "constitutive" dimensions through which actors "define the boundaries and distinctive practices of a group."[49] Put differently, instead of analyzing idiosyncratic views of particular national leaders, one needs to examine a larger domestic debate on the nation's proper role as contested in each country and its manifestation in specific policy contexts.

East Asian countries' understanding of the North Korean challenge illustrates this point. For the regional countries, the North Korea question is inescapably linked to their pursuit of new regional roles and greater regional status. Specifically, South Korea's "sunshine" policy of engaging North Korea and promoting inter-Korean reconciliation began in the late 1990s when the Kim Dae-jung administration sought to expand South Korea's regional role in the wake of the Asian financial crisis and the rise of multilateral regional frameworks such as the ASEAN Plus Three (APT). His regional strategy not only culminated in the inter-Korean summit in 2000 but also was consolidated into a broader regional vision that was adopted by his successor Roh Moo-hyun. The regional master plan, *Dongbuka Jungsim Gukga-ron* (or the strategy of transforming the Korean Peninsula into the focal point of Northeast Asia), sought to position South Korea at the hub of regional economic integration and security cooperation.[50] North Korea, in this vision, is a key partner for greater regional integration centered on the Korean Peninsula rather than the main enemy to fight.

Similarly, even before the second North Korean nuclear crisis, Japan's pursuit of a greater regional role was also tied to the North Korean question. As an enduring controversy over Japan's past role as colonizer and the regional suspicion of its future role cause its regional diplomatic space to narrow,[51] Japan's deep involvement in the North Korean question provides it with a unique opportunity "to rejuvenate its troubled regional status."[52] By participating in the Six Party process, a former senior Japanese diplomat reasons, Japan can redefine its relations with participating countries, opening "a new strategic position in the region."[53] In this context, the Korean Peninsula is "the gateway to Asia or even to 'normalcy' in international relations," where Japan can "solidify a longstanding role in the emergent Northeast Asian regionalism."[54] Former Japanese Prime Minister Koizumi Junichiro's efforts to normalize Japan's diplomatic relations with Pyongyang were the epitome of that yearning and an important steppingstone to becoming an independent regional player.[55]

In China as well, maintaining ties to North Korea is part and parcel of its larger efforts to enhance Beijing's regional clout. From a Chinese perspective, the Korean Peninsula represents a place where China's ambitions to become a regional "hegemon" will be tested.[56] In this view, the Six Party process can serve as a launch pad for an alternative regional security structure that would go beyond the current U.S.-centered regional order and enhance China's regional status accordingly. As Figure 1.1 illustrates[57], for

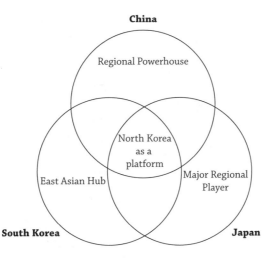

China

Regional Powerhouse

North Korea
as a
platform

East Asian Hub

Major Regional
Player

South Korea

Japan

Figure 1.1:
North Korea and Regional Roles

the East Asian states, North Korea is not a clear-cut threat but a staging ground for each nation's respective new regional role and vision.[58]

In a close parallel with the East Asian case, Iran's nuclear pursuit and the global response led by the Bush administration also intersected with Middle Eastern states' search for a new regional role. In contrast to the familiar narrative of Iran's nuclear ambition as a key global proliferation challenge, most of Iran's neighbors not only improved their diplomatic relations with Tehran but also expanded economic and social exchanges with Iran in the hopes of playing a greater regional role and enhancing their regional status.

Turkey, for instance, has pursued a new regional vision centered on Ankara's active involvement in regional affairs and Turkey's independent regional role. In this strategic shift, Turkey's threat perception also changed as the ruling Justice and Development Party (AKP) deemphasized "Islamic threat" in the region and engaged Iran and Iraq as regional neighbors.[59] Moreover, despite Turkey's status as a U.S. ally, its efforts to improve ties with anti-Western regional players such as Iran, Hamas, and Syria also strengthened Ankara's status within the Middle East.[60]

Similarly, Gulf states such as Oman, Qatar, and the United Arab Emirates have intensified their engagement with Iran with the larger goal of enhancing their regional status and promoting their regional autonomy. This regional drive continued in the face of the nuclear standoff between Washington and Tehran and the threat of the U.S. military strikes on Iran. While expanding their ties with Tehran both politically and economically,

Turkey and the Gulf states refused to follow the hardline position of the Bush administration and Israel. Overall, given the salience of North Korea and Iran in the local actors' regional role conceptions, it is difficult to assume that they would unproblematically accept the U.S. threat perception of North Korea and Iran as global rogues and follow whatever path the United States would take in dealing with the nuclear question.

Role Conflict and Domestic Contestation over the Meaning of North Korea and Iran

In advancing an argument based on role conceptions, this book does not assume that the mere presence of certain role conceptions would dictate policy outcomes in a deterministic fashion. The domestic process of articulating the nation's roles is often a competitive one, since various political groups may have different, contending ideas about the role of their nation in a region.[61]

While some scholars during the first wave of role theory noted the possibility of conflict among various roles, they did not investigate role conflict in a systematic manner.[62] Michael Barnett's study on pan-Arabism is a notable exception.[63] Based on the case study of the pre–1967 Arab states system, he demonstrates the way "overlapping institutions produce contradictory demands on Arab states' foreign policy and contribute to regional instability."[64]

Breaking from the earlier role analyses that tended to assume elites as a single unit, recent scholars also maintain that internal discords among policy elites over a proper role can trigger role conflict.[65] Examining the EU's role in the post–Cold War context, for instance, Rikard Bengtsson and Ole Elgstrom identify "the complex and dynamic interplay between an actor's own role conception, on the one hand, and the structurally guided role expectations of others, on the other hand."[66] Similarly, Cristian Cantir and Juliet Kaarbo argue that different regional roles can be "generated from different institutional contexts, both domestic and international."[67] While insightful in their plea for going beyond the first-wave role analyses' rather deterministic stance on the effects of role conceptions on policymaking, their analysis nonetheless stop short of exploring how such competing roles are domestically contested, with consequences for policymaking and regional relations.

In unpacking the domestic political process behind contending regional roles, it is helpful to reflect on the relationship between agent and structure in world politics.[68] In this vein, a group of scholars made a worthwhile effort to link political psychology, which privileges individual agencies, and systemic constructivism, which stresses structural domains.[69] This book's analytical framework builds on this insight by examining the interaction between regional states and external structure with respect to regional role conceptions. Specifically, while this book highlights the importance of particular regional roles pursued by regional actors themselves, it does not overlook the structural dimension in which regional actors have to consider the roles expected of their nations by external—often more materially capable—powers.

Specifically, two such regional roles are of particular importance in both East Asia and the Middle East: internally shaped regional roles, which are conceived and pursued internally by local actors themselves, and externally shaped regional roles, which are expected by external actors (e.g., strategically important external powers such as the United States).[70] The question that naturally arises is: Which types of role prevail, and under what conditions? Early role theorists generally assumed that in case of role conflict, internally shaped roles would be more influential than externally expected ones in shaping state behavior.[71] Without empirical testing, however, we cannot be certain whether internally or externally shaped roles will triumph at a given moment in time.

In East Asia, the existing power structure, in which the United States maintains a substantial military and economic presence, powerfully conditions regional role conceptions through the U.S.-centered roles. In fact, even the region's biggest power, China, focuses on the state of Sino-American ties as a main foreign policy priority because "the United States holds the key to China's international recognition."[72] Given this structural reality of the region, evidenced in the U.S.-led hub-and-spokes system, all the regional countries, albeit to varying degrees, seek approval from the de facto regional hegemon, the United States, by cooperating with it on various security issues, including the North Korean nuclear challenge.

At the same time, however, they seek foreign policy autonomy by engaging North Korea in their own ways. As a consequence, rather than internally generated role conceptions dictating policy behavior in a predictable manner (as the early literature on role conceptions assumed), a constant balancing act between seeking U.S. recognition and pursuing regional autonomy characterizes regional role conceptions in East Asia, a pattern echoed in the Middle East over the Iranian challenge. The higher the levels of congruence between internally shaped regional roles (e.g., independent regional player or regional powerhouse) and externally shaped regional roles (e.g., U.S. ally or strategic partner), the more likely that the regional countries will support the U.S. approach toward North Korea. But if there were a conflict between the two roles, regional actors would either resist or try to weaken the U.S. approach.

In East Asia, domestic debates on regional role conceptions began to intensify in the post-9/11 era as America's regional role changed.[73] As the Bush administration zeroed in on the role of global counterproliferation enforcer, resorting to coercive means and rhetoric, its traditional role as regional stabilizer was increasingly in question. The role shift worried the regional actors who prized regional stability and their respective regional visions tied to North Korea. In fact, during the first North Korean nuclear crisis, the Clinton administration adopted a strategy of gradual escalation, seeking regional understanding and support in the process and thus fulfilling its role as regional stabilizer. In contrast, the Bush administration turned to a simplifying, unilateral approach in its global strategy and applied it to the North Korean situation, often with little consideration for regional views and repercussions. Rejecting the rogue frame, the regional countries soon moved to challenge the Bush administration's approach toward North Korea.

The stage was then set for a battle between the United States and regional countries on the proper handling of the North Korean challenge. As one Chinese expert succinctly put it, while there was "no regional agreement on the North Korean threat, there [was] a regional consensus on maintaining regional stability."[74] A senior South Korean defense analyst of a government-affiliated research institute observed that in the process of preventing a U.S. preemptive strike on North Korea in the early period of the second crisis, "China, South Korea and Japan got much closer, while alliance coordination between the U.S. and its allies, Japan and South Korea, became much more difficult."[75] A senior Chinese expert predicted in 2004 that as long as the Bush administration maintained an aggressive approach toward North Korea, "the regional consensus [on North Korea] would be maintained."[76] Against this backdrop, as explored in chapter 5, regional cooperation among the East Asian countries improved during the early rounds of the Six Party talks.

However, as the Six Party talks reached a stalemate with no signs of immediate resolution, the prolonged crisis gradually gave rise to domestic contestation over the North Korean threat and competing regional roles in each East Asian country.[77] This regional uncertainty pushed domestic actors to "compete to frame the event because how the event is understood has important consequences for mobilizing action and furthering their interests."[78] Once changing external circumstances called into question the prevalent regional vision, other groups challenged the hitherto dominant view, leading to a domestic jostling for a prevailing narrative that would shape the nation's collective regional vision. In the process, different political actors projected different regional role conceptions that mirrored their own ideational preferences.[79]

Despite political leaders' North Korea-anchored regional visions and their objection to the U.S. frame, the continued stalemate at the Six Party talks and North Korea's nuclear tests enabled the domestic actors who stressed stronger ties with the United States and the U.S.-centered regional roles to challenge the reigning view and to re-amplify the North Korean threat.[80] Specifically, while Japanese moderates saw North Korea as a potential "bridge" for Japan to reenter East Asia, Japanese conservatives called it a "threat" armed with Nodong or Taepodong missiles.[81] South Korean liberals' view of their northern neighbor as a regional "partner" was also challenged by conservatives who continued to call Pyongyang "jujeok" (the main enemy of the nation). In China as well, the mainstream position of North Korea as a strategic "buffer" in the U.S.-centered regional order was questioned by other policy elites who began to see its fellow Communist as a "liability" as Beijing joined the world economy and became a "stakeholder" in the international system.[82]

What followed was domestic contestation between those who sought to ride on the Bush administration's drive to demonize North Korea by emphasizing U.S.-centered roles and those who remained focused on internally shaped roles and the meaning of North Korea as a platform for their nation's greater regional role and foreign policy autonomy. Different interpretations of the North Korean challenge then fit neatly into competing narratives about a proper regional role. Each group accepted the aspects of North Korea that conformed to its own regional role, while rejecting the contradicting one. Although "North Korea engagers" in each country maintained their benign view of North Korea as a focal point of their regional vision, "North Korea bashers" began to latch onto the U.S. position and inflated the North Korea threat to promote U.S. ties and enhance their political standing in their countries and the region, a pattern echoed in the Middle East as well.[83] In other words, irrespective of the objective nature of the North Korean threat, domestic political groups in each country tailored the North Korean issue to their competing regional visions.[84]

As shown in Table 1.1, in each East Asian country, those who stressed foreign policy autonomy and a greater regional role tended to downplay the North Korean threat (e.g., South Korean liberals, including Presidents Kim Dae-jung and Roh Moo-hyun; the People's Liberation Army and the International Liaison Department of the Communist Party in China; Japanese Prime Ministers Koizumi, Murayama Tomiichi, Fukuda Yasuo, and Hatoyama Yukio). Instead, they highlighted the positive meanings of

Table 1.1. REGIONAL ROLE CONCEPTIONS AND THREAT PERCEPTIONS
OF NORTH KOREA IN EAST ASIA

	Internally shaped role conceptions	Externally expected role conceptions
South Korea	Regional hub, independent player (*North Korea (N.K.) as "partner"*) • Building the Korean Peninsula as the hub of regional integration • Securing foreign policy autonomy	U.S. ally (*N.K. as "the main enemy"*) • Strengthening alliance with the U.S. • Coordinating with U.S. global strategy
China	Regional powerhouse (*N.K. as "buffer/platform"*) • Improving regime security • Enhancing regional influence	Global "stakeholder" (*N.K. as "liability"*) • Strengthening Sino-U.S. ties • Showcasing China's new global image
Japan	Major regional player (*N.K. as "bridge/platform"*) • Increasing regional influence • Securing foreign policy autonomy	U.S. ally, "normal" state (*N.K. as a "major threat"*) • Strengthening alliance as a global pact • Building a normal defense posture

North Korea in their larger regional visions, such as partner, buffer, or bridge. Other domestic groups tended to focus on ties with the United States (e.g., conservatives, including the Grand National Party (GNP) and later the New Frontier (Saenuri) Party in South Korea; the Foreign Ministry in China;[85] what Richard Samuels calls "a new generation of revisionists" in Japan, such as Prime Ministers Abe Shinzo and Aso Taro).[86] They tended to emphasize the North Korean threat, while using the North Korea bashing as a means to strengthen ties with the United States and improve their domestic political standing.[87]

Similar domestic contestation over different regional roles emerged in the Middle East. For instance, hardliners in Israel such as Prime Minister Netanyahu objected to any deal with Iran for fear of losing Israel's strategic edge, stressed the externally expected role as a U.S. ally, and latched onto and even magnified the U.S. threat perception of Iran and the global rogue frame. However, as elaborated in chapter 6, other moderate political actors publicly opposed Israel's aggressive rhetoric, especially a preemptive strike against Iran, and tried to engage Iran with Tel Aviv's long-term relations with Tehran in mind. Contestation over different regional roles existed among the Gulf states as well. Saudi Arabia's growing rivalry with Iran over sectarian issues (i.e., Sunni vs. Shia) and regional status in the Middle East led to Riyadh's emphasis on Iran as a major regional threat and its externally shaped regional role as a U.S. ally, while other Gulf states and Turkey sought to balance between the externally expected regional role as U.S. ally and their internally shaped regional role as independent regional actors who hoped to complement the U.S.-centered Gulf security architecture with their own engagement policy toward Tehran.

Regional Role Conceptions and Regional Order

The converging and diverging nature of the regional responses to the North Korean and Iranian challenge suggests that regional role conceptions with respect to North Korea and Iran have broader regional implications. A key question here is how domestic-level attributes, such as particular national aspiration for a new regional role, interact with international circumstances to yield distinctive regional outcomes. An analysis of regional role conceptions can help us better understand the evolving regional order in East Asia. As different domestic actors in each regional country either reject or latch onto the U.S. position, competing regional roles in turn affect regional interactions with the United States and regional actors among themselves. In short, the regional order is shaped not only by a collective regional approach that was markedly different from that of the United States in the early years of the nuclear crises but also by intra-regional variation over time. This finding also contributes to the scholarly debate on the international relations of East Asia.

In the literature on East Asian security, for instance, one of the key debates since the end of the Cold War has been conceptualizing the post–Cold War regional order.[88] Drawing on the prewar European experiences, Aaron Friedberg, for one, projects an image of East Asia as "the cockpit of great power conflict," where an emerging multipolar East Asian order would lead to regional instability.[89] In contrast, basing his argument primarily on the historical experiences of East Asian countries, David Kang forecasts a stable East Asian hierarchy centered on China.[90] East Asian dynamics surrounding North Korea, however, raise questions about such deterministic accounts. Simply put, the East Asian security order is not preordained to be conflictual or stable. Instead of inferring from different, largely dissimilar social contexts (e.g., prewar European or premodern Asian), I argue, an analysis of the regional order should be subject to empirical testing in specific policy domains as regional actors interact among themselves and with external powers in various political contexts.

Existing studies also tend to privilege the effects of extra-regional systemic forces at the expense of local responses. For instance, John Ikenberry demonstrates how the United States, after its victory in World War II, structured and operated a stable postwar international order by binding itself to multilateral institutional mechanisms.[91] From this vantage point, the regional order in East Asia is a natural outgrowth of that U.S.-led global order, with the United States stabilizing the regional order through its bilateral alliances and U.S.-led institutional mechanisms. While systemic, external forces remain important, others have shown that in the face of similar external challenges states may respond differently due to the effects of domestic politics. For instance, Randall Schweller argues that one of the key factors shaping balancing behavior is "elite consensus [or discord] about the nature and extent of the threat."[92] What is crucial, in other words, is not just the presence of external forces but how they "interact with dominant ideas in particular ways to shape enduring patterns of national behavior."[93]

Contrary to the traditional view of regional order as a material reality deduced unproblematically from the power structure at the system level, regions are "social constructs" shaped by political practices by various actors.[94] In other words, the construction of order is a dynamic process,[95] where the "boundaries and salient features" of a region are constantly in the making, depending on the nature of interaction between external and internal dynamics.[96] Hence, instead of focusing on either external or internal forces, we need to explore their interplay as a key factor shaping regional order. An analysis of regional role conceptions is particularly well suited to capture both the external and internal dimensions of regional order building. It helps us unpack the domestic political mechanism by which external factors interact with different political actors' regional role conceptions, affecting individual state's policymaking and shaping the larger regional order.

Specifically, if the two regional role conceptions were deemed compatible, regional actors would be able to expand their regional roles within the U.S.-led regional order. If not, the regional actors would resist the U.S. approach, and the resulting order would be more conflictual. An underlying mechanism for this dynamic is the regional perception of the legitimacy of the existing regional order, as legitimacy is one of the crucial pillars of any successful political order.[97] By the same token, the regional order would be particularly unstable when the legitimacy of that order is in question.[98]A yawning gap between the regional actors' externally shaped and internally shaped regional roles marked the beginning of a legitimacy crisis in the U.S.-led regional order.

While the Clinton administration's North Korea policy complemented South Korea's sunshine policy and Japan's and China's greater regional aspirations around the Korean Peninsula, the Bush administration's approach conflicted with the regional yearning for greater roles, setting in motion a gradual transformation in the regional order.[99] Specifically, the Clinton administration's approach during the 1998 North Korean missile crisis, commonly known as the Perry Process, showed a mutually reinforcing mechanism between the United States and East Asian countries. For instance, President Kim Dae-jung did not have to balance between alliance ties and South Korea's regional policy. Instead, South Korea's regional vision thrived under the leadership of the United States.

Regional consultation during the Perry Process also enabled the regional actors to play a greater role in dealing with North Korea, while at the same time allowing them to support U.S. leadership, which ensured role congruence between the U.S.-centered and internally shaped roles. No serious domestic contestation emerged over relationships with the United States and North Korea. Compatible understandings of the North Korean challenge and the practices of coordination and consultation during the Perry Process served to mitigate mutual suspicion among East Asian countries and promote regionalism in the process. In this way, alliance coordination via the Trilateral Coordination and Oversight Group (TCOG) among the United States, Japan, and South Korea and regional cooperation among China, Japan, and South Korea through the APT improved markedly.

In contrast, during the Bush presidency, the gap between the United States and regional understandings of the North Korean question caused conflict between the U.S.-centered regional roles and the internally shaped regional roles. Specifically, the rogue frame and the coercive U.S. policy stance toward North Korea complicated East Asian countries' efforts to expand their regional roles by engaging North Korea. By intensifying role conflict, the Bush administration's approach strained alliance ties, especially with South Korea. As for regionalism, by late 2004, a shared regional understanding of North Korea and the collective regional resistance to the Bush administration's approach facilitated regional cooperation. But as the rise of conservatives in Japan and later in South Korea pushed the government in the other direction, the earlier pattern of regional cooperation deteriorated. As a result, the U.S. alliances in East Asia have been losing a trilateral dimension, at the same time as regionalism fragmented.

In short, the degree to which regional roles become congruent or not influences the level of regional cooperation.

Under these circumstances, trilateral cooperation of the TCOG became the first victim of growing tensions among U.S. allies. In China, in the face of President Bush's inflexible approach toward North Korea, many suspected that the United States was trying to rebuild the regional order to its liking via the Six Party talks.[100] In the process, the domestic group portraying North Korea as a liability dwindled, while the leadership moved to emphasize the traditional ties with North Korea. In June 2008, for instance, Xi Jinping, then Hu Jintao's designated successor (later president), made his first official foreign visit to Pyongyang. During his visit, he reiterated to Kim Jong Il that "the China–DPRK friendship is inalterable and has withstood international flux," while agreeing with the North Koreans to celebrate the year 2009 as "the DPRK–China friendship year."[101] Meanwhile, Japan's earlier efforts to improve its regional status and to gain regional momentum faltered. As the conservatives assumed key government positions in Tokyo, trilateral cooperation with the United States and South Korea was replaced by an increasing focus on the global role of the U.S.–Japan alliance.[102]

In sum, the Bush administration shaped the regional order in two ways: in the early rounds of the Six Party talks (by the end of 2004) it provoked a *collective* regional response. Such regional reactions made alliance coordination very difficult, though they improved the pattern of regional consultation and cooperation developed during the Perry Process. As the stalled Six Party process and North Korea's nuclear tests intensified role conflict and fueled domestic contestation over North Korea after 2005, a *contested* regional dynamic emerged, pitting Japan against China and South Korea. In the process, the earlier momentum for greater regional cooperation was replaced with mounting tensions, including a renewed rivalry between China and Japan and a strained relationship between South Korea and Japan. Overall, as summarized in Table 1.2, while a more inclusive and cooperative regional order emerged in the late 1990s, during the second crisis the region became more fragmented and conflictual.

As elaborated in chapter 6, similar regional dynamics of alliance tension and fragmented regionalism emerged in the Middle East when role conflict intensified during the Iranian nuclear crisis. The alliance ties between Turkey and the United States suffered when Ankara came into conflict with Washington over Iran, especially after a deal brokered by Turkey and Brazil was rejected by the United States. Ankara in return voted against additional sanctions against Iran at the UN Security Council. Division and role

Table 1.2. REGIONAL ROLE CONCEPTIONS AND REGIONAL ORDERS

	The Perry Process	The Bush Doctrine
The interaction between the U.S. approaches and regional role conceptions	*Congruence* between U.S.-directed roles and internally shaped roles	*Conflict* between the U.S.-directed roles and internally shaped roles
Shape* of regional order	Broadened, multi-tiered • Institutionalized trilateral alliance coordination • Inclusive regionalism	Narrowed, fragmented • Ad hoc bilateral alliance ties • Exclusive regionalism
Character** of regional order	*Cooperative* • Alliance cooperation (TCOG) • Open regionalism (APT, ARF)	*Conflictual* • Alliance problem (end of TCOG) • By 2004: regionalism (APT) • Post-2005: regional rivalry (weak APT)

*The structural dimension refers to the underlying organizational template of the regional order, such as a bilateral hub-and-spokes order built around U.S. alliances and a fusion of trilateral alliance mechanism and broader, open regionalism.

**The character of the regional order concerns whether patterns of regional interaction are conflictual or cooperative.

conflict with regard to Iran among members of the Gulf Cooperation Council (GCC) also led to fractured regional relations in the Middle East.

1.5 RESEARCH DESIGN AND THE ROADMAP OF THE BOOK

This book employs a comparative analysis of regional perceptions and policies concerning the North Korean and Iranian nuclear challenges over the past two decades. This is not to deny that there are several important differences between the two cases. For example, North Korea withdrew from the Nuclear Nonproliferation Treaty (NPT), whereas Iran is still a member. The two countries also diverge in terms of the stage of nuclear development (i.e., North Korea with three nuclear tests and weapon-grade fissile materials vs. Iran with no testing or accumulating of weapon-grade fissile materials) or their regional status (i.e., North Korea is a relatively small state with the poorest economy in East Asia, whereas Iran, with its sizable population and abundant natural resources, is a major regional power in the Middle East).[103]

While primarily focused on the East Asian cases, this book conducts a comparison of the two regions for a number of reasons. First, while North Korea and Iran are widely viewed as the two most serious threats to the global nonproliferation regime, regional threat perceptions have fluctuated significantly in the past two decades. Despite their differences, North Korea and Iran are also similarly creating both problems and opportunities for various local actors in regions where U.S. alliances have traditionally been the linchpin of regional order and stability. This dual nature of the North Korean and Iranian problems, both global and regional, has not been examined systematically through a comparative lens in the scholarly literature.[104] A cross-regional comparison of the two regions would help to uncover similarities and differences in the regional understandings of the proliferation challenge and their effects on regional order and global security.

To assess the impact of role conceptions and the changes in regional order in East Asia, I compare the political dynamics in both the spatial dimension (i.e., global, regional, national contexts) and the temporal dimension (i.e., the North Korean missile crisis and the Perry Process in 1998–2000; and the second nuclear crisis of 2002–present). The research for this book benefited from multiple data sources gathered from China, Japan, South Korea, and the United States. First, I rely on a wide range of official documents concerning the North Korean issue in each country. With the exception of Japanese, I use materials in both the local language and in English.[105] Second, I draw on fifty-seven in-depth interviews that I conducted with government officials and experts in the three East Asian countries, as well as scores of interviews of relevant policymakers by the local media. I also utilize a wide range of secondary literature, local newspapers, and opinion pieces concerning the North Korean challenge in each East Asian country.

For the Middle Eastern case, I examine the regional views of the Iranian challenge in the past two decades with special reference to Turkey, Israel, and the six Gulf Cooperation Council states. I compare regional dynamics before and after Iran's nuclear crisis that began in late 2002 and explore their impact on U.S. alliance relations with the regional states and regional interaction within the Gulf Cooperation Council. I draw on the extensive scholarly literature on the history and security relations of the Middle East and the Persian Gulf. Along with the scholarly materials, I also make use of various media interviews of regional officials, government documents, and press reports from countries in the Middle East. Throughout the empirical chapters, I employ a method of process tracing which tracks the policymaking process to identify the mechanism by which role effects lead to policy behavior.

Based on a comprehensive survey of policy documents, speeches, and interview data, in chapters 2 and 3 I examine and compare the American and East Asian understandings of the North Korean challenge in different political contexts and trace how such understandings interacted with different regional role conceptions and policy behavior. Chapter 2 delineates the similarities and differences in the American and regional understandings of the North Korean challenge during the first nuclear crisis and the second nuclear crisis. More specifically, chapter 2 explores how 9/11 and the specter of nuclear terrorism gave new meaning to the problem of rogue states and the threat of WMD proliferation, altering previous understandings and policy trajectories laid out by the Clinton administration. In contrast to the perceptional fluidity in East Asia on what North Korea represents, there was an increasing rigidity in the U.S. perception of North Korea as an urgent, global security problem. This perceptional rigidity/fluidity contrast led to different policy orientations toward North Korea. Unlike the Clinton administration, the Bush administration made more risk-taking, inflexible choices vis-à-vis North Korea. In East Asia, where traditional threat perceptions of North Korea were lowered amid the search for greater regional roles, that U.S. policy shift was seen as problematic for the pursuit of such role.

After mapping out broader global and regional patterns with respect to the North Korean challenge, I explore, in chapter 3, the particular meanings attached to North Korea in domestic debates in East Asia. By delving into domestic contestation over North Korea in South Korea, China, and Japan, chapter 3 delineates the link between regional role conceptions and policy orientations toward North Korea in the three countries. This chapter seeks to identify the sources of different regional role conceptions in each country and to show how the roles so conceived led to particular policies. I devote particular attention to the policymaking process on North Korea in each country by "triangulating" various data sources such as interviews, opinion polls, regional scholarly journals, and official documents.[106]

Chapters 4 and 5 turn to the impact of role congruence and role conflict on the regional order in East Asia. To demonstrate the causal effects of regional role conceptions on regional order, I compare alliance politics and regionalism during the Clinton and Bush presidencies. More specifically, I assess the contrasting regional dynamics shaped by different U.S. approaches toward North Korea and see how alliance management and community building worked out differently in different global contexts, transforming the shape and character of regional order in East Asia. Chapter 4 traces the Clinton administration's approach toward North

Korea during the North Korean missile crisis and North Korea's suspected nuclear activities and reactions to the U.S. approach at the time, demonstrating how the interaction between the Clinton administration and the regional countries affected alliance relationship and regionalism. Chapter 5 turns to the regional order as shaped by the Bush administration's policy toward North Korea and shows how alliance cooperation and regional frameworks changed.

Chapter 6 extends the regional role framework to the Middle East. It explores how different regional strategies of several Middle Eastern countries shaped their understandings of and policies toward Iran. Specifically, this chapter examines U.S. alliance dynamics in the Middle East and the Gulf Cooperation Council (GCC) as a manifestation of the shifting regional order impacted by Iran's nuclear challenge. Chapter 7 then concludes the book with a summary of findings and a discussion of theoretical and policy implications. This chapter also analyzes similarities and differences between the two regions and considers the extension of the regional role framework to other issue areas. The book ends with an epilogue that discusses the latest regional developments and the future prospects of the two nuclear challenges amid new regional dynamics such as political transitions in the three East Asian countries and the Arab uprisings in the Middle East.

CHAPTER 2
The Global Proliferation Approach

2.1 INTRODUCTION

Throughout the post–Cold War period, U.S. responses to North Korea's nuclear ambitions have been based on a simple premise: a nuclear North Korea would destabilize regional stability and thus cannot be permitted under any circumstances. At the height of each of the North Korean nuclear crises, both the Clinton and Bush administrations imposed a series of economic sanctions and considered military options.[1] The similarities, however, go no further. During the first North Korean nuclear crisis, the Clinton administration relied primarily on bilateral negotiations with North Korea. The underlying assumption was that the North Korean threat, while dangerous, was manageable, requiring long-term political solutions. In contrast, the Bush administration took a unilateral, coercive approach on the assumption that North Korea represented a global challenge—both urgent and unconventional in nature—demanding immediate, decisive measures.

This chapter explores how 9/11 and the specter of nuclear terrorism gave new meaning to the problem of rogue states and the threat of WMD proliferation, altering previous understandings and policy trajectories laid out by the Clinton administration. With its almost exclusive focus on the global, nuclear dimension of the North Korean and Iranian challenges, I argue, the current U.S. approach has in essence "globalized" what have traditionally been regional security problems.[2] Unlike the Clinton administration, the Bush administration decided to take a more risk-prone, inflexible policy vis-à-vis North Korea.

The different U.S. understandings of and approaches toward North Korea, in turn, shaped the nature of East Asian reactions in each crisis.

While largely bilateral in scope, the Clinton administration's approach was to secure multilateral backing in the form of alliance cooperation from Japan and South Korea. During the first crisis, the Chinese government also provided support for the Clinton administration's approach on many occasions. A completely different picture emerged in the aftermath of the second crisis. While the Bush administration put negotiations with North Korea into a multilateral setting, Michael Armacost observed that it was the United States that was pressured by regional countries to take a more conciliatory approach.[3] When Secretary of State Condoleezza Rice raised the idea of imposing economic and political penalties against North Korea, referring to what she called "other options in the international system," her message fell on deaf ears in East Asia. Throughout the second crisis, wrote Glenn Kessler, it had been "the United States, not North Korea that seemed isolated."[4]

This chapter takes a systematic look at the Bush Doctrine in general and its application to the North Korean case in particular. The Bush Doctrine represents a radical shift in the perception of and policy toward potential proliferators such as North Korea and Iran. Underneath this transformation was a new assessment of the uncertainty surrounding the proliferation challenge.[5] From the Bush administration's perspective, the terrorist attacks of September 11 and the ensuing specter of nuclear terrorism demanded a new sense of urgency in addressing the proliferation challenge. Put simply, the post-9/11 context enabled "a new American vision of national security that has redefined both the nature of the threat and the U.S. response."[6] Different understandings then led to different policy prescriptions. Unlike the Clinton administration, the Bush administration opted for confrontational and hardline policy choices vis-à-vis North Korea. The abrupt and drastic shift in the U.S. policy toward Pyongyang also diverged from the preferences of the regional actors. In East Asia, where the North Korean threat became a matter of domestic political contestation as nations search for greater regional roles and status, the U.S. policy shift was seen as problematic and threatening to regional stability.

In what follows, I locate the changes in U.S. policy toward global rogues in the broader global strategic context. With an empirical focus on the East Asian dynamics, it examines how that shift prompted a distinct regional response. In doing so, this chapter maps out broad patterns in the global and regional understandings of and policy behavior toward the North Korean challenge. I pay particular attention to similarities and differences in American and regional understandings of the North Korean challenge during the first and the second nuclear crises. The next section provides a brief overview of the contrast in the regional responses to the different U.S. approaches during the first and second crises. The following section explores the nature of the Bush Doctrine as it relates to the post-9/11 global security vision, proliferation strategy, and the North Korean challenge. Particular emphasis is placed on the contrast between the Bush administration's strategy and that of the Clinton administration. The chapter then moves to the regional level, examining East Asia's assessment of the Bush Doctrine during the second crisis, followed by a concluding section summarizing the chapter.

2.2 DIFFERENT REGIONAL RESPONSES TO SIMILAR CRISES

In 1992, when the North Korean government rejected a request for special inspections of suspicious nuclear facilities in North Korea by the International Atomic and Energy Agency (IAEA), the newly formed Clinton administration found itself in the first nuclear crisis of the post–Cold War era. In striking similarity to the second crisis, North Korea announced in early 1993 its intention to withdraw from the Nuclear Nonproliferation Treaty (NPT). In May 1994, when North Korea began removing fuel rods from its 25-megawatt reactor, the Clinton administration made public its intention to propose economic sanctions on North Korea at the UN Security Council, prompting Pyongyang to respond with a warning that sanctions would provoke military actions by North Korea.[7] Concerned about rapidly developing tensions on the Korean Peninsula, the Clinton administration adopted a strategy of gradual escalation as it attempted to build a coalition with its regional allies and China.

With the issues of greater regional roles and foreign policy autonomy and a regional vision linked to Pyongyang hardly a factor for the domestic debate in each East Asian state, North Korea's regional neighbors did not question the U.S. approach to North Korea. The U.S. allies, Japan and South Korea, quickly endorsed the escalation strategy. In response to North Korea's announcement of its withdrawal from the NPT, Japanese Chief Cabinet Secretary Kono Yohei made it clear that Japan would support sanctions should efforts to forestall North Korea's withdrawal fail.[8] Similarly, the Kim Young-sam government in South Korea not only declared that it would take "all necessary steps" to support sanctions, in June 1993, it unilaterally suspended trade with the North and banned South Korean companies from contacting North Koreans altogether. At the time, those supporting sanctions in South Korea included Kim Dae-jung, then the leader of the main opposition party and later the architect of the sunshine policy of engagement toward the North.[9] The message from South Korea was unmistakable: "unless and until North Korea cleared itself of all suspicions by way of inspections, there would be no progress in inter-Korean economic exchanges and cooperation."[10]

At their meeting in 1994, Japanese Prime Minister Hosokawa Morihito and President Kim Young-sam reiterated their shared view that unless North Korea allowed IAEA inspections of the Yongbyon nuclear facilities, the two countries would join the international sanctions against North Korea.[11] Throughout the crisis, South Korea and Japan sided with the United States over the North Korean issue.[12] During a tripartite meeting in June 1994, for instance, the United States and its two Asian allies formed "a united front against North Korea" and urged the UN Security Council to consider sanctions on North Korea.[13]

Meanwhile, Kim Jong Il's planned visit to China in early 1993 was reportedly canceled, as China refused to accept North Korea's request for support for its position on the issue of nuclear inspection.[14] In June 1994, in a meeting with a North Korean ambassador, China's Vice Foreign Minister Tang Jiaxuan even suggested that China's role in resolving the issue of expected sanctions at the UN Security Council was "limited," with the unmistakable implication that North Korea should not count on China's veto at the UN Security Council.[15] As Japan's Foreign Minister Kakizawa Koji put it, "it was important for Japan, South Korea and China—as Pyongyang's neighbors—to send North Korea the right message together."[16] Overall, with no effects of the regional role conceptions vis-à-vis North Korea, the regional response at the time was not very different from that of the Clinton administration.[17] As summed up in a Congressional testimony by Ambassador Robert L. Gallucci, the chief U.S. negotiator with the North Koreans at the time, the regional response during the first crisis and after the Geneva Agreement was in accord with that of the United States: "We stayed in touch with allies . . . [W]e are, all three, together on this agreement."[18]

In contrast, even prior to 9/11, the Bush administration's attitude toward North Korea caused friction between the United States and East Asian countries. When the new administration in Washington refused to follow through on the engagement policy of the Clinton administration, which was largely in accord with the evolving regional visions of East Asian states anchored to North Korea, the regional concerns began to grow.[19] Despite Secretary of State Colin Powell's initial interest in the engagement policy, neo-conservatives in the Pentagon and the White House from the beginning had no desire of continuing the Clinton administration's policy on North Korea. In his first meeting with South Korea

President Kim Dae-jung, President Bush himself made clear that "he would not resume missile talks with North Korea anytime soon, putting aside the Clinton administration's two-year campaign for a deal and the eventual normalization of relations."[20]

The situation took a turn for the worse as a new post–9/11 global strategic blueprint took shape in Washington and Bush's "axis of evil" speech signaled a new direction in addressing the proliferation challenge. In this vein, 9/11 provided the Bush administration and its neo-conservative officials with an impetus for redefining the threat of WMD and pushing the larger goal of regime change in Iraq and other rogue states. In these rapidly changing circumstances, the second North Korean nuclear crisis hardened the Bush administration's position. Alarmed about its potential effects on their regional visions and internally shaped regional roles, East Asian countries quickly demanded flexibility from Washington. Under the pressure from South Korea and Japan, the Bush administration briefly relaxed its stance in a US-South Korea-Japan statement issued on January 7, 2003, which expressed a willingness to meet with North Koreans and discuss the nuclear issue.[21] But the hardline position intensified as the crisis deepened. Soon the Bush administration found itself "on a collision course not just with Pyongyang, but more importantly with U.S. allies in northeast Asia."[22] Before examining the escalating tension between the Bush administration and the East Asian countries, however, the next section analyzes the nature of the Bush Doctrine and its application to the proliferation challenge, including North Korea.

2.3 THE BUSH DOCTRINE AND THE NORTH KOREAN CHALLENGE

The Bush Doctrine: 9/11 and Global Strategic Context

With the strategic blueprint laid out in the 2002 *National Security Strategy*,[23] the Bush administration gave a decidedly militaristic turn to America's global strategic posture. The main assumption of that document was that the United States faced undeterrable, irrational regimes bent on threatening their neighbors and disrupting the global nonproliferation regime to satisfy their nuclear ambition. In an era when nuclear proliferation increases the danger of nuclear terrorism, so the argument goes, the business-as-usual approach is untenable. Such a drastic change in threat perception necessitated a new, proactive approach based on preemption[24] (rather than deterrence), counterproliferation (rather than nonproliferation), and military means (rather than diplomatic options).

In this radical strategic shift, 9/11 proved to be a watershed moment, a transformative event that paved the way for a new frame of reference in U.S. global strategy. In fact, John Lewis Gaddis called the Bush Doctrine "the most sweeping shift in U.S. grand strategy since the beginning of the Cold War."[25] In a remarkable similarity to the Truman Doctrine, which laid out a new strategic doctrine of containment and the building of a national security state after World War II, President Bush effectively "[turned] the crisis of 9/11 into an opportunity to secure the endorsement of the American public for a new kind of national security strategy encapsulated in the slogan 'the war on terror.'"[26] As one prominent neo-conservative put it, "[September 11] changed the world, and changed our understanding of the world." In this post-9/11 world, he continued, neo-conservatism is "the most plausible explanation of the new reality and the most compelling and active response to it," while warning of "the danger of a foreign policy centered on the illusion of stability and equilibrium."[27]

However, the origins of the strategic transformation reflected in the Bush Doctrine date further back than September 11. Christian Reus-Smit, for example, links the Bush Doctrine to the ideological underpinnings of the Reagan administration: "deep-rooted politico-cultural conceptions of American exceptionalism, democratic mission and security through world order tutelage; and the chance confluence of historical events."[28] However, it was only after the end of the Cold War that a concrete strategic blueprint based on such beliefs took shape. In 1992, the Pentagon worked on the first biennial National Defense Planning Guidance (NDPG), a document that, for the first time since the end of World War II, did not highlight the Soviet Union as the main threat. Written by key neo-conservatives who would later become high-ranking officials in the George W. Bush administration, such as Paul Wolfowitz, Zalmay Khalilzad, and L. Scooter Libby, the 1992 NDPG envisioned a formidable global superpower so dominant that it would "sufficiently account for the interests of the advanced industrial nations" and would dissuade any potential competitors from "challenging [U.S.] leadership or seeking to overturn the established political and economic order."[29]

The document listed proliferation of weapons of mass destruction, ballistic missiles, and terrorism as the main threats, singling out Iraq and North Korea as primary cases. In dealing with these countries, the report made it clear that the United States would act unilaterally.[30] When the document was leaked to the media, it caused a firestorm of controversy, with the rest of the world criticizing it as "a blueprint for American hegemony." President George H. W. Bush and other government officials soon dismissed the document altogether. However, Dick Cheney, then Secretary of

Defense, saw its potential for transforming the global order and told Khalilzad, "You've discovered a new rationale for our role in the world."[31]

Although completely discredited during the Democratic administration of the 1990s, the ideas behind the 1992 NDPG survived, only to resurface with a vengeance during the George W. Bush presidency. With the proponents of the 1992 NDPG now in key government positions, after 9/11 the Bush administration moved swiftly to a new agenda of reshaping the global order and regional dynamics in key parts of the world. The combination of power, fear, and perceived opportunity, according to Robert Jervis, enabled the Bush administration to "seek to reshape global politics and various societies around the world." Absent U.S. intervention, from this perspective, "the international environment will become more menacing to the United States and its values, but strong action can help increase global security and produce a better world."[32] In fact, the 2006 *Quadrennial Defense Review* epitomized a new U.S. strategic focus:

> [The U.S. strategic goal is] to ensure that *no foreign power can dictate the terms of regional or global security*. It will attempt to dissuade any military competitor from developing disruptive or other capabilities that could enable regional hegemony or hostile action against the United States or other friendly countries.[33] (Emphasis added)

The Bush Doctrine and Nuclear Proliferation

In its new global strategic blueprint, the Bush administration put particular emphasis on the proliferation challenge and the threat from "rogue states." Such a framing in turn would have ripple effects on global and regional affairs, as a single objective reality can be interpreted in myriad ways by different political actors, all with implications for subsequent policy decisions.[34] Crucial in this regard are not just the specific terms political actors use (e.g., rogues, or axis-of-evil), but "who has the ability to shape the international agenda and how they choose to shape it." In the post–Cold War era, it is the United States that, as the sole superpower, has "the ability to put forward new ideas, to define (or redefine) international society, and to exclude those states that do not comply."[35] In this process, whether a particular regime actually has the wherewithal to inflict substantial damage on the United States or how its regional neighbors view them becomes secondary. What matters instead is the type of regime the United States designates as a threat: a regime that is considered hostile to the United States and its regional strategy.

Along with its new framing of rogue states and WMD as the central threat, the Bush administration unveiled a new policy approach to proliferation by shifting its emphasis from nonproliferation to counterproliferation.[36] The doctrine of preemption[37] figured prominently in President Bush's speeches and *The 2002 National Security Strategy* symbolized such a shift.[38] Since its inception in 1968, the nonproliferation norm, the ideational backbone of the Nuclear Nonproliferation Treaty (NPT) regime, has been largely successful in prohibiting the possession and proliferation of weapons of mass destruction, including nuclear, biological, and chemical weapons. In the nuclear domain, the nonproliferation norm has been relatively effective for more than three decades, with the notable exception of the South Asian cases—India and Pakistan.[39]

Technically speaking, however, India and Pakistan are not in breach of the rules and regulations specified by the nonproliferation regime, since the two have never been signatories of the NPT. Nevertheless, they were not free from global condemnation as norm violators. Referring to the Indian and Pakistani nuclear tests in 1998, Spurgeon Keeny noted that both countries violated "the 30-year international norm against new nuclear-weapon states and the newly established taboo against nuclear testing."[40] Although critics questioned both the enforcement mechanism of the nonproliferation regime and the effectiveness of international sanctions against proliferators, the effects of the nonproliferation norm in curbing the temptation to go nuclear were generally viewed in a positive light during the Cold War period.

The first sign of change emerged in the early years of the Clinton administration when the Pentagon began to use the term "counterproliferation." With the specter of Saddam Hussein's WMD retaliation in the First Gulf War still vivid in 1993, then Secretary of Defense Les Aspin launched the Counterproliferation Initiative (CPI) to explore military options for dealing with WMD-armed adversaries.[41] While the program was further developed through various counterproliferation plans and programs in subsequent years, the Clinton administration's initiative remained "subordinate to a larger national strategy predicated primarily on traditional and more recent nonproliferation measures."[42] The term counterproliferation was carefully "embedded within a comprehensive non-proliferation policy that included non-military instruments," and thus was viewed as an effort to complement, rather than supplant, existing nonproliferation options.[43] Furthermore, the Clinton administration's counterproliferation initiative did not include "nuclear first strikes or preventive war aimed at stopping a regime from acquiring WMD. Intra-war attacks on enemy WMD facilities were envisaged, but not starting a war itself— and certainly not a nuclear war."[44]

The Bush administration added a whole new dimension to U.S. proliferation policy with the 2002 *National Security Strategy*. The report framed the new strategic environment in a way that emphasized WMD threats and required proactive actions, including preemptive strikes. The basic assumption was that the post–Cold War threat environment was fundamentally different from that of the Cold War years:

> In the Cold War, weapons of mass destruction were considered weapons of last resort whose use risked the destruction of those who used them. Today, our enemies see weapons of mass destruction as weapons of choice.[45]

While the nonproliferation norm, with its related policies, was "multilateral at its core" and "primarily a diplomatic strategy," the 2002 *National Security Strategy* called for proactive and, if necessary, unilateral actions.[46]

Parallel to the doctrinal change, a series of action plans included the use of nuclear weapons. While briefly mentioning the problem of "rogue states," the previous *Nuclear Posture Review* published in 1994 concluded, "the threat they posed did not warrant significant changes in U.S. nuclear forces or policies."[47] However, the 2002 *Nuclear Posture Review* called for, if necessary, specific nuclear options targeted at countries, including North Korea and Iran.[48] In December 2002, the U.S. Department of Defense also set out a policy for combating the proliferation of nuclear, biological, and chemical (NBC) weapons in *The National Strategy to Combat Weapons of Mass Destruction*.[49] The report declared that the "primary objective of a response is to disrupt *an imminent attack* or an attack in progress, and eliminate the threat of *future attacks*" (Emphasis added).[50]

Overall, the Bush administration's counterproliferation drive had two distinctive features that represent a sharp break from the nonproliferation campaign. First, as the above quote from *The National Strategy to Combat Weapons of Mass Destruction* shows, the new strategy made no distinction between the threats of "imminent" and "future" attacks. Effectively conflating the terms preemption and prevention, the Bush administration's proliferation drive was focused on the mere *possibility*, not the *probability*, of imminent enemy attacks. John Lewis Gaddis attributed the blending of the terms to the impact of 9/11: "In mounting its post–September 11 offensive, the Bush administration conflated these terms, using the word 'preemption' to justify what turned out to be a 'preventive' war against Saddam Hussein's Iraq."[51] Donald Rumsfeld himself admitted at a congressional hearing, "the coalition did not act in Iraq because we had discovered dramatic new evidence of Iraq's pursuit of weapons of mass destruction. We acted because we saw the evidence in a dramatic new light—through the prism of our experience on 9/11."[52] The bottom line was that WMD threats acquired *an ever-present sense of urgency.*

Secondly, the main targets of the Bush administration's counterproliferation drive were not *weapons*, but *regimes* that seek such weapons. The main rationale for setting up the NPT system in the first place was a belief that the existence of nuclear weapons themselves was the main source of the problem.[53] The emphasis on removing weapons, not regimes, continued in the Clinton administration, which described the main security threat as the one "posed by the proliferation of nuclear, biological and chemical weapons and their means of delivery."[54] The Bush administration dramatically shifted focus in proliferation policy. As Bill Keller wrote, from the Bush administration's perspective, "the main problem is not nuclear weapons themselves, but bad regimes armed with nuclear weapons."[55] When Saddam's regime collapsed, President Bush proclaimed:

> By a combination of creative strategies and advanced technology, we are redefining war on our terms. . . . In this new era of warfare, we can target *a regime*, not a nation.

> Terrorists and tyrants have now been put on notice, they can *no longer feel safe* hiding behind innocent lives.[56] (Emphasis added)

Laying out the rationale for the doctrine of preemption, President Bush went further by declaring that containment policy was of little use in the face of rogue states and dictators bent on using nuclear weapons.

> [N]ew threats also require new thinking . . . Containment is not possible when *unbalanced dictators* with weapons of mass destruction can deliver those weapons on missiles or secretly provide them to terrorist allies.

> We cannot put our faith in the word of *tyrants*, who solemnly sign nonproliferation treaties, and then systemically break them. If we wait for threats to fully materialize, we will have waited too long . . . In the world we have entered, *the only path to safety is the path of action. And this nation will act.*[57] (Emphasis added)

The Bush Doctrine and the North Korean Challenge

The shifts in the broader strategic focus and proliferation policy of the United States directly affected the country's policy toward North Korea. Even before the doctrinal change, the Bush administration's approach toward North Korea was confrontational. After its refusal to endorse South Korea's sunshine policy and continue Clinton's engagement policy toward North Korea, the Bush administration in June 2001 issued a long-awaited policy review on North Korea. It proposed a "comprehensive approach" toward North Korea, including the issues of ballistic missiles, conventional forces, and nuclear issues. While the Bush administration expressed an interest in addressing a wide range of issues with North Korea, it called for North Korea's compliance on all these aspects prior to a U.S. counter-offer.[58] As such, the expanded agenda itself amounted to "a marked stiffening of U.S. policy from that of the Clinton administration." North Korea in turn reacted sharply by depicting the Bush administration's approach as "an attempt to disarm [North Korea] through negotiations . . . hostile in its intention" and a major shift from the Clinton administration's approach that, from a North Korean perspective, was "in conformity with the interests of both sides."[59]

Worth noting here is that behavior did not matter much in the Bush administration's designation of threat. As Jae-Jung Suh observed, the change in the Bush administration's perception of the North Korean threat came without significant changes in North Korea's material capabilities or regime behavior. In the broader global campaign against proliferation, the Bush administration viewed North Korea only as a global proliferation threat, while discounting its willingness to cooperate with the Clinton administration on a number of issues.[60] As a matter of fact, North Korea's reaction after 9/11 was anything but provocative. One day after the attacks in New York and Washington, the North Korean government issued a public statement denouncing all forms of terrorism, while conveying, through Swedish diplomats based in North Korea, a private message of condolence to the United States. Moreover, it signed a number of international protocols on terrorism.[61] Some observers interpreted North Korea's behavior as an expression of interest in renewing contacts with the United States.[62]

Nonetheless, nothing came of North Korea's diplomatic initiatives toward the Bush administration. Instead, a few months later, President Bush opted to denounce North Korea as part of the axis of evil. Still, North Korea did not give up hopes of renewing talks with the United States. In September 2002, North Korea announced an indefinite extension of the moratorium on testing long-range missiles as long as dialogue continued with the United States. Again, positive North Korean behavior did not trigger similar reactions from the United States. The Bush administration simply responded with a White House statement that Assistant Secretary of State James Kelly would visit Pyongyang and "explain U.S. policy and seek progress on a range of issues of long-standing concern to the United States and the international community."[63] Regional actors who expected that the Bush administration would finally make progress on a variety of issues with North Korea were disappointed by Kelly's confrontation with his North Korean counterpart over North Korea's alleged uranium enrichment program, which sparked the second North Korean nuclear crisis.

What followed was the end of the Agreed Framework, which in turn led to chain reactions from North Korea, including reprocessing of materials from the Yongbyon reactor and withdrawal from the NPT. Despite similarities in early developments of the two crises, the different approaches by the Clinton and Bush administrations were emblematic of a broad contrast in their assumptions about how the North Korean challenge could be managed. Whereas the Clinton administration pursued a policy of "deepening engagement with North Korea," the Bush administration sought a policy of "rigidity and toughness."[64] Secretary of Defense Rumsfeld was adamantly opposed to U.S. engagement with North Korea and argued in a series of memos that the United States should focus on the collapse of the North Korean regime, not on dialogue with Kim Jong Il.[65] Secretary of State Condoleezza Rice also maintained a similar position in regard to the North Korean regime. In an interview in May 2006, a reporter asked her whether North Korea was still part of the axis of evil. With little hesitation, she responded, "absolutely."[66]

The different understandings of the North Korea challenge led to different means of addressing it. While the Clinton administration engaged in a series of direct talks with North Korea, the Bush administration, until 2007, did not allow its representatives at the Six Party Talks to have bilateral meetings with their North Korean counterparts. While the Clinton administration considered the use of force only as a last resort, the Bush administration did not hesitate to single out North Korea as a potential target of U.S. attacks, even nuclear attacks as revealed in the 2002 *Nuclear Posture Review*.[67] This policy orientation stood in stark contrast to that of the Clinton administration, which agreed to provide a "negative security assurance" of not using nuclear weapons against North Korea as long as it remained a member of the NPT.[68] With extension of the NPT hanging in the balance, the Clinton administration was both determined to resolve the first North Korean nuclear crisis and willing to seize an opportunity to "conduct the first truly international diplomatic campaign to promote nonproliferation."[69]

Although the Bush administration used the multilateral Six Party framework, it did so mainly as a venue for putting unified pressure on North Korea. Washington hardliners, including those in Vice President

Dick Cheney's office and Robert C. Joseph, the nonproliferation director at the National Security Council, prohibited direct talks between the U.S. delegation and North Koreans even on an informal basis. The chief U.S. delegate James Kelly's talking points prepared by the State Department were often replaced with a harsher White House version.[70] The hardliners viewed the Six Party talks mainly as a site "for the United States to set out its nonnegotiable demands with the support of the other four partners."[71] According to Lawrence Wilkerson, Colin Powell's chief of staff, Cheney ensured that U.S. negotiators in their meeting with North Korean counterparts would be able to "say little more than 'welcome and good-bye.'"[72] Again, this was a far cry from the Clinton administration's stance. As U.S. negotiators at the time revealed in their memoirs, the Clinton administration at times appeared to focus too much on multilateralism, "being too deferential to Seoul and Vienna."[73]

Moreover, documents associated with the Bush Doctrine used preemption and counterproliferation "almost synonymously" in their discussion of military actions on WMD targets.[74] This allowed greater emphasis on military means in proliferation strategy. The 2006 *Quadrennial Defense Review* thus emphasized "WMD elimination operations that locate, characterize, secure, disable and/or destroy a state or non-state actor's WMD capabilities and programs in a hostile or uncertain environment."[75] Similarly, in September 2005, Secretary Rumsfeld urged a resumption of "studying the feasibility of an earth-penetrating nuclear warhead," which can be used against underground targets.[76] Amid this series of events, even some prominent members of the Republican Party began to question the validity of the post–9/11 U.S. global strategy. For instance, former State Department Middle East negotiator Dennis Ross expressed concern about the Bush administration's "instinct toward regime change" rather than changing regime behavior.[77]

In a rare off-the-record interview in November 2002, a Bush administration official specifically linked the focus on regimes to the North Korean case.

I think we need to stop thinking about what we're going to give [North Korea]. Instead, we need to think about how we're going to change this [Kim Jong Il] regime. How are we going to bring this government down? That's the threat, the government. That's what our President thinks. Our diplomats are uneasy with it but that's what our President thinks. He's very clear on that. He was quoted in the Post and on Sixty Minutes saying that he loathed the leader, "the dear leader." That's our President. That's what he thinks! There's not much mystery in this. *Change the regime.*[78] (Emphasis added)

While acknowledging the need for diplomatic channels, President Bush did not rule out military options: "If they don't work diplomatically, they will have to work militarily. And military option is our last choice."[79] Under Secretary of State John Bolton made the same point, "If rogue states are not willing to follow the logic of nonproliferation norms, they must be prepared to face the logic of adverse consequences. It is why we repeatedly caution that no option is off the table."[80] In another speech, Bolton went further in saying that "North Korea and Iran would be the next targets after the war with Iraq ended."[81] Secretary Rice also suggested that Kim Jong Il ruled "a wounded, isolated nation that can be enveloped by troops and unhappy neighbors, and squeezed until its bleeding economy shatters."[82] In fact, an early 2003 column revealed a "planning for a possible military strike" on North Korea's nuclear facility. Although U.S. officials downplayed them as "no more than contingency plans," they included a host of military scenarios ranging from "surgical cruise missile strikes to sledgehammer bombing," and "even talk of using tactical nuclear weapons to neutralize hardened artillery positions aimed at Seoul."[83]

All in all, the combination of 9/11 and America's preponderance enabled the Bush administration to uphold a new strategic doctrine aimed at reshaping the world order. In this sense, Stephen Walt argued that the Bush Doctrine was not a policy of preemption, but "a war fought to forestall a shift in the balance of power, independent of whether or not the opponent was planning to attack."[84] In the long term, he predicted, the strategy would fail since "the key is not power but persuasion" that U.S. primacy is in fact better than other scenarios for the rest of the world.[85] To East Asian countries, the Bush administration's global strategy in general and its applications to North Korea in particular were anything but persuasive.

2.4 THE EAST ASIAN RESPONSE TO THE BUSH DOCTRINE

Regional Understanding of the North Korean Challenge

Despite the U.S. perception of North Korea as an urgent global threat, East Asian countries have viewed the North Korean challenge as integral to an evolving regional order and have sought to "regionalize" the issue from the onset of the second crisis. From a regional perspective, the North Korean question is intricately linked to the continuation of the Cold War tensions surrounding the Korean Peninsula, rather than a novel and imminent challenge to regional stability. As a consequence, the

Bush administration's narrative of an urgent and unconventional threat emanating from Pyongyang had little resonance in East Asia. Even in the immediate aftermath of the second crisis, one Japanese expert predicted, the North Korean problem could serve as a "basis for stabilizing the rest of East Asia."[86]

The widening gulf between the United States and regional understandings of the North Korean challenge was also evident in the fact that East Asian states thought less about the nuclear issue itself than the impact of the North Korean question on broader regional security dynamics such as the China–Japan rivalry and anti-U.S. sentiments on the Korean Peninsula.[87] For instance, to many Chinese, the greatest threat remains Taipei, not Pyongyang.[88] The main challenge associated with North Korean nuclear question would primarily be its potential to create a regional nuclear arms race that might result in a nuclear-armed Taiwan. Similarly, South Korean policymakers expressed concern about the impact of the North Korean factor on Japan's path to a becoming a "normal state."[89] As a former Japanese ambassador and high-ranking Foreign Ministry official put it succinctly, "the regional perception of the North Korean threat is to a large degree a function of regional security dynamics."[90]

This rather fluid, contingent nature of the regional threat perception of North Korea—in contrast to the fixed, unduly simplistic global narrative of an unpredictable and uniquely dangerous rogue nation—stemmed from the regional understanding of the North Korean challenge as a complex regional security question that had "both profound historical origins and complicated realistic factors."[91] For instance, one Chinese expert contended that "the remaining shadows of the Cold War in the Korean Peninsula" and the lack of mutual trust between the United States and North Korea were the root cause of the North Korean nuclear crisis.[92] Another Chinese analyst concurred when he wrote that North Korea's nuclear ambitions derive from "its acute sense of insecurity and vulnerability and, hence, any resolution must address this issue."[93]

Such an understanding was not confined to the views of Pyongyang's sole communist ally. Even South Korean President Roh Moo-hyun revealed in his speech in 2004 that he was sympathetic to the North Korean stance that its pursuit of nuclear weapons stemmed from its need to deter external threats.[94] The Japanese, for their part, maintained that the North Korean issue represented the last chapter of Japan's postwar settlements with its East Asian neighbors, a key factor that motivated Japanese Prime Minister Koizumi's stated goal of diplomatic normalization with North Korea.[95] Despite the abduction scandal and the subsequent anti–North Korean sentiment in Japan, Prime Minister Koizumi repeated his willingness to normalize diplomatic relations with North Korea before the end of his term as prime minister in September 2006.[96]

Regional Response to the Bush Administration's Approach

As for the proper response to the North Korean challenge, both the Western media and policymakers tended to stress the importance for coercive measures and China's backing to that end. Calling on China to use its leverage over North Korea, for instance, Fareed Zakaria wrote, "Washington is right to urge [China] to act boldly."[97] Similarly, Thomas Friedman lamented that were China to put pressure on North Korea "the proliferation threat from Pyongyang would be over."[98] In the face of China's resistance to the use of pressure tactics, then U.S. Under Secretary of State Robert Joseph even threatened that if China did not take more action "there possibly could be very significant consequences for U.S.–Chinese relations."[99]

In this vein, the allegation of a North Korea–Libya link over uranium hexafluoride gas in February 2005 provides a unique window into the way the Bush administration used the Six Party talks as a platform for applying unified pressure on North Korea. Just as North Korea was expected to resume the Six Party talks, Bush's top Asian officials visited China, Japan, and South Korea to brief their counterparts about the alleged link. Given that the allegation was first made almost a year earlier, David Albright, a prominent U.S. proliferation expert and a former UN inspector, said, "the timing has to make one suspicious that the information is being used to pressure allies to take a tougher line with North Korea."[100] Some South Korean observers thus viewed the Six Party meetings primarily as "a unilateral offensive in the guise of a multilateral modality to strangulate North Korea."[101]

Despite the single-minded U.S. focus on using coercion to disarm North Korea's nuclear arsenal, East Asian countries "want[ed] above all to keep their neighborhood peaceful."[102] China's active diplomacy in the second crisis, a dramatic change from its passivity during the first crisis in 1993–1994, was not because of Pyongyang's nuclear provocation per se but because of a fear that the standoff between North Korea and the United States was "heading toward a certain clash that would be disastrous for China."[103] Put differently, it was not the imminent danger of the North Korean nuclear threat but "the clear and present danger of Pyongyang being next on the U.S. hit list" that partly drove China's proactive role in the second crisis.[104]

A Chinese expert warned that if the Bush administration stuck to its position of "exercising pressure on North Korea and bringing about an eventual regime change," U.S.–China cooperation could not be maintained.[105] In the early weeks of the war in Iraq, a South Korean defense analyst even hoped for a lengthy operation there to avoid U.S. preemptive strikes on North Korea.[106] The Bush doctrine of a preemptive war also made a Japanese expert lamented, "The United States had become a destabilizing factor in international affairs."[107] Warning against America's "leanings toward the use of force and unilateralism," a Japanese columnist declared, "If Bush and company mean to peddle freedom in a package with missiles and artillery shells, I wish they would keep out of the global square."[108]

As a consequence, at the beginning of the crisis, Japan worked with South Korea "to nudge the Bush administration towards negotiations with North Korea."[109] Another Japanese expert and advisor to the government warned of the Bush administration's "uncompromising stance toward Pyongyang, which involves the risk of pushing the North Korean leadership into a corner." He suggested instead that through negotiations and diplomacy, Japan and South Korea should "take approaches toward Pyongyang that are different from that of the United States."[110] In fact, the Koizumi government stated that its objective was not "to overturn the regime in North Korea but to gradually change the nature of its political and economic systems."[111] After his second trip to Pyongyang, Prime Minister Koizumi even conveyed to President Bush the North Korean concern about U.S. policy. A few months later, he suggested to Bush that the U.S. government consider direct negotiation with North Korea. With no response from Bush, both sides had to agree not to include this issue in their joint press briefing.[112]

China's Foreign Ministry spokesman Kong Quan directly linked the Bush administration's pressure tactics to regional instability: "we do not believe in resorting to sanctions or pressure. These measures would not solve problems but instead could complicate the situation."[113] South Korean President Roh also blamed the call for regime change in Pyongyang by U.S. hardliners for the difficulty in resolving the North Korean crisis.[114] His Unification Minister Chung Dong Young soon announced that the South Korean government would play a leadership role in managing the North Korean issue, rather than meekly embracing the U.S. approach.[115]

Given the different understandings of the North Korean challenge, East Asian countries showed little interest in U.S.-led counterproliferation initiatives such as the Proliferation Security Initiative (PSI). Both Beijing and Seoul refused to join the global drive that garnered broad support from various countries in the world.[116] Even Japan, one of the few East Asian members of the PSI, expressed apprehension about the possibility of the initiative provoking North Korea too much.[117] Mentioning the North Korean fear that the Negative Security Assurance (NSA) included in the 1994 Agreed Framework was no longer valid in the wake of the newest U.S. nuclear posture review, a report submitted by the Foreign Ministry–sponsored Japan Institute of International Affairs called for providing North Korea with multilateral security assurances.[118] With Japan's plea for moderation added to the regional chorus of a negotiated solution, the Bush administration "for the first time presented elements of a 'roadmap' for settlement" at the third round of the Six Party Talks in July 2004.[119]

All in all, central to the regional understanding of the North Korean challenge was not so much the nuclear issue per se as its impact on regional order. Relating North Korean nuclear ambitions to China's own experiences in the early Cold War years, a leading Chinese arms control expert expressed his understanding of North Korea's nuclear pursuit and even called for "accepting a nuclear North Korea."[120] A former Chinese Foreign Ministry official made a similar point that China might tolerate a nuclear North Korea if its impact on the regional security order were minimal.[121] In 2003, South Korean president Roh's envoys to Washington shocked Bush advisers by revealing that they "would rather have a nuclear North Korea than a chaotic collapse of the government there."[122]

Throughout the second North Korean nuclear crisis, South Korean Presidents Kim Dae-jung and Roh Moo-hyun and Japanese Prime Minister Koizumi Junichiro all sought to use quiet bargaining and the promise of economic assistance in dealing with North Korea. Along with its potential to disrupt the regional status quo, from an East Asian perspective, the Bush Doctrine was also seen as impeding the momentum toward regionalism. Focused on the global and nuclear dimensions, the Bush administration gave short shrift to South Korea's reconciliation policy toward Pyongyang and the regional initiative centered on North Korea. Similarly, as one Japanese expert put it, the Bush administration never liked Koizumi's visits to Pyongyang and intended to mitigate the impact of such visits.[123] Soon, regional frustration led to growing questions about U.S. strategic intentions in the region.

Regional Concerns about U.S. Intentions and Regional Order

As the stalemate at the Six Party Talks continued in the midst of the Bush administration's inflexible position toward North Korea, regional countries grew more alarmed about possible motivations behind the hard line stance. Instead of accepting the U.S. rationale for the post–9/11 strategic context, East Asian countries began to view the Bush Doctrine as a new U.S. regional strategy aimed at reshaping the regional order to its liking.[124] For example, one South Korean analyst suspected the Bush administration was not forthcoming in its dealings with North Korea because it feared a loss of U.S. influence in the region and a negative impact on a planned missile defense scheme in East Asia.[125] One Chinese expert of the Communist Party School seemed to agree when he observed that the crisis would "serve the U.S. goal of maintaining its predominant security posture in the region."[126]

Paradoxically, despite the pervasive sense of urgency and the crisis metaphor in the U.S. narrative of North Korea, many regional actors suspected that the Bush administration might not be interested in resolving the crisis anytime soon.[127] From a regional perspective, resolution of the crisis hinged crucially on whether the United States and North Korea "can be reasonable in presenting their concerns and in appreciating the concerns of others."[128] Instead of taking a leadership role at the Six Party Talks, one regional expert protested, the United States delegated the job of resolving the crisis to East Asian countries.[129] Others also suggested that the Bush administration's main goal in the Six Party Talks might be "to wreck the talks in order to pave the way for more coercive actions," particularly given the region-wide view that President Bush expressed "less sensitivity and respect than Clinton toward the views and approaches of South Korea in dealing with the North."[130]

Overall, there was an acute sense in the region that the Six Party Talks had little prospect of success unless the United States showed greater willingness to negotiate.[131] Even if the United States made some progress on the nuclear front, one Chinese expert predicted, there would be another stalemate since having "some levels of tension on the Korean Peninsula would be helpful for the Americans" in their regional strategic plans.[132] Similarly, others observed, had the United States acted properly in the region (i.e., had they not threatened the Kim regime), the situation would have been different and might have been resolved more quickly.[133] One analyst at the State Council–affiliated Chinese Institute of Contemporary International Relations (CICIR) even suggested that if regional countries alone had participated in the talks, the crisis would have already been defused.[134] It was in this context that a former South Korean unification minister complained that the United States found fault with North Korea over the nuclear issue whenever a mood of reconciliation surfaced on the Korean Peninsula.[135]

The regional suspicion of the U.S. role at the Six Party Talks also revealed a more alarming trend in the regional perception of long-term U.S. roles in the region. For instance, another analyst at the China Institute of Contemporary International Relations observed that the ultimate U.S. goal with regard to proliferation issues was not "the resolution of nuclear crises but securing a hegemonic position in various parts of the world" in the Middle East (e.g., Iraq and Iran) and East Asia (e.g., North Korea).[136] From this vantage point, the U.S.-led counterproliferation drive was indeed a hegemonic means to interfere in the sovereignty of other states and to spread democratic regimes.[137] In the East Asian context, such a campaign manifested itself as a hardline U.S. stance on North Korea, with a broader regional goal of consolidating "the all-round US-Japan and US-ROK alliances."[138] From a Chinese perspective, the U.S. defense realignment scheme in East Asia (e.g., changes in the U.S.-Japanese alliance and U.S. military deployments, etc.) was part of larger "U.S. efforts to hinder China's rise in Asia."[139] As a result, the Six Party Talks became the battleground of different narratives and strategic visions. As an analyst at the Chinese Academy of Social Sciences suggested, while regional countries viewed the multilateral venue as a site for genuine regional institution building, the United States was "using it as a platform for strengthening its own alliance posture."[140]

More broadly, regional experts suggested that the fundamental question in addressing the North Korean challenge was how to perceive U.S.–China relations in the region.[141] Many Chinese analysts expressed their concern about "the uncertainties in United State's unilateral attempt to remold the world and its impact on the Sino-American relationship."[142] Among other questions, the Chinese asked about U.S. hegemony, power politics, and unilateral behavior in international relations.[143] Focusing on different perceptions of the North Korean challenge, Liu Ming maintained that "China values the stability of the Korean Peninsula with lesser preconditions, while the United States may become more willing to intervene directly to alter the status quo."[144] This is problematic for the Chinese given China's "deep-seated skepticism about the United States' strategic designs in the region."[145] Some even suggested that it would be easier for the Bush administration to use the North Korean threat than the more controversial China threat.[146]

Sensing the skewed U.S. threat perception in Bush's axis-of-evil speech, the Chinese government immediately issued a warning in a Foreign Ministry statement: "consequences will be very serious if [the United States] proceeds with this kind of logic."[147] As the crisis worsened, even high-ranking officials directly challenged the U.S. approach. In November 2004, for instance, the *China Daily* carried a controversial article by Chen

Qichen, a highly influential former Chinese foreign minister, entitled "U.S. strategy to be banned." In it, Chen offered a harsh rebuke of the Bush Doctrine: "The philosophy of the 'Bush Doctrine' is, in essence, force. It advocates the United States should rule over the whole world with overwhelming force, military force in particular."[148]

The Bush Doctrine worried the Japanese as well, as Tokyo was expected to play a greater regional role and to be "further integrated into the U.S. global strategy."[149] However, for the Japanese, the fear of entrapment in a U.S. military campaign appeared to be far greater than the fear of abandonment.[150] Pointing to a lack of public discussion on the implications of such a shift, a Japanese editorial called for "cautious and prudent behavior" in order to "reduce possible tensions and to foster mutual trust with neighbors."[151] Given Prime Minister Koizumi's close friendship with President Bush, a group of Japanese experts suggested that Koizumi might be "the best and only person who can persuade President Bush to have serious negotiations with the North Koreans."[152] However, if Japan simply follows the Bush administration's approach, another Japanese expert pointed out, Japan's "channels for cooperation with South Korea and China will be narrowed."[153]

2.5 CONCLUSION

The overall narrative and responses of East Asian countries with respect to the Bush administration's approach toward North Korea demonstrate that East Asian countries did not share the Bush administration's understanding of the North Korean threat and, thus, sought to weaken the U.S. approach in various dimensions. In contrast to the U.S. discourse about the urgent nature of the North Korean challenge, the regional sense of urgency derived not from North Korea's nuclear ambitions but from the global context where the traditional focus on nonproliferation was overshadowed by the counterproliferation drive of preemption and regime change.

As the outbreak of the second North Korean nuclear crisis coincided with a radical shift in global proliferation efforts, the U.S.-North Korean action-reaction dynamics reached a volatile point at which East Asian countries, the bystanders in the first crisis, decided to act, both bilaterally and through the Six Party process. Such activism stemmed from an understanding that regional stability rests more on managed or improved coexistence with the cumbersome neighbor than on coercion and preemption aimed at regime change in Pyongyang.

A comparison between the first and second North Korean nuclear crises illustrates this point. Absent the global rogue/counterproliferation frame, the first North Korean nuclear crisis featured a relatively small gap between the United States' understanding of the North Korean issue and the regional understanding of the same issue. Under these circumstances, regional actors felt no particular need to get involved in resolving the crisis, except by endorsing the Clinton administration's position and offering support for the United States along the way. With the new global narrative about counterproliferation and regime change fully at work, the second crisis brought into sharp relief the gap between global and regional understandings of the North Korean challenge, prompting the regional actors to resist the U.S. counterproliferation drive and its application to the North Korean case.

To be sure, there were many critics of the Bush Doctrine in the United States as well. Contemplating effective ways to deal with rogue regimes, Nicholas Kristof contrasted "engagement and deal-making" during the Clinton presidency with "confrontation and isolation" by the Bush administration. While Clinton's approach stopped North Korea from producing "a single ounce of plutonium during his eight years in office," Kristof predicted that North Korea would be able to amass "enough plutonium for about 10 weapons" in Bush's presidency.[154] The nuclear dimension, however, was hardly the only area where the Bush administration failed miserably. With its exclusive focus on proliferation and regime change, the Bush administration found few supporters in East Asia. As documented in this chapter, the regional resistance was sparked by the Bush administration's failure to grasp the East Asian understanding of what North Korea represents in and for the region. Examining how the meanings of North Korea were linked to the regional strategies of China, Japan, and South Korea is the subject of the next chapter.

CHAPTER 3

The North Korean Challenge and Regional Role Conceptions in East Asia

3.1 INTRODUCTION

This chapter explores the origins and nature of the regional understanding of the North Korean challenge. It shows that despite their seemingly disparate bilateral issues with North Korea, East Asian countries have engaged Pyongyang with the goals of playing a greater regional role and ensuring foreign policy autonomy. Although their efforts to enhance regional roles (i.e., internally shaped roles) must be made within the broader context of U.S. power and influence in the region (i.e., U.S.-directed regional roles), for the East Asian states North Korea is far more than a *short-term* proliferation question. It is inextricably linked to their *long-term* strategic priorities and regional visions. Hence, instead of unproblematically accepting the U.S. narrative, they view the North Korean challenge as a unique opportunity to recast their regional roles and overcome strategic dependence on the United States.

It is telling that specific policy overtures toward Pyongyang proliferated even after the outbreak of the second North Korean nuclear crises. Specifically, from the expansion of the joint Kaesung Industrial Zone in North Korea to the second inter-Korean summit in October 2007, the Kim Dae-jung and Roh Moo-hyun governments in Seoul were persistent in seeking reconciliation with North Korea. China also enhanced its strategic and economic ties with North Korea, while at the same time skillfully playing a mediating role between Pyongyang and Washington. During his tenure, Japanese Prime Minister Koizumi not only visited Pyongyang twice but also maintained his willingness to normalize Japan's troubled relationship with North Korea until he stepped down as prime minster in 2006.[1]

The internally shaped regional roles premised on greater engagement with Pyongyang, however, do not always dictate the domestic debate about the North Korean challenge. Evolving external circumstances also create an opening for different domestic political actors who seek to project different, U.S.-directed regional roles. For instance, as the crisis reached a stalemate in late 2004 and especially after North Korea's nuclear test in 2006, the U.S. approach and the rogue rhetoric served to empower domestic political groups that raised questions about the ruling government's regional visions linked to North Korea.

While similar tensions emerged between North Korea engagers and North Korea bashers in each East Asian country, the degree of domestic contestation was particularly high in Japan. Exploiting the public uproar against North Korea concerning the abduction issue and latching onto the global rogue narrative, Japan's conservatives made inroads into the national political scene. The ensuing political contestation reshaped domestic coalition dynamics in Japan, where the U.S.-directed regional role as an ally and an alternative regional vision centered on the U.S.-Japan alliance gained wide currency, making the earlier regional convergence on North Korea difficult to sustain.

The chapter probes deeper into the sources and evolution of these competing regional roles and contending regional visions in the following manner. The next section discusses the main drivers behind the search for new regional roles in East Asia and examines the nature of regional role conceptions and domestic contestation over the North Korean question. The following three sections take a closer look at the link between regional role conceptions and threat perceptions vis-à-vis North Korea in each of the three East Asian countries.

3.2 THE ORIGINS AND THE NATURE OF REGIONAL ROLE CONCEPTIONS

The abrupt ending of the Cold War erected a new regional order in Europe, which encompassed former Soviet satellite states. Few changes took place in the regional strategic landscape in East Asia. Instead, the region was quickly engulfed in a series of crises, including the first North Korean nuclear crisis and the Taiwan Strait Crisis of 1995–1996. Despite initial predictions of a gradual withdrawal of the United States from the region, both crises were managed mainly by the United States. By the mid-1990s, all the regional talks about an impending shift in the regional order quickly disappeared as the United States reiterated its regional commitment by pledging the maintenance of one hundred thousand troops in the region and by renewing the U.S.–Japan alliance. As a result, post–Cold War East Asia has remained virtually the same as before, with the U.S.-centered hub-and-spokes system of alliances largely intact.

The continuation of the U.S.-centered regional order, however, did not stop East Asian countries from seeking new regional roles and independent regional visions. Indeed, incessant calls for a new regional security framework in the 1990s reflect a region-wide yearning to go beyond the Cold War–based regional security structure in which their strategic dependence on the United States and limited regional roles persist. Specifically, Japan, the world's third largest economy, is a defeated nation that is permanently denied the right to use combat force beyond its territories. The postwar legacy still continues in the form of the pacifist constitution, which limits Japan's armed forces to a purely self-defense posture, thereby preventing it from assuming global and regional roles commensurate with its economic prowess. Its past roles as a colonizer in Korea and an invader in China make its regional status even more problematic.

Similarly, South Korea, the twelfth largest economy in the world and a global leader in information technology, also remains a long-time client of an alliance in which its wartime operational control is surrendered to a U.S. commander. China, the second-largest economy in the world and a member of both the UN Security Council and the exclusive nuclear club, is a divided socialist nation in which the ruling Communist Party's political legitimacy hinges critically on economic "catch-up" with the West and improving regional and international status. In short, all the East Asian countries have been eager to play greater and more independent regional roles and, in the process, to expand their diplomatic space and regional autonomy.

Each country's drive to redefine and enhance regional roles involves an effort to readjust troubled relations with North Korea. For the East Asian countries, that relationship is of great significance as it holds out the promise of enhanced diplomatic influence and regional status. Despite years of ups and downs, Japan's efforts to normalize its diplomatic relationship with North Korea have been persistent since the first round of the talks began in 1992. Prime Minister Koizumi's normalization efforts and the Pyongyang Declaration in 2002 illustrated Japan's regional strategy that continued to include North Korea as a key part of Japan's regional vision. South Korea's engagement policy toward North Korea, known as the sunshine policy, was not just about promoting inter-Korean reconciliation but also about positioning the Korean Peninsula at the center of East Asian economic and political integration.[2] Although showing communist solidarity was no longer a strategic necessity for China's fourth-generation leaders, Beijing's close relationship with Pyongyang had the potential for enhancing China's influence on the Korean Peninsula, "a geostrategic focal point of East Asia."[3]

While pursuit of greater regional roles and autonomy surfaced in earlier periods, the current regional overture toward North Korea began in earnest in 1998. With the adoption of the sunshine policy toward North Korea, the South Korean government set in motion a process of regional initiatives converging on the Korean Peninsula. With its new diplomatic campaign toward the North, the Kim Dae-jung government hoped to play a leading role on the regional scene. Concerned about the emergence of a regional order dictated by the United States and its alliances, the Chinese were also intent on reshaping the regional order and expanding its own role in the process.[4] Were it not for China's greater regional influence on the Korean Peninsula, they believed, the prospect of forging a new regional order would be slim.[5] China's active mediating role in the Six Party talks stemmed in part from this strategic thinking.

Japan's positive response to the sunshine policy was also prompt and consistent. In his summit with then South Korean President Kim Dae-jung in 1998, Japanese Prime Minister Obuchi Keizo suggested that Japan and Russia participate in "a six-party Northeast Asian security forum" which would address the issue of Korean Peninsula stability.[6] Prime Minister Mori Yoshiro, Obuchi's successor, also exchanged his views on North Korea with South Korean President Kim and updated him on the status of the Japan-DPRK normalization talks, while his foreign minister expressed Japan's support for the sunshine policy.[7] Prime Minister Koizumi's 2002 visit to Pyongyang also came with the realization that Japan was "left on the periphery" of the regional diplomatic scene in the midst of the first inter-Korean summit and Kim Jong Il's visit to Beijing right before the Korean summit.[8] Apart from bilateral issues with North Korea such as resolution of the colonial past and the abduction issue, Japan had broader "regional aspirations" concerning North Korea, "aiming to shape the future of the Korean peninsula, to expand Japan's regional security role, and to channel the rise of China as a regional power."[9]

It is worth pointing out, however, that despite the region-wide efforts to enhance regional roles and foreign policy autonomy, there were important differences among the East Asian countries in their domestic political dynamics, which, in conjunction with changing external circumstances, affected their domestic debate on regional roles and their approach toward North Korea. A case in point is the rise of the conservatives and anti-North Korean public sentiment in Japan, which came to the fore after North Korea's admission about the abduction of Japanese citizens by its agents in the 1970s and 1980s. The Bush Doctrine and the North Korean nuclear test in 2006 played into the anti-North Korean sentiment that had been a powerful domestic force since the revelation about the abduction. There is also no denying that the regional countries still played their roles under the influence of the United States. This is why the regional actors needed to balance externally and internally shaped regional roles.

Interestingly, East Asian countries' efforts to ensure role congruence between the two regional roles often took the form of double-talk. In a September 2003 speech at the UN General Assembly, for instance, Japanese Foreign Minister Kawaguchi Yoriko publicly called for the dismantling of North Korean nuclear programs and a speedy resolution of the abduction issue before Japan could proceed with the normalization of its diplomatic relations with North Korea. However, a few months later, a four-member Japanese official delegation made a secret trip to Pyongyang for further negotiations. Similarly, when then South Korean Foreign Minister Ban Ki-moon made a speech at the UN General Assembly in September 2004, he called for North Korea to immediately forgo all nuclear programs, while at the same time declaring that bilateral exchanges and cooperation between the two Koreas had reached *"a point from which there [was] no turning back."*[10]

More broadly, the East Asian states' pursuit of greater regional roles reflects their desire to escape from their dependence on the United States.[11] For reasons of security and economic development, Japan and South Korea have been dependent on alliance relationship with the United States. However, as a former Japanese ambassador and high-ranking foreign ministry official puts it, the United States has "its own parochial national interests," which may not always be in tune with those of its regional allies.[12] China has also been relying on friendly ties with the United States for continued economic growth and regional stability. Accompanying this sense of dependency was a persistent feeling of compromised regional status and a lack of foreign policy autonomy. It is this fervent desire of the regional actors to overcome their strategic dependency and to chart their own regional visions that shaped the East Asian understandings of, and policy behavior toward, North Korea. The following sections explore each country case in greater detail.

3.3 SOUTH KOREA

The Search for New Regional Roles

As the Cold War was drawing to an end, the South Korean government for the first time in its modern history set out an independent regional policy initiative. In the early 1990s, the Roh Tae-woo government launched a foreign policy blueprint called *"Nordpolitik,"* seeking diplomatic rapprochement with the Soviet Union and China.[13] Although the diplomatic charm offensive was aimed mainly at the two Communist neighbors, the key priority was "finding an opening with North Korea."[14] In late 1991, the two Koreas signed the "Basic Agreement, which includes a nonaggression pact and allows for exchange programs."[15] Although the diplomatic initiative went no further in the aftermath of the first North Korean nuclear crisis, the whole process demonstrated South Korea's willingness to play a greater regional role by taking an autonomous stance toward North Korea.

The first serious opportunity for South Korea to play such a regional role came in 1996 when President Clinton and South Korean President Kim Young-sam agreed to hold a "four party meeting," involving the two Koreas, the United States, and China. A joint statement from their meeting stated, "South and North Korea should take the lead in a renewed search for a permanent peace agreement."[16] For this new regional plan to succeed, South Korea had to persuade neighboring countries to join the regional exercise. This strategic consideration facilitated a bold initiative to improve relations with Japan and China.[17] Former South Korean Foreign Minister Hong Soonyoung implied this logic when he declared that South Korea's engagement policy was "not just aimed at North Korea."[18]

The South Koreans also sought to link inter-Korean engagement to a larger regional framework to ensure political and even financial support for a gradual reunification on the Korean Peninsula.[19] In this regard, the South Koreans proposed to hold a summit for the two Koreas and four regional powers "to focus international attention on Korea and to jumpstart the Korean peace process."[20] They envisioned the summit not only as "a breakthrough in the Korean peace process," but also as a platform for a broader regional security framework.[21] Given that previous regional tragedies such as Japan's colonization and the Korean War originated in the Korean Peninsula, a prominent South Korean scholar wrote, it would be only natural that the Peninsula should serve as a platform for rebuilding a new regional order.[22]

Internally Shaped Regional Role: The Sunshine Policy, the Hub of East Asia, and North Korea

Based on this long-standing regional vision, the Kim Dae-jung government proposed the sunshine policy of engagement toward North Korea. While seeking a peaceful coexistence of the two Koreas in the short term, the central tenet of the sunshine policy was to gradually transform "the reclusive regime in North Korea into a cooperative partner in peace and prosperity."[23] The Kim government linked the prospect of regime survival in Pyongyang and the reduction of regional tension to North Korea's integration into the region.[24] In the process, South Korea hoped to change both inter-Korean relations and to play a larger and proactive regional role.

South Korea's efforts during the Perry Process illustrate this point. Despite a crisis situation in the wake of North Korea's 1998 missile launch and suspicions about secret nuclear facilities in North Korea, the Kim administration persuaded the United States to reach a negotiated deal with North Korea, while frequently sending officials to Washington to discuss the North Korean situation.[25] Chinese President Jiang Zemin and Japanese Prime Minister Hashimoto Ryutaro repeatedly expressed their support for the sunshine policy, which further strengthened South Korea's efforts to change the U.S. policy toward North Korea. In this way, one South Korean expert observed, the sunshine policy effectively regionalized the North Korean issue, which had initially been seen in a global frame.[26]

After the first inter-Korean Summit in 2000 and the awarding of the Nobel Peace prize to President Kim, South Korea's engagement toward North Korea gained further momentum. President Kim, however, did not confine his focus solely to the inter-Korean level and sought to utilize Seoul's newfound links to Pyongyang with South Korea's greater regional role and a larger regional dimension in mind. A case in point was his effort to facilitate North Korea's relations with Japan. According to Lim Dong Won, the Unification Minister during the Kim government, in April 2002, just a few months before Koizumi's first visit to North Korea and the Pyongyang Declaration, President Kim sent Lim as a special envoy to Pyongyang and encouraged Kim Jong Il to acknowledge the abduction incidents and move ahead with diplomatic normalization with Japan.[27]

The engagement policy toward North Korea continued with the "Peace and Prosperity policy" of the Roh Moo-hyun administration. While seeking reconciliation with the North, the Roh government actively encouraged other regional countries to engage North Korea. A senior official of South Korea's Ministry of National Unification explained the rationale behind such a regional drive: depending upon the way the North Korean situation is settled, he predicted, "China-Japan relations may change, as well as regional dynamics."[28] The Roh government also encouraged Japan's efforts to normalize diplomatic ties with North Korea as a useful way to dampen tension between North Korea and the United States.[29] At the same time, the South Korean government made a series of efforts to improve its own relations with the North, including a 2004 decision to make the Minister of National Unification the head of South Korea's National Security Council.[30]

South Korea's regional drive aimed at North Korea also reflected and was reinforced by the general mood among the South Korean public, which was shifting in favor of inter-Korean relations. Against this backdrop, the two Koreas engaged in the joint operation of an industrial park in the North Korean border city of Kaesong, which was characterized by the governments "as an experiment with market reforms."[31] As of 2008, there were 150 South Korean companies in operation in the complex.[32] Encouraged by a series of exchanges with North Korea, the majority of South Koreans supported the reconciliation effort. More than at any time since the end of the Korean War, a general consensus emerged among the South Korean public that coexistence with North Korea accompanied by a gradual change of the North aimed at unification was the only viable option.[33]

The spread of inter-Korean nationalism (*minjok gongjo*) in turn affected South Korea's regional policy and alliance relationship with the United States.[34] Those who supported the government position held that North Korea was "part of the Korean ethnic community" and thus raised questions about the U.S. role and its policies toward North Korea, which may not be in tune with South Korea's national interests.[35] Many South Koreans also maintained that inter-Korean relations and the future of the Korean Peninsula should be controlled by Koreans themselves, including the North Koreans.[36] This "pan-Korean nationalism" and South Korea's internally shaped regional role as an independent regional actor was increasingly on a collision course with the Bush administration's hardline approach toward the North.[37] A 2003 poll showed that 35.4 percent of South Koreans in their twenties chose the United States as the least favored country while only 4.1 percent chose North Korea. Overall, over 40 percent of Koreans in their twenties thought that "inter-Korean cooperation should take precedence over South Korea's cooperation with the United States."[38]

Given this nationwide support for the engagement policy toward the North, it is not surprising that U.S. policy toward North Korea was seen as "driving North Korea into a corner, risking provocation and unnecessary harm to the policy of inter-Korean reconciliation."[39] A former South Korean minister of unification even suggested that the United States had found fault with North Korea over the nuclear issue whenever reconciliation efforts were underway.[40] As a consequence, there has been "a shift in the popular image of the U.S. from a protector of South Korea's security to a potential impediment to inter-Korean reconciliation."[41] Under these circumstances, South Korea's role as an independent regional actor outweighed its role as a U.S. ally. The resulting gap between the United States' and South Korea's approaches toward the North also made coordination between the two allied nations all the more difficult.

Echoing South Korea's sense of strategic dependency, inter-Korean nationalism (*minjok gongjo*) was also tied to the "anti-great power-ism" borne out of South Korea's yearning to break away from exploitation by greater powers in its modern history.[42] The majority of the South Korean public, mostly post–Korean War generations, were sympathetic to this interpretation of South Korea's history. From this vantage point, the Bush administration's approach toward the North was viewed as "hostile, and unaccommodating to South Korea's interests."[43] Instead, the South Koreans were eager to realize their vision of "a Korea that is master of its own fate and destiny," a vision premised on the gradual unification of the two Koreas.[44] The salience of inter-Korean nationalism within South Korean society put the South Korean government in a difficult position in which it needed to strike a balance between inter-Korean relations and cooperation with its long-time ally, the United States.[45]

Role Conflict and Tension between Inter-Korean Relations and Alliance Ties

As the crisis reached a stalemate, increasing tension between South Korea's different regional roles opened up larger domestic contestation about South Korea's regional security priorities. At a deeper level, South Korea's domestic debate revolved around the two faces of the North Korean challenge: as the *raison d'être* of the U.S.–South Korean alliance and as the ultimate partner for inter-Korean reconciliation and unification.[46] During the Bush presidency, the main contention in South Korea was whether South Korea should focus more on its externally shaped regional role and its strategic ties with the United States (*hanmi gongjo*), as proposed by conservatives, or its internally shaped regional role and inter-Korean reconciliation (*minjok gongjo*), as promoted by liberals. As a South Korean expert at the government-affiliated Korean Institute for National Unification characterized, the domestic political battle between the two camps essentially came down to the issue of national identity.[47]

As the Roh government's engagement policy made little progress in the face of the standoff between the United States and North Korea, South Korean conservatives began to challenge the government position. While sympathetic to inter-Korean nationalism, the conservative groups, including the opposition Grand National Party, reiterated the importance of alliance ties with the United States. From their viewpoint, South Korea's policy of engagement with the North was a risky strategy, "endangering both U.S.–[South Korean] relations and South Korean security."[48] For example, one expert at the Foreign Ministry–affiliated Institute of Foreign Affairs and National Security observed that while other countries took into account broader regional issues, South Korea remained myopic in its exclusive focus on inter-Korean relations.[49]

However, given broadening popular support for the engagement policy and widespread opposition to Bush's hardline approach, the conservative challenge failed to alter the government's emphasis on an internally shaped regional role. Instead, President Roh went further to propose South Korea's balancer/mediator role (*gyunhyungja-ron*) in the region, an attempt to pursue "a more independent foreign policy that would avoid alignment with the United States in containing China or North Korea."[50] In this regional vision, North Korea constituted a key anchor for South Korea's "assertive and constructive role for Korea throughout Asia."[51] Instead of siding with Washington, President Roh expressed his willingness to offer more concessions to North Korea to achieve reconciliation with the North.[52] Lee Jong Seok, then the head of South Korea's National Security Council and national unification minister, depicted Roh's position as "his determination that our government must play a more active role to break the current stalemate."[53] South Korea's efforts finally came to fruition in 2007 as the Bush administration changed its approach toward North Korea and the second inter-Korean summit took place in October 2007.

In the first year of his presidency, Roh's successor, President Lee Myung-bak of the conservative Grand National Party, criticized his predecessors' North Korea policy as "unconditional support" that failed to achieve reciprocal cooperation from North Korea. However, the Lee government soon moderated its position on North Korea, announcing that it would be willing to provide fifty thousand tons of corn to North Korea.[54] The Unification Minister Kim Hajoong also attended a ceremony commemorating the anniversary of the first inter-Korean summit, while reiterating the Lee government's interest in the Kaesong industrial complex in North Korea.[55] President Lee also expressed his interest in visiting Pyongyang for an inter-Korean summit. Echoing President Roh's earlier efforts for regional cooperation with China, the Lee government also began to promote regional integration. For instance, in January 2010, Yu Woo-ik, South Korea's ambassador to China, suggested that China and South Korea should work with China to facilitate East Asian integration.[56]

Later in the same year, however, the external circumstances around South Korea turned decisively to the worse. Amid a political uncertainty associated with the leadership succession, North Korea launched a series of attacks on South Korea. They included the sinking of a South Korean naval ship, *Cheonan*, with the killing of forty-six South Korean sailors, and artillery attacks on a South Korean island involving civilian deaths. The new developments strengthened the conservatives' hardline position and their emphasis on the U.S.-shaped regional role. The Lee government responded with a virtual freeze in inter-Korean relations. While alarmed by North Korea's aggression, however, the South Korean public answered Lee's confrontational approach with reservations, defeating the Lee's party in local elections. Ryoo Kihl-jae, a South Korean expert on North Korea, suspected that South Koreans "interpreted Lee's response to the Cheonan to be like a new Cold War. But now it is the 21st century, and that kind of thinking is seen as old-fashioned, as well as harmful to the economy and people's standard of living."[57]

The Lee government moderated its hardline position in 2011 when it replaced the unification minister who had been hawkish toward the North with Yu Woo Ik, who took a more flexible approach by resuming exchanges with North Korea.[58] In his first speech after the death of Kim Jong Il, President Lee also hinted at his willingness to improve ties with the North, announcing that "there should be a new opportunity amid changes and uncertainty. If North Korea shows its attitude of sincerity, a new era on the Korean Peninsula can be opened."[59] In an interesting about-face and a sign of the continuing salience of its internally shaped regional role, the Lee government also tried to block anti–North Korean activists' attempts to send pro-democracy leaflets to North Korea by balloon. The apparent effort to de-escalate came just two months prior to the presidential election in which the three leading candidates, including that of the ruling party, had all proposed a rapprochement with North Korea. As one South Korean analyst suspected, given that the earlier confrontational approach only led to more North Korean provocations, "any North Korea–related problems now can be burdensome for the ruling party."[60]

3.4 CHINA

China's Search for Greater Regional Roles

Like South Korea, China started its quest for new regional roles in 1989, when China unveiled its surrounding area (*zhoubian*) diplomacy as a coherent regional strategy.[61] A key driver behind the strategic shift was the need to "project China's national identity as an up-and-coming superpower in the Asia-Pacific region so as to make up for the domestic legitimization and security deficits."[62] Unlike revolutionary nationalism in the past, Chinese nationalism also became "moderate and conservative, placing a premium on stability and a peaceful international context."[63] With this new strategic focus and foreign policy outlook, Chinese leaders hoped to rejuvenate China's image from "a revolutionary country that rejected the existing international regime to a responsible power within the system."[64] As a result, there has been "a shift of the gravity of its diplomacy from the Third World to major powers."[65]

In this sense, China's constructive role at the Six Party talks was part of larger efforts to demonstrate "how important China is in international affairs."[66] For the fourth-generation leadership led by President Hu Jintao, the adoption of China's "peaceful rise" (*heping jueqi*) strategy was not only an effective means to alleviate the "China threat" thesis but also a strong signal to the world that China is willing to play a constructive role in the international system.[67] In fact, the Chinese began to highlight China's active mediating role during the second North Korean nuclear crisis as a prime example of China's embrace of constructive international roles.[68]

At a deeper level, however, the change in strategic and foreign policy direction was rooted in China's need to address its "dual national identity": the image of a great nation in both the historical (due to its long history and rich cultural traditions) and contemporary senses (given its nuclear power status and its veto power at the United Nation Security Council) on the one hand, and the image of a developing socialist nation that still lags behind the level of the West on the other.[69] The problem of the dual national image was compounded by the U.S. support of Taiwan, a quintessential symbol of compromised sovereignty. Despite Chinese leaders' initial expectations for the emergence of a multipolar system in the post–Cold War era, by the mid-1990s it became abundantly clear to the Chinese leadership that a prolonged American unipolarity would be the order of the day, and China should readjust to this new strategic reality by actively pursuing multilateral diplomacy and carving out its role in the region and beyond.[70]

Given "China's outlier status vis-à-vis the U.S.-centered great power group," especially in the wake of the Tiananmen incident, a stable relationship with the United States became even more important.[71] Hence, no serious Chinese analyst denied that the United States might be the most important country for China's modernization.[72] Despite concerns about China's new strategy of "peaceful rise (*heping jueqi*)," the rationale behind the strategy was to "enhance cooperation and minimize conflicts with the US."[73] At the same time, however, many Chinese suspected that the hardline U.S. approach to China was an attempt to "prevent it from achieving great-power status."[74] In this view, instead of cooperating with the United States, China had to promote multipolarization as a counterweight to U.S. hegemony.

The competing regional strategies reflected a broader strategic dilemma for China: how to navigate between cooperating with the United States and guarding against U.S. interference with China's core national interests. In other words, Chinese foreign policy orientation was essentially a balancing act between the conflicting demands of integrating with the international system and unifying the divided nation.[75] Although China's rapid economic growth satisfied the needs of both modernization and integration with the world, an understanding of how best to maintain national unity and territorial integrity remained elusive, especially in the context of Taiwan's move toward *de jure* independence. The situation was complicated all the more by the reality that the United States, while publicly acknowledging a "one China" policy, was still bound by the 1979 Taiwan Relations Act to intervene in a Taiwan contingency. Given the rising nationalist sentiment among the Chinese public, particularly on the issues of Taiwan and Japan, Chinese leaders had to be as assertive in their foreign policy as possible without disrupting their modernization drive or endangering regional stability.[76]

Cooperative Security, the New Security Concept (NSC), and North Korea

It was against this strategic backdrop that China has been seeking greater regional roles and a new regional vision. More specifically, China has sought to enhance its regional influence under the rubric of "cooperative security," a broad diplomatic initiative pitched as a "counterweight to traditional military alliances and other forms of the 'Cold War mentality.'"[77] Specifically, since the late 1990s, the Chinese government has set out a new foreign policy vision premised on "the new concept of security."[78] Officially introduced at the 1997 ASEAN Regional Forum, the new security concept (NSC) was offered as "an alternative vision of how nations should pursue national security in the post-Cold War world order."[79] While stressing the importance of "mutual trust, mutual benefit, equality and cooperation," it also called for "safeguarding the global and regional strategic balance and stability" and upholding "the principle of non-interference in each other's internal affairs."[80] The NSC also reflected Beijing's desire to circumvent Washington's well-established alliance networks in East Asia by associating those structures with a "Cold War mentality" (lengzhan siwei) ill-suited to the twenty-first century.[81] More importantly, the NSC regarded the Asia-Pacific region as "China's geopolitical priority and expressed China's support for more actively pursuing its national interests through multilateral international organizations."[82]

In this broader strategic formulation, the Korean Peninsula symbolizes the "core problem" (hexin wenti) of Northeast Asia.[83] In modern history, the Korean Peninsula was the site of various pivotal events that altered the fate of modern China. During the Pacific War, Imperial Japan used the Korean Peninsula as a launch pad for its military invasion into the Chinese territory.[84] More importantly, the Peninsula is inextricably connected to painful historical memories such as the Sino-Japanese War over Korea in 1894, which led to the cession of Taiwan, and the outbreak of the Korean War in 1950, which deprived the Chinese of an opportunity to regain control over Taiwan, resulting in national disunity ever since.[85]

As a consequence, the Korean Peninsula was, and remains, one of China's primary arenas for achieving expanded regional roles.[86] In this vein, Beijing's increasing role around the Korean Peninsula could be viewed as "the starting point for a return to Pax Sinica in the region,"[87] or, as one Chinese policy advisor put it, "a 'test stone' for [a] rising China."[88] Another Chinese analyst even suggested that it is on the Peninsula that Beijing's chances of becoming a major global power and a regional "hegemon" would be tested.[89] In short, China's active role during the second North Korean crisis can be understood in this broader context of changing strategic calculation in China. From the outset, China's response to the second crisis was markedly different from its lukewarm attitude during the first crisis. As the second crisis escalated in March 2003, the Chinese government for the first time established a Leadership Small Group on the North Korean Problem (Chaoxian Wenti Lingdao Xiaozu) headed by President Hu Jintao himself.[90]

Externally and Internally Shaped Regional Roles: North Korea as a Liability or a Buffer

Similar to the South Korean case, the Chinese understanding of North Korea was hardly universal. In fact, with the tension mounted around the Peninsula, a group of Chinese called "the liability school" began to highlight the negative side of the North Korean challenge. From their perspective, as China pursued continued economic growth and regional stability, North Korean provocations on its borders have increasingly become a burden to both China's regional strategy of cooperative security and its relations with the United States.[91] The longer the current stalemate in the Six Party Talks continued, so the reasoning went, the more China would lose, especially in the context of a worsening relationship with the United States.[92] In retrospect, early signs of the liability school emerged even before the outbreak of the second crisis. Speaking in 1997, then Premier Li Peng reportedly told a group of Americans, "North Korea is neither an ally of the PRC nor an enemy, but merely a neighboring country."[93] What was new in the latest manifestation of China's concerns about North Korea, however, was the direct link made between North Korea's provocations and China's relations with the United States, highlighting the importance of the U.S.-centered regional role in dealing with Pyongyang.

Recognizing China's limited options in an era of American hegemony, for instance, a prominent Chinese expert and frequent foreign policy commentator at Renmin University pointed out that cooperation with the United States on the North Korean crisis was in China's national interest and even suggested "a policy of bandwagon, which means that China should accept and participate in the U.S.-led global regimes."[94] Similarly, pointing to the new global situation facing China, another expert at the Chinese Academy of Social Sciences called for deleting the military alliance clause (or *junsi dongmeng*) in China's half-century-long bilateral treaty with North Korea.[95] In a controversial article published in 2004, a Chinese expert at the Tianjin Academy of Social Sciences openly criticized Kim Jong Il's domestic policy and nuclear ambitions and described North Korea as a key obstacle to Sino-American ties, resulting in a temporary suspension of publication of the journal *Strategy and Management [Zhanrue yu Guanli]*.[96] Zhang Liangui of the Central Party School was even more blunt, declaring, "North Korea is China's biggest foreign policy failure of the past 50 years."[97]

The Chinese tendency to view the North Korean question through the prism of the U.S.–China relationship[98] was also found in the different approaches toward North Korea between the International Liaison

Department of the Central Committee of the Communist Party (*Zhongli-anbu*) and the Chinese Foreign Ministry. According to a senior Chinese arms control expert, while *Zhonglianbu* was keen on maintaining various exchanges with its North Korean counterpart, the Foreign Ministry tended to be "more sympathetic" to the global frame pushed by the United States.[99] After the first North Korean nuclear test in 2006, for instance, Chinese Foreign Ministry spokesman Liu Jianchao made a rare rebuke of North Korea, saying, "the test was carried out flagrantly" and "will undoubtedly exert a negative impact on our relations."[100]

Interestingly, however, the Chinese coverage of Liu's remark on the same day in *China Daily*, a Communist Party–controlled, state–run English newspaper, was different in tone. With the headline of "Developing friendly ties with DPRK unchanged," the report quoted Liu as saying that "China will continue to develop good-neighborly and friendly cooperation with the DPRK and this policy is unshakable."[101] This episode illustrates both the marginal status of the liability camp in China and the continuing significance of North Korea in China's regional strategy. In fact, the majority of Chinese experts subscribed to the so-called "buffer zone" school, which values the strategic importance of North Korea in China's regional vision.[102]

For both the "liability" and the "buffer zone" camps, the first and foremost priority for China was maintaining regional stability.[103] The main difference, however, lay in the types of regional roles they promoted and the perceived connection between the North Korean crisis and regional instability. While the liability camp tended to emphasize the danger of North Korean provocations to regional stability (and the U.S.-directed regional role of China as a responsible global player), the buffer zone camp stressed the internally shaped regional role as an independent regional actor and tended to believe that the crisis was not only manageable but that China could also benefit from actively coping with it.[104] What was more alarming, from the perspective of the buffer zone camp, was the Bush administration's approach aimed at regime change and preemption.[105]

More broadly, many Chinese experts maintained that North Korea could be a base on which China could rebuild a regional security structure.[106] In fact, back in 2003 when the Six Party mechanism was established as the first multilateral security framework, including all the major powers in the region, the Chinese hoped that the framework could develop into a permanent multilateral security framework.[107] In doing so, they hoped to move beyond the Washington-led hub-and-spokes system centered on the U.S. alliances with Japan and South Korea.[108] For instance, in the same volume of the journal that published the article on deleting the military alliance clause, another Chinese analyst stressed the need to help North Korea to move out of the Cold War structure.[109] Considering the historical and practical complexities of the North Korean problem, the author contended, it would be crucial for regional countries to build a web of multilateral security systems that would include a U.S.–North Korea channel; the four-party system of U.S., China, and the two Koreas for transforming the armistice into a permanent peace mechanism; and a six-party system with Japan and Russia for establishing a nuclear-free Northeast Asia.[110]

As the nuclear crisis intensified in the face of the standoff between North Korea and the United States, the Chinese began to question the regional role of the United States as well. Traditionally, the majority view in China was that China had benefited from the balancer role held by the United States in the region, especially between China and Japan, where it prevented the latter from becoming more militaristic.[111] With its uncompromising approach to North Korea, however, the Bush administration was seen in China as using the nuclear crisis to strengthen its alliance posture (e.g., building a missile defense system with Japan and expanding the regional scope of the U.S.–Japan alliance).[112] While the Chinese acknowledged the U.S. need to seek alliance support in the war on terror, they increasingly viewed the restructuring of U.S. military alliance mainly through Japan's expanded cooperation with the United States as a means to "guard against" and "pin down" China.[113] With that, the debate came full circle: those who pointed out the burden of the North Korean problems were largely sidelined, and a *People's Daily* column even warned against "sacrificing relations with other countries for the sake of stable Sino–U.S. ties."[114]

The internal debate on North Korea, however, played out in the changing external circumstances. After the second North Korean nuclear test in 2009, the voices of the liability camp quickly resurfaced and latched onto the global frame of highlighting the North Korean threat. China's Foreign Ministry thus declared, "The DPRK ignored universal opposition of the international community and once more conducted the nuclear test. The Chinese government is resolutely opposed to it."[115] In June 2009, China also voted for UN Security Council Resolution 1874, which "extended the financial sanctions and arms embargo which were implemented via Resolution 1718 in late 2006."[116] Eventually, however, the buffer zone camp ultimately won the domestic debate. As the rest of the world effectively halted aid to North Korea, China's trade and aid have increasingly served as a vital lifeline for North Korea. At the same time, North Korea's military became the central actor in the state-run economy, making a lucrative mineral sales deal with China.[117] In October 2009, Prime Minister Wen Jiabao made a visit to Pyongyang and agreed on "unprecedented large-scale investment and aid" to the North, including Beijing's pledge to support the development of special economic zones (SEZ) in North Korea.[118]

China's focus on regional autonomy gained further momentum in the subsequent years. After the North Korean shelling on the Yeonpyong Island, Chinese President Hu Jintao "called for calm and rational response from all sides to prevent the deterioration of the fragile security situation on the Korean Peninsula," maintaining that "dialogues and negotiations are the only right way to solve the issues and achieve lasting peace and stability of the Korean Peninsula."[119] In response to China's lukewarm approach to the North Korean attacks in 2010, South Korean President Lee Myung-bak "urged Beijing to play a role befitting its newfound international prestige," but to no avail.[120] Echoing the earlier view of the liability camp and the U.S.-shaped regional role, a Beijing University expert warned that China's approach to North Korea "seems to present to the wider world an image of a China obsessed with her own narrow interests."[121]

Such concern about China's global role notwithstanding, its leaders appeared to have zeroed in on its regional role and foreign policy autonomy. In the period of 2010–2011 alone, Chinese President Hu hosted Kim Jong Il three times, an unprecedented chain of events solidifying their relationship further. Mirroring the strengthening political ties, China–North Korea trade increased more than 16 percent to reach $1.29 billion in the first half of 2010.[122] China's response to Kim Jong Il's death is a further testimony to the importance of North Korea in China's regional vision. Soon after the announcement of the death, all nine members of the Standing Committee of the Chinese Party's Politburo, including President Hu Jintao, Premier Wen Jiabao, and then Vice President and current President Xi Jinping, paid their tribute to Kim Jong Il at the North Korean Embassy in Beijing, signaling that "China is working to reassure Pyongyang of the strength of ties and retain its influence amid an uncertain leadership transition."[123] When Wang Jiarui of the Communist Party's International Relations Department visited Pyongyang in August 2012, Kim Jung Un called for the strengthening of bilateral relations between the two countries. In return, Wang said, "We are ready to work jointly with [North Korea] to maintain high-level contacts, strengthen party-to-party exchanges, and boost practical cooperation."[124] Two weeks later, Kim Jong Un's Uncle Jang Song-taek led a large delegation to Beijing and agreed with China on the development of special economic zones in North Korea. Wang Jiarui also confirmed with Jang that China had plans to "deepen cooperation in all areas, including the economy and trade."[125] Positively assessing the renewed cooperation and North Korea's potential for China's regional vision, a Chinese columnist called for "encourag[ing] North Korea's opening up instead of repeatedly creating tensions that will only intensify Pyongyang's caution and vigilance" and inviting North Korea into regional economic integration.[126]

3.5 JAPAN

The Search for Greater Regional Roles

Japan's post–World War Two strategic landscape has been shaped by the two U.S.-imposed realities: the Peace Constitution and the U.S.–Japan alliance. What is striking about this security mechanism is the asymmetric nature of alliance relations, where Japan's commitment to its share of the collective defense is abrogated to maintain the war-renouncing constitution. As a result, there has been an inevitable discrepancy between Japan's desire for a more active, greater role in regional and global affairs and the legal constraints of Article 9 of the constitution, which prevents Japan from playing such roles. Moreover, Japan's status as an economic powerhouse is often "contrasted with its low visibility in global military and political affairs," prompting a debate about its proper role in the changing global and regional context.[127] Consequently, a central feature of the strategic narrative in Japan has been how to adjust the abnormal state of its security posture to the post–Cold War strategic context.

Specifically, the debate has revolved around the goal of "establishing [Japan's] own identity" in the region and the types of roles Japan should play in the post–Cold War era.[128] Japanese conservatives, on the one hand, have pushed for becoming "an independent state with a monopoly of force," thereby restoring a "lost or suppressed identity."[129] For Japanese moderates, on the other hand, Japan's move toward a "normal state" is problematic in the region because its neighbors harbor suspicions of Japan due to its past and uncertain future roles in the region. Hence, while the conservatives tend to brush aside the regional concern about Japan's move toward a "normal state," many others, most notably regionalists and pacifists, have thus been loath to transform Japan's defense posture in haste. In other words, the crux of the Japanese debate on regional roles has been centered on the two national images: a normal state with strengthened alliance ties with the United States and an autonomous East Asian player within an integrated regional framework.

The first signs of Japan's search for regional and international roles emerged in the immediate aftermath of the Cold War. In the new strategic context, Japanese elites began to reconsider the rationale for maintaining security ties with the United States.[130] Finding a new regional role became a national obsession after the allegation of "checkbook diplomacy" during the First Gulf War, when the Japanese government was criticized for providing only financial support.[131] In the first post–Cold War challenge, Japan's support was viewed as "too little and too late" and widely considered a "defeat for Japan,"[132] provoking "a sense of national humiliation."[133]

The Prime Minister's Office soon commissioned a special advisory committee to make a blueprint for Japan's post–Cold War security. The committee released its final report in August 1994 under the title of "The Modality of the Security and Defense Capability of Japan: The Outlook for the 21st Century."[134] It called for utilizing not only the U.S.–Japan alliance but also other mechanisms such as the United Nations and various regional frameworks for security cooperation. It envisioned two complementary regional roles for Japan, both as an independent regional actor and a U.S. ally, as part of "a two-pronged approach on multilateral security frameworks and the U.S.-Japanese bilateral alliance at the same time."[135] With this expanded regional vision, the report marked a strategic shift from a "cold war defense strategy," placing the alliance within the broader framework of a multilateral regional security structure.[136]

The efforts at diversifying Japan's security mechanism and Japan's search for a new regional role, however, lost momentum in the mid-1990s as the U.S.–Japan alliance was bolstered with the passage of the U.S.–Japan Defense Cooperation Guidelines. In February 1995, the U.S. Department of Defense released the East Asian Strategy Report (EASR), also known as "Nye Initiative," reaffirming the maintenance of U.S. troops in East Asia and bolstering U.S.–Japan security cooperation.[137] Nevertheless, Japan's pursuit of regional roles and its balancing act between the U.S.–Japan alliance and a regional security framework continued, and the Japanese increasingly believed that Japan should strive to establish a multilateral security framework in East Asia.[138] The "regionalists" were concerned about Japan's strategic dependence on the United States and hoped that regional economic integration would facilitate a regional security mechanism to supplement the U.S.–Japan alliance.[139]

An Internally Shaped Role: Reentering Asia, Normalization, and North Korea

The regional initiatives in the early years of the post–Cold War period, however, lacked an overarching strategic vision for regional order and Japan's role within it.[140] While Washington urged Tokyo to take a new role as a major partner in global and regional security affairs, its identity as an Asian power and the persistent sense of dependency on the United States called for another role as an autonomous regional player.[141] A senior analyst at the Defense Ministry–affiliated National Institute of Defense Studies observed that instead of "relying solely on the United States," many Japanese elites endorsed Japan's efforts toward regional cooperation with its neighbors.[142]

Government officials began to echo such views. For instance, Yamamoto Ichita, Parliamentary Vice Foreign Minister, observed that the U.S.–Japan alliance, albeit important, has also restricted Japan's efforts toward multipolar diplomacy: "Now, Japan's homework is to find ways to pursue its own diplomacy without hurting its ties with the U.S."[143] Sakakibara Eisuke, the influential former vice finance minister known as Mr. Yen, also stressed that "standing on its own feet while maintaining an alliance is not incompatible."[144]

Japan's persistent efforts to normalize its diplomatic relations with North Korea are part of its larger regional vision aimed at "reentering" Asia and playing a greater, independent regional role. For reasons of history and geographical proximity, Japan's regional strategy has centered on the Korean Peninsula. Yamagata Aritomo, the grand old man of the Meiji government, once famously declared, "The Korean Peninsula is a dagger pointed at the heart of Japan."[145] Throughout history, the Peninsula represented "the gateway" to Asia, and decades after their ill-fated regional dominance, the Japanese were seeking "to secure a new, if different, foothold there in order to solidify a longstanding role in the emergent Northeast Asian regionalism."[146] Given the strategic importance of the Korean Peninsula, Japanese leaders were determined not to foreclose the possibility of forging a new relationship with North Korea, consistently refusing to accept the South Korean demand that it recognize South Korea as the only legitimate government for the entire Peninsula.[147]

Japan's first initiative toward North Korea came from Prime Minister Takeshita Noboru. In his 1989 statement to the Japanese Diet, Takeshita expressed "deep remorse and apology (*ikan*) to all people in this area" for Japan's colonial rule. Given Japan's unspoken tradition of offering formal apologies only to South Korea, not to the North, such a move signaled that he was not only addressing both South and North Korea but was specifically interested in enhancing Japan's relations with North Korea.[148] In 1990, then Liberal Democratic Party heavy-weight Kanemaru Shin made a visit to Pyongyang, setting in motion a series of efforts toward diplomatic normalization with North Korea.[149] Within thirteen months starting in January 1991, both sides held eight rounds of normalization talks, only to be stalled in 1993 amid the first North Korean nuclear crisis. The normalization effort, however, was quickly resumed after the signing of the Agreed Framework, which defused the first crisis. In March 1995, a delegation led by another Liberal Democratic Party (LDP) leader Watanabe Michio visited Pyongyang and agreed that "there wasn't any precondition to resume the negotiations for the normalization of the relationship."[150]

Japan took a more direct role as a player in Korean Peninsula affairs via its vital financial backing for the Korean Peninsula Energy Development Organization (KEDO) framework and enhanced status in trilateral consultations.[151] In 1998, Japan also proposed a six-party security forum consisting of the two Koreas, Japan, and China, Russia, and the United States.[152] As one senior foreign ministry official argued, "Japan must have its own place for negotiating with North Korea" and must "engage actively in the problems of the Korean Peninsula."[153] Even after the 1998 Taepodong missile launch that flew over the Japanese archipelago, Tokyo's normalization efforts continued as Prime Minister Obuchi Keizo expressed his determination to reopen diplomacy with the North in his January 1999 speech at the Diet.

In December 1999, as the Perry Process reduced tension with North Korea, former Prime Minister Murayama Tomiichi led a sixteen-member multi-party Diet delegation to Pyongyang to jumpstart the stalled normalization talks.[154] Prime Minister Mori Yoshiro also showed similar determination. While stressing the significance of the U.S.–Japan alliance, he said it was important for Japan to "make even further diplomatic efforts toward the realization of peace in Asia, centered particularly in Northeast Asia."[155] He specifically linked his plea for pursuing a "rebirth of foreign policy" to the situation on the Korean Peninsula:

With regard to the situation on the Korean Peninsula, which has witnessed significant developments such as the historical North-South Summit, I will channel all my efforts into achieving the advent of a new era in Northeast Asia. I will continue to make the maximum endeavor towards the resolution of pending issues, including the normalization of relations with North Korea.[156]

Despite repeated interruptions caused by various regional contingencies in the 1990s, the fact that successive Japanese governments have persistently sought diplomatic normalization with North Korea is a testimony to Tokyo's eagerness to alter its troubled relationship with Pyongyang and to play a greater regional role. A former Japanese diplomat even placed Japan–North Korea relations in the historical context of the Japanese colonization of the Korean Peninsula. To fully "overcome this past," he argued, normalization and diplomatic relationship with the North must be established.[157] Not only is North Korea "the last and remaining chapter" of Japan's postwar settlement since World War II,[158] it has the potential to improve Japan's regional status amid regional controversy over the history issue.[159]

Prime Minister Koizumi's normalization drive was the culmination of decade-long efforts at enhancing Tokyo's regional status and autonomy by engaging Pyongyang. A senior analyst at the National Institute of Defense Studies observed that Koizumi's two visits to Pyongyang stemmed from the premise that Japan should play a greater role in the region.[160] In addition to the issue of resolving the history issue once and for all, Koizumi maintained that the normalization would strengthen Japan's regional status and give it "greater diplomatic leverage" in the region.[161] While addressing the issue of abducted Japanese, Koizumi "sought to establish Japan as a major actor in the jockeying over North Korea's evolution."[162] An expert at the Japan Institute of International Affairs even asserted that Koizumi's normalization efforts came even at the risk of weakening its ties with the United States.[163]

In fact, Koizumi's first visit to Pyongyang in 2002 came to fruition after Foreign Ministry officials had been "quietly exploring [the possibility of a visit] for more than nine months without telling the United States." Even after U.S. officials revealed Washington's suspicion of North Korea's secrete uranium enrichment program, Koizumi did not cancel the trip.[164] More striking in the 2002 visit was the central role of a foreign ministry official—Tanaka Hitoshi, then Director General of the Asian and Oceanian Bureau—rather than influential political figures.[165] As the public perception of North Korea turned negative due to the abduction scandal and the 1998 missile launch, secrecy was crucial in realizing the summit in Pyongyang. Tanaka limited updates on the preparations for the summit to only a handful of top officials, including Koizumi and Chief Cabinet Secretary Fukuda Yasuo, and bypassed the usual chain of command, including then Foreign Minister Kawaguchi Yoriko and Deputy Chief Cabinet Secretary Abe Shinzo, who was then known for his hawkish attitude toward North Korea.[166] Even as the second North Korean nuclear crisis broke out,

Koizumi's normalization drive did not falter, as manifested in his second visit to Pyongyang in 2004.

Overall, Japan's role in the second crisis was a far cry from the role it played during the first crisis. According to a former Foreign Ministry official, its proactive role was rooted in the hope that through its participation in the Six Party processes "Japan might be able to strengthen her relations with each of the member countries," paving the way for Japan's "new strategic position in the region for many years to come."[167] A Japanese commentator also called for the remedying the "abnormal" relations with North Korea with "a sense of mission, a determination to build a new order in Asia and a political capacity to conduct diplomacy under a long-term strategy."[168] Through its approach toward North Korea, the Japanese government zeroed in on "establishing Japan's regional policy, particularly centered on the Korean Peninsula."[169]

Most Japanese policymakers and experts praised the normalization effort as a regional roadmap in the right direction.[170] Okonogi Masao, a leading Korea specialist in Japan, portrayed Koizumi's Pyongyang trip as a bold step that "skillfully blended two stances, one of cooperating with Washington and the other of acting independently of it."[171] Taniguchi Makoto, a former Japanese ambassador and high-ranking foreign ministry official, touted the summit as "the first positive, independent and multilateral diplomatic initiative to be taken in recent years."[172] Koizumi's visit was widely viewed as a pathbreaking regional initiative, with the potential for "revolutionizing East Asian security dynamics," comparable in significance to Nixon's visit to China in 1972.[173] Koizumi himself reiterated the importance of the normalization "for both countries, for the Korean Peninsula, for Asia and the world."[174]

What is particularly significant was the link, made explicitly by several Japanese experts, between Japan's normalization with the North and the formation of a new regional order. In fact, in the Pyongyang Declaration signed between Koizumi and Kim Jong Il, the term "Northeast Asia" appeared for the first time since 1945 in a Japanese diplomatic document.[175] It was an official endorsement of a policy recommendation by Japanese experts to "take concrete steps to apply normalization principles to a broader, more multilateral framework" and to "create a 'community of nations' in the region" on the basis of reconciliation between Japan and North Korea.[176] In the words of Wada Haruki, a prominent liberal scholar of Tokyo University, the Pyongyang Declaration was "the first occasion for Japan to raise the banner of a new regionalism since the tragic years of the Great East Asian Co-prosperity during World War II."[177] Japanese neighbors in turn welcomed Japan's engagement toward North Korea.[178]

Regionalists soon formed the National Movement for Normalization of Japan-DPRK Relations (*Nitcho Kokko Sokushin Kokumin Kyokai*) headed by former Prime Minister Murayama, with the following declaration:

> Normalization of Japan-DPRK relations and economic assistance to the DPRK from Japan, linked with North-South cooperation in the Korean Peninsula, should build the basis for peace in Northeast Asia, and is in the interest of all the countries and people of our region.[179]

Domestic Contestation over North Korea's and Japan's Competing Regional Roles

As the Six Party Talks reached a stalemate and anti–North Korean sentiments grew stronger in Japan, "a new generation of revisionists" rose to prominence by "[capitalizing on] the changing regional dynamics."[180] Then Chief Cabinet Secretary Abe Shinzo led the conservative campaign. Since 2003, Abe had successfully taken advantage of the abduction issue, first to secure an LDP victory in the parliamentary election in November 2003, and "in the process became a formidable political actor on the national stage."[181] As the conservative camp dominated the domestic political scene, North Korea engagers were increasingly marginalized.[182] Over time, the Japanese conservatives turned to the North Korean threat as a new focus upon which to build their regional vision.[183] What followed was a surge of North Korea bashing throughout Japan and increasingly anti-North Korean media coverage in Japan.[184]

Under these circumstances, the National Association for the Rescue of Japanese Kidnapped by North Korea expanded its stature within Japanese society. As the abduction issue continued to occupy Japan's domestic debate, many of the association's regional leaders have become active members of Nippon Kaigi, "Japan's largest nationalist organization, which rejects postwar pacifism, embraces the imperial system and defends Japan's past wars in Asia."[185] In other words, the abduction incidents that took place decades ago gave the conservatives "a new opportunity to highlight how Japan has been ill-prepared" in security and to persuade the public about "the need for change."[186] In short, the perceived North Korean threat served as "a convenient excuse to justify the abandonment of the Peace Constitution" and Japan's move toward becoming a "normal" state.[187]

It was against this changing domestic political context that Abe, by then having ascended to premiership, made a strong push for constitutional revision. In May 2007, on the sixtieth anniversary of the Peace Constitution, Abe made a speech that was markedly different from the 1997 statement by then Prime Minister Hashimoto Ryutaro. While Hashimoto promised Japan would make "contributions to the peace and prosperity of the international community under the philosophy of the Constitution," Abe proposed that "a bold review of Japan's postwar regime and an in-depth discussion of the Constitution toward realizing a 'new Japan' would create a spirit for laying a new path to a new era."[188] Under this new regional vision, the long-time conservative goal of upgrading the Self Defense Agency to a full-fledged defense department was finally realized in January 2007. In the process, along with Japan's regional role as a "normal state," the U.S.-directed role as a global ally was stressed.

Lost in the domestic whirlwind of North Korea bashing and Abe's new regional blueprint was Japan's search for an independent regional role. Instead, the strategic focus was shifted to the U.S.–Japan alliance. For instance, the 2005 *East Asian Strategic Review*, issued by Defense Agency's National Institute for Defense Studies, characterized Japan's regional role as "the pivot of the United States' alliances" so that the United States will be able to "deploy its forces in a 'more agile and more flexible' manner."[189] After the 2006 North Korean nuclear test, the Abe government bypassed the regional route altogether and coordinated directly with the United States and other UN Security Council members to pass UNSC Resolution 1718, levying new sanctions on North Korea.[190]

At the same time, however, other Japanese politicians and analysts began to suggest that Japan's preoccupation with the abduction issue was "counterproductive, arguing the Japanese public and government [were] allowing it to interfere with its broader diplomatic goals with respect to North Korea."[191] While the conservatives generally welcomed the move toward a global alliance primarily because it would speed up the move toward a "normal" state, others expressed their concern by warning that Japan, under the new plan, "[would] be further integrated into the U.S. global strategy."[192] After Abe resigned in 2007, however, signs of change emerged in both Japanese politics and the domestic security debate. For instance, Ozawa Ichiro, then head of the opposition Democratic Party of Japan (DPJ), renewed emphasis on engaging Asia. In explaining his diplomatic vision, Ozawa even stressed the role of Japan as "the bridge between China and the United States."[193] Following in Koizumi's footsteps regarding North Korea, Prime Minister Fukuda Yasuo in 2008 decided to "seek a resolution to the North's nuclear programs, missile threats and the abductions in a 'comprehensive' manner."[194] As positive developments emerged in the Six Party process, in June 2008 Japan resumed its negotiation with North Korea.[195]

However, the political use of the North Korean threat continued as well. In August 2009, just a few days before a Lower House election, Prime Minister Aso Taro visited the site of the alleged abduction of Yokota Megumi, the most widely publicized abductee in Japan, to draw attention to the abduction issue.[196] It was only after Hatoyama Yukio, from the DPJ, became prime minister that North Korea expressed the hope that both sides would hold official meetings to improve their strained bilateral relations during the Abe and Aso administrations.[197] The meetings did not materialize, however, as Japan sided with the hardline stance of the conservative Lee government in Seoul and the United States after North Korea's attacks on South Korea. Nonetheless, Japan's efforts to engage North Korea quickly resumed. In August 2012, the Noda Yoshihiko government announced that it would hold meetings with North Korea, the first since 2008, to discuss "various pending issues." Chief Cabinet Secretary Fujimura Osamu expressed his hope that the two sides "[would] be able to comprehensively solve pending issues and settle their 'unfortunate past' so they can establish diplomatic ties."[198]

3.6 CONCLUSION

This chapter has shown that the regional understanding of the North Korean challenge has little to do with the nuclear dimension. Instead, East Asian countries view the North Korean question with their greater regional roles in mind. Far from eliciting a converging debate as to how to address the nuclear challenge, the North Korean crisis sparked a divergent and highly contested set of domestic debates. Contrary to the global narrative of the North Korean nuclear challenge, the regional narrative has been shaped by the complex interaction between the internally shaped and U.S.-directed regional roles, which in turn influences each country's respective responses to the U.S. approach toward North Korea.

In all three countries, the main focus of their regional visions was linked to North Korea, while they cautiously navigated between their respective relations with the United States (i.e., the U.S.-directed regional role) and North Korea (i.e., the internally shaped regional role). While the U.S. pressure and external circumstances occasionally drove some domestic actors to latch onto the global frame and to bolster the role of a U.S. ally or partner, countries in East Asia have consistently been seeking to alter the traditional relationship with North Korea with an eye toward greater regional status and foreign policy autonomy, which would help them go beyond the confines of dual national identity and strategic dependency.

Throughout the process, the three East Asian countries pursued new regional visions that would supplement, if not supplant, the U.S.-centered regional order of the hub-and-spokes system.

To be sure, the emerging regional security order is far from clear, especially in view of the still unfolding crisis on the Korean Peninsula. However, by focusing only on the nuclear issues and, thus, neglecting complex regional dynamics surrounding North Korea, the United States risks both overlooking a major shift in the regional security landscape and losing its legitimacy as a regional hegemon in East Asia. In the following chapters, I demonstrate the broader implications of the competing regional role conceptions for the East Asian regional order. I do so by comparing alliance politics and regionalism during the 1998 North Korean Missile Crisis during the Clinton administration and the second North Korean nuclear crisis during the Bush administration.

CHAPTER 4

The Clinton Administration and the East Asian Regional Order

The beauty of the Perry process was that we formulated with South Korea and Japan a common strategy with an agreed set of goals, and then an allocation of responsibilities as to how we could achieve those goals through our individual dialogues or negotiating processes with North Korea. And that indeed is what we need now.

—Stephen Bosworth, *former U.S. Ambassador to South Korea.*[1]

4.1 INTRODUCTION

On August 31, 1998, North Korea reignited a full-blown regional crisis by test-launching an intermediate-level ballistic missile, which flew over Japanese territory and landed in the Pacific Ocean. The missile crisis set in motion a yearlong process of comprehensive policy review and consultation, later known as the Perry Process, as it was named after its leader, former U.S. Defense Secretary William Perry. Unlike the first North Korean nuclear crisis during which regional actors were largely sidelined from the bilateral negotiation between the United States and North Korea, the 1998 missile crisis coincided with region-wide efforts to seek new regional roles through redefined ties with North Korea. Contrary to the Bush administration's understanding and policy behavior vis-à-vis North Korea during the second nuclear crisis, the Clinton administration approached the North Korean challenge in a way that both reflected and reinforced such regional initiatives in East Asia. As a result, the Perry Process not only successfully resolved the missile crisis but also ensured the compatibility between U.S.-directed and internally shaped regional role conceptions. Overall, the Perry Process yielded a new, positive pattern of alliance coordination between the United States and its Asian allies, Japan and South Korea, while helping facilitate a new regional pattern of cooperation and consultation among China, Japan, and South Korea.[2]

A mutually reinforcing dynamic between the Clinton administration's approach toward North Korea and the regional initiatives vis-à-vis North Korea reshaped the structure of the regional order into trilateral alliance coordination and broadened regionalism. This regional order was also cooperative in nature, opening new avenues for regional rivals to work together on a number of issue areas. From a U.S. perspective, the Perry Process was also emblematic of positive multilateral initiatives that engaged countries in East Asia to deal with "regional security affairs without undermining the hegemonic strategy."[3] The Trilateral Coordination and Oversight Group (TCOG) among the United States, Japan, and South Korea was a prime example of successful alliance relations. Cooperation among East Asian countries through a variety of multilateral regional venues also multiplied in scope and number. Regional frameworks such as the ASEAN Plus Three (APT) meetings demonstrated the viability of a broader, more open regional security mechanism, paving the way for trilateral cooperation among China, Japan, and South Korea and the formation of a new regional forum called the East Asia Summit.

In what follows, this chapter documents the role congruence promoted by the Perry Process and its regional consequences with respect to alliance politics and regionalism. The first section provides the development of the Perry Process with a brief comparison to regional dynamics during the first North Korean nuclear crisis. I pay particular attention to how externally and internally shaped regional role conceptions in East Asia became compatible in this period. The following two sections, in turn, assess the impact of the Perry Process on the regional order by exploring alliance politics and regionalism in East Asia. I demonstrate patterns of alliance coordination reflected in the Korean Peninsula Energy Development Organization (KEDO) and the TCOG. I then explore the rise of regionalism in East Asia and a region-wide search for a multi-layered regional order. The final section concludes with a summary of findings and a brief discussion of policy lessons.

4.2 REGIONAL ROLE CONCEPTIONS AND THE EMERGENCE OF THE PERRY PROCESS

To get a better sense of the regional dynamics shaped by the Perry Process, it is worth comparing regional dynamics between the first North

Korean nuclear crisis of 1993–1994 and the 1998 missile crisis. During the first nuclear crisis, North Korea took a series of provocative steps, such as refusing UN inspections of its nuclear sites, extracting plutonium from fuel rods, and threatening to withdraw from the Nuclear Nonproliferation Treaty (NPT).[4] The situation became so volatile that then U.S. Chairman of the Joint Chiefs of Staff General John Shalikashvili called it the "most dangerous crisis" the United States had encountered since the end of World War II.[5] While the global rogue frame became a catchphrase of the Bush administration, the imagery and rhetoric of rogue states—backlash states, nuclear outlaws, etc.—were also evident during the Clinton administration.[6] Indeed, at the height of the crisis in June 1994, President Clinton seriously considered a military strike on the Yongbyon nuclear facilities.[7]

While alarmed about the prospect of a nuclear North Korea, East Asian countries remained passive bystanders during the first crisis. Instead of taking a leading role in resolving the crisis, they were generally content to play second fiddle to the Clinton administration's bilateral approach toward Pyongyang. Although concerned about the possibility that the crisis could wreak havoc on the still evolving post–Cold War strategic landscape,[8] both U.S. allies, namely Japan and South Korea, as well as China, did not actively seek a regional approach to defuse the crisis, nor did they engage in serious domestic debates about North Korea. Once the crisis was resolved through the Agreed Framework between the United States and North Korea in October 1994, the East Asian countries fully endorsed the bilateral deal, while Japan and South Korea paid most of the financial bills for the implementation of the U.S.-led nuclear deal.

The signing of the Agreed Framework formally ended the first North Korean nuclear crisis. In its aftermath, various multilateral venues emerged to address the North Korean question. These included KEDO, a multilateral mechanism for the implementation of the Agreed Framework, and the Four Party Talks to establish a peace regime on the Korean Peninsula. By the time these new multilateral frameworks surfaced in East Asia, regional actors, who had been largely passive during the first nuclear crisis, began to express willingness to play greater roles in regional security affairs.

In South Korea, the Kim Young-sam government was determined to play "a legitimate and equal role in any further discussions on the Korean questions and to find a way to resume direct official contact with North Korea."[9] In 1996, the South Korean government, in consultation with the Clinton administration, proposed a four-party regional forum among the United States, the two Koreas, and China with the goal of turning the Korean Armistice Treaty into a permanent peace treaty consisting of all the signatories of the armistice that ended the Korean War. Still fresh from its own crisis in the Taiwan Strait in 1995–1996,[10] the Chinese, for their part, were eager to play a greater regional role by joining the four-party talks. In December 1997, after holding three preparatory meetings, the four countries held the first formal session of the Four Party Talks in Geneva. However, the talks were not smooth sailing, as Pyongyang repeated its usual demand for the United States to change its military posture in the region. Despite several rounds of formal meetings and agreements on working groups to discuss specific issues, no tangible results ensued.[11] Moreover, South Korean President Kim Young-sam was merely insistent on South Korea's leading role in Korean Peninsula issues, rather than reaching out to North Korea with a broader regional role in mind.

The situation changed drastically in 1998, when the Kim Dae-jung government came to power with a novel approach to North Korea. The "sunshine" policy of engagement and reconciliation toward North Korea began in earnest a process of widening inter-Korean ties. Kim did so by linking inter-Korean relations to a broader regional framework and envisioning South Korea's greater regional role in that context. This is why President Kim quickly moved to expand the Four Party talks. The Kim government's proposal for a "Two Plus Four formula and the establishment of a Northeast Asian security cooperation regime" came about specifically to shape the regional security environment and facilitate inter-Korean relations.[12] To this end, unlike his predecessors, President Kim did not insist on the traditional South Korean position of improving inter-Korean ties ahead of U.S.–North Korean relations. Instead, he urged both the United States and Japan to speed up the process of normalization with North Korea.[13] In this sense, President Kim's sunshine policy marked "a radical departure from previous policies toward North Korea," demonstrating that South Korea's foreign policy can be "proactive and assertive rather than reactive and defensive."[14]

Such South Korean efforts could not have been more timely, as both the United States and other regional countries were interested in new regional security frameworks. From the vantage point of U.S. policymakers, such regional formats could serve to reduce the Chinese sense of uncertainty about the future role of the U.S.–Japan alliance.[15] The Chinese, for their part, began to assess multilateral regional frameworks positively and used the regional venues to dampen fears of the "China threat," which was developing in the region after the former Middle Kingdom's remarkable economic growth and military modernization.[16] Breaking away from its previous passivity in regional diplomacy, China began to take an active role in a broad array of regional affairs. Determined to play a new regional role as "a more responsible and cooperative player," the Chinese embraced various multilateral venues, including those designed to deal with the North Korean nuclear issue.[17] China's active participation in the Four Party Talks in the late 1990s and the Six Party Talks afterward exemplifies such efforts.

As in the Chinese case, Japan's pursuit of a greater regional role in multilateral frameworks began with an instrumental reason in mind: In this case, the purpose was to mollify regional concerns rooted in Japan's role as a colonizer and invader in the early twentieth century. In fact, due to regional suspicions of Japan's renewed militarism, some scholars have proposed the U.S.–Britain or U.S.–German model as future scenarios for the U.S.–Japan alliance. According to John Ikenberry and Takashi Inoguchi, Germany is a model for playing an active regional role, while simultaneously being bound into various regional multilateral frameworks, "thereby providing stabilizing reassurances to neighboring countries."[18] Another regional expert maintains that rather than relying solely on the United States, Japan should consider the roles of Britain and Germany in Europe, the former as a model for effectively balancing strategic ties with the United States and its regional role in Europe and the latter as a model for redeeming its past with its neighbors.[19] In this vein, one Japanese expert even cites Japan's contribution to the KEDO and its participation in regional institutions as examples of Japan's new role as a "global civilian power."[20]

A closer look at Japan's activities in regional frameworks, however, shows that its emphasis remained regional, specifically expanding its regional role by normalizing ties with North Korea and gaining diplomatic leverage around the Korean Peninsula. Despite a widely accepted scholarly view of Japan as a "reactive" state,[21] the Japanese became more proactive and assertive in their regional initiatives in the late 1990s. In addition to alliance-based institutions, such as the KEDO, the TCOG and the Japan–U.S. security treaty, Japan promoted the idea of a six-party forum, involving the United States, China, Japan, Russia, and North and South Korea, on the assumption "that resolving the North Korean problem must be approached in a broader framework."[22] Around the same time, in August 1997, the Japanese government resumed the long-mothballed negotiations over diplomatic normalization with North Korea.[23] Later in November 1997, a Japanese Diet delegation, representing the ruling coalition of the Liberal Democratic Party, the Social Democratic Party, and the New Party Sakigake and headed by a high-ranking LDP official and future Prime Minister Mori Yoshiro, visited Pyongyang. In December of the same year, then Foreign Minister Obuchi Keizo expressed his enthusiasm toward the regional initiative by declaring that "negotiations for diplomatic normalization will be reopened as soon as possible."[24]

However, the East Asian countries' efforts to redefine their relations with North Korea and improve their regional roles in the process met their first major hurdle during the 1998 missile crisis. As the tension developed, the pursuit of greater regional roles appeared to be in jeopardy. Rather than forcing its own view of the situation and policy stance, however, the Clinton administration from the start approached the mounting crisis with close coordination with its regional counterparts. This allowed the regional countries to continue with their respective initiatives toward North Korea, ensuring role congruence between the U.S.-directed and internally shaped regional roles. The positive developments in turn helped improve the regional order, both in alliance mechanism and regionalism.

The North Korean Missile Crisis and the Perry Process

Even before the outbreak of the missile crisis, the Republican-dominated U.S. Congress voiced concerns about North Korea and the validity of the Agreed Framework that resolved the first North Korean nuclear crisis. As the implementation of the bilateral deal did not proceed as scheduled, the North Koreans also began to question U.S. intention and decided to ratchet up pressure on the United States to lift the sanctions levied against them.[25] Against this backdrop, in July 1998, a congressionally mandated commission headed by Donald Rumsfeld issued a bipartisan report warning of growing missile threats from rogue states, including North Korea.[26] In addition, one month later, in August 1998, the New York Times ran a front-page story about a suspected secret underground nuclear facility near Kumchangri, North Korea.[27] It was amid this increasing U.S. suspicion about North Korea's intentions that Pyongyang test-launched the Taepodong missile.

For the hardliners in Washington, the combination of North Korea's long-range ballistic missiles and its potential to produce nuclear bombs immediately conjured up an image of impending danger from the Korean Peninsula.[28] The U.S. Congress soon called for a comprehensive review of U.S. policy toward North Korea.[29] In October 1998, the U.S. Congress issued "a new provision in the 'Omnibus Consolidated and Emergency Supplemental Act' (Public Law 105–277)," which mandated:

> not later than January 1, 1999, the President shall name a North Korea Policy Coordinator, who shall conduct a full and complete interagency review of US policy toward North Korea, shall provide policy direction for negotiations with North Korea related to nuclear weapons, ballistic missiles, and other security related issues, and shall also provide leadership for US participation in KEDO.[30]

In response, President Clinton appointed former defense secretary William Perry as North Korea Policy Coordinator. In October 1998, the United States and North Korea started negotiations, formally setting in motion a yearlong process. After a series of meetings, North Korea, in May 1999, agreed to allow an on-site inspection of the suspected nuclear site by the United States.[31] Upon confirming that the suspected site was not nuclear-related, the Clinton administration continued negotiations on North Korea's missile issue. In May 1999, Perry himself visited Pyongyang. After several months of negotiations with North Korea and extensive consultations with regional countries, in September 1999 the United States and North Korea signed the Berlin Agreement. With the signing of the agreement, North Korea announced that as long as talks between the United States and North Korea continued, it would put a moratorium on missile testing. In return, the Clinton administration lifted some of the economic sanctions on North Korea.

Role Congruence During the Perry Process

According to Ambassador Wendy Sherman, who was Perry's advisor and later successor as U.S. policy coordinator on North Korea, Perry initially thought that he would spend only two or three months working on the review. Instead, he ended up spending nearly a year to engage in "a very wide range of consultations with Congress, experts on all sides, allies, almost everyone in government, other interested parties."[32] More importantly, his team made numerous trips to Seoul, Tokyo, and Beijing for coordination and consultation, not to mention his own visit to Pyongyang.[33] Stanley Roth, then Assistant Secretary of State for East Asian and Pacific Affairs, attributed the success of the Perry process to "repeated consultations with the Japanese and Korean governments." Perry's recommendations were crucial precisely because "they reflect the thinking of leaders in Tokyo and Seoul as well as Washington."[34]

For instance, within a ten-month period following Perry's appointment, Lim Dongwon, then South Korean President Kim Dae-jung's special adviser and later unification minister, met Perry eight times for policy consultation.[35] Through these meetings, the South Korean government proposed to Perry a package deal with North Korea, linking North Korea's dismantling of WMD programs to economic assistance, which eventually became the core of the 1999 Perry Report.[36] The U.S. endorsement of South Korea's engagement policy toward North Korea and Perry's efforts to "synchronize U.S. policy with that of South Korea" promoted "a sense of compatibility" in the policies of the two countries.[37] As Perry himself later recalled, such close consultation among allies, including six tripartite meetings with South Korea and Japan, contributed to the success of the multilateral process. He not only discussed the recommendations in his final report with President Clinton, South Korean President Kim, and Japanese Prime Minister Obuchi but also briefed the Chinese and the Russians to seek their support as well.[38]

As mandated, in September 1999 Perry and his team submitted a completed report to President Clinton and the U.S. Congress. In contrast to the Bush administration's view of the North Korean regime as an irrational and unpredictable rogue state, the central premise of the Perry Report was that deterrence against North Korea was working and, therefore, the United States "must deal with the DPRK regime as it is, not as [the United States] would wish it to be."[39] In essence, the report recommended a two-path strategy. First, if North Korea were "willing to forgo its long-range missile program as well as its nuclear weapons program, [the United States] should be willing to move step-by-step on a path to a comprehensive normalization of relations, including the establishment of a permanent peace." But, if not, "[the United States] must take actions to contain that threat."[40] In a deliberate effort not to provoke North Korea, the unclassified version of the Perry Report did not specify the type of measures the United States and its allies would take in the second scenario.[41] Afterward, the Clinton administration pursued a comprehensive engagement policy toward North Korea.

As the relationship between the United States and North Korea took a positive turn, regional countries were also able to continue their initiatives toward North Korea. Shortly after the publication of the Perry Report, Beijing quickly moved to repair its somewhat estranged relationship with Pyongyang. China's Foreign Minister Tang Jiaxuan's "good will" visit to Pyongyang in October 1999 was the first high-ranking official visit since 1996.[42] In a new sign of improvement in inter-Korean ties, a South Korean government-sanctioned tour to North Korea's Mount Keumkang began to flourish. President Kim Dae-jung viewed the Perry Report and the Clinton administration's approach toward North Korea "as vindicating his efforts to dismantle a decades-long threat-driven policy on the peninsula."[43]

As the United States and South Korea sought their own paths to enhanced relations with North Korea during this period, there was an implicit understanding among the ruling LDP leadership in Japan that it could not afford to be sidelined in the region-wide drive to improve ties with Pyongyang.[44] In December 1999, a parliamentary delegation led by former Prime Minister Murayama Tomiichi made a three-day visit to North Korea. During this visit, both sides agreed to resume talks for diplomatic normalization that had been stalled since 1992. Prime Minister Obuchi was also eager to forge ahead with normalization efforts. Working closely with Nonaka Hiromu, then LDP deputy secretary general who had broad connections with the North Koreans, Obuchi sought a breakthrough with Pyongyang.[45] Trilateral coordination with the United States and South Korea, in turn, enabled Japan to play a greater role in Korean Peninsula affairs.[46] Instead of blocking Japan's proactive approach toward North Korea, both the United States and South Korea welcomed the Murayama mission.[47] In short, trilateral coordination during the Perry Process ensured role congruence, which in turn resulted in enhanced alliance cooperation and enthusiastic support for the 1999 Berlin Agreement. In the process, "a great deal of optimism" emerged in Japan as it, "in consultation with South Korea and the United States, reenergized its normalization diplomacy toward North Korea in 2000."[48]

The historic inter-Korean summit in 2000 was the result of this positive regional momentum. Tellingly, the focus of the summit was not just on inter-Korean relations but also on the region.[49] From a South Korean perspective, permanent peace would require a formal end of the Cold War rivalry on the peninsula and a dramatic transformation of inter-Korean relations with the full endorsements by the region's great powers. To that end, the Kim Dae-jung government strongly encouraged the United States and Japan to normalize their ties with the North.[50] By making South Korea's external and internal regional role conceptions congruent, the Clinton administration, in turn, facilitated South Korea's expanded role in the region. Under this permissive regional context, President Kim was able to forge ahead with inter-Korean reconciliation.

As the two Kims shook their hands with smiles at the first summit between the two long-time archenemies, the Cold War tension in the region appeared to subside on the troubled peninsula. Regional leaders shared the upbeat mood emanating from the two Koreas. Japanese Prime Minister Mori, for instance, declared the summit to be an East Asian equivalent of "the fall of the Berlin Wall."[51] China's Foreign Affairs Ministry called it "a major event of historic significance."[52] U.S. Secretary of State Madeleine Albright was equally optimistic when she said, "The United States strongly supports South Korea's policy of engagement, and we will do all we can to encourage further reconciliation . . . so the full promise of the summit can be achieved."[53] The United States, the guarantor of a Cold War peace in the region, finally reached a major turning point in its relationship with a long-time enemy against which it fought the very first war of the Cold War era.

U.S.–North Korean Reconciliation and the End of the Perry Process

In July 2000, only a month after the inter-Korean summit, U.S. Secretary of State Madeleine Albright and North Korean Foreign Minister Baek Namsoon had their first high-level meeting between the two countries at the annual ASEAN Research Forum (ARF) meeting in Bangkok. In return for Perry's 1999 visit to Pyongyang, they discussed the possibility of a Washington visit by a high-level North Korean envoy.[54] In October 2000, Kim Jong Il sent Vice Marshal Jo Myong Rok, the second man in charge of the North Korean military, as his special envoy to President Clinton. During his visit to Washington, Vice Marshall Jo singled out the Perry Process as "important contributions" and spoke highly of the recommendations made in the report.[55] Both sides also issued the U.S.-DPRK Joint Communiqué. As shown in Table 4.1, the Joint Communiqué not only addressed specific U.S. concerns about North Korea's WMD capability but also featured prominently inter-Korean and regional dimensions.[56]

In his meeting with President Clinton, Vice Marshall Jo invited Clinton to visit Pyongyang. Jo maintained that through the visit by President Clinton, "[the United States and North Korea] will be able to find the solution to all problems." In return, President Clinton asked Secretary Albright to "go first to prepare the ground."[57] Before her visit to Pyongyang, Albright consulted South Korean President Kim Dae-jung, who strongly endorsed the visit. Secretary Albright made her official visit to Pyongyang from October 23 to 24, 2000. She was, and remains, the highest U.S. official to visit the North in the history of U.S.–North Korean relations. In Pyongyang, Kim Jong Il unexpectedly joined Albright in a series of meetings and events that lasted more than six hours. Secretary Albright characterized her meetings with Kim Jong Il as "serious, constructive, and in-depth."[58] As quoted below, Albright's speech in a reception hosted by Kim Jong Il was upbeat and promising.

Mr. Chairman, the process in which we are now engaged . . . *can lead to reconciliation and reunification of the Peninsula and to more normal and prosperous relations* between your government and others in the region and the world.

We each must strive to open new avenues of communication, commerce and contacts. We *must each do our part if the Cold War is truly to end and along with it the divisions* that have caused such suffering to the people of Korea.[59] (Emphasis added)

Through the Perry Process, North Korea finally showed willingness to get out of its siege mentality. Sensing Kim Jong Il's determination to make a

Table 4.1. THE U.S.–DPRK JOINT COMMUNIQUÉ (EXCERPT)

Dimension	Content[123]
Regional	• "the United States and the Democratic People's Republic of Korea have decided to take steps to fundamentally improve their bilateral relations *in the interests of enhancing peace and security in the Asia-Pacific region.*" • "the two sides agreed there are a variety of available means, including *Four Party talks*, to reduce tension on the Korean Peninsula and *formally end the Korean War by replacing the 1953 Armistice Agreement with permanent peace arrangements.*"
U.S.-North Korean	• "the two sides stated that *neither government would have hostile intent toward the other* and confirmed the commitment of both governments to make every effort in the future to *build a new relationship free from past enmity.*" • "the two sides reaffirmed that their relations should be based on the principles of *respect for each other's sovereignty and non-interference in each other's internal affairs,* and noted the value of regular diplomatic contacts"
Inter-Korean	• "Special Envoy Jo Myong Rok *explained to the US side developments in the inter-Korean dialogue* in recent months, including the results of the historic North–South summit. • "The U.S. side expressed its firm commitment to *assist* in all appropriate ways the continued progress and success of ongoing *North–South dialogue* and initiatives for reconciliation and greater cooperation, including increased security dialogue."
WMD	• "the D.P.R.K. informed the U.S. that *it will not launch long-range missiles of any kind* while talks on the missile issue continue." • "the US and the D.P.R.K. strongly affirmed its importance to achieving peace and security on *a nuclear weapons free Korean Peninsula.*"

deal with the United States, South Korean President Kim Dae-jung strongly urged President Clinton to visit Pyongyang.[60] According to Albright, the Clinton administration at the time was "reasonably confident that North Korea would agree to a deal ending the potential threat posed to [the United States] by long-range missiles and nuclear arms."[61] Perry himself later revealed that based on his judgment "the United States was within a few months of getting the desired agreement from North Korea."[62] Yet the White House could not make a final decision due in large part to "the scheduling chaos" caused by ongoing negotiations in the Middle East.[63] The unforeseen and prolonged controversy over the result of the 2000 U.S. presidential election at the time did not help matters either. President Clinton himself lamented his decision not to visit Pyongyang: "I hated to give up on ending the North Korean missile program but I simply couldn't risk being halfway around the world when we were so close to peace in the Middle East."[64] President Clinton later said to William Perry that "it was his 'biggest regret' that he did not visit North Korea."[65]

4.3 ALLIANCE POLITICS DURING THE PERRY PROCESS

While the Perry Process could not bring a permanent solution to the tension on the Korean Peninsula, it elevated alliance coordination to a new high, opening up an unprecedented pattern of trilateral cooperation among the U.S. allies. The consultation process not only institutionalized a new alliance coordination mechanism but also strengthened existing ones such as the KEDO, a key regional mechanism for addressing the North Korean issue prior to the Perry Process. Along with the United States and its East Asian allies, Japan and South Korea, even the European Union joined the organization. By 2002, KEDO's membership had expanded to thirteen countries, with sixteen countries making financial contributions to the implementation project.[66]

The Korean Peninsula Energy Development Organization

As an issue-specific, ad hoc multilateral framework, KEDO became a main venue for alliance coordination on the North Korean issue. One scholar even considered KEDO to be "the most important multilateral security institution" in the region.[67] Its significance, however, was not confined to the stated goal of implementing the Agreed Framework. Under the permissive condition of regional role congruence, it served as "an important mechanism to give South Korea and Japan a 'seat at the table' in dealing with a critical regional security issue" and offering a regional forum for trilateral cooperation among U.S. allies.[68] As the Japanese deputy director to KEDO observed, the organization was not only crucial to stopping North Korea's nuclear programs but also served "as a model for U.S.-ROK-Japan cooperation."[69]

Such practices in alliance cooperation proved to be very useful during the Perry Process. It was upon this institutional foundation that the United States and South Korea were able to maintain trilateral cooperation even after the Taepodong launch by North Korea. Flying directly over the Japanese archipelago, North Korea's missile caused outrage among the Japanese public. Many Japanese experts agreed that the launch made the strongest impact on the Japanese perception of security in the postwar period. One former Japanese diplomat even compared the missile launch to a hypothetical Cuban missile launch over Florida.[70] After the launch, the Japanese government initially threatened to suspend its commitment to KEDO. A withdrawal of the up to $1 billion Japanese contribution to KEDO would have both risked the collapse of the multi-year project and undermined the engagement policies of the Clinton administration and the South Korean government.[71] It was the Perry Process that helped Japan to return to KEDO and narrowed the perception gap between the United States and South Korea on the one hand and Japan on the other.[72]

Along with the immediate goal of addressing North Korea's WMD challenges, the Perry Process yielded a greater and longer-term benefit as well. The agreement to replace the Armistice Treaty in the U.S.–North Korean Joint Communiqué was a case in point. While previous U.S. policies were geared toward short-term goals such as resolving the nuclear and missile issues, the Perry Process expanded Korean Peninsula issues to include a larger and long-term goal of achieving a permanent peace regime in the region.[73] Crucially, Washington's approach to Pyongyang at the time permitted Seoul to pursue a greater regional role without compromising the U.S.-centered regional role. The role congruence was possible mainly because the Perry Report fit nicely with "the operating principles of the Sunshine policy."[74] Before the inter-Korean summit in 2000, South Korean Minister of Unification Park Jae Kyu frequently met U.S. Ambassador Thomas Hubbard to update Washington on the progress of inter-Korean contacts and negotiations. After the summit, President Kim also dispatched his senior secretary for foreign affairs and national security to brief President Clinton on the summit. In this way, the inter-Korean summit also "justified and buttressed Clinton's own engagement policy toward North Korea."[75]

More broadly, as one senior South Korean Unification Ministry official recalled, what followed was "a virtuous circle or a mutually reinforcing dynamic between inter-Korean ties and US-Korean alliance ties, and the Perry report was the best illustration of such a link."[76] One long-time watcher of U.S.-Korean relations also noted that the Clinton administration's support for the sunshine policy and the inter-Korean summit led to "the best period in U.S.-South Korean relations."[77] The enhanced alliance coordination between the United States and South Korea also enabled the establishment of a broader, trilateral institutional mechanism for alliance coordination that included Japan.

The Trilateral Coordination and Oversight Group

In hindsight, Japan's ultimately abandoned decision to withdraw from KEDO was a blessing in disguise. Japan's threat compelled the United States and South Korea to conclude that a high-level trilateral coordinating mechanism among the three allies would be key to successful negotiations with North Korea.[78] In April 1999, the United States, Japan, and South Korea established the TCOG for the specific purpose of discussing and coordinating the implementation strategy of the Perry Process among the three Asian allies.

As a novel consultation mechanism for the three Asian allies, the TCOG was institutionalized in several ways. First, it held numerous meetings by senior-level government officials to coordinate their specific policies toward North Korea. At the ministerial level, foreign ministers of the three allies also held separate meetings on the North Korean question and other regional security issues. Finally, Presidents Clinton and Kim, and Prime Minister Obuchi held a trilateral summit meeting in September 1999.[79] Rather than merely reflecting a particular U.S. position on North Korea, the Perry report was a byproduct of the burgeoning institutional mechanisms and practices of trilateral coordination.[80] Remarkably, within the first eighteen months, the group held fourteen meetings.[81] Through the process, the TCOG vastly improved alliance coordination.

Moreover, true to its form, the TCOG genuinely promoted trial cooperation, rather than repeating the traditional pattern of parallel bilateral channels between the U.S.–Japan alliance and the U.S.–South Korea alliance, with the United States serving as the intermediary. As one Japanese expert assessed, the trilateral cooperation on the North Korean question at the time was "the most commendable achievement" precisely because traditionally the long-held enmity between Japan and South Korea prevented such a close working relationship among the three allies.[82] During this period, however, South Korea's bilateral ties with Japan were improving rapidly, as evidenced in President Kim's decision to allow the imports of previously restricted Japanese cultural products to South Korea.[83] At the 1998 summit between Japanese Prime Minister Obuchi and South Korean President Kim, both sides announced the "Japan-Republic of Korea Partnership Toward the 21st Century Declaration." The declaration aimed to "formalize security consultative meetings, acknowledge greater defense-official exchanges, and sanction bilateral security dialogues expressly, as a way to create a more stable security relationship."[84] As the Perry Process yielded positive outcomes in October 1999, Japan and South Korea agreed to have regular dialogue on regional security at their ministerial talks.[85] A few months later, President Kim told Prime Minister Mori that South Korea's cooperation with Japan was conducive to peace on the Korean Peninsula and expressed his strong support for Japan's normalization efforts with North Korea.[86]

A virtuous circle between stronger alliance relations and the continued engagement drive toward Pyongyang epitomized the role congruence between the U.S.-centered and internally shaped regional roles during the Perry Process. On the one hand, the TCOG heralded a new pattern of alliance cooperation by enabling "the extension and deepening of security dialogue beyond the relatively narrow purview of the respective bilateral alliance networks."[87] The trilateral alliance cooperation in turn "harmonized the U.S.'s proliferation concern, South Korea's sunshine policy and Japan's wary stance toward North Korea" in a synergistic way.[88] While jointly helping to defuse the crisis on the peninsula and reinforcing South Korea and Japan's regional role as U.S. allies, the Perry Process also allowed South Korea and Japan to pursue their own regional roles centered on North Korea. Through the process of close coordination, South Korea's efforts toward inter-Korean reconciliation resulted in the first inter-Korean summit in 2000, while Japan jumpstarted its own regional drive to normalize its diplomatic ties with North Korea. The compatibility between the U.S. approach toward North Korea and the regional initiatives in turn contributed significantly to trilateral cooperation among the U.S. allies.

4.4 EAST ASIAN REGIONALISM DURING THE PERRY PROCESS

Along with alliance cooperation in the region, the Clinton administration's approach toward North Korea also facilitated greater regional cooperation. Compared to Europe, regionalism in East Asia had tradition-ally been characterized as underinstitutionalized and underperform-ing.[89] Asia's open regionalism in the economic realm was also widely attributed to the dominance of the United States in the region.[90] During the Perry Process, however, a new pattern of expanded regionalism emerged in the security arena as well. As the Perry Process ensured re-gional consultation and promoted regional attempts to engage North Korea, externally shaped regional roles, as U.S. allies or partners, did not conflict with internally shaped roles linked to North Korea. In other words, a region-wide pursuit of greater regional roles in multilateral re-gional settings coexisted nicely with the renewed U.S. engagement toward North Korea. As a result, unlike earlier calls for exclusive Asian regional-ism such as the East Asian Economic Caucus,[91] regionalism in this period took a more expansive form, simultaneously benefiting alliance coordina-tion and broader regional cooperation among East Asian countries. The development of the APT as a new multilateral regional forum illustrates this point.

The ASEAN Plus Three and Various Regional Frameworks

It is no coincidence that East Asian regionalism via the APT and other multilateral regional frameworks gained momentum in the late 1990s when the Perry Process and the three East Asian countries' initiatives toward Pyongyang substantially reduced tension on the Korean Penin-sula. At the 1998 APT summit in Vietnam, South Korean President Kim Dae-jung proposed a plan to establish the East Asian Vision Group (EAVG) to facilitate regionalism in the economic and security arenas. A year later in October 1999, China, Japan, and South Korea, along with members of the Association of Southeast Asian Nations (ASEAN), formally launched EAVG. It was through EAVG that the idea of the East Asia Summit was first developed and extended.[92]

The group held five meetings between 1999 and 2001 and delivered its report to the 2001 APT meeting in Brunei. The Report "envisions East Asia moving from a region of nations to a bona fide regional community where collective efforts are made for peace, prosperity and progress."[93] As an institutional mechanism, the report also recommended the develop-ment of the annual summit of the APT into the East Asian Summit and the establishment of an East Asian Forum, including Track I and II mecha-nisms, with the goal of providing an institutional channel for broad ex-changes and cooperation.[94]

Coupled with South Korea's efforts for EAVG activities, the 2000 inter-Korean summit facilitated regional cooperation in a systematic fashion. At the November 2000 APT meeting in Singapore, for instance, leaders of China, Japan, and South Korea "agreed to make 2002 the year of people's exchanges and to hold annual trilateral summits."[95] Along with its normalization efforts, in July 2000, Japan also added a regional dimension to inter-Korean relations by persuading ASEAN members to invite North Korea into the activities of the ARF.[96] During these positive regional developments, the United States and China were also able to adopt "reinforcing policies in support of further Korean cooperation."[97] The transformation of inter-Korean relations provided an opening for a new regional security structure in which U.S. alliances continued to flourish, "but in a way that China can live with."[98]

This regional trend was particularly beneficial for the Chinese leadership, given the widely shared view in Beijing that China's regional status was contingent on the state of Sino-American relations and that the key factor behind the relationship is the "compatibility of strategic interests with" the United States.[99] If the United States prevailed in a military contingency on the Korean Peninsula with China on the sidelines, it would expose "China's inability to parry U.S. post–cold war international dominance even in Beijing's own front yard."[100] In this vein, the Perry Process served as a useful channel for the Chinese to coordinate their approach with the United States on North Korea. As one U.S. Asia expert noted at the time, it was remarkable that the Chinese government was able to maintain such "working level U.S.–PRC consultations" despite the heightened bilateral tension in the wake of the NATO bombing of the Chinese embassy in Belgrade and the publication of the Cox Report accusing China of espionage on military technologies in 1999.[101]

The compatibility between the United States and China on the question of North Korea soon led to China's reevaluation of the regional security environment. In his August 2000 speech, China's UN ambassador, Sha Zhukang, observed:

> The overall situation in the Asia-Pacific region is moving towards relaxation. [North Korea] is improving its relations with the United States, Japan and other Western countries. It remains the main trend in the region to enhance dialogue and mutual understanding, build confidence and to solve problems through consultation.[102]

In his 2000 visit to Japan, Prime Minister Zhu Rongji changed China's traditional position and agreed to have a friendly exchange of naval vessels between the People's Liberation Army Navy (PLAN) and Japan's Maritime Self-Defense Forces.[103] Speaking in 2001, Chinese Foreign Minister Tang Jiaxuan also declared that the ARF, which includes not only East Asian countries but also the United States, was "the most important venue in the Asia Pacific region for the discussion of regional security issues."

With growing confidence in their regional role, Chinese leaders began to offer various proposals for regional framework at the APT meetings. At the 2000 APT meetings in Singapore, Chinese premier Zhu suggested that the APT be turned into a key channel of East Asia regional cooperation, and Japanese Prime Minister Mori and South Korean President Kim agreed to enhance trilateral cooperation on a variety of issues.[104] From that point on, the leaders of China, Japan, and South Korea have met separately at the APT annual meetings, ushering in a new era of trilateral regional consultation. The Japanese also grew more confident in their regional role and participated more actively in multilateral regional frameworks.

Broadening Regionalism and a Multi-layered Regional Order

As the three East Asian countries expressed greater interest in broadened regionalism, the United States also made efforts to expand the bilateral alliance mechanism into broader multilateral regional frameworks on the basis of the North Korean question. For instance, Kurt Campbell, then deputy assistant secretary of defense, promoted the concept of "minilateralism," issue-specific, ad-hoc small multilateral security mechanisms (e.g., KEDO and the TCOG), as a steppingstone toward a more institutionalized multilateralism.[105] The U.S. interest in multilateral regional frameworks also permitted the regional countries to go beyond the traditional bilateral focus anchored to alliance ties or partnerships with the United States. As a result, the regional countries envisioned a broadened, multilayered regional order encompassing both existing and new institutional arrangements.

In Japan, for instance, the multi-tiered regional order had four components. While the core of the order remained the U.S.–Japan alliance, other arrangements expanded outward to feature ad hoc groupings for specific regional issues such as KEDO and the TCOG (second tier), broader regional frameworks for security dialogue (third tier), and similar frameworks for non-security issues such as economic cooperation (fourth tier).[106] A foreign ministry official in Japan characterized the concept of multi-layered order as "something beyond the hitherto hub-and-spoke," and later, Japan's 2002 *Diplomatic Bluebook* specifically referred to the "promotion of multi-layered regional cooperation in the Asia-Pacific" as a major agenda for Japanese foreign policy.[107]

While differing in specifics, the Chinese were also thinking about a new regional security architecture that had several dimensions. Guarding against the strengthened U.S.–Japan alliance, the Chinese government called for a new security arrangement based on several pillars, which included "a concert of major powers" in the region (e.g., the United States, China, Japan, and Russia), "ad hoc coalitions on specific issues" (e.g., the North Korean nuclear issue), "existing security alliances," (e.g., U.S. regional alliances), and "regional or subregional mechanisms" (e.g., the ARF and the APT).[108] To the extent that the U.S. alliance system is not geared toward containment of China, a Chinese analyst observed, Beijing would be willing to "live with it and even work with it on certain issues of common interest," including stability on the Korean Peninsula.[109] Similarly in South Korea, analysts viewed that "a multilayered, multidimensional forum of bilateral, trilateral, quadrilateral, and multilateral security dialogues" would play a useful supplementary role for the traditional bilateral security structure.[110]

All in all, a new pattern of expanded regionalism grew out of the Perry Process in the form of broadened regional security frameworks and the gradual embrace of a multi-layered regional order. This outcome was possible because the Clinton administration's approach during the Perry Process did not force regional actors to choose between the U.S.-centered and internally shaped regional roles. Instead, both external and internal regional roles became congruent and mutually reinforcing, benefiting the East Asian countries. For instance, Japan was able to improve U.S.–Japan ties and regional cooperation alike,[111] as the Perry Process promoted Japan's dual role as alliance partner and regional player active in various multilateral regional venues. Similarly, the Kim Dae-jung government was able to actively reach out to its neighbors. Along with South Korea's aforementioned diplomatic overture to Japan, in July 1999, for instance, South Korean Defense Minister Cho Sung-tae visited Beijing for the first time and launched the first defense ministerial meeting with his Chinese counterpart.[112] All along, however, South Korea's alliance ties with the United States remained strong.

For China as well, the Perry Process was conducive to assuming a greater regional role, while at the same time helping it to improve its ties with the United States. Although emphasizing multipolarity to overcome the U.S.-centered order, the real focus for the Chinese was on "a strategic partnership or condominium with the United States in which it is one of two co-managers of Asian security."[113] Chinese experts have generally confirmed this view with their hope for the United States to actively participate in regional frameworks.[114] In this regard, the Perry Process closely approximated their preferred regional roadmap, with the greater potential for promoting regional cooperation and improving regional stability. Echoing China's expectations, Perry himself called for cooperative relations between the United States and China, based on the notion of "preventive defense." Contrary to the containment policy, which would prevent China from playing a greater regional role, preventive defense "encourage[d] Chinese participation and influence" in the region where Sino–American cooperation on the Korean issue could serve as a roadmap for broader regional cooperation in the future.[115]

4.5 CONCLUSION

As the East Asian countries sought to enhance their regional roles by changing their terms of engagement with North Korea, the renewed crisis on the Korean Peninsula in 1998 was particularly alarming. If the threat perception of North Korea were the sole determinant of regional behavior, we would expect the rise of alliance and/or regional mechanisms tailored specifically to reduce tension on the Korean Peninsula. Until the perceived threat from North Korea subsided, region-wide efforts to enhance regional roles by engaging North Korea would have been put aside. The threat perception was particularly high in Japan as the missile flew over its territories.

Despite an increase in the perceived threat and the domestic uproar against North Korea, however, the Japanese government soon resumed contacts with North Korea for negotiations. Even before the North Koreans announced their decision on the missile moratorium, Prime Minister Obuchi reaffirmed his willingness to improve ties with North Korea.[116] Rather than building an ad hoc regional framework to address the North Korean threat, the regional countries called for broader regional frameworks that would include North Korea. Throughout the 1998 missile crisis, China's participation in the Four Party Talks continued because of its desire "to play a positive and even-handed role in diplomatic activities relevant to the Korean Peninsula."[117] South Korea's engagement policy toward North Korea also persisted throughout the process.

As documented in this chapter, the continuation and progress of the regional initiatives toward North Korea was due in no small part to the

Perry Process, which enabled the regional countries to pursue their internally shaped regional roles without damaging their existing U.S.-centered regional roles. As the Perry Process ensured congruence between externally and internally shaped regional role conceptions, alliance ties expanded and regional cooperation proliferated. This dynamic in turn reinforced the regional efforts to engage North Korea. The overall compatibility between the U.S. and regional approaches not only helped to reduce the tension on the Korean Peninsula but also shaped an expanded and cooperative regional order in East Asia.

Ezra Vogel, a leading authority on Asian politics, touted KEDO and the Perry Process as models for regional cooperation. He singled out the Perry Process as an epitome of "what [the United States] can do when [the U.S. administration has] high-level leadership that goes about Asian policy on a very systematic basis."[118] Instead of boxing North Korea into a corner through coercive rhetoric and policies, the Perry Report offered North Korea an incentive to work with the United States and eventually helped the North to agree on the Joint Communiqué and a missile moratorium. However, a larger benefit from the Perry Process was its contribution to the regional order. The United States began the process by regionalizing the North Korean question through alliance coordination at the TCOG on the one hand and consultation with the regional actors including China on the other. As Clinton's second term neared the end, William Perry insisted that the approach recommended in his report "must be sustained into the future, beyond the term of this Administration."[119]

With George W. Bush in the Oval Office, however, Perry's hope was dashed almost overnight. Bush's unstated policy of "anything but Clinton's" on North Korea effectively stalled the regional momentum begun by South Korean President Kim Dae-jung's sunshine policy. At a private meeting with Secretary Albright in November 2002 when the second North Korean nuclear crisis began to intensify, President Kim indirectly expressed his frustration to Albright: "We had our best chance for a breakthrough in the last days of your administration. You understood the situation here and how much was at stake. You devoted your full energy. I will always be grateful to you and President Clinton for the support you gave."[120] In her own interview, Albright also bemoaned the consequences of the Bush policy toward North Korea:

Just imagine what would have happened if the Bush administration had picked up the hand of cards that we left on the table six years ago. In these six years, the North Koreans have been able to develop enough material to have eight to ten nuclear weapons whereas when we left it was one or two.[121]

This is a particularly unfortunate development, given reports about the possibility of intelligence hype on North Korea's enriched uranium program, which sparked the second crisis.[122] A more ominous consequence of the Bush administration's approach toward North Korea, however, was regional: a worsened regional order and the weakened U.S. influence in East Asia. The next chapter examines the nature of the East Asian order during the George W. Bush presidency.

CHAPTER 5

The Bush Doctrine and the East Asian Regional Order

5.1 INTRODUCTION

The arrival of a Republican administration in 2001 marked the end of the Perry Process. The subsequent changes in U.S. policy toward North Korea had "larger policy consequences that have redefined the East Asian political and security landscape."[1] The main objective of this chapter is to explore how the George W. Bush administration's approach transformed the East Asian order. As with chapter 4, I examine two dimensions: alliance politics and regionalism. Compared to the Clinton administration during the Perry Process, the Bush administration showed little respect for a region-wide yearning for expanding regional roles by redefining relations with North Korea. The global priority of countering proliferation was implemented without due consideration of such role conceptions.

As a consequence, no mutually reinforcing mechanism existed between externally shaped and internally shaped regional roles. Instead, the hardline U.S. approach during this period interacted with domestic debates about proper regional roles in each country. While North Korea engagers continued to emphasize internally shaped regional roles, North Korea bashers latched onto the global rogue frame and began to push for the U.S.-centered regional roles. This domestic dynamic was particularly strong in Japan, where the emergence of anti–North Korean conservatives stymied the cooperative regional relations engendered by the Perry Process. By intensifying role conflict and helping domestic groups "renationalize" the North Korean challenge, the Bush administration altered the nature of regional role conceptions and transformed the regional order into a narrowed, exclusive alliance structure and fractured regionalism in East Asia.

This chapter proceeds in the following manner. The next section examines how the Bush administration's approach toward North Korea interacted with regional role conceptions in China, Japan, and South Korea, engendering role conflict. The subsequent two sections explore the impact of the role conflict prompted by the Bush Doctrine on alliance relations and regionalism in East Asia. In brief, during the second North Korean nuclear crisis, America's alliance mechanisms in East Asia became strained, as the United States and South Korea clashed over the North Korean question and South Korea's relations with China markedly improved. As a consequence, the Trilateral Coordination and Oversight Group (TCOG) among the United States, Japan, and South Korea ceased to function and disappeared altogether. The presence of role conflict also made regional cooperation among East Asian countries more difficult. The chapter ends with a brief summary of findings.

5.2 REGIONAL ROLE CONCEPTIONS DURING THE BUSH PRESIDENCY

The prolonged controversy over the election results and the ultimate victory of George W. Bush in the 2000 presidential election dashed the last hope of President Clinton's Pyongyang visit. With his strong rebuke of the Clinton administration's foreign policy agenda,[2] President Bush was in no mood to continue the momentum toward U.S.–North Korea reconciliation. Sensing a wind of change in the U.S. policy on North Korea, South Korean President Kim Dae-jung wasted no time in his efforts to persuade his U.S. counterpart to endorse the sunshine policy of engagement and continue cooperative regional relations. In March 2001, when President Kim made a hurried visit to Washington he became the first Asian leader to meet with President Bush.[3] President Kim's personal plea for a speedy U.S.–North Korea negotiation, however, was met with Bush's deep skepticism of Kim Jong Il and strong reservations about any deals with North Korea.

The Bush administration's dramatic about-face on North Korea was vividly captured in a rare diplomatic flip-flop involving U.S. Secretary of State Colin Powell. As President Kim was arriving in Washington for the summit, Powell initially expressed his willingness to "pick up where President Clinton and administration left off" on the North Korean question. As soon as Powell's view was reported in the news media, hawkish members of the Bush administration, most notably Vice President Dick Cheney and National Security Advisor Condoleezza Rice, immediately took issue with Powell's assessment and forced Powell to correct his earlier remark with the following statement:

> We are undertaking a full review of our relationship with North Korea, coming up with policies that build on the past, coming up with policies unique to the administration, the other things we want to see put on the table . . . [Despite the expectation that] imminent negotiations are about to begin, that is not the case.[4]

With this public rejection of an early dialogue with Pyongyang, President Kim's efforts to persuade the United States to join the regional drive to engage North Korea collapsed in what the South Korean media called "a diplomatic disaster."

Even prior to the second North Korean nuclear crisis, the Bush administration's policy toward North Korea was on a collision course with the regional currents surrounding the Korean Peninsula. A few months after the summit between Presidents Kim and Bush, a much-anticipated U.S. policy review was issued in June 2001, which formally set the tone for a difficult time ahead. It laid out a set of new conditions for political reconciliation between the United States and North Korea. While the Clinton administration's policy on North Korea complemented and reinforced South Korea's sunshine policy, the U.S. policy review was "the anti-thesis of the Clinton policy," creating friction between the two allies.[5] While the review stressed the importance of close cooperation with South Korea and Japan, references to the Perry Report or the U.S.–North Korea Joint Communiqué were nowhere to be found.[6] A few months later, in his 2002 State of the Union address, Bush dismissed North Korea as part of an "axis of evil," effectively sealing off any road to reconciliation between Washington and Pyongyang.

The Bush administration's 180-degree turn in dealing with North Korea initially did not alter the domestic debates about North Korea and regional role conceptions in East Asia. If anything, the axis-of-evil speech stirred up anger among the majority of the South Koreans, strengthening the internally shaped regional role of Seoul as an independent regional player. The South Koreans viewed the hardline U.S. stance as a tactic of "dragging them into unnecessary conflict with Pyongyang and sabotaging President Kim Dae-jung's efforts to engage Pyongyang."[7] South Korea's then ambassador to the United States, Yang Sung Chul, publicly questioned the validity of the speech. Referring to Bush's scheduled visit to Seoul in February 2002, he demanded that President Bush "clear up this lack of clarity on the issue."[8] Reactions from the South Korean public were equally negative. A Gallup poll surveyed in February 2002 revealed that in a radical shift from previous surveys, only one-third of respondents expressed favorable opinions of the United States, while 60 percent of respondents viewed the United States unfavorably. Moreover, 62 percent deemed the axis-of-evil speech "an excessive statement to escalate tensions in the Korean peninsula."[9]

In Japan, even as Prime Minister Koizumi's support for the United States in Afghanistan and Iraq markedly enhanced Japan's alliance ties with the United States, others called for an "Asian diplomacy as a base and South Korea as the entry point."[10] Given South Korea's reconciliation policy toward North Korea and calls for others to follow suit, Japan's own efforts to engage North Korea were thought to have the potential to enhance Japan's regional role and status. In this regard, Koizumi's normalization negotiations with North Korea were widely perceived as "a break out from the old security arrangement" with the United States.[11]

Even after U.S. Assistant Secretary of State James Kelly briefed South Korea and Japan about North Korea's alleged enriched uranium program, the two governments did not slow down their efforts to engage North Korea. While the South Korean government proceeded with its planned ministerial talks with the North, the Koizumi government in Japan forged ahead with a resumption of normalization talks.[12] Taken aback by the Japan–North Korean summit, the Bush administration proceeded with the much-delayed official visit to North Korea a few weeks later. Instead of discussing issues of political reconciliation and exchanges, however, Kelly, under the instruction of hawkish officials in Washington, confronted his North Korean counterpart with the accusation that North Korea was pursuing an enriched uranium program. The first meeting between Bush administration officials and North Korea quickly turned into a diplomatic fiasco between the two countries. After the failed meeting, the United States accused North Korea of violating the Agreed Framework. Yet again, the Korean Peninsula became the epicenter of an evolving nuclear crisis.

By the end of 2002, the tension intensified in a dangerous action-reaction dynamic between the United States and North Korea. In November 2002, the Bush administration suspended delivery of heavy fuel oil to North Korea and soon effectively ended the implementation of the Agreed Framework. Undeterred, the North Koreans worsened the situation further by expelling UN inspectors and resuming the processing of spent fuel rods. As the year 2003 dawned, the situation grew even more alarming. In April 2003, North Korea became the first country ever to withdraw from the Nuclear Nonproliferation Treaty (NPT). Even in the early months of the Iraq War, the Bush administration dispatched military reinforcements to the vicinity of the Korean Peninsula, reaffirming that the United States would be willing to deal simultaneously with two different regional military contingencies.

The Bush Doctrine and Role Conflict in East Asia

Given their yearning for playing greater regional roles and the salience of North Korea in their respective regional visions, the rapidly developing crisis on the Korean Peninsula was particularly vexing for China, Japan, and South Korea. Faced with the possibility of a military confrontation between the United States and North Korea, the regional countries quickly moved to dampen the mounting tension on the peninsula. After hosting the unsuccessful three-party talks in April 2003, the Chinese government launched a series of shuttle diplomacy meetings across the region and played a vital role in setting up the Six Party Talks. Long eager to join such a regional mechanism on the Korean Peninsula, Japan became an active participant and "worked with South Korea to nudge the Bush administration towards negotiations with North Korea."[13] The common understanding of North Korea as a regional platform and the collective regional response to the Bush administration helped facilitate regionalism in the first phase of the second crisis.

The regional efforts failed to cohere, however, as the Bush administration's confrontational stance accentuated role conflict between externally and internally shaped regional roles and affected the domestic debate about North Korea in each country. Despite the regional call for greater flexibility toward North Korea, the United States continued to insist on the complete, verifiable, and irreversible dismantling (CVID) of North Korea's nuclear programs prior to any discussion on various bilateral issues between the two countries. The inflexible U.S. position provoked equally hostile reactions from North Korea, with the Six Party processes reaching a stalemate by the end of 2004. The end result was a loss of the regional momentum since the beginning of the Perry Process.

As the Bush administration moved to turn the Six Party Talks into a unified front against North Korea, efforts to enhance internally shaped regional roles, such as Koizumi's normalization drive and South Korea's engagement policy, became the first victims of the unfolding crisis. The situation jeopardized South Korean President Roh Moo-hyun's plan to expand the sunshine policy and turn South Korea into a "hub" of regional cooperation in East Asia.[14] To change the tide of the emerging crisis on its borders, the South Korean government proposed a gradual and reciprocal approach aimed at achieving North Korea's denuclearization in exchange for security assurances and economic assistance by the regional actors.[15]

As President Roh himself described, South Korean efforts at crisis resolution were rooted in South Korea's broader regional vision of establishing "a Northeast Asian community through a new regional order of cooperation and integration that transcends old antagonisms and conflicts among countries in this region" and "[linking] the resolution of the North Korean nuclear issue to the establishment of a peace regime" on the Korean Peninsula and regional cooperation.[16] Hence, despite the intensifying crisis, the Roh government continued with its joint industrial project with North Korea in Kaesung. Roh also urged Japanese Prime Minister Koizumi to continue his efforts to normalize diplomatic relations with North Korea, while encouraging China's constructive role at the UN Security Council over the North Korean issue.[17] Given Seoul's efforts aimed at expanding its independent regional role in a new regional order, the U.S. stance on Pyongyang exacerbated role conflict for South Korea, which was torn between "the nationalistic bond between the two Koreas and the alliance security bond between the United States and South Korea."[18]

The Bush administration's hardline approach toward Pyongyang also put Japan in a difficult position. U.S. Deputy Secretary of State Richard Armitage, in his meeting with then Liberal Democratic Party (LDP) Secretary General Abe Shinzo, declared, "the Japanese-American alliance [was] going after North Korea."[19] The U.S. framing of Japan as an ally working in tandem with the United States to pressure North Korea, however, was no easy sell for the Japanese since they wanted to maintain a degree of autonomy in their alliance relationship and wished not to be held hostage to U.S. global strategy.[20] Morimoto Satoshi, an adviser to the government on foreign policy and security affairs, described Japan's dilemma in the following observation:

> [There is] the clear emergence of the United States' unilateralism as the sole superpower and the increasing domination and hegemony in its interaction with other countries . . . We are faced with a difficult challenge: to incorporate U.S. unilateralism into broader trends of multilateralism and regionalism, and persuade it to act in harmony with them.[21]

Japan's strategic quandary was based on the fear that "a closer alliance relationship would draw them, as the junior partner, into supporting a U.S. agenda that would deprive them of their autonomous approach and complicate the independent pursuit of their own interests, particularly in

Asia."[22] Hence, a Japanese expert and government advisor lamented that the Bush administration was "able to halt the normalization negotiations between Japan and [North Korea] and restore US dominance in the resolution of issues on the Korean Peninsula."[23] Instead of following the Bush administration's approach of refusing to deal with North Korea, another prominent international relations expert at Keio University argued for "preserving a framework for normalization talks and spearheading a breakthrough in Northeast Asian politics."[24]

In China as well, the Bush administration's counterproliferation policy and its approach toward North Korea were viewed as part of a hegemonic strategy of using "military power to impose U.S. interests."[25] The Bush administration's drive to build an anti-rogue coalition was particularly sinister for the Chinese, since the Six Party Talks could serve as "a regional framework to prevent China and others from challenging US hegemony."[26] Although the immediate post-9/11 period witnessed better China–U.S. relations, especially regarding cooperation in fighting terrorism, the Chinese did not conceal their concerns about the United States. For instance, Chu Shulong, a Tsinghua University expert known for his relatively moderate view of U.S.–China relations, pointed to the Chinese concern over a wide range of U.S. global and regional policies: among others, U.S. hegemony and unilateral behavior, U.S. policy toward North Korea, and a leaked U.S. *Nuclear Posture Review* that named China and North Korea as potential targets against which the United States may use nuclear weapons.[27] As such, from a Chinese perspective, the Bush administration's call for China to play the role of a responsible stakeholder in dealing with North Korea sounded hypocritical.

Over time, China began to pursue a new regional order, one that would be vastly different from what the Bush administration had in mind with the adoption of the Bush Doctrine. In a marked departure from Deng Xiaoping's motto of "*tao guang yang hui*" (hide its ambitions and disguise its claws), the Chinese began to openly seek the role of "a more substantial player in a region where the United States traditionally [held] far more sway."[28] In the face of a unilateral approach by the Bush administration, the Chinese also accepted regionalism as a tool to counterbalance the United States, albeit in a way that was "a more-charming and less-threatening form of exercising China's influence."[29] As one Chinese expert put it, "increasing regionalism [would be] an important way to restrain American hegemonism."[30]

This was an unexpected development because the Chinese, at the outset of the second crisis, were more interested in turning the Six Party Talks into a viable regional security mechanism. In fact, since the second round of the Six Party Talks in early 2004, the Chinese delegation pushed for the construction of a permanent regional security mechanism.[31] More broadly, Beijing's effort, which mirrored Seoul's vision of a multilateral peace regime on the Korean Peninsula, was rooted in a region-wide assumption that integrating the U.S. alliances with a broader regional mechanism would be critical to long-term regional stability. This was also why Japan and South Korea were seeking to balance alliance ties and participation in broader regional forums.[32] The Chinese, for their part, expressed greater interest in a multi-tiered regional order, including existing military alliances and new regional security mechanisms.[33]

As the Bush administration forced the regional actors to follow its hardline approach toward North Korea, they found themselves in a strategic predicament where internally shaped regional roles were to be sacrificed in favor of U.S.-directed roles. By insisting on its own stance over North Korea and intensifying role conflict in East Asia, the Bush administration made regional efforts to balance relationship with the United States and regionalism difficult to sustain. Moreover, by emboldening North Korea bashers in each country and influencing domestic political dynamics, the Bush administration reshaped the regional order in East Asia, especially in alliance politics and regionalism.

5.3 THE BUSH DOCTRINE AND ALLIANCE POLITICS

For more than half a century, the United States has served as the backbone of regional stability in East Asia. The so-called hub-and-spokes system of its alliances with Japan and South Korea has not only maintained regional stability but also lessened the security dilemma among regional actors. With the doctrine of preemption and the Global Posture Review (GPR), the Bush administration charted a whole new course in alliance politics. As demonstrated in various U.S.-led multilateral security measures, such as the Proliferation Security Initiative (PSI), more than ever before, the United States utilized ad hoc, fluid coalitions, rather than a permanent, fixed alliance mechanism. At the same time, without much discussion with its regional allies, the Bush administration was eager to transform its traditional alliances into a global military pact to address various global challenges. This trend stood in stark contrast to the close alliance coordination between the United States and its two Asian allies during the Perry Process.[34]

As the Bush Doctrine conflicted with the regional approach toward North Korea, transformative changes took place in alliance dynamics in

East Asia. Overall, the U.S. alliances lost regional focus, with the U.S.–South Korean alliance strained over North Korea and the U.S.–Japan alliance focusing more on global dimensions. In the process, the trilateral cooperation mechanism among the United States, Japan, and South Korea, established under the banner of the TCOG, faced difficulties and ceased to exist. The task of alliance management grew even more difficult as Sino–South Korean security ties improved substantially and South Korea talked of the role of regional balancer.

As a result, the U.S.–South Korea alliance was on the verge of "unraveling due to diverging perceptions of the principal threat, coordination problems regarding policies toward North Korea" and what Michael Armacost calls "a significant erosion of public support for the alliance among elites in both countries."[35] The South Korean concern was first and foremost directed at the impact of the Bush administration's approach on inter-Korean relations. Most South Koreans felt that the United States was "sabotaging North-South interactions."[36] Specifically, the South Koreans viewed Bush's policy toward North Korea as "aggressive, even hostile, and unaccommodating to South Korea's interests," sparking anti-U.S. sentiment among the South Korean public. Instead of respecting the regional approach, from a South Korean perspective, the Bush administration was "trying to project and impose its own understanding and approach on others."[37] In his 2003 meeting with Secretary of State Powell, then South Korean Foreign Minister Yoon Young Kwan even warned that if the United States were not more forthcoming at the Six Party Talks, the South Korean government might not send troops to Iraq.[38] Clearly irritated by the unexpected ultimatum from a long-time ally, Powell shot back, "That is not how allies deal with each other."[39]

The Koizumi government in Japan was also alarmed by the Bush administration's approach. Immediately after the outbreak of the second nuclear crisis, Japan played a crucial "mediating role between South Korea and the United States" over the North Korean issue.[40] The South Korean government positively assessed Japan's efforts in "inducing peaceful negotiations between the U.S. and North Korea."[41] For instance, during respective bilateral summits with President Bush and South Korean President Roh in May and June 2003, Prime Minister Koizumi attempted to "bridge the gap between South Korea and the United States," while using its participation in the TCOG as a chance to harmonize "the disparate views and attitudes of South Korea and the United States."[42] In this way, at the beginning of the second crisis, the TCOG offered U.S. Asian allies an additional benefit of ensuring that "the United States will not move unilaterally on policy toward [North Korea]."[43]

The Collapse of the Trilateral Cooperation at the TCOG

From 1999, when the TCOG began, to September 2004, there were thirty-five meetings among the three allies.[44] The frequency of meetings attests to the level of commitment to maintaining trilateral alliance cooperation among the Asian allies. As the second crisis deepened, however, the TCOG was transformed into an "informal caucus among allies" within the broader Six Party process.[45] Growing signs of tension emerged among the three allies at the TCOG meetings. For instance, Lee Soo Hyuck, former South Korean representative at the TCOG and the Six Party Talks, admitted that there were disagreements on specific issues at the TCOG meetings that required the use of "indirect and implicative" language in an attempt to paper over the differences.[46]

Even before the outbreak of the second crisis, signs of trouble emerged over the apparent inconsistency in U.S. policy toward North Korea. At the January 2002 TCOG meeting, U.S. Assistant Secretary of State James Kelly expressed his willingness to meet North Korean officials "any time, any place without preconditions." But only four days later, President Bush delivered his axis-of-evil speech, effectively nullifying Kelly's remark and further delaying Kelly's visit to Pyongyang. The three countries also used subsequent meetings in April and September 2002 mainly as a venue for post-hoc management of South Korea's special envoy's visit to Pyongyang and Koizumi's North Korea visit and not as opportunities for formulating a coordinated policy toward North Korea. In particular, the announcement of Koizumi's planned Pyongyang trip "took almost everyone by surprise, and it underscored how the TCOG was not a forum for discussing such sensitive information."[47]

Soon, the TCOG began to "take on characteristics more of a trilateral negotiation process than of a means to coordinate their respective North Korean policies."[48] Most importantly, some South Koreans argued that the trilateral meeting could be better used to "help soften the Bush team's harder line."[49] One Japanese analyst seemed to agree when he maintained that President Roh's emphasis on South Korea's "leadership role" in dealing with the North might be "an attempt to restrain the United States from launching a Bush-style preemptive strike."[50] Not surprisingly, the meetings were soon relegated to a channel for covering the widening gap between the allies, particularly between the U.S. call for suspension of the Agreed Framework and South Korea's push for a U.S. nonaggression pledge to North Korea. As the Bush administration stressed the externally shaped regional role as a U.S. ally at the expense of internally shaped regional roles linked to North Korea, the subsequent role conflict, especially in South Korea, led to the collapse of trilateral alliance cooperation. It was in this changing regional context that the three countries began to characterize the trilateral meetings as informal, dropping the name TCOG altogether. Soon, the U.S. State Department, which formalized Perry's recommendation into the TCOG in 1999, started downplaying the importance of the meetings, simply stating that they are "just informal consultations between allies."[51]

South Korea's Growing Ties with China

Another source of difficulty for alliance management was an improving relationship between South Korea and China. Since the normalization of diplomatic ties in 1992, the Chinese and South Korean governments had substantially expanded their cooperation in various areas, particularly in economic affairs. Faced with a unilateralist U.S. approach toward North Korea, some Koreans began to call for "closer relations with China as providing an attractive counterweight to possible U.S. unilateralism on the Korean Peninsula."[52] Trapped between its alliance ties with the United States and its efforts to improve relations with North Korea, South Korea was gradually drawn to the idea of combining "its leverage and influence on North Korea with that of China in pursuit of a diplomatic breakthrough."[53] In this way, the North Korea crisis served to shape "a new alignment in East Asia, with China and South Korea moving closer toward each other on one side and the United States on the other."[54]

Early signs of South Korea's deference to China on regional security issues date back to March 1994. During the first North Korean nuclear crisis, then South Korea's ambassador to China, Hwang Byung-Tae, caused a stir by making the following statement:

> South Korea–China cooperation over the issue of North Korea's nuclear program should go beyond the current level of simply notifying Beijing what has already been decided between Seoul and Washington . . . South Korea's diplomacy should break out of its heavy reliance exclusively on the United States.[55]

Although the South Korean government immediately dismissed his view and the ambassador retracted his remark, South Korea's increasing consideration of China's regional position was clearly on display.[56] In the late 1990s, Chinese–South Korean ties further improved with regular defense ministerial meetings taking place since August 1999 and mutual naval port calls in October 2001 and in May 2002.[57]

After the second North Korean nuclear crisis broke out, China's proactive role in the Six Party processes elevated the relationship between China and South Korea to a new high. With the North Korean challenge driving them in a similar direction, both governments increasingly "defer[red] to each other's preferences," along the way making their policies toward North Korea "nearly identical."[58] In fact, many South Korean and Chinese officials observed at the time that "no discernible differences existed between themselves as far as the North Korean nuclear issue was concerned."[59] Most of the Chinese officials and experts I interviewed subscribed to this view.[60] The Chinese maintained that the ending of the Cold War on the Korean Peninsula would be "the key to the peace of the peninsula" and that a comprehensive partnership between China and South Korea would be critical to the ending of such Cold War tension on the Peninsula.[61]

The similar views on North Korea led to bilateral cooperation in a more concrete manner. At the November 2005 summit, President Roh Moo-hyun and Chinese President Hu Jintao declared that cooperation between the two neighbors entered "a new stage." Some of the joint agreements at the time included the setting up of a hotline between their foreign ministries, the establishment of a regular discussion channel between vice foreign ministers, expansion of military cooperation, and the doubling of bilateral trade to $200 billion by 2012.[62] The positive view of Sino–South Korean relations was widely shared by the Chinese policy elites. From a Chinese perspective, the bilateral ties not only prevent formation of a "Cold War mentality" in the region but also open the way for regional cooperation in security and economic areas. In this view, the comprehensive partnership between China and South Korea during this period also "upgraded [South Korea]'s political status and influence in the Northeast Asian region immensely," along the way contributing to the summit and the subsequent reconciliation drive between the two Koreas.[63]

Amid these developments, a report by South Korea's Presidential Commission on Policy Planning called for establishing "an 'Asian Union' that would include North Korea," and transforming the status of South Korea "from a [South] Korea that is focused on the United States to one focused on Asia, inclusive of both China and North Korea."[64] According to an April 2004 survey of the 204 newly elected members of the South Korean National Assembly, 50 percent of the ruling Uri party members listed China as South Korea's most important ally, whereas 42 percent chose the United States.[65]

Enhanced China–South Korean ties also meant that South Korea would be "a reluctant participant at best in any possible U.S.-led effort to pressure or constrain China and that the U.S. ability to establish a future order on the Korean peninsula contrary to Chinese interests also will be curbed."[66] In fact, China's preferred policy outcome is inter-Korean reconciliation without unification, or what can be called the "status quo plus" outcome: a peaceful coexistence between the two Koreas, ensuring not only a stable North Korean regime but "the peninsula being drawn into a Chinese sphere of influence."[67] As such, improving inter-Korean reconciliation would put China in an enviable position since it can fully cooperate with South Korea on a wide range of issues while, at the same time, keeping its traditional ties with North Korea largely intact.[68] All in all, during the Bush presidency, China took advantage of difficulties in U.S.–South Korean relations and moved even closer to Seoul, both politically and diplomatically, with the potential "to influence the security environment to its advantage in a post-unification Korea."[69]

A Fractured Alliance System: South Korea's Regional Balancer Role and Japan's Global Focus

South Korea's tension with the United States and its increasing cooperation with China also had implications for broader U.S. regional strategy. At a Senate Armed Services Committee hearing, then U.S. Commander of the Pacific Command, William Fallon, argued that the U.S.–South Korean alliance must adapt to "the changing security environment" represented by "China's military modernization." By cooperating more closely with the United States and Japan, he reasoned, South Korea would be able to shift its strategic focus from a North Korean contingency to "a more regional view of security and stability."[70] In a sign of role conflict, however, the U.S. call for a South Korean supporting regional role based on the U.S. strategic blueprint was met with South Korea's pronouncement of a new regional role. Instead of taking the U.S.-centered regional role and joining the U.S. regional campaign to balance against China, the South Korean government proposed a new role of regional balancer.

In March 2005 President Roh publicly declared: "we will not be embroiled in any conflict in Northeast Asia against our will. This is an absolutely firm principle we cannot yield under any circumstances."[71] With this remark, President Roh essentially rejected the U.S.-directed regional role that was part of the U.S. regional plan to counter China. Instead, he expressed his willingness to seek a multiparty security regime that would include China. His view is well reflected in his interview with a South Korean newspaper:

> Some suggest that South Korea should remain in "camp diplomacy" to defend itself and have a deterrent to a war on or around the peninsula . . . but my administration's policy is that we should overcome the Cold War confrontation and march along with our neighbors toward a multilateral security regime on the basis of expanding economic cooperation in the region.

> If the U.S. manages the strategic structure based on confrontation with the U.S. and Japan on one side and China and Russia on the other, tensions would hang over the region and something miserable could take place.[72]

The culmination of this regional vision was made public in 2005 when Roh declared South Korea's "balancer role" (*gyunhyungja-ron*): "Korea will play the role of a balancer, not only on the Korean peninsula, but throughout Northeast Asia."[73] The speech immediately stirred up controversy in both Washington and Seoul, complicating further alliance management between the United States and South Korea.[74] Meanwhile, a senior Chinese security expert at Renmin University positively assessed Roh's manifestation of South Korea's regional policy by commenting that his speech "could mark a significant change" for the region.[75]

While the Bush Doctrine drove South Korea to the internally shaped regional role that strained alliance ties with the United States, it emboldened Japan's North Korea bashers who started to challenge the hitherto mainstream view that Japan should engage more fully in regional security cooperation.[76] The stalled Six Party process and North Korea's nuclear test enabled Japanese conservatives to latch onto the U.S. frame. As they rejected the regionalist vision and embraced the U.S. threat perception of North Korea, what followed was "a de facto globalization" of the US–Japan alliance.[77] In the November 2003 parliamentary elections, for instance, the key foreign policy agenda was not East Asia, but the strengthening of the U.S.–Japan alliance, which contrasted sharply with South Korea's emphasis on Northeast Asian cooperation.[78] The most worrisome development, according to Gavan McCormack, was "the 2005/06 agreement to the fusion of command and intelligence between Japanese and U.S. forces." This agreement effectively subordinated Japan to U.S. global strategic leadership and committed it to collective defense, one of the remaining security taboos that Washington has been eager to eliminate.[79] Overall, instead of the internally shaped regional role as an independent regional player, the conservative government in Tokyo pushed for the U.S.-centered regional role as a junior partner of the U.S.–Japan alliance.

By then Abe Shinzo, a leading North Korea basher, became prime minister, declaring that "the changing security environment for Japan and the world call[ed] on Japan to contribute to global challenges."[80] To this end, he proposed to establish what he called the "Arc of Freedom and Prosperity," including the United States and other democratic countries.[81] In a specific move, in January 2006, Foreign Minister Aso Taro met with U.S. Secretary of State Condoleezza Rice and Australian Minister for Foreign Affairs Alexander Downer for the first ministerial-level security talks between the three countries. At the meeting, they discussed the possibility of joint military exercises between the three allied countries.[82] As the U.S.–Japan alliance increasingly focused on concerns beyond the region, the traditional U.S. regional alliance, which was aimed at deterring the Soviet Union, was "being replaced by a nascent anti-China US-dominated multilateral alliance system."[83] However, given the fact that South Korea refused to join this new regional arrangement, wrote Richard Tanter, the "new tripartite security architecture [was] decidedly wobbly."[84]

5.4 THE BUSH DOCTRINE AND EAST ASIAN REGIONALISM

In contrast to the fractured alliance ties caused by the Bush Doctrine, there were signs of broadening regionalism during the earlier periods of the second crisis, an indication that internally shaped regional roles were as important as U.S.-directed regional roles expected by the Bush administration. Tellingly, the push for larger multilateral regional frameworks came from senior Japanese government officials. For instance, at the 2002 Asia Security Conference, commonly known as the Shangri-la Dialogue, then Japan's Defense Agency Director Nakatani Gen suggested that the Conference be developed into "a formal Asia–Pacific Defense Ministerial Meeting to complement the largely foreign ministry–centered [ASEAN Regional Forum]."[85] More importantly, he also proposed a new security framework that would include China, the two Koreas, and the United States and, in his official visit to Seoul in April 2002, put forward joint research with South Korea on a regional security framework.[86] Even after the outbreak of the second crisis, Japan, while at a trilateral summit in November 2002, joined China and South Korea in promoting regional cooperation in a wide range of areas and exchanging views on the situation on the Korean Peninsula.[87]

Writing about the prospects for regionalism in East Asia around that time, Gilbert Rozman, a prominent sociologist and leading Asia watcher, envisioned a "Korean peninsula becoming the center of an entire region in search of a community that the United States may not easily accept."[88] In fact, in response to the U.S. plea to forge a unified front against North Korea, President Roh attempted to build an alternative regional coalition with China and Japan against the United States. At the ASEAN Plus Three (APT) meeting in October 2003, for example, Roh met with Chinese Premier Wen Jiabao and Japanese Prime Minister Koizumi and issued, for the first time, a joint statement calling on the parties to seek "a peaceful resolution of the North Korean nuclear issue and to cooperate for the second round of the Six-Party Talks."[89] More importantly, the statement, entitled "Joint Declaration on the Promotion of Tripartite Cooperation among China, Japan, and South Korea," called for a strengthening security dialogue among the three Asian countries.[90]

The Rise of the ASEAN Plus Three (APT), 2001–2004

The idea of having the APT meetings first emerged in the early 1990s with Malaysian Prime Minister Mahathir Mohamad's proposal for forming an East Asian Economic Grouping (EAEG) and later an East Asian Economic Caucus (EAEC). These suggestions failed to materialize owing much to U.S. opposition and the emergence of the Asia Pacific Economic Cooperation (APEC) as a larger regional alternative. The idea later resurfaced in December 1997 when leaders of the Association of Southeast Asian Nations (ASEAN) as well as of China, Japan, and South Korea convened an informal meeting on the sidelines of the Second ASEAN Informal Summit in Malaysia. The APT process was formally institutionalized at the Third Summit in 1999 with a Joint Statement on East Asia Cooperation.[91] During this early period, however, cooperation among East Asian countries remained marginal and limited.

The regional interaction facilitated by the Perry Process enabled trilateral cooperation among China, Japan, and South Korea through the APT mechanism. In November 2000, at the APT meeting in Singapore, Chinese Premier Zhu Rongji, Japanese Prime Minister Mori Yoshiro, and South Korean President Kim Dae-jung agreed to enhance trilateral cooperation on a variety of issues. The first joint statement by the three countries features "[t]he five-point agreement on environmental, economic, cultural, and information technology (IT) cooperation, and transnational efforts at combating crime and piracy."[92] Chinese Premier Zhu also suggested that the APT "could become the main channel of East Asia regional cooperation." In 2001, Zhu expanded China's vision for the APT to include "dialogue and cooperation to political and security fields."[93]

For its part, Japan also contributed to the regional effort by hosting the first trilateral foreign minister–level meeting in July 2002. Japan's regional role was boosted by the successful co-hosting of the 2002 World Cup with South Korea, as well as by trilateral cooperation among China, Japan, and South Korea during trilateral leaders' summits at the APT. At the 2002 APT meeting, the three countries held a trilateral summit, agreeing to deepen China–Japan–ROK trilateral cooperation in various issue areas and exchanging their views on the North Korean situation.[94] The Japanese also stressed the importance of the joint statement on North Korea at the 2003 APT meetings, with a Foreign Ministry website highlighting that the three East Asian countries "reaffirm[ed] their commitment to a peaceful solution of the nuclear issue facing the Korean Peninsula through dialogue and to the denuclearization of the Korean Peninsula, while addressing all the concerns of the parties and working together to maintain peace and stability on the Peninsula."[95] In November 2003, Chinese Vice Foreign Minister Dai Bingguo visited Japan and said that "China intended to cooperate closely with Japan" for peaceful resolution of the North Korean situation.[96]

Overall, compared with the dismal failure of the Trilateral Coordination and Oversight Group (TCOG) among America's Asian allies, the APT seemed to be evolving into a valuable regional venue for security cooperation. A new pattern of regional cooperation among China, Japan and South Korea continued in the wake of the second crisis. For instance, in July 2004, foreign ministers of China, South Korea, and Japan held a trilateral meeting on the sidelines of the APT meeting, discussing East Asian regional cooperation and North Korea's nuclear crisis.[97] As late as the November 2004 APT summit in Laos, the three countries reiterated their commitment to a peaceful solution of the nuclear issue through dialogue.[98]

Although facilitated in part by the need to discuss the North Korean issue, regional cooperation went beyond Korean Peninsula issues. In fact, even at the height of the second crisis, many South Koreans, including President Kim Dae-jung, believed that the Six Party framework should go beyond the nuclear issue to become a permanent regional organization.[99] Early signs were promising as the three East Asian countries discussed regional security issues with a broader regional security framework in their minds. On June 18, 2003, for instance, the foreign ministers of China, Japan, and South Korea held a trilateral meeting in Cambodia.

During the meeting, South Korean Foreign Minister Youn Youngkwan and Japanese Foreign Minister Kawaguchi Yoriko explained to Chinese Foreign Minister Li Zhaoxing the results of the June 2003 TCOG meeting and discussed the prospect of expanding the three-party talks involving China and the United States, to a five-party system including South Korea and Japan.[100]

Soon, meetings and consultations among the high-ranking foreign ministry officials of China, Japan, and South Korea became a regular feature of regional diplomacy.[101] For instance, the three countries' foreign ministry officials in charge of Asian affairs held a tripartite meeting in Seoul and Beijing in November 2003, and a "Japan-ROK-China Director-General-level Meeting" was held in Seoul in December 2003.[102] Along with official meetings, the three East Asian countries facilitated a flurry of semi-governmental Track II and nongovernmental meetings. Table 5.1 illustrates these regional developments, as manifested in several key governmental and Track II activities among the three countries.

Role Conflict, The Decline of Regionalism, and China–Japan Rivalry

However, positive developments in East Asian regionalism did not last long, as the nuclear crisis reached a stalemate in late 2004 and Japan's North Korea bashers rose to power in the midst of anti–North Korean sentiments in Japan. Hamstrung by an unprecedented level of anti–North Korean feelings on the domestic front and Bush's unwavering hardline stance toward North Korea, the Koizumi government was unable to find a breakthrough over the North Korean issue. Signaling role conflict, Japan's pursuit of a greater regional role by engaging North Korea was increasingly challenged by the Japanese right, who reasserted the externally shaped regional role of Japan as a U.S. ally.

Nonetheless, Koizumi made another attempt at jump-starting the normalization talks in September 2004 when he held an unusual meeting with a North Korean vice foreign minister on the sidelines of the UN General Assembly. Koizumi asked the North Korean minister to convey his message to Kim Jong Il that "it is important to both normalize ties between the two countries and get on with six-party talks." While the North Korean minister stressed the importance of the Six Party process, he made clear that North Korea could not attend the talks due to what they viewed as "a hostile U.S. policy."[103] The subsequent stalemate in turn provided an opening for North Korea bashers to push for the U.S.-directed regional role and an alternative regional vision centered on the U.S.–Japan

Table 5.1. EAST ASIAN REGIONAL SECURITY MEETINGS (2002–2004)

Venue	Main Features
The 2002 Korea–Japan Millennium Symposium October 26, 2002, Tokyo, Japan	• Participation by former South Korean President Kim Young-sam and former Japanese Prime Ministers Mori Yoshiro, Nakasone Yasuhiro, and regional experts. • Okonogi Masao of Keio University called for sharing regional identity, not just systems (democracy, market economy, and U.S. alliances). • Former Chairman of CSCAP Korea Kim Dalchoong called for regional multilateral cooperation led by China, Japan, and South Korea.[142]
The First Conference of the Network of East Asian Think-Tanks (NEAT) September 29–30, 2003, Beijing, China	• The inaugural meeting of the NEAT, one of the two multilateral consultation agendas proposed in the previous APT meetings (the other one is the East Asian Forum below). • The conference was designed to promote Track II cooperation in East Asia, with the aim of providing intellectual support and policy recommendations on key economic and security issues. • Discussed the establishment of a regional cooperation organization suited to the regional conditions.[143]
The First East Asia Forum (EAF) December 16, 2003, Seoul, South Korea	• Hundreds of members of the ASEAN Plus Three (APT) participated in the inaugural meeting of the EAF. • South Korean President Roh declared, "Resolving the North Korean nuclear challenge and the peaceful settlement of the Korean Peninsula would contribute to the peace and prosperity in East Asia."[144]
Symposium on Northeast Asian Security Cooperation and the Six Party Talks May 28, 2004, Seoul, South Korea.	• Hosted by South Korea's *Donga Ilbo*, Japan's *Asahi Shimbun*, and China's State Council's Chinese Institute of Contemporary International Relations. • Participants shared a similar view of the situation regarding the Six Party Talks. • While admitting different interests of each country at the talks, participants assessed the Six Party processes as a good starting point for regional cooperation.
The First China, Japan, South Korea Forum for Peaceful Development and Security October 11, 2004, Beijing, China.	• In this forum, about seventy governmental and nongovernmental security experts from the three East Asian countries participated. • Participants exchanged their views of such diverse issues North Korea's nuclear programs, China–Japan rivalry, and forging a Northeast Asian security framework.[145]

alliance, both ominous signs for trilateral regional cooperation among China, Japan, and South Korea.

The Bush administration's hardline position on North Korea also dampened Beijing's earlier hope of transforming the Six Party talks into a broader regional security framework. As the Six Party talks reached an impasse, a senior Chinese foreign policy advisor lamented that China and Japan did not seem to seize the opportunities for regional cooperation.[104] Given Koizumi's close personal ties to President Bush, some regional actors also hoped that Japan would play a bridge-building role between the hawkish United States and more moderate regional countries.[105] By late 2004, however, the stalled Six Party process and the growing dominance of conservative voices in Japan left the Koizumi government with few options. As a result, previous efforts at balancing Japan's internally shaped regional role and externally expected regional role gradually gave in to the Japanese right's regional vision anchored to the alliance ties with the United States.

As Japanese moderates who emphasized the internally shaped regional role were losing ground over the issues of normalization with North Korea and East Asian regionalism, the conservative LDP lawmakers led by then Deputy Secretary General Abe Shinzo and relatives of the abductees quickly joined forces to push an anti–North Korean campaign and economic sanctions on North Korea.[106] The Japanese right stressed the U.S.-directed regional role by seeking to expand Japan's defense role within the revitalized U.S.–Japan alliance. In this context, in November 2004, the LDP's investigative committee on constitution finalized a draft constitution calling for the exercise of collective self-defense within the U.S.-Japan alliance and the use of the Japanese military overseas in the name of contributing to the international community.[107] The conservatives also considered an expanded role of Japan's defense forces for regional contingencies. In an effort to "revamp the national defense strategy," Defense Agency officials even stipulated "three scenarios in which China attacks Japan," which include "attacks stemming from disputes over ocean resources and claims over the Senkaku Islands as well as a clash across the Taiwan Strait."[108]

Taken aback by the explicit language aimed at China, the Chinese promptly responded with a warning against Japan's "Cold War mentality" and suggested that President Hu Jintao's summit with Prime Minister Koizumi at the 2004 APEC meeting might be difficult.[109] In the midst of the mounting tension between the two countries, it was also reported that a Chinese naval submarine intruded into Japan's territorial waters near Okinawa.[110] While the Chinese Navy cited a technical problem, the damage had already been done. In a draft version of a New Defense Program Outline

(NDPO) presented to the ruling LDP in 2004, Japan for the first time named North Korea and China as threats to its security:

> North Korea's military moves are a grave destabilizing factor in the region. At the same time, Japan must pay close attention to China's modernization of its military and the expansion of its activities in the sea.[111]

In response, the Chinese wasted no time in expressing their anger, as asserted in a Foreign Ministry statement:

> Official Japanese documents openly play up the so-called 'China threat," which is completely baseless and irresponsible . . . China expresses strong dissatisfaction with this, and hopes Japan will do more to improve mutual trust and the healthy and stable development of bilateral ties.[112]

The Communist Party's official *People's Daily* also warned, "Japan appear[ed] to be following the United States in security strategy."[113] In another opinion piece in the same paper, a columnist claimed that Japan was becoming "the frontline of U.S. Asian policy" of containing China, which "entirely [went] against the trend of the times featuring peace and development."[114] The timing of the Sino-Japanese tension was particularly unfortunate as East Asian countries were about to meet for another APT meeting and the first East Asian Summit in Malaysia. Citing the negative turn in Sino-Japanese relations, the Chinese government ruled out meetings between Chinese Premier Wen Jiabao and Prime Minister Koizumi at the meetings.[115]

As the Bush administration accentuated role conflict and regional role conceptions played out differently in each capital, cooperative regional dynamics engendered by the Perry Process fell victim to a full-blown regional rivalry between Beijing and Tokyo. By late 2005, the Sino-Japanese tension was morphed into a new "conflict between Japan and China over the form of a future East Asian community." Whereas the Chinese stressed the boundaries of an East Asian community within the framework of the APT centered on China, Japan, and South Korea, the Japanese insisted on building a regional community based on the broader East Asian summit including Australia, New Zealand, and the United States.[116] Breaking away from a previous tendency not to publicly discuss the Taiwan issues, Japanese officials also began to state that they shared with the United States "a common concern about the future of Taiwan," while publicly criticizing China's growing military buildup in the region.[117] Appearing on a national television in April 2006, Japanese Foreign Minister Aso Taro even called China a military threat.[118] Citing a U.S.–Japan pronouncement that both the Taiwan and Korean Peninsula issues were part of their "common strategic objectives," the Chinese warned that Japan was held hostage to U.S. global strategies.[119]

Tension between Japan and South Korea and Failed Regionalism

Regional tension also spread to the relationship between South Korea and Japan. In early 2005, the two countries faced off over the small islets known as Tokdo/Takeshima, which had been annexed to Japan during the colonial period and later in the postwar years placed under South Korea's administrative control.[120] South Korean resentment toward Japan was amplified by Seoul's belief at the time that the Japanese government was "building up its military and taking a hard line position toward North Korea."[121] From South Korea's perspective, Japan's emphasis on North Korea bashing and the U.S.-directed regional role came at the cost of South Korea's internally shaped regional role as a regional hub and independent regional player. Feeling betrayed by Tokyo's seemingly abrupt volte-face on North Korea, the South Korean government publicly opposed Japan's plan to become a permanent member of the UN Security Council. The South Korean ambassador to the UN, Kim Samhoon, made it clear that a country not trusted by its neighbors would not be worthy to play a greater role in the international community.[122]

As Japan's relationships with China and South Korea headed toward the worst level in the postwar period, earlier regional developments toward forging an inclusive regional security mechanism were soon replaced with a narrowed, exclusive focus on the U.S.-Japan alliance. In a major shift from the region-focused Higuchi Report of 1994, the 2004 strategic report, known as the Araki Report and issued by a blue-ribbon prime ministerial advisory council, proposed a markedly different foreign policy blueprint for Japan. Its main recommendations included "strengthening Japan's security alliance with the United States and changing the Self-Defense Forces into a 'multifunctional, flexible defense force.'" The report proposed an "'integrated security strategy' that deals more actively with international security issues as well as self-defense under the alliance with the United States."[123] In this way, the transformation of the bilateral alliance took concrete form, but in a manner designed "to reaffirm the US-dominated hegemonic framework of security in the region."[124] The Chinese in turn blamed America's "effort to encourage Japan to take a more activist regional and global security role" for the tension between China and Japan.[125]

After years of refusal to engage in direct, bilateral talks with North Korea and the coercive approach toward the North, the Bush administration finally softened its hardline position in late 2006. The immediate catalyst was North Korea's nuclear test in October 2006. The subsequent defeat of the Republican Party in the 2006 congressional elections further necessitated a new breakthrough in foreign policy, paving the way for the U.S. "reverse-course" policy toward North Korea.[126] In January 2007, the Bush administration held its first official meeting with North Korea since the outbreak of the second crisis in 2002. In a series of events reminiscent of the Perry Process, the Bush administration pledged that, should North Korea forgo its nuclear path, the United States would be prepared to pursue "a bilateral process" to establish "a normal relationship" with North Korea.[127] In return, in July 2007, North Korea shut down the Yongbyon reactor and readmitted a permanent UN inspection team.[128] Later, North Korea also submitted a declaration regarding its nuclear programs in exchange for the United States' lifting sanctions and taking North Korea off the list of states that sponsor terrorism.[129]

Along with its contribution to the nuclear dimension and the progress at the Six Party Talks, the Bush administration's policy shift toward North Korea, albeit briefly, enhanced role congruence and regional dynamics. After the nuclear breakthrough between the United States and North Korea, for instance, the two Koreas also achieved their own diplomatic milestone, successfully holding the second inter-Korean summit in October 2007. Both sides issued a joint declaration signed by President Roh Moohyun and Chairman Kim Jong Il. In it, the two Koreas agreed, "[they] should end the current armistice and establish a permanent peace regime."[130]

As Prime Minister Abe's hardline position toward North Korea put Japan at odds with its neighbors, many Japanese elites also began to express concern that Japan was "losing an opportunity to influence the talks and help shape the future of Northeast Asia."[131] Dismissing the Abe administration's hardline stance as "a simplistic policy" in light of the recent thaw between North Korea and the United States and between the two Koreas, an editorial in *Asahi Shimbun* declared, "Japan must not miss the bus" and urged Abe's successor Fukuda Yasuo to produce a comprehensive North Korea policy.[132] Prime Minister Fukuda eventually decided to "seek a resolution to the North's nuclear programs, missile threats and the abductions in a 'comprehensive' manner."[133] Along the way, Japan's relations with its regional neighbors also briefly improved. South Korean Foreign Minister Song Minsun spoke highly of the change in Japan's stance toward

North Korea.[134] Chinese Defense Minister Cao Gangchuan also visited Japan in August 2007, the first visit by a Chinese defense minister since February 1998.[135]

The rekindled interest in regionalism in the last years of the Bush presidency, however, was short-lived. By 2008, for different domestic political reasons, the conservative Lee Myung-bak and Aso Taro governments came to power in South Korea and Japan, respectively.[136] Given their emphasis on the political transition and respective domestic political agendas, resuscitating moribund regionalism was hardly a priority. More importantly, years of distrust and mutual suspicion between the Bush administration and North Korea proved to be difficult to overcome, particularly so in the last year of the Bush presidency. Despite the initial successes such as the disabling of the Yongbyon reactor and the demolition of its cooling tower in May 2008, the disputes over the verification of North Korea's nuclear inventory and the subsequent suspension of the U.S. provision of heavy fuel oil effectively torpedoed the bilateral agreement between the United States and North Korea. President Bush left Washington with the legacies of failed nuclear diplomacy with Pyongyang and the decidedly negative effects on the regional order in East Asia.

5.5 CONCLUSION

Comparing the Clinton and Bush administrations' approaches to North Korea, one regional expert maintained that while Clinton was interested in reformulating the regional order, Bush seemed to have had no such interest.[137] As examined in this chapter, however, the Bush administration did have a regional plan of its own. It was rooted in a new global strategy of countering proliferation threats and reshaping the regional security structure in a mold that was markedly different from what the regional countries had in mind. By shifting the strategic focus away from "intraregional issues toward a common global threat," the Bush administration effected a transformation of the East Asian regional order.[138] It did so by intensifying role conflict and enabling the rise of the Japanese right, which latched onto the U.S. hardline stance and promoted an alternative regional vision that turned Japan away from regional cooperation and toward the U.S.–Japan alliance.

As a result, the Bush era witnessed a sea change in the U.S.-centered hub-and-spokes regional alliance structure, in particular the U.S.–South Korean axis. The South Korean government not only rejected the U.S. call for pressuring North Korea and joining the global coalition against proliferation but also frequently aligned itself with China. At the beginning, the Japanese also emphasized the importance of balancing the U.S.–Japan alliance and the trilateral cooperation among Asian allies.[139] If Japan simply followed the American neo-conservatives, one Japanese expert warned, its channels for cooperation with South Korea and China and the chance to forge a broader regional security framework would be lost.[140] In the wake of growing anti–North Korean sentiments and the dominance of "revisionist" voices on the domestic political stage, the Koizumi government's normalization drive aimed at enhancing Japan's internally shaped regional role was eventually hijacked by the conservative agenda of redefining Japan's security role in the regional and global realms on the basis of the externally shaped regional role as a U.S. ally.

Such a transformation did not bode well for the regional cooperation launched by the Perry Process. The Chinese government, which had had high expectations of developing the Six Party talks into a new regional security mechanism, found itself in a rapidly worsening conflict with Japan over their respective strategic influence and the proper format of a regional security framework. Failing to realize its regional strategy of turning the Korean Peninsula into a new hub of regional integration and cooperation, the Roh Moo-hyun government envisioned South Korea's balancer role in the region, while complaining about anti–North Korean sentiments in Japan. Under these regional circumstances, the APT and the East Asian summit ended up on the diplomatic backburner.

In his critical assessment of the Bush Doctrine as applied to the region, Amitav Acharya, a leading scholar on Asian regionalism, contends that the Bush administration's approach undermined regional "hopes for a more robust multilateral security order" in East Asia.[141] This chapter has shown one such mechanism during the Bush presidency. By intensifying role conflict and forcing the regional actors to adopt its preferred role as U.S. partners in the anti–North Korean counterproliferation coalition, the Bush administration stalled regional efforts to forge a broader cooperative regional security order and helped erect a narrowed and conflictual regional order in East Asia. As the next chapter explores, however, that momentous legacy is hardly confined to one region.

CHAPTER 6

Iran's Nuclear Pursuit and the Shifting Regional Order in the Middle East

6.1 INTRODUCTION

While this book has thus far focused primarily on the East Asian case, this chapter extends the argument beyond the East Asian dynamics. It demonstrates that the regional patterns identified in East Asia are also applicable to the Middle East, with regard to the Iranian nuclear challenge. Similar to the East Asian case, regional dynamics in the Middle East since the beginning of the Iranian nuclear crisis in 2003 show that regional countries' regional role conceptions and distinctive regional visions have shaped their policies toward Iran. Just like the decade-long crisis on the Korean Peninsula, Iran's nuclear pursuit and the Bush administration's response intersected with Middle Eastern states' search for a new regional role and foreign policy autonomy, reshaping the regional order in the Middle East.

After years of U.S. sanctions and rumors about an impending Israeli preemptive strike, talks between the P5 + 1 and Iran renewed debates about how to resolve the long-running nuclear crisis in a volatile region. In the common narrative in the United States and Europe, Iran's nuclear pursuit, just like the North Korean challenge, represents a straightforward global problem endangering global nonproliferation efforts and the global oil market. For regional countries, however, the issue is far more complex, as Iran's nuclear ambition coincided with the shifting regional order in the wake of the U.S. withdrawal from Iraq and the Arab uprisings spreading through the region. This chapter examines the interplay between global nuclear proliferation and regional order by demonstrating how issues critical to the regional order in the Middle East, such as competition for status, Sunni-Shia rivalry, and geopolitics involving external great powers, shape the perceptions and policy behavior of Iran and its neighbors, complicating nuclear diplomacy at the global level.

In the past decade, however, both the Bush and Obama administrations have remained consumed by the nuclear question, overlooking larger regional dynamics surrounding Iran. In order to cope better with the nuclear crisis and fully grasp the changes in the Middle East, it is essential to understand the regional views of Iran and their impact on the regional order. Mirroring the East Asian case, Iran's neighbors think more about regional order, both in security and economic terms, than about the nuclear equation. Investigating this crucial yet underappreciated regional story is the central objective of this chapter.

To their credit, a handful of analysts have pleaded for greater attention to the views of Iran's neighbors. In addressing Iran's nuclear challenge, James Lindsay and Ray Takeyh write, it is imperative to examine "not only how Iran is likely to act but also how other states will react to this outcome—and what the United States could do to influence their responses."[1] Kenneth Pollack, who served on the Clinton administration's National Security Council as its Iran expert, also warns that despite the continued U.S. strategy of containment against Tehran, its success ultimately depends on "how Iran's neighbors and other interested countries will respond."[2]

Few analyses, however, explore the regional dimension of the Iranian nuclear challenge in a systematic manner.[3] This chapter aims to do just that in the following ways. The next section examines the evolution of Iran's nuclear ambition, which itself was a byproduct of Tehran's search for a greater regional role, and the U.S. responses. The following sections in turn investigate several regional countries' own perceptions and policies with regard to Iran and their links to regional role conceptions and broader regional visions. The penultimate section examines the impact of regional role conceptions on the regional order in the Middle East. The chapter concludes with a summary of the findings and a brief discussion on the prospects for regional order in the wake of the Arab uprisings that have swept through the region since early 2011.

6.2 IRAN'S REGIONAL ROLE, NUCLEAR PURSUIT, AND CLASH WITH THE UNITED STATES

Historically, Iran has been a major regional force in the greater Middle East. Given its past glory as the Persian Empire and the size of its territory and population, Iranian leaders continue to believe that Iran has "the right to dominate the region."[4] The Shah of Iran came closest to achieving the elusive goal in the 1970s when his regime became a de facto regional powerhouse in the aftermath of Nixon's détente policy and the withdrawal of British forces from the region. During this period, the U.S. strategy toward the Middle East was based on two pillars: Tehran's military power and Riyadh's oil wealth.[5] As a regional buffer against the Soviet expansion and a major ally of the United States, Shah's Iran was vital to "the stability of the region and to international security."[6]

After the Iranian Revolution deposed the Shah regime, Iran continued to play a pivotal role in the formation of the current regional order as the revolution in Tehran spread Islamist ideology throughout the region.[7] In particular, the creation of the Gulf Cooperation Council (GCC) was a regional response to instability sparked in the wake of the Iranian Revolution and the Soviet invasion of Afghanistan.[8] Supreme Leader Ruhollah Khomeini's drive to export the revolutionary Islamist zeal and to expand Iran's regional influence failed to materialize only because Tehran was consumed by the ruinous eight-year war with Iraq throughout the 1980s.

Iran's efforts to enhance its regional influence quickly resumed in the 1990s. In its desperate efforts to recover from the devastating war, Tehran began to normalize its ties with neighboring Arab states, a remarkable diplomatic move given that some of those Arab states sided with Iraq throughout the Iran–Iraq War. However, Iran struggled to improve relations with the United States, a de facto regional hegemon with a growing military presence and alliance ties with all of the Gulf monarchies. One of the main stumbling blocks was Iran's alleged quest for nuclear programs. Going beyond the realm of nuclear proliferation, however, bilateral tension was rooted in competing regional visions between the United States and Iran.

Iran's pursuit of nuclear programs dates back to the Shah's rule in the 1970s during which the United States provided support for civilian nuclear reactors. After the revolution, the clerical regime initially halted the nuclear program. But the Iran–Iraq War and Saddam Hussein's use of chemical weapons rekindled Tehran's interest in the nuclear programs.[9] In the early 1990s, an allegation of Iran's nuclear activities prompted an International Atomic Energy Agency (IAEA) inspection on Iran's nuclear facilities, which found no illegal activities. In January 1995, however, the announcement that Russia agreed to complete the moribund nuclear reactors at Bushehr renewed suspicions about Iran's nuclear ambition.[10]

The rapidly evolving tension with Iran interacted with the U.S. efforts to reassert its regional hegemony in the post–Cold War context. As Gary Sick, a former National Security Council staffer in charge of Iran, admitted, after the Gulf War "there was also a palpable yearning within the Washington establishment for an all-purpose enemy that would provide a focus for our strategic planning and justify agency budgets in a period of retrenchment."[11] Along with Saddam Hussein's Iraq, Tehran became a convenient regional foe against which the U.S. military forces could be arrayed. In June 1995, the Clinton administration put its regional strategic blueprint into action by establishing a main base for the U.S. Navy's Fifth Fleet in Bahrain and pre-positioning military installations in several Gulf states.[12]

It is worth noting, however, that—similar to the North Korean case—the U.S. approach toward Iran was not always confrontational and coercive. Echoing the Perry Process in coping with North Korea, in the late 1990s Iran's relations with the United States improved markedly, following the emergence of the moderate President Mohammad Khatami. He not only called for dialogue with the United States and the West but also expressed regret about the traumatic hostage crisis that has since bedeviled Tehran's relations with Washington. U.S. Secretary of State Madeleine Albright responded with a roadmap for "normal relations" between the two countries, acknowledging the U.S. responsibility for the 1953 coup that deposed Prime Minister Mohammad Mosaddeq. It was under this changing political dynamics that the United States stopped calling Iran a "rogue" or "outlaw" state.[13]

As was the case during the Perry Process, the hope for reconciliation between the old foes, however, was dashed as the Bush administration questioned the validity of the Clinton administration's engagement policy around the world, including the Middle East. After 9/11, hawkish members of the Bush administration began to depict Iran as "an existential threat to Israel and opposed any dialogue with Iran that might 'legitimize' the regime in Tehran."[14] In his 2002 State of the Union address, President Bush himself declared that Iran was part of an "axis of evil." As with the North Korean case, the Bush administration focused on regime change, not regime evolution. Flynt Leverett, a Middle East expert who served on the National Security Council at the time, revealed that the Bush administration had consistently refused to consider serious negotiations with Iran over its nuclear and regional ambitions:

> The dirty secret is the administration has never put on the table an offer to negotiate with Iran the issues that would really matter: their own security, the legitimacy of the Islamic republic and Iran's place in the regional order.[15]

Not surprisingly, Iranian President Khatami was enraged by the axis-of-evil speech, given Iran's cooperation with the United States at the onset of the war in Afghanistan.[16] While bilateral relations have deteriorated ever since, there were missed opportunities during the first term of the Bush presidency as well. In fact, there are a range of shared interests between the United States and Iran, including regional stability. One scholar thus characterizes U.S.–Iran cooperation as the single most important factor in improving "U.S. capacity to redress the power balance in the Middle East."[17] With this potential in mind, Iran in 2003 approached the Bush administration via a Swiss diplomat with an offer to help with capturing terrorists and stabilizing Iraq, to stop support for Hezbollah and Hamas, to moderate its position toward Israel, as well as to resolve Iran's nuclear crisis. In return, Tehran asked for the lifting of U.S. sanctions and for better ties with the United States.

While some U.S. officials showed interest in the idea of potential U.S.–Iran cooperation on such wide-ranging issues, hawks in the Bush administration thought otherwise. They not only rejected the offer but also sent the Swiss ambassador a diplomatic cable, rebuking him for relaying the Iranian message to Washington.[18] With the failed attempt at reconciliation further weakening the moderate camp in Tehran, Iran's domestic dynamics turned worse in 2004 as its new parliament was filled with hardliners who were determined to continue the nuclear enrichment program.[19] The Bush administration exacerbated the situation by insisting on "the language of regime change, which went straight to the heart of Iran's security concerns."[20] According to former IAEA Director General Mohamed ElBaradei, whenever possible diplomatic breakthroughs emerged, "the Americans found a way to block progress."[21] The missed opportunity led to Iran's aggressive moves to challenge U.S. interests in the region and to expand its nuclear enrichment program to more than eight thousand centrifuges during the Bush presidency.[22]

A more ominous consequence of the Bush administration's confrontational approach was regional. In a striking similarity to its approach toward Pyongyang, the Bush administration demonized the clerical regime in Tehran, refusing to even have bilateral meetings with Iran. Some Bush officials later conceded that they had considered setting up a regional meeting, modeled after the Six Party Talks, mainly to confront Iran. As was the case in East Asia, however, such a coercive move was destined to fail since "none of Iran's neighbors are willing and able to play the decisive role alongside the United States."[23] A major source of regional concerns about the U.S. policy on the Middle East was role conflict between what U.S. policymakers expected from Iran's neighbors and the regional actors' own perceptions of proper roles in the region. While Iran's neighbors are undoubtedly worried about Iran's nuclear pursuit, they are more concerned about America's regional agenda manifested in the course of the ongoing war in Iraq.

In fact, the current regional order in the Middle East was created as the United States backed up "one coalition in the Middle East—Egypt, Israel, and Saudi Arabia—against another—Syria, Libya, and Iran," and the latter has been eager to expel U.S. forces and undermine U.S. regional allies.[24] The Middle Eastern security order, however, has been shattered by the wars in Afghanistan and Iraq, which resulted in the downfall of Saddam Hussein's Iraq and of the Taliban, the two archenemies of Iran. The collapse of the two Sunni-led regimes in turn enabled what Iran expert Vali Nasr called the "Shia revival" that was led by the Islamic Republic.[25] With two of its main enemies out of the picture and the regionally unpopular United States mired in the insurgency in Iraq, Iran was able to frame its regional strategy as a "resistance to the American-dominated regional order."[26]

Tehran's pursuit of nuclear programs is part and parcel of its strategy of "asserting its regional influence."[27] The nuclear program is even viewed in Iran as "a symbol of Iranian independence—comparable to oil's nationalization in the 1950s."[28] The Iranian view of its nuclear program is also shaped by a widely shared perception of injustice toward Iran compared to Israel. The Iranian public is particularly disturbed by the fact that Iran has been subject to the Additional Protocol of the Nuclear Nonproliferation Treaty (NPT), while Israel, Pakistan, and India, though they have nuclear weapons capability, have never been subject to it, and the Iranian sentiment is broadly shared by its regional neighbors.[29] More broadly, there is a gulf between how the U.S. frames the Iran question and how Iran's neighbors perceive it. From a U.S. perspective, the threat of Iran's nuclear pursuit is based on a number of worst-case scenarios: an immediate regional nuclear arms race, transfer of nuclear technologies to hostile regimes and terrorists, and a greater likelihood of conventional aggression and coercion from Tehran.[30]

Such threat perceptions, however, do not resonate with most of Iran's neighbors. While some Arab governments, such as Saudi Arabia, express concern about Iran's nuclear potential, the Arab public in general shows little worry about the prospect of Iran acquiring nuclear arsenal. For instance, a 2010 Arab Public Opinion Poll showed that "57% of respondents to view Iran's achievement of nuclear weaponry as having a positive effect in the region, with only 21% viewing this potential development negatively."[31] Moreover, regional actors tend to view Iran as a highly rational actor. Robert Baer chronicles how the Iranians transformed from their early role as radical supporters of terrorism to "Machiavellian statesmen."[32] To improve its regional standing, Iran sought to enhance its ties with Arab neighbors, even "willing to overlook the fact that Saudi Arabia and most of the Persian Gulf states were strong financial and logistical backers of Saddam Hussein's Iraq throughout the bloody 1980–88 war."[33] Iran's effort to engage its Arab neighbors was not a one-way street. As examined below, most countries normalized their political relations and expanded economic and social ties with the Islamic Republic with the goal of playing a greater regional role and enhancing their regional status.

6.3 TURKEY: A NEW REGIONAL VISION AND RENEWED TIES WITH IRAN

Just as the Iranians seek to expand their regional influence by wielding the nuclear card, other countries in the Middle East pay greater attention to their regional roles and status in the region. Among them, Turkey has been at the forefront of transforming its regional role in the past decade. Given its status as a member of NATO and its increasingly prosperous economy, Turkey is a natural powerhouse in the region. For various reasons, however, Turkey, another prominent non-Arab state like Iran, has until recently failed to make inroads into the Arab world. With an ambitious and proactive regional vision put forth by the ruling Justice and Development Party (AKP in Turkish), however, Turkey has emerged as a force to be reckoned with in the regional strategic landscape.

As Turkish leaders reentered the regional scene, Iran was a particularly important player to work with. In fact, in recent decades the two countries avoided direct confrontation and shared a wide range of interests. In a region dominated by the United States, Turkey and Iran have also shown their ability "to sustain themselves, albeit by very different policies and methods, as sovereign, unoccupied powers against the hegemonic demands, political threats and economic intimidation of the U.S."[34] After the Iranian revolution, however, Turkey, a Western-oriented, secular country, found itself in a strained relationship with Tehran. Similar to the South Korean and Japanese cases during the Cold War period, the U.S.-directed regional role of Turkey as a U.S. ally prevailed over its internally shaped regional role as an independent regional player. Turkish leaders were particularly worried about the prospect of the Islamist trend spiraling into the secular Kemalist state and the potential for a failed revolution leading to the collapse of Iran and the subsequent emergence of a Kurdish state spilling over to its country.[35]

At the same time, however, the perceived link between Turkey's domestic problems and its regional relations with its neighbors, especially the

Kurdish issue and radical Islamic movements on the one hand and increasing economic ties with regional countries on the other "forced Turkey to break the shell of its traditional isolation in the region and to seek more active involvement in Middle Eastern affairs."[36] The first serious attempt at playing a greater regional role came in the 1980s. Eager to expand Turkey's economic relations with the region, President Turgut Ozal pursued an "activist and internationalist approach" toward the Middle East, facilitating Turkey's business interest in the region and drawing Arab capital to Ankara.[37] Along the lines of this regional approach, Turkey's policy toward Iran was shaped by three goals: "to coexist with Iran, to maintain strict neutrality in the Iran–Iraq war and to take advantage of the war to expand its economic ties with Iran."[38]

The end of the Cold War and the 1991 Gulf War brought Turkey a new strategic reality, calling into the question its traditional regional role as a U.S. ally. During the U.S.-led coalition efforts against Saddam Hussein, Turkey was forced to suspend the use of oil pipeline connected to Iraq and had to forgo most of its trade ties with Baghdad. Coupled with the economic costs, the Gulf War sparked a major humanitarian crisis involving numerous Kurdish refugees fleeing from Iraq, causing "Turkish ambivalence about the costs and benefits of close strategic support for U.S. policies in the region."[39] More fundamentally, the demise of the Cold War dramatically reduced Turkey's geostrategic value for the United States, prompting Ankara to search for a new role in the changing regional context.[40] As a result of this broad strategic reflection, Turkey began to take "a more assertive and independent foreign policy within its region."[41]

Under this new regional vision, Turkey's relations with Iran improved markedly. Ankara had strategic and economic interests in cooperating with Iran, especially over the issue of Kurdish rebels and "Iran's potential participation in an international consortium of companies to build a natural gas pipeline from Turkmenistan to Turkey."[42] In the mid-1990s, Islamist Prime Minister Necmettin Erbakan opened a new chapter in Turkey's inroads into the Muslim world when he made a state visit to Iran. The visit reflected his "clear desire to break away from the restrictions of a Washington-centric view of the region."[43] A few months later, in December 1996, during Iranian President Hashemi Rafsanjani's return visit to Ankara, Erbakan even pursued "a defense cooperation agreement" with Tehran, angering the Turkish military's General Staff.[44] Unlike a new cadre of civilian leaders who envisioned the internally shaped regional role of Turkey as an independent regional actor and more autonomous regional strategy, Turkey's military remained focused on the externally shaped regional role as a U.S. ally. Mirroring South Korea's domestic debate between moderates and conservatives, Turkey's domestic contestation over a proper regional role triggered role conflict between the U.S.-directed and internally shaped regional roles. In response to Erbakan's attempts to improve ties with Tehran, for instance, the military sought close strategic relations with Israel, another key U.S. ally in the region.[45]

However, Turkey's efforts to expand its relations with Muslim neighbors intensified in the twenty-first century. Even Ankara's pursuit of EU membership was shaped in part by its search for a greater regional role as a bridge between Eurasia and the Middle East, "a self-image as a bridge over troubled lands, connecting cultures."[46] As Turkey's efforts to join the EU faltered amid lukewarm responses from some of the EU members, the AKP turned increasingly to an independent foreign policy. The central premise of the new approach was that Turkey must overcome its strategic dependence on external powers and "actively seek ways to balance its relationships and alliances so that it can maintain optimal independence and leverage on the global and regional stage."[47] Ankara's pursuit of regional autonomy and an internally shaped regional role also affected the way it perceived regional threats. Specifically, the effort to "re-engage" the region led to "a de-emphasis of the 'othering' and 'Islamic threat' in Turkey's view of the region," enabling Turkey to see Iran, Iraq, or Syria not as regional foes or "others" but as eastern neighbors with which Turkey could have mutually beneficial relations.[48]

Broadly speaking, Turkey's regional vision, initially put forth in a book entitled *Stratejik Derinlik* (or Strategic Depth), by Ahmet Davutoglu, a scholar who later became Foreign Minister and Prime Minister, rejected the notion of "regional power" that simply followed the United States and promoted instead the idea of a nation that sought to chart its own regional strategy.[49] In its National Security Policy document, the Recep Tayyip Erdogan government emphasized "peaceful coexistence and security cooperation" with neighbors such as Russia, Iran, Greece, and Iraq.[50] In particular, having better relationships with anti-Western Muslim political entities, such as Iran, Syria, and Hamas, bolstered Turkey's status within the Muslim world.[51]

Turkey's calls for moderation toward and dialogue with Iran were part of its larger regional vision called "zero problems with neighbors," a policy premised on the assumption that a dispute in Turkey's extended neighborhood "threatens peace and limits chances for regional development; all are therefore of urgent concern to Turkey."[52] Even after 9/11 and the Bush administration's confrontational turn regarding Iran, Turkey's ties with Tehran grew closer. For instance, Turkey's President Ahmet Necdet Sezer made an official visit to Iran in 2002 right after the axis-of-evil speech and "signed two protocols on economic and cultural cooperation."[53] Turkey's economic ties continued to improve, especially in the energy sector, while Ankara's free-visa policy allowed more than half a million Iranians to visit Turkey annually.[54] In this vein, it is not surprising that the AKP government was among the first governments to convey a congratulatory message to President Mahmoud Ahmadinejad after the controversial election victory in June 2009.[55] In a striking similarity to South Korea's sunshine policy of engagement toward North Korea, Turkey "sought to bring Iran into regional organizations and, by doing so, secure Iran's commitment to a shift in behavior toward greater cooperation—that is, check Iran's influence and change its foreign policy by integrating Iran into the region through diplomacy and trade."[56]

The regional integration strategy was also appealing to Turkish leaders for several reasons. First, Turkey's prospering economy has benefited substantially from its growing regional ties.[57] Foreign Minister Davutoglu himself stressed that the main goal of the ruling party was to build "a peaceful and prosperous Middle East integrated through trade and investment."[58] In addition, Turkey's "soft power" was spreading throughout the Middle East, "exporting pop culture and serious ideas and attracting visitors, including one and a half million Iranians a year, to gape at the Turkish miracle."[59] With its positive regional role, Turkey's regional status also soared in the region during the Erdogan years. For instance, Palestinian leader Mahmoud Abbas touted Turkey as "a model on the way to democracy."[60]

It was in the context of this growing regional confidence that Turkey confronted Iran's nuclear question. Turkish President Abdullah Gul even called his nation "the only country that can have a very important contribution to the diplomatic route" concerning Iran.[61] To be sure, Iran's nuclear pursuit is a matter of concern for the Turks as well. However, it is not on the list of top foreign policy priorities.[62] Given Ankara's regional vision linked to its neighbors, including Iran, it is not surprising that Turkey questioned the effectiveness of the hardline U.S. approach toward Iran. Overall, Turkish leaders have maintained that "the U.S. approach will be counterproductive and will negatively affect Turkey's overall relations with Iran—its neighbor in perpetuity."[63]

As it pursued an independent regional policy and engagement toward Iran, Turkey's threat perception of Iran also remained very low. In the wake of the Iraq War, many Turks viewed the United States "as the chief destabilizing factor" in the region. In a 2004 opinion poll on Turkey's threat perception conducted by Turkey's International Strategic Research Organization (ISRO), the United States was ranked first, while Iran only ninth.[64] Some may downplay Turkey's threat perception of the United

States as a temporary effect of its strong opposition to the Iraq War. However, another survey conducted in early 2011 by MetroPOLL, an Ankara-based polling organization, also showed that 43 percent of the Turkish respondents named the United States as the biggest threat facing Turkey, while only 3 percent viewed Iran as a threat.[65]

Distancing itself from the U.S. or Israeli position, Turkish leaders tended to view Iran's pursuit of nuclear programs as "legitimate given the country's energy needs."[66] Hence, although the United States pushed for more sanctions, even with a reminder of Turkey's "obligations as a member of NATO," Turkey pressed ahead with its own negotiations with Iran.[67] In 2009, Turkey agreed with the IAEA Secretary General Mohammed ElBaradei that the enriched uranium in Iran could be transferred to Turkey.[68] When the United States opposed the Iranian uranium swap deal mediated by Turkey and Brazil, Ankara made its discontent abundantly clear by casting a vote against more sanctions on Iran in the UN Security Council.[69] Turkey's new regional vision and its attendant policy toward Iran became a major source of discord between Turkey and the United States.[70]

6.4 ISRAEL, SAUDI ARABIA, AND BAHRAIN: REGIONAL RIVALRY AND TENSIONS WITH IRAN

Not all countries in the Middle East seek to engage Iran with a new regional vision in mind. Historically, in the region Iran conjured up the specter of regional turmoil and destruction as it served as the main route for invasion by external forces, such as the Mongols and Russia.[71] The Persian Empire itself was at times the main contender in the regional power struggle. Soon after Britain withdrew from the Persian Gulf, Iran also occupied three strategically important islands in the Gulf, and later intervened in Oman's civil war in Dhofar, provoking the Arab fear of "Iranian expansionism."[72] In fact, one of the key impediments to building a collective regional security mechanism has been the Gulf Arab states' apprehension of Iran's regional dominance.[73] The regional fear is now echoed most often and loudly in Israel where Iran's nuclear pursuit has been depicted as an "existential threat," necessitating a preemptive strike on Iran's nuclear facilities.

At the same time, however, it is important to note that Israel's dire threat perception of Iran is only a recent phenomenon, which is shaped in part by Israel's changing regional role conceptions. Despite Israel's turbulent relations with Arab states, Israel and Iran often found themselves in a mutually beneficial strategic relationship, especially during the Cold

War period. Iran was one of the few regional states that had solid strategic ties with Israel under the so-called Periphery Doctrine, a regional strategy aimed at non-Arab states in the Middle East and beyond.[74] Even after the Iranian revolution, which strained Iran's ties with most Arab states, Israel maintained good strategic relations with Iran. During the Iran–Iraq War, Israeli leaders were concerned mainly about Saddam's Iraq, and, in the words of a leading Iran expert in Israel, David Menashri, "no one in Israel said anything about an Iranian threat—the word wasn't even uttered."[75]

Israel's threat perception of Iran changed abruptly in the post–Cold War context as Tel Aviv reconsidered its regional strategic plan linked to a cooperative relationship with Tehran and recast its regional role as a staunch U.S. ally. As the Cold War's sudden demise reduced "Israel's strategic utility" for the United States, new measures were called for: "Israel needed to make peace with the Palestinians to reduce friction with the United States, and it needed to redirect its resources toward the potential Iranian threat to convince Washington to confront Tehran."[76] Similar to the abrupt change in Japan's threat perception of North Korea and without any discernable changes in Iran's behavior, Israel began to frame "Iran and Shia Islamic fundamentalism as a global threat" in a campaign to prevent "a U.S.–Iran rapprochement," which, according to a former Israeli ambassador to the United States "could come at the expense of Israel's strategic relationship with the U.S."[77]

For the Israelis, Iran's nuclear pursuit is problematic not because of the prospect of a nuclear conflict between Iran and Israel, but because of "the regional and strategic consequences that nuclear parity in the Middle East will have for Israel," which in turn "could force Israel to accept territorial compromises with its neighbors." Moreover, from the perspective of Israeli hardliners, Iran's nuclear capability, be it weapons capability or achieving the nuclear fuel cycle, might "compel Washington to cut a deal with Tehran in which Iran would gain recognition as a regional power and acquire strategic significance in the Middle East at the expense of Israel."[78] This is why Israeli hardliners have increasingly stressed the U.S.-directed role as the major U.S. ally and latched onto the U.S. frame of Iran as an urgent threat. In this vein, Prime Minister Benjamin Netanyahu and Defense Minister Ehud Barak often evoked a sense of "an imminent 'existential threat' from Tehran, comparable to that of the Nazis in 1939, and warn[ed] that the Iranian nuclear program [was] fast approaching a 'zone of immunity.'"[79]

The Israeli campaign to inflate Iran's threat echoes its earlier attempt in the 1990s to garner support from its Western allies "by emphasizing the alleged suicidal tendencies of the clergy and Iran's apparent infatuation with the idea of destroying Israel."[80] This time, however, Israel's regional predicament in the wake of the Arab uprisings seemed to have made it push for an even tougher position on Iran. As the Hosni Mubarak's regime in Egypt lost power and Jordan's King Abdullah II faced fierce domestic protests, Israel's ties with the two Arab treaty partners and "its strategic position in the Middle East reached a particularly low point."[81] Israeli's regional standing was further eroded when Turkey improved its regional position by getting close to Iran and Syria.[82]

It was against this changing regional strategic backdrop that the domestic political pendulum swung to the hawkish side. Israel appeared to be "dominated by a nationalist, right-wing muscular view of Israel, the region, and the world."[83] Akin to the Japanese hardliners' North Korea bashing, the conservative political actors latched onto and pushed further the global frame of the Iranian challenge. Prime Minister Netanyahu himself launched his reelection bid in 2012 by highlighting that Israel has "new unspecified 'capabilities' to act against Iran's nuclear threat, an issue he said he had placed at the heart of the global debate."[84] In Netanyahu's telling, by threatening a war against Iran, he "succeeded in shifting the world's focus, including that of the Obama administration, from the Israel-Palestine question to Iran," and "hope[d] to compel the United States and the European Union to impose ever-stricter sanctions on Iran."[85]

However, with the exception of Netanyahu and Barak, most Israeli policy elites, including "the majority of Israel's cabinet and virtually all of its top national security officials," opposed Israel's preemptive strike against Iran.[86] Most prominently, President Shimon Peres and former Mossad Chief Meir Dagan joined other cabinet and intelligence officials who publicly opposed Israel's attack on Iran. According to a 2012 opinion survey conducted in Israel, 61 percent of Jewish Israelis opposed the attack, with only 27 percent in favor.[87] Dagan himself cautioned that a preemptive strike would only embolden Tehran, thus "intensify[ing], not diminish[ing], the danger posed by Iran."[88] Beyond short-term military options, the moderates continue to engage Iran with a long-term regional plan in mind. In March 2014, for instance, President Peres made the following remarks in his *Nowruz* (or New Day) greeting to Iranians and subsequent interviews:

> The Jewish people and the Iranian people have a very long history and are going to have a long future. The relations between your people and our people were more than good . . .

> We must talk to one another and march together toward a future of prosperity and wellbeing. Israelis and Iranians can live in peace. There's no reason why they couldn't.[89]

Domestic contestation about the nature of the Iranian threat is figured prominently in Arab politics as well. In fact, the main source of Iran's threat to the Arab world is political, not military, in nature. The Arab governments are worried about Iran "not because they fear invasion, but because of Iran's political appeal to elements of their own populations, which could challenge their grip on power at home."[90] In particular, Shia Islam has historically been a key source of threat to regimes in such Arab regimes as Iraq, Kuwait, Bahrain, and Saudi Arabia.[91]

Among Iran's immediate regional neighbors in the Persian Gulf, Saudi Arabia has one of the most troubled relationships with Iran. In fact, their strained ties are not entirely surprising given the ethnic (Persian and Arab) and political/religious (i.e., "a revolutionary Shiite republic and a reactionary Sunni Wahhabist monarchy") differences between the two.[92] Saudi Arabia's rivalry with Iran is long running, but the Iranian revolution "lent the rivalry an ideological dimension and transformed it into outright hostility."[93] Iran's potential for spreading revolutionary Islam directly challenges the Islamic legitimacy of the Gulf monarchies, particularly the royal family in Riyadh.[94] This is why Saudi Arabia provided major financial support for Saddam Hussein during the Iran–Iraq War.

Despite the treacherous bilateral relations, the end of the Gulf War and Iran's more pragmatic approach to the Arab monarchies led to a gradual thawing of tension between the two regional rivals. The bilateral ties improved further in 1997 when reformist Mohammad Khatami was elected as President, which led to "a policy of normalization with Iran's Arab neighbors in the Persian Gulf."[95] In this period, Iran's relations with Gulf states "improved considerably, and Iran reached security accords with Saudi Arabia in 2001 and Kuwait in 2002."[96] The reconciliation process, however, was short-lived, and the rivalry seemed to have returned in the 2000s when Syria grew strategically closer to Iran amid Tehran's expanding regional role, a particularly troubling development to Saudi Arabia and Egypt as it represented "the disappearance of the regional axis."[97] The time was ripe for Riyadh's more active role in the region.

By 2007, Saudi Arabia transformed itself from "its long-established role as a low-profile, behind-the-scenes, regional player" into a proactive regional player seeking to pursue an independent foreign policy, especially in Lebanon and the Palestine territories.[98] Paradoxically, due in part to Tehran's cooperation, Riyadh assumed a key role in defusing the political struggle between the Lebanese government led by then Prime Minister Fouad Siniora and the opposition camp.[99] As Iran's regional influence grew in the Middle East, however, Saudi Arabia became more anxious about its status in the region. Its dwindling regional influence was particularly irksome to Saudi leaders because Iran derided the oil rich monarchy as "the agent of the U.S." in the Persian Gulf.[100] Riyadh's decision to purchase more weapons from the United States betrayed its growing sense of insecurity in the region. Overall, Saudi Arabia has increasingly emphasized its externally shaped regional role as a U.S. ally and latched onto the global frame and approach vis-à-vis Iran. The renewed emphasis on the externally shaped regional role is likely to continue as Riyadh believes that Tehran "challenges the U.S.-dominated order in the region—an order under which the United States seeks to guarantee the survival of its allied Sunni Arab dictatorships."[101]

From the domestic political standpoint, Saudi Arabia, Bahrain, and Kuwait have "the largest Shiite communities in the GCC, and consequently view Iran through the prism of their internal security as well as of regional stability."[102] Among them, Bahrain was particularly worried about Iran's potential for exploiting its internal economic and social divisions.[103] Ever since the alleged Iranian support for the 1981 coup attempt, Bahraini leaders have been suspicious of the connection between Iran and their Shia majority population.[104] As a consequence, Bahrain remained one of the strongest supporters of the GCC mechanism and emphasized strategic relations with Saudi Arabia.[105] Due to its financial and military dependence on Saudi Arabia, Bahrain was eager to "prove its usefulness to the Al Saud in their rivalry with Iran," while portraying Iran's defense buildup as "a regional threat."[106]

Saudi-Bahraini ties grew even stronger after the Arab uprisings. After massive domestic protests led by the disgruntled Shiites in Manama, both Saudi and Bahraini leaders claimed that Iran was masterminding the Shia unrest in Bahrain. Suspecting that "the unrest in Bahrain and elsewhere in the region strengthen[ed] the hand of its rival" in Tehran, Saudi Arabia increasingly turned to "inflammatory sectarian rhetoric to paint Iran and Arab Shiite in the region as hostile forces."[107] Saudi Arabia also proposed a formal union with Bahrain at the GCC summit in May 2012, while seeking "closer political, economic, and security relations amid regional instability and the perceived threat posed by Iran."[108]

6.5 OMAN, QATAR, AND THE UNITED ARAB EMIRATES

Unlike their larger counterparts, the smaller Gulf states have historically been "locked in a state of mutual dependence."[109] GCC states' relations with Iran were at the lowest point during the Iran–Iraq War, when most Arab regimes backed the Saddam Hussein regime. Even in this period, however, most small Gulf states were careful not to antagonize Iran. As a result, there was a divergence between Saudi Arabia and Kuwait, both of which supported Iraq, on the one hand, and the other states in the southern Gulf region, which maintained "actual or semi-neutrality," on the other.[110] While most Gulf states remained worried about the spread of ideological zeal from Tehran to their fragile monarchies, "none was willing to ignore possibilities of improving relations with the Islamic Republic."[111] After the Iran–Iraq War, Iran's ties with the Gulf states quickly recovered. Iran's flight and maritime connections with the Gulf states were soon resumed.[112] After Saddam's invasion of Kuwait, Iran–Gulf relations improved further, as Tehran denounced Iraq's adventurism and remained neutral during the Gulf War.[113]

Meanwhile, there were increasing signs of a problem in the relationship between Gulf states and the United States. The most potentially troublesome issue was a regional sense of growing strategic dependence on the United States. Specifically, one of the most direct regional effects of the U.S. Gulf War victory was the dominant security role of the United States and a permanent U.S. military presence in the region, "constraining the freedom of action that the local states had enjoyed and presenting them with new challenges to regime and state security."[114] As a consequence, some of the Gulf states took an ambivalent stance on the Clinton administration's dual containment by maintaining positive relations with Iran.[115] In the 1997 GCC summit, for instance, Kuwait even suggested that Iran's participation in a regional security framework would be crucial, given that its defense cooperation with the United States "would not last forever."[116]

Reflecting their overall approach toward Iran, most countries in the Gulf do not share the U.S. view of Iran as a major security threat. In the narrative popular in the West, Iran's threat is multi-fold: "a five-pronged threat with its nuclear program, its meddling in Iraq, its support for international terrorism, its opposition to Middle East peace, and its clampdown on its own citizens."[117] Such a dire warning, however, was not shared by small Gulf states. According to Dubai-based analyst Riad Kahwaji, no GCC states have ever prepared for civil defense in anticipation of an Iranian strike, and he depicts the overall regional view of the Iranian nuclear issue as "indifferent."[118] This is particularly significant given that the Gulf states do have various conflicts of interest with Iran, including the UAE–Iran dispute over three islands in the Gulf and Kuwait's misgivings about Iran's exploitation of the Dorra gas field.[119] The Arab public also expressed broad sympathy for "what is widely seen as a double standard by which only Israeli is allowed to possess nuclear weapons."[120]

What worried the Gulf states the most about Iran was not the nuclear threat but its impact on the regional order: "an intense concern about the restructuring of the region's power relations—old security norms could be thrown into question and states will have to renegotiate or reaffirm their ties to outside patrons."[121] It was in the context of this seemingly fluid regional order that Kuwait, Qatar, and Oman grew "more tolerant of the Iranian nuclear program," while viewing "accommodation with Iran as the key to their own prosperity and security and generally [opposing] Western efforts to further isolate Iran."[122] For instance, Muhammad al-Sabah, the Kuwaiti Ambassador to the United States, remarked, "Kuwait is not concerned about Iran's nuclear program," while H. H. Sayyid Haitham, Secretary General of the Omani Foreign Ministry, expressed his understanding of the Iranian situation:

> Iran after its war with Iraq [felt] very weak. They think that the US forces in the Gulf are directed against them. So they have a reason to arm. It is an internal Iranian affair. There are no grounds for us to feel threatened. We are not in confrontation with them.[123]

To be sure, this regional view appeared to be at odds with the regional security posture centered on the U.S. military in the Gulf. Similar to the East Asian case, however, Gulf states were faced with two different regional role conceptions: the externally shaped regional role as a U.S. ally and the internally shaped regional role as independent regional actor. In this vein, a major conundrum for the Gulf states was that the existing U.S.-led Gulf security framework was inherently unpopular among the public due in part to its heavy dependence on the U.S. forces and a lack of foreign policy autonomy in the region. Although the GCC maintained its own defense force, the Peninsula Shield Force, its effectiveness and actual performance in Gulf crises were far too limited, with no prospect of overcoming strategic dependence on the United States anytime soon. The irony of the continuing reliance on the United States was that coupled with its potential damage to the domestic political legitimacy of the ruling monarchies, the U.S. military might "be less effective against political threats and subversion," a kind of challenge Iran represented to the Arab monarchies, not its nuclear program.[124]

Moreover, smaller Gulf states were worried that the much larger Saudi Arabia might be "seizing on U.S.-Iranian tensions and the uncertainty of a post-drawdown Iraq to reassert its hold over GCC affairs."[125] The limited institutionalization of the GCC was a reflection of "lingering unease within the smaller member-states at potential Saudi hegemony within the organization."[126] In the face of the powerful yet unpredictable Saudi Arabia, other Gulf states were "emerging like vassals in different stages of revolt against their Saudi master."[127] Among them, Dubai, a mega-global city in the UAE, has been at the forefront of "quietly thawing the geopolitical freeze" between Iran and its Gulf neighbors.[128] Lacking a politically sensitive Shiite minority problem, Qatar and the United Arab Emirates have maintained close economic relations with the Islamic Republic.[129] More importantly, the Gulf states refused to "become a spearhead for, or rather a puppet of, either Saudi Arabia or the United States in their dispute with Iran."[130] Instead, they have been stressing their internally shaped regional roles as independent regional players and seeking to chart their own course by engaging Tehran.

Among others, Oman's relations with Iran epitomize southern Gulf states' search for autonomous regional foreign policy. Oman's quest for an autonomous regional role stemmed from its historical experience since the 1930s, during which it often lost its sovereignty and authority to external powers, including its neighbors such as Saudi Arabia, Egypt, and Iraq.[131] Even when Sultan Qaboos came to power in 1970, Oman was not part of "the mainstream of Arab affairs," a situation he wanted to remedy by seeking an independent foreign policy toward Iran.[132] In the early 1970s, the Shah of Iran provided support for Oman during the Dhofar War "in exchange for privileged relations for the Shah on the Arabian Peninsula." Sultan Qaboos in return achieved a regional status "to be treated as an equal by the then most powerful ruler in the region."[133]

Even after the Iranian revolution, Oman's policymakers were determined to keep "its carefully nurtured relationship with Iran."[134] Oman refused to view Iran as a major regional threat, instead arguing that "a prosperous and stable Iran would enhance and consolidate the chances of comprehensive peace in the Persian Gulf and the whole of the Middle East." As a result, Oman continued to serve as Tehran's mediator and supporter within the GCC, facilitating the normalization of diplomatic relations between Iran and Saudi Arabia in 1991.[135] During Iranian President Khatami's visit to Muscat in October 2004, Oman and Iran signed various bilateral agreements, while emphasizing "the right of nations to develop their nuclear capacities for peaceful purposes in accordance with the nonproliferation treaty of the IAEA" and criticizing Israel's refusal to get nuclear inspections.[136]

Mindful of Saudi Arabia's regional dominance in the Gulf and in their search for autonomous regional roles, both Oman and Qatar "pursued common diplomatic initiatives in improving relations with Iran."[137] Specifically, Qatar maintained close economic ties with Tehran, especially regarding cooperation on the Kish and North field/South Pars gas fields.[138] Based on the export of natural gas and financial assets, Qatar benefited enormously from "the internationalization of the Gulf and its emergence as the center of gravity in the Middle East," asserting its new-found regional role.[139] A similar pattern emerged in the United Arab Emirates. Driven by its extensive commercial ties, the UAE has also sought good relations with Iran.[140] As Dubai sought its new role as a major hub of business, trade, and tourism in the Middle East, its trading ties with Tehran increased. One analyst even called Dubai "Iran's offshore business center."[141]

6.6 REGIONAL ROLE CONCEPTIONS AND THE REGIONAL ORDER IN THE MIDDLE EAST

Similar to the East Asian case, different role considerations and the pursuit of foreign policy autonomy had implications for the regional order in the Middle East. By affecting alliance ties and regional cooperation, the role conflict between the U.S.-centered regional role and the regional actors' own regional role conceptions led to a more exclusive and conflictual regional order. As for alliance management, there were growing signs of strain between the United States and its regional allies. The tension was most pronounced in the case of U.S.–Turkey relations as Ankara often clashed with Washington over the proper course of action in dealing with the Iranian challenge. Most GCC states, especially Oman and Qatar, also refused to go along with the U.S. approach. Regional integration among the Gulf states was another victim during the past decade, in which members of the GCC divided over their relationships with the United States and Iran alike, fracturing the GCC unity.

Regional alliance ties with the United States were already strained after the outbreak of the War in Iraq, but no other country experienced more tumultuous relations with Washington than Turkey. With its new focus on Muslim neighbors and autonomous regional strategy, Ankara's ties with Western allies and Israel were also tested, signaling a shifting strategic relationship between Turkey and its NATO allies. As Turkey turned more to its internally shaped regional role as an independent regional player, it was willing to break away from a "transatlantic consensus" on Iran and saw its alliance ties with the United States and other NATO members "through the prism of its regional priorities."[142]

This is not to suggest that the U.S.-directed role as a NATO ally was no longer valid. In September 2011, for instance, Turkey agreed to install an early warning radar in its territory as part of NATO's missile defense system. The agreement came on the heels of Turkey's condemnation of the Assad regime, which was engaged in a brutal civil war with rebel forces in Syria.[143] However, given its continued emphasis on regional role and regional integration, Turkey announced the plan only after the United States and Turkey agreed that the missile shield "should not worsen its relationship with neighboring countries," especially by not naming Iran and Syria as specific threats.[144] Breaking away from its traditional strategic relations with Israel, the Turkish media also revealed Ankara's objection to sharing information collected by the early warning system with Tel Aviv.[145]

Similar considerations of enhancing regional autonomy and improving regional ties were at work among the Gulf states, hindering alliance ties with the United States. On the whole, they shared the goals of maintaining their domestic rule and stable oil exports and preventing the region from great power rivalries.[146] However, the strategic dependence of the Gulf states on the United States increasingly challenged the legitimacy of monarchic rules in the midst of geostrategic shifts in the Persian Gulf. The central dilemma for the Gulf leaders was that "the American presence [was] both vital to regime survival yet also the lightning rod for oppositional discontent," and this dilemma emanated from the public's opposition to U.S. policies in Iraq and Afghanistan, the close relations of the United States and Israel, and the perceived inability of the United States to jump-start the moribund Arab-Israeli peace process.[147]

The GCC states' strategic quandary was particularly vexing with respect to Iran. Since 1979, the U.S.-led order in the Persian Gulf was that of containment aimed at Iran and, later, the dual containment of Iran and Iraq. The regional order aimed at containing Tehran "helped to maintain authoritarian rule in most of the region, which in turn help[ed] to fuel popular Arab unrest and create[d] domestic vulnerabilities for Iran, Islamists and others to exploit."[148] In the 1990s, the Gulf states thus questioned the validity of the U.S. approach toward Iran, which was centered on containment and isolation. Eager to restore the shattered economy after the Iran–Iraq War, Tehran was also willing to mend political relations with the Arab world and to promote economic ties with its Gulf neighbors.[149] In the process, Iran made frequent high-level visits to the Arab world and even proposed a "regional security pact."[150]

Similar to countries in East Asia, however, the Gulf states had to strike a balance between their growing ties with Iran and their strategic partnerships with the United States. In other words, the question was how to ensure congruence between internally and externally shaped regional roles. Instead, the hardline U.S. approach toward Tehran and a gradual shift in the Gulf's strategic focus to the East revealed "an emerging disconnect between the eastward orientation of economic and commercial linkages and the continuing political and security interdependence with the western powers."[151] As a result, it became increasingly difficult for the Gulf states to reconcile the traditional U.S.-centered regional order and a new regional security framework, a daunting task that "may best be achieved through engaging economically and commercially with Iran and a potentially resurgent post-occupation Iraq while regulating their power through an inclusive security arrangement."[152]

The same rationale underpinned Turkey's vision for regional integration. In Davutoglu's telling, "a peaceful and prosperous Middle East integrated through trade and investment" would benefit Turkey even at the risk of diverging from the U.S. regional vision.[153] In a similar vein, Oman refused to view the GCC as "a military force directed at Tehran." Sultan Qaboos himself insisted that "there [was] no alternative to peaceful co-existence between Arabs and Persians in the end."[154] Echoing Turkey's regional vision, Oman thus called for "the re-integration of Tehran into both the Gulf and the international community."[155]

However, the U.S. approach to Iran complicated such regional efforts, intensifying role conflict between U.S.-directed regional roles and internally shaped regional roles and negatively affecting regionalism in the Middle East. In fact, the majority of U.S. policymakers tended to view the regional order in the Middle East as neatly divided between "a moderate, pro-American camp that ought to be bolstered and a militant, pro-Iranian one that needs to be contained," an outdated regional vision that overlooked the regional role of new actors such as Turkey and Qatar.[156] Added to the rapidly shifting regional strategic landscape was Iran's growing regional influence. Previously hemmed in by the Pakistan–Taliban axis in the East and Iraq in the West, the Shia revival led by Tehran had the potential to bolster Iran's regional status and its nuclear drive.[157]

Under these circumstances, the hardline U.S. approach toward Iran would be ill-suited to meet a variety of regional challenges, including situations in Iraq and Afghanistan and Iran's regional role.[158] Worse yet, the Bush administration's anti-Iran campaign provoked regional discord. For instance, Saudi Arabia, alarmed about Iran's increasing role and status, latched onto the U.S. frame and stressed the U.S.-directed role, calling for the GCC cooperation against Iran.[159] From an Iranian perspective, however, the concept of role (*naqsh*) did not refer to "a means for domination in an offensive way," instead it referred to "an indication of *inclusion* for defensive purposes."[160] In fact, this fit nicely with the regional visions of most of the Gulf states and boded well for an inclusive regional order in the Gulf. As such, inviting Iran and regulating its rising power within an inclusive regional-security architecture would be a more effective approach to address both the nuclear and regional challenges.[161]

6.7 CONCLUSION

The findings of this chapter support the argument advanced in chapter 1. As was the case in East Asia, local actors in the Middle East were primarily concerned with their regional roles and autonomy and the impact of Iran's growing clout on the regional order. Apart from the regional actors who latched onto the U.S. framing and continued to stress the U.S.-directed regional role, issues of Iran's nuclear capability and the prolonged, yet unsuccessful, nuclear diplomacy between the West and Iran were hardly a concern for those countries that sought to enhance their regional role and autonomy by engaging Tehran. Regional visions centered on different types of regional roles, which in turn put the local actors in contention over the nature and shape of the Middle Eastern order.

Like conservatives in Japan and South Korea, Middle Eastern countries seeking both a dominant regional role and close security ties with the United States, such as Israel and Saudi Arabia, inflated the Iranian threat. Despite their close strategic ties in the past and even prior to Iran's nuclear pursuit, Israel's policy toward Iran turned to sheer hostility. Ever fearful about Iran's regional influence and effects on its Shiite minority, Saudi Arabia was also eager to frame Iran's challenge in the sectarian terms as a regional struggle between Sunni Arabs and Shiite Persians. Similarly, Bahrain, another close U.S. ally with the majority Shiite population, also highlighted the danger emanating from the other side of the Persian Gulf.

In contrast, Turkey's search for a new role in the Middle East and Oman's pursuit of an autonomous regional policy allowed them to forge a new relationship with Iran. Other Gulf states also engaged in a delicate balancing act between alliance ties with the U.S. and their own relations with Iran. Even Egypt, a former rival of Iran for regional influence, sought a greater regional role in the new regional order after the Arab uprisings. In explaining Cairo's proactive initiative to Tehran, an Egyptian presidential spokesman echoed the Gulf states' regional vision, which was centered on regional role and autonomy.

> We're not competing with anyone and we don't seek to form alliances, but we're pursuing a real role for Egypt that it deserves. This is what's meant by redefining Egypt's regional role and national security.[162]

Similarly, more "independent-minded states such as Qatar and Turkey have built solid working relations with Iran and sought a role as mediators" in a changing regional strategic environment, while other Gulf states were increasingly reluctant "to cooperate with an America whose new policies they detest and fearful of anything that might trigger popular protests."[163] Under this shifting regional context, containment against Iran was difficult to sell, even in countries in the pro-U.S. and anti-Iran camp, such as Saudi Arabia and Bahrain. The regional threat perception after the Arab uprisings bore this reality out. In a July 2011 public survey conducted in twelve Arab countries, most respondents did not view Iran as a regional threat. The meager 5 percent of participants listed Iran as a threat, while 22 percent and 51 percent named the United States and Israel respectively. Even in Saudi Arabia, only 8 percent of the respondents viewed Iran as a threat to their country.[164]

In sum, the region-wide pursuit of a greater regional role and foreign policy autonomy in the past decade shaped the way the regional actors perceived and coped with the Iranian challenge. As a result, the U.S.-directed regional role as a U.S. ally was increasingly challenged. Furthermore, the emergence of the Arab public after the Arab uprisings "mark[ed] the end of those days when America could enforce an unpopular regional order."[165] A sensible U.S. strategy for the Middle East would require greater attention to the delicate inner workings of regional dynamics surrounding the Iranian challenge and the increasing gulf between the U.S. regional expectations and the regional understanding of the Iranian question. As with the North Korean case, focusing narrowly on the nuclear dimension and the failed policy of coercion and containment and, in the process, overlooking a larger shift in the regional strategic landscape was detrimental to both U.S. Middle East strategy and regional stability.

CHAPTER 7

Proliferation and Future Regional Orders in East Asia and the Middle East

7.1 INTRODUCTION

This book has explored how the global campaign to defuse the North Korean and Iranian nuclear crises interacted with the local efforts to enhance regional roles and foreign policy autonomy, shaping the regional order in East Asia and the Middle East. While the United States framed the two crises as a quintessential global proliferation challenge, the regional actors viewed them as part and parcel of an emerging regional order and sought to recast their relations with the purported global rogues. These contrasting narratives not only undercut the global nonproliferation efforts but also helped shape the regional order in the two regions. Two specific mechanisms for such regional patterns were at work: (1) Regional understanding of and policy responses to the proliferation challenge were shaped less by outside pressures than by the types of regional role conceptions (i.e., externally or internally shaped regional roles) that were prevalent at a given time in each country; and (2) The subsequent role congruence or conflict altered regional order by affecting the levels of alliance coordination and regional cooperation in each region.

Hence, global proliferation challenges cannot be addressed in isolation from larger regional dynamics surrounding proliferators. Instead of evoking the specter of a common global threat as claimed by the Bush administration, the two nuclear crises intensified domestic debates about the nature of the North Korean and Iranian challenges and their impact on regional order. Rather than a venue for defusing the nuclear crisis, the Six Party Talks became a site of competing logics between the U.S. framing of

North Korea as a clear-cut global challenge and the East Asian view of it as a complex regional problem whose solution would have repercussions for the East Asian order. As one expert observed, the Six Party Talks have failed to resolve the crisis in part because "North Korea figure[d] very differently in the regional plans" of the countries involved.[1] The question is precisely how North Korea and Iran were linked to the regional strategies of their neighbors and with what regional consequences. As evidenced in the book, regional role considerations played a crucial role in assessing the threats and shaping policy responses with respect to North Korea and Iran.

As such, we need to evaluate the impact of the Iranian and North Korean nuclear crises in a much broader sense than the nuclear angle. By focusing only on the nuclear aspects, the United States runs the risk of missing a gradual shift in the regional order and along the way losing its status as a regional hegemon in East Asia and the Middle East. Its tension with Turkey over Iran's nuclear swap deal and the UNSC resolution, and several years of strain in the U.S.–South Korean alliance over North Korea not only symbolize the clash between the global and regional approaches (which in turn exacerbates role conflict between the externally and internally shaped regional roles) but also suggest the long-term, potentially corrosive effects on the regional influence of the United States in these two vitally important regions.

This concluding chapter proceeds in the following steps. The next section provides a brief summary of the findings. The following section discusses both theoretical and policy implications. I then consider the possibility of applying the analytical framework advanced in this book to other issue areas and suggest possible avenues of further research and extension, such as the prospects of China–U.S. relations and East Asian regionalism.

7.2 FINDINGS AND THEORETICAL IMPLICATIONS

Summary of Findings

This book provides a systematic account of the regional understandings and consequences of the proliferation challenge in two key regions of the world. As North Korea and Iran have been depicted as two archetypal rogue states bent on disrupting the global nonproliferation regime and destabilizing their respective regions, understanding how their regional neighbors perceive and grapple with their challenges is key to successful nuclear diplomacy and regional stability. East Asia and the Middle East are also two strategically important regions where the United States has served as a de facto regional hegemon whose influence, as evidenced in this book, is now being increasingly challenged in the changing regional contexts. An analysis of the interplay between the global proliferation challenge and regional order helps us to discern distinctive regional patterns surrounding the two nuclear crises.[2]

In this book, I have put forth an argument that stresses the role of ideational factors, especially regional role conceptions. By examining the East Asian regional order, as affected by the North Korean challenge, and by observing the Middle Eastern regional dynamics with respect to Iran, I have shown that regional role conceptions—the way political elites articulate their nations' regional roles—influence the understanding of threat and national interests vis-à-vis North Korea and Iran. Two regional roles are crucial: the externally shaped, U.S.-directed regional roles as U.S. allies or strategic partners and the internally shaped regional roles linked to North Korea and Iran. The more congruent the externally and internally shaped regional roles become, the more stable and inclusive regional order emerges in the form of greater alliance cohesion and broader regional cooperation. Conversely, the greater the conflict between the two roles, the more conflictual and exclusive regional order ensues.

In the East Asian context, the search for new regional roles by South Korea, China, and Japan shaped their understanding of and policy behavior toward North Korea. It also influenced the way the three East Asian countries responded to the Bush administration's approach toward North Korea. They not only questioned the validity of the Bush Doctrine as applied to the North Korean case but also tried to persuade the United States to take an alternative, more flexible approach. Such a regional response is a radical departure from East Asian behavior during the Perry Process of the Clinton presidency. During this period, East Asia's quest for greater roles vis-à-vis North Korea blended well with the U.S. approach, facilitating role congruence in East Asia. Along with positive outcomes after the resolution of the crisis, the regional order in this period became more stable as new patterns of alliance cooperation and regionalism emerged. As the Bush administration took a hardline position toward North Korea and triggered role conflict, alliance relations faltered and regional cooperation stalled. Similar regional dynamics emerged in the Middle East over the Iranian nuclear challenge.

More broadly, this study has demonstrated how the same objective reality of facing North Korea is interpreted differently by different political actors. Regional role conceptions powerfully shape the ways they understand the nature of threats and employ the appropriate means to address them. By forcing the East Asian countries to adopt the global frame of fighting rogues and to play the roles it preferred, the Bush administration put itself on a collision course with the regional actors. At the domestic level, however, it also ignited domestic contestation in which different political actors competed for different regional roles and regional visions. In the process, earlier collective regional resistance to the U.S. approach was replaced with regional rivalries. All in all, the Bush administration's approach toward North Korea and regional role conceptions in East Asia set in motion a transformation in the regional strategic landscape, blurring traditional boundaries between friends and foes, while creating new ones between allies and neighbors.

As examined in chapter 6, the regional actors in the Middle East have also focused primarily on their regional role and foreign policy autonomy, rather than Iran's nuclear challenge per se. Despite the global rhetoric, regional threat perceptions of Iran remained largely unaltered, with the only small minority with their own political agendas inflating the Iranian threat. Different regional visions put forth by various regional actors also affected the nature of the regional order in the Middle East, as they pushed for competing policies toward Iran based on their considerations of alliance ties with the United States and regional autonomy. In the process, the long-held U.S. strategy of containment toward Iran has been increasingly challenged in the region and its regional standing substantially curtailed.

Alternative Explanations and Regional Outcomes

Existing accounts are useful for elucidating certain aspects of the regional outcomes, but they provide only partial insight into the regional situations surrounding North Korea and Iran. For instance, this book's argument, which is centered on regional role conceptions, does not dismiss the relevance of external, systemic forces in influencing policy behavior. In fact, exogenous factors, such as the sudden shifts in U.S. policy toward the North Korean and Iranian nuclear challenges, play a crucial role in affecting regional dynamics. As analyzed in chapter 2, the Bush administration's post–9/11 global counterproliferation campaign aimed at "global rogue states" was one such external shock, with significant implications for the ways regional actors perceived the North Korean and Iranian challenges.

However, systemic forces alone rarely determine policy outcomes. Instead, such shifts are filtered through domestic variables.[3] Specifically, the effects of external factors are often conditioned by the degree of domestic contestation over the proper regional role and the nature of the North Korean and Iranian threat.[4] Given the importance of internally shaped regional roles linked to North Korea and Iran, the Bush administration's approach was hard for regional actors to accept. The ensuing role conflict not only thwarted the U.S.-led nuclear diplomacy but also shaped the nature of the regional order in East Asia and the Middle East. In this regard, the analytical framework advanced in this book offers a more systematic and nuanced account of the varied regional outcomes.

Moreover, the account of regional role conceptions better explains why regional actors responded differently to the U.S. approaches in different time periods, despite Washington's continuing power dominance and hegemonic status in the region. As demonstrated in the empirical chapters, it was not the perceived power itself, but the perceived legitimacy of power that turned out to be crucial. Of particular importance in securing the authority of the ruler is "the consent of the ruled."[5] The East Asian response to the United States during the Perry Process represented a type of authority relationship where "shared understanding allows the powerful to exert legitimate control."[6] However, the Bush administration's approach toward North Korea caused role conflict on the part of the regional actors, weakening the U.S. authority and prompting regional resistance.

The explanation based on threat perception is also useful in explaining the regional resistance to the coercive U.S. approach during the second crisis. One could also point out the different threat perceptions of North Korea and Iran *among* the regional actors as a factor influencing regional outcomes. For instance, one might attribute Japan's hardline approach toward North Korea since 2005 to its heightened threat perception of North Korea. As examined in the empirical analysis, however, threat perception itself is a function of regional role conceptions. In other words, the types of prominent regional roles (i.e., externally shaped or internally driven regional roles) in different political contexts affect the degree of perceived threat. When South Korea and China focused on their internally shaped regional role linked to Pyongyang, North Korea's provocation did not increase their threat perception of the North.

Even in the case of Japan, where the North Korean threat was supposedly most palpable, it was evoked for political purposes. It is worth noting in this regard that while Japanese Prime Minister Abe Shinzo set up a separate office in his cabinet to manage the abduction issue that took place decades ago, he did not even consider establishing an office in charge of addressing North Korea's nuclear or missile programs.[7] Similarly, Japan's persistent efforts to raise the abduction issue at the Six Party Talks, even to the point of disrupting nuclear negotiation at the multilateral meetings, indicate that Japan's threat perception of North Korea was shaped by political considerations. Specifically, a former high-ranking Japanese diplomat pointed out that talks about the North Korean threat in Japan resurfaced whenever the need to stress Japan's ties with the United States emerged.[8]

Moreover, as evidenced in chapter 3, there is an element of elasticity in regional threat perceptions of North Korea: the North Korean threat is voiced by the regional actors who identify with the United States and latch onto the U.S. frame, while it is substantially weakened in the assessments made by those in conflict with the U.S. approach. As such, East Asian countries' threat perception of North Korea is largely a function of how the regional countries perceive their regional roles. The salience of particular regional role conceptions (e.g., external or internal role conceptions) then provides clues about whether or not the North Korean threat is (de) amplified in the region. In short, the regional threat perception of North Korea itself is endogenous to regional role conceptions, a pattern echoed in the Middle East over the threat perception of Iran.

With its focus on the regional countries' disparate national interests vis-à-vis North Korea, the national interests account seems to be more convincing in explaining the regional divergence during the latter half of the second crisis. But it ignores the fact that, despite divergent national interests among regional actors, the actors converged on the importance of North Korea as a regional focal point during the Perry Process and the early rounds of the Six Party Talks. As evidenced in chapters 4 and 5, the explanations that are centered on regional role conceptions and role congruence/conflict account for the variation in regional outcomes in both the Perry Process and the second crisis, while shedding light on the reasons for the regional divergence since 2005.

Regional Role Conceptions as a Variable and Its Validity in Explaining Regional Order

Building on the constructivist literature, this book highlights an ideational factor—regional role conceptions—as a key determinant in interstate behavior. As examined in the empirical chapters, how policymakers view their proper regional role can have substantial effects on their threat perceptions and national interest formation. To be sure, material considerations and external structural variables remain important, especially for those regional actors who emphasize the strategic relationship with the United States, as well as the U.S.-centered regional role.

However, focusing only on the material side of the ledger will be insufficient to explain regional patterns identified in the book. Despite the continuing material capabilities of the United States, the degree of the regional resistance to the U.S. approach varied depending on the nature of regional role conceptions at the domestic level. The challenge to the United States was strongest when an internally shaped regional role was dominant at the domestic level. Overall, the regional debates over North Korea and Iran show that threat perceptions and policy discussions were contested not on the basis of external structural conditions or material factors but on the basis of contending domestic views of what their nation's regional role should be like.

Beyond the proliferation issue, the analysis offered in the book highlights the importance of the regional level as an analytical focus in International Relations theorizing. Examining regional role conceptions can be a useful way to conceptualize regional orders. Despite the expectations of systemic theories, both realist and liberal, regional orders are neither preordained nor a simple outgrowth of systemic forces such as the balance of power or economic interdependence. As Peter Katzenstein observes, regions are not merely material objects within the world system. They are also "social and cognitive constructs that are rooted in political practice."[9] Constantly in the making through social interaction among regional actors, there are neither fixed regions nor fixed regional interests. Rather, they are formed "in the process of interaction and intersubjective understanding."[10]

This book has demonstrated how the North Korean and Iranian challenges affect the pattern of regional interaction in a far more complex way than the existing literature leads us to expect, creating new sources of both cooperation and division in the region. While useful in explaining the regional order during the Cold War period, realist and liberal/institutionalist theories of regional order are hampered by their largely static and deterministic claims about the future of the East Asian order. What is also common in the realist and liberal institutionalist analyses is the central role accorded to the United States in shaping the future of the region.

From a realist perspective, many scholars argue that the strengthening of the U.S.-centered hub-and-spokes system of alliances is the key to regional stability in East Asia.[11] Pointing to the absence of formal multilateral frameworks in the region, however, liberal institutionalists stress the importance of broadening the current U.S.-alliance system.[12] In their article on the U.S–Japan alliance, for instance, Mike Mochizuki and Michael O'Hanlon argue that America's Asian alliances need to be tightened up, "not against threat, but in the name of common interests and values."[13]

They reason that the United States and Japan, as with the case of the U.S.–U.K alliance, should pursue a "liberal agenda that serves the goals of democracy, human rights, economic development, and regional inclusiveness," thus laying the groundwork for a multilateral collective-security arrangement for the region.[14] John Ikenberry and Michael Mastanduno concur by suggesting that rather than turning to "the realpolitik effort to prevent the deterioration of the Asian security environment," it is time to take a "progressive step" toward a regional security community.[15]

However, the growing gap between the United States and regional understandings of—and responses to—the North Korean challenge suggests an increasing difficulty in realizing U.S.-centered regional designs. Given the contested nature of the North Korean problem at different levels and the importance of the North Korea factor in regional role conceptions in East Asia, improving regional cooperation among U.S. allies and broader regional integration will be difficult. By locating contested regional role conceptions at the center of analysis, this book explains both the regional resistance to the U.S. approach and a lack of progress in building a broader regional security framework.

At a deeper level, regional role conceptions can help us better understand regional actors' different understandings of a proper regional order. In Europe, for instance, different members have different understandings about regional order building. The British tend to view European integration largely as "a process without a specific end." In contrast, the French tie it to "the vision of a powerful independent Europe as a major player in world politics," while the Germans consider it a steppingstone to an "eternal peace" in Europe. Given these different perceptions of region making process and visions for the future, Lisbeth Aggestam argues, European stability hinges in large part on how its members harmonize their role conceptions and ensure stable expectations among themselves.[16] My research extends this insight to East Asia and the Middle East.

The prospects of creating a new regional order in East Asia by harmonizing regional role conceptions were growing rapidly in the late 1990s. As inter-Korean reconciliation began new regional momentum, some scholars began to call for dialogue between the United States and East Asian countries on "how to move toward a more self-sustaining and stable regional order."[17] Writing in early 2001, Kent Calder also predicted that the combination of regional meetings on North Korea and the U.S.–Japan–South Korea policy coordination processes via the Trilateral Coordination and Oversight Group (TCOG) would bring about "an institutional basis for the new geopolitics" in East Asia.[18] Such initial expectations, however, did not materialize, as the Bush administration took a hardline approach toward North Korea.

In this vein, in the late 1990s the Perry Process provided a rare opportunity to build such a new regional framework that would make the existing U.S.-centered order more stable, while satisfying regional actors' yearning for greater regional roles. The Bush administration not only failed to seize the opportunity but also ran the risk of disrupting the existing regional order. Frustrated by dwindling U.S. influence in East Asia during the Bush presidency, several International Relations scholars called for a "forward-looking foreign policy" aimed not only at managing crises but also at proactively shaping "the context for future policy choices." In this context, Francis Fukuyama recommends that the United States turn the Six Party framework into a permanent regional organization.[19] As discussed in chapter 6, most regional actors in the Middle East also call for a new, inclusive regional order. I argue that paying attention to regional role conceptions in general and role congruence/conflict in particular would be critical in making sense of a new regional order in East Asia and the Middle East.

A New Approach to Proliferation: Renewed Focus on Demand-Side Measures

In the literature on nuclear proliferation, scholars have traditionally explored the sources and consequences of proliferation. Specifically, some of the key works analyze motivations behind states' seeking or giving up nuclear ambitions,[20] while others address the question of whether or not proliferation contributes to stability in the international system.[21] In the post-9/11 world, however, the analytical focus has shifted decisively to the question of how best to contain the danger of nuclear proliferation.[22] As a consequence, scholarly and policy debates have been fixated on addressing supply-side measures (e.g., what policy tools should be used to contain the spread of Weapons of Mass Destruction) at the expense of the demand-side of the ledger (e.g., how to mitigate permissive conditions, such as regional security concerns, that drive nuclear developments in the first place, etc.).[23]

Traditionally, U.S. nuclear policy utilized various demand-side measures. For instance, the Carter administration offered negative security assurances (i.e., reassuring potential adversaries against a nuclear first strike). Such assurances, however, have been substantially weakened by the Bush administration. Along with the axis-of-evil rhetoric, the doctrine of preemption and a renewed focus on new-generation nuclear weapons, as manifested in the December 2002 *National Strategy to Combat Weapons of Mass Destruction*, signaled to other nations that nuclear weapons would play "a growing, not diminishing, role in U.S. security decisions."[24] Instead of relying too much on "the overmilitarized means" for meeting the proliferation challenge, critics argue, the United States should utilize various resources to shape the incentive structure of rogue states.[25]

In this regard, the East Asian and Middle Eastern cases suggest that for proliferation strategy to be effective, the United States should consider not only the incentive structure of rogues but also that of their neighbors, who may complicate the global counterproliferation approach in a myriad ways. Guarding against the ubiquitous U.S. involvement in various global crises, Charles Kupchan calls for greater reliance on countries closer to a crisis, not only because of their proximity but also due to the support and legitimacy for regional involvement.[26] Unless regional countries closely align their interests with that of the United States over the proliferation challenge, successful nuclear diplomacy will remain a daunting task. The United States can improve its odds by gaining a deeper understanding of regional dynamics surrounding proliferation challenges.

More broadly, the Six Party process was not just a global campaign to prevent nuclear proliferation; more importantly, at stake was "the vigor of [U.S.] alliances, the future of northeast Asia, America's stature and standing in East Asia."[27] Given the East Asian interest in engaging North Korea, another way to solve the rogue states problem would be to "[embed] them in regional security orders that constrain them while offering them the stability and encouragement needed for successful economic development." Engagement in this sense can be "a part of a larger multilateral process of establishing a new security order involving great power cooperation."[28] Given the regional interest in such a multilateral, multi-layered order, similar efforts can be made in the Middle East. In the predominant narrative about the Iranian challenge, however, containment and isolation have been the default strategy. Most analyses have been focused primarily on what Israel and the United States should or should not do. It is almost as if no other regional actors were involved in the nuclear saga with Iran. A similar emphasis has been placed on what China should do in dealing with North Korea. This book has demonstrated a far more complex regional narrative about the meanings of North Korea and Iran. Even in Israel and China, contending views exist. As such, paying attention to the regional visions of different actors and seeking to deftly influence domestic debates would be far more effective than imposing the global proliferation frame.

7.3 POLICY IMPLICATIONS

The findings of this book yield a number of policy implications in both regional and global respects. First, to address the proliferation challenge more effectively, U.S. policymakers should use America's power and influence prudently, that is, in ways that are not in conflict with regional role conceptions in each region. Conversely, facilitating role congruence can both contribute to the success of global proliferation policy and enhance the stability of regional order. At the heart of the matter lies role conflict on the part of United States: its traditional regional role as a stabilizer and its new global role as an enforcer of counterproliferation and anti-terror strategies.

Ensuring Role Congruence between America's Global and Regional Roles

As argued in this book, despite its dominant material position, the United States cannot dictate the terms of engagement vis-à-vis proliferators. Regional following will depend on the compatibility between the U.S. approach toward proliferators and their neighbors' regional role conceptions. Just as East Asian and Middle Eastern countries are mulling over their proper regional roles, it is time for U.S. policymakers to think about how to reconcile the U.S. role as a global proliferation enforcer with its traditional role as a regional stabilizer.[29] The promulgation of the Bush Doctrine caused tension between these two roles. How to cope with this contradiction is a central task in effectively addressing nuclear proliferation and securing a viable U.S. strategy in East Asia and the Middle East. At a minimum, efforts to solve a global problem should not come at the expense of America's decade-long regional role in the two regions, a guarantor of regional stability throughout the Cold War.

Writing about a US regional force realignment plan under the Global Posture Review (GPR), Kurt Campbell and Celeste Ward cautioned against "collateral damage to long-standing arrangements and relationships" in the region. As they argued, it is pointless "to gain marginal benefits for possible future operations at the cost of undermining close existing alliances or causing important countries to question their security ties to the United States."[30] The same lesson can be applied to the U.S. approach to the proliferation issues.

During the Clinton presidency, the United States made conscious efforts to balance global proliferation strategy and U.S. regional influence. For instance, during the first North Korean nuclear crisis, the Clinton administration at times promoted inter-Korean relations for nonprolif-eration reasons: as the United States needed South Korea's support in its nuclear negotiations with North Korea, the Clinton administration bar-gained hard for South Korea's request that it not be "excluded from nego-tiations on the peninsula."[31] More importantly, the Clinton administration approached the proliferation issue in ways that were not in conflict with regional stability. As Robert Gallucci, the chief U.S. negotiator during the first crisis, observed, the Agreed Framework held out the "possibility of gradually opening the way for all countries in the region to establish more normal political and economic ties with North Korea," which "would serve our broader interests in regional stability and prosperity."[32]

A key problem with the Bush administration's approach was its empha-sis on global priority in ways that negatively affected regional security. Its relentless focus on the war on terror and the global counterproliferation campaign not only endangered regional stability but also undermined U.S. influence in East Asia. For instance, William Odom lamented that the Bush administration pursued "a destabilizing and feckless nonprolifera-tion policy at the expense of regional stability" in the Middle East and East Asia.[33] Ironically, the U.S. influence has dwindled most substantially in the two regions with the most militarized U.S. presence: East Asia and the Middle East.[34] In restoring the U.S. influence in the two regions, U.S. policymakers should pay more attention to the congruence between its global and regional roles.

In this regard, the Obama administration's U.S. strategic rebalancing toward the Asia-Pacific—the so-called Asia pivot—has the potential to ensure the role congruence and improve the U.S. regional role in East Asia.[35] In the words of then Secretary of State Hillary Clinton, the Asia pivot is a "forward-deployed diplomacy" designed to "lock in a substan-tially increased investment—diplomatic, economic, strategic, and otherwise—in the Asia-Pacific region."[36] The Obama administration high-lighted two underlying motivations for the strategic rebalancing toward the Asia-Pacific: (1) the region's increasing importance for the U.S. econ-omy, which led to the promotion of the Trans-Pacific Partnership (TPP) as a new regional trade mechanism and (2) the U.S. need to reassure regional countries about America's regional commitment.[37] Overall, the Asia pivot was a major strategic shift to enhance the U.S. role and to restore its legit-imacy, which was damaged during the Bush administration.

The U.S. strategic rebalancing, however, has affected the regional role conceptions of the three East Asian countries as well. For instance, the Chi-nese increasingly viewed the U.S. pivot to Asia as a counterbalancing coali-tion against China, jeopardizing its internally shaped regional role as a rising regional powerhouse.[38] The tension between Beijing and Washington also triggered role conflict between South Korea's internally shaped regional role as an independent regional player and externally shaped regional role as a U.S. ally. In Japan, the Abe government welcomed the U.S. rebalancing, as it promoted Japan's greater regional role, which is centered on the U.S.–Japan alliance. Overall, the varied regional responses to the U.S. pivot to Asia have thus far diminished the effects of the U.S. strategic shift.

The Bush versus Obama Years on Proliferation

In many respects, the foreign policy orientations of the George W. Bush and Barack Obama administrations are a study in contrast. While the Bush administration was known for its unilateral, military-centered approach, the Obama administration has taken a multilateral approach with a strong emphasis on international institutions and treaties. Gone are the Manichean dichotomy of "us vs. them" and the "war on terror" campaign.[39] Despite the vast differences in their foreign policy outlooks, however, the two administrations adopted a very similar stance toward North Korea and Iran, relying predominantly on coercive measures against these defiant regimes.

In his first two rounds of the State of the Union address, President Obama also highlighted the two nuclear crises as major global challenges and called for more sanctions and a common global approach. Echoing the Bush administration's rationale, Vice President Joe Biden's call for China's efforts toward North Korea and Iran was based on his assumption that both the United States and China would benefit from "global stability, which includes preventing Iran and North Korea from obtaining nuclear weapons."[40] Having failed to make a breakthrough in nuclear diplomacy, the Obama administration turned to a hardline stance on Iran in 2010.[41] Mirroring the Bush administration's coercive policy, the Obama administration not only rejected the nuclear swap deal with Iran negotiated by Turkey and Brazil but also announced, the very next day, a series of sanctions against Iran.[42] A similar coercive drive has been a central feature of the Obama administration's approach toward Pyongyang, with no discernable success, as manifested in North Korea's several missile launches and the third nuclear test in February 2013.[43]

For the past decade, the same coercive approach taken by the Bush and Obama administrations has failed to make meaningful breakthroughs, while both North Korea and Iran continued to accumulate their fissile materials.[44] According to former director of Los Alamos National Laboratory

Siegfried Hecker, who has visited North Korea's nuclear facilities several times, North Korea is likely to have about twelve nuclear weapons as of January 2015. Given its estimated capacity to build four to six bombs annually, North Korea's nuclear arsenal may increase to twenty nuclear weapons by the time Obama leaves office in early 2017.[45] By the time the Obama administration resumed negotiation with the Hassan Rouhani government in 2013, Iran had also installed about twenty thousand centrifuges in their nuclear facilities, with an increasing stockpile of enriched uranium, some of which was "enriched to nearly 20 percent, which is well on the way to weapons level."[46]

Worse yet, the United States also caused unnecessary tensions with some of the regional actors, which resulted in the weakening of its alliance ties in East Asia and the Middle East. As simultaneous political transitions in China, Japan, and South Korea, as well as the Arab uprisings in the Middle East, rekindled discussions about the regional order in the two regions, it is time for a new thinking and a fresh restart. The Obama and future U.S. administrations can do so by paying greater attention to the regional debates on the multidimensional challenge of North Korea and Iran. I examine latest developments in the two regions and their effects on regional role conceptions and regional order in the epilogue.

U.S. Regional Strategy

The analysis in this book also suggests that the U.S. strategy to turn its bilateral alliances with East Asian and Gulf states into coherent regional alliance networks would be difficult to achieve, especially in the context of alliance tension between the United States and South Korea and South Korea's growing ties with China. It is in this context that the 2007 Armitage Report stressed the importance of maintaining "a robust, dynamic relationship with the new Asia," with the central aim of "defining a regional architecture that will be consistent with U.S. interests."[47] Noting a discord between the United States and South Korea, the Report also called for the United States and Japan to improve ties with South Korea, while raising questions about China's regional intentions.[48] Similarly, referring to a regional community centered on East Asian regionalism, a high-ranking U.S. official expressed concern that China hoped to dominate the region via such an exclusive regional mechanism, and, hence, he warned, "Japan cannot possibly afford to advocate Asian regionalism."[49]

Such American attitudes, with their emphasis on the U.S.-directed regional roles at the expense of internally shaped roles, were not well received in the region, especially during the Roh presidency. Instead, regional actors prefer a U.S. regional strategy that harmonizes both externally and internally shaped roles. This is why Yoichi Funabashi argues that the U.S.–Japan alliance and East Asian regionalism are compatible, "not a matter of choosing one or the other."[50] From this vantage point, Japan's ideal approach in the region is to promote an "Asia Pacific fusion,"[51] or, as one Japanese business executive puts it, "*Shin-Bei Nyu-A* (close to America and entering Asia)."[52]

While acknowledging that Japan's search for an Asian identity could conflict with its geopolitical interest in keeping strong alliance ties with the United States, a former Japanese diplomat nonetheless makes the following statement.

> [T]he harmonization of [Japan's] power, efficiency, and identity can ultimately be achieved through its two fundamental postwar policy objectives: *strengthening its alliance with the United States and reentering Asia.* If the international situation compels Japan to choose one of the two, the consensus is clear: alliance will be given precedence. But this kind of zero-sum picture is not desirable for Japan. It *must achieve both objectives in order to maximize its diplomatic posture and satisfy its national interest.* (Emphasis added)[53]

7.4 EXTENSION AND FURTHER RESEARCH

This book is the first systematic attempt at exploring the interaction between the U.S.-led global proliferation campaign and the regional dimensions of the North Korean and Iranian nuclear challenges. Through this analysis, it shows the generalizability of the book's analytical framework across different regions and over time. In this final section, I suggest possible avenues of further research based on the analytical framework offered in this book.

The Rise of China and China–U.S. Relations in East Asia

The findings of the book can be added to the ongoing scholarly debate on the rise of China.[54] Paying due attention to the contingent nature of China–U.S. relations, Jeffrey Legro rejects deterministic claims such as the China threat thesis and the interdependence argument. Instead, he points out that such systemic factors are filtered through "enduring foreign policy ideas in domestic politics and subsequent national behavior."[55]

The key question is what kinds of foreign policy ideas will prevail in China and under what conditions? My research suggests that one way of discerning a prevailing foreign policy idea in China is to examine its role conceptions—how Chinese political elites think about China's role in the region and how certain regional issues (e.g., the North Korean question) are linked to that vision, shaping foreign policy decisions.

In fact, some have suggested that the North Korean question can be a useful starting point for a new regional security framework in East Asia. Noting that China has both immediate security concerns and longer-term strategic objectives on the question of North Korea and the Korean peninsula, for instance, Henry Kissinger proposes a China-U.S. strategic dialogue aimed at discussing "the political evolution of the Korean Peninsula and of Northeast Asia."[56] Despite their common interest in stability on the Korean Peninsula, the long-term goals of China and the United States tend to diverge. While the United States seeks to resolve the situation in ways that preserve and enhance its regional influence, China pursues "a post–Cold War security architecture that is less U.S.-centric."[57]

In this regard, ensuring role congruence between the U.S.-directed and internally shaped roles can be conducive to achieving stable Sino-American relations. Singling out the Korean issue as a potential model case for U.S.-China relations and future cooperation on broader East Asian security issues, Ashton Carter and William Perry argue that U.S. regional leadership should engage in "catalyzing cooperative action" with China in ways that can be viewed by the Chinese as "being used to defend precisely those interests that China will share with the United States."[58] Thomas Christensen concurs by suggesting that a sensible U.S. Asia strategy would be the maintenance of a regional presence anchored to its regional alliances "without attempting to undercut China's diplomatic relationships with other regional actors, even with U.S. allies."[59]

If the United States and China, along with other regional powers, were able to produce a positive outcome on the North Korean question, I argue, it would signal "a long-term strategic convergence between Washington and Beijing."[60] The Clinton administration was indeed close to this best-case scenario on a variety of issues, including stability on the Korean Peninsula, while the Bush administration's approach was fixated on the broader agenda of prolonging U.S. primacy even at the risk of endangering regional stability.[61] Prolonging tension on the Korean Peninsula or relying solely on coercive measures would only intensify role conflict in China, with negative implications for China-U.S. relations in the future.

Conversely, facilitating role congruence can be an effective way for the United States to secure legitimacy in the era of the U.S. global retrenchment.[62] As Stephen Walt observes, "the key [in maintaining U.S. primacy] is not power but persuasion," through which the United State should demonstrate to the world why American primacy is better than possible alternatives.[63] This view is echoed in the notion of a benign hegemonic order that John Ikenberry and others advance.[64] Michael Mastanduno also follows this line of reasoning: without "a reasonable degree of acceptance or acquiescence on the part of other major states in the system," hegemonic order is bound to disintegrate. In this sense, hegemony differs from power preponderance, which is based on brute force, rather than "the legitimate exercise of power."[65]

Curiously though, existing literature pays limited attention to how hegemonic power becomes legitimate in the eyes of local actors. As the United States faces a gradual decline and the rise of other great powers, we need to look at various regional processes in which the power-based framing gets shared or rejected. The findings of this research provide one way to achieve legitimacy at the regional level: conduct global and regional strategies in ways that ensure role congruence on the part of regional countries. Devoting greater attention to China's own regional role conceptions and promoting compatibility between the respective regional visions of the United States and China would increase the likelihood of restoring U.S. legitimacy in the region, while ensuring stable Sino-American relations.

Sources of Discord on East Asian Regionalism

An extensive analysis of regional role conceptions in East Asia can be useful in explaining a lack of progress in East Asian regionalism despite the expressed desire on the part of East Asian countries. Since the end of the Cold War era, various regional politicians and pundits have emphasized regionalism and multilateral frameworks in East Asia, but with little success. How can we explain the apparent gap between the region's incessant calls for regionalism and multilateral frameworks and the regional realities centered on bilateral relations with the United States? For regionalism to be successful, regional countries need to foster elements of cohesive regional awareness, a gradual "shifting of national and individual consciousness of state to a new center—a region."[66] As it stands, East Asian regionalism lacks such a shared vision. For instance, as Jitsuo Tsuchiyama observes, the majority of the Japanese public tend to view multilateral frameworks "as an academic argument partly because there appears to be no such common identity as 'we' in East Asia."[67] Without a common conceptual framework for the region, chances of developing a common vision for the region will remain slim.[68]

The findings of this book indicate that the main problem with East Asian regionalism is a lack of consensus on the nature and the proper shape of regional order. One possible reason for the discord may be the regional countries' varying conceptions of regional roles and role conflicts during the Bush presidency. It is worth noting in this regard that China, Japan, and South Korea managed to work toward trilateral cooperation in late 2008 when the Bush years came to an end. For instance, the three countries held the Trilateral Summit in December 2008, unveiling the "Action Plan for Promoting Trilateral Cooperation."[69] Since then, they met several times to work together for the Chiang Mai Initiatives for currency swaps and probed into a China-Japan-Korea Free Trade Agreement.[70] If the United States conducts regional policy in ways that are sensitive to internally shaped role conceptions, it would not only help U.S. policymaking but also facilitate regionalism. Absent such considerations, and with the U.S. push for U.S.-centered roles, East Asian countries will be prone to role conflict, with a growing difficulty in reaching a mutual understanding on regionalism.

This is indeed what has been taking place in the region. The Chinese, for instance, now tend to view regionalism as a way to balance the U.S. regional influence. The South Koreans often approach regionalism as a channel to revamp the stalled inter-Korean relations, whereas the Japanese regard regionalism as a hedging option in case of America's withdrawal from the region. Lacking common threads or narratives about regionalism, East Asian regionalism is increasingly adrift. A careful survey of the different narratives about regionalism in each country in the past decade would help us to better understand the sources of difficulty in forging an effective regional framework. A similar analysis of the regional narratives about the post–Arab uprisings regional order in the Middle East would be illuminating not only in making sense of the shifting tectonic plates in the region but also in coping better with the decade-long challenge from a "global rogue."

Epilogue

Events on the [Korean] peninsula and the reactions they evoke from China and the United States seem certain to play an important role in defining the security architecture of East Asia for the twenty-first century.

—Avery Goldstein[1]

The "Arab Spring" has brought to the fore the critical fault lines in the region. . . . creating possibilities for new alignments and an as yet undetermined new political and security order in the region.

—Rajeev Agarwal[2]

In 2013, both the second North Korean nuclear crisis and the Iranian nuclear crisis have passed the ten-year mark. It was also the year when President Barack Obama began his second term in the rapidly changing global and regional contexts, which included the arrival of a new generation of leaders in China, Japan, and South Korea, as well as widening regional divisions and turmoil in the Middle East after the Arab uprisings. Hence, it is particularly useful to assess the current U.S. approach to the two nuclear challenges and examine how regional actors have responded.

As latest regional developments add to the complexities of the two regional cases, the jury is still out on the ultimate outcomes of the decade-long proliferation conundrums. If the findings of this book are any guide, however, regional dynamics will be shaped to an important degree by the nature of regional role conceptions and the level of role congruence and conflict. In the following pages, I seek to demonstrate how the analytical framework advanced in this book may illuminate latest regional developments in East Asia and the Middle East.

In East Asia, the passage of power in the three East Asian countries coincided with the abrupt passing of Kim Jong Il and the emergence of his young and inexperienced son Kim Jung Un as the ruler of North Korea. The new regime in Pyongyang added a greater sense of uncertainty and volatility to the already tortuous process of nuclear diplomacy. A far more consequential series of events has engulfed the entire region of the Middle East. Popular uprisings in 2011 sparked "the most dynamic transformation" since the 1916 Sykes–Picot agreement, which artificially split the region into separate colonial zones ruled by the British and the French.[3]

Despite early predictions, however, the end of the Kim Jung Il era "did not result in any fundamental change in the nature and leadership of the regime."[4] In the Middle East as well, continuing political upheavals in Egypt, Iraq, and Syria have not significantly affected the region's understanding of the Iranian nuclear challenge. Overall, the seemingly transformative regional developments have not altered the regional dynamics documented in this book. As of this writing, the two nuclear challenges persist and the regional actors' efforts to play a greater role continue, albeit in a much different regional environment. What has changed in the past few years is the nature of regional role conceptions in each country and their impact on the regional order in each region.

In East Asia, the change in regional role conceptions was most prominent in South Korea. The conservative Lee Myung-bak government's emphasis on the U.S.-centered regional role led to its willing adoption of the U.S. frame and its hardline position on North Korea. While partly spurred by Pyongyang's provocations, including the sinking of a South Korean naval ship in 2010, the Lee government's about-face on inter-Korean relations ended Seoul's decade-long campaign to play a proactive regional role and ensure regional autonomy. A former South Korean foreign minister lamented that the South Korea–led efforts to build a multilateral security framework eventually failed as the Lee government focused solely on improving the U.S.–South Korean alliance.[5]

During the 2012 presidential election campaign, the political backlash resulted in a weakening of the U.S.-centered regional role and a renewed effort to engage North Korea. Moon Jae-in, the opposition Democratic Party's candidate, promised to put an end to Lee's stance on North Korea and promote reconciliation between the two Koreas.[6] Emboldened to break away from Lee's U.S.-centered regional strategy and seek South Korea's greater regional autonomy, Moon called for "balanced diplomacy" between the United States and China.[7] Park Geun-hye, the ruling New Frontier party candidate and Lee's eventual successor, also expressed her willingness to consider large-scale economic projects with the North and hold a summit with Kim Jung Un to improve inter-Korean relations.[8]

President Park's "trustpolitik" toward North Korea led to some initial success in August 2013 when Pyongyang agreed to resume operation at the Kaesung joint industrial complex and restart family reunions of selected North Koreans and their relatives in South Korea.[9] Echoing the Kim Dae-jung government's sunshine policy, the Park government's policy is also aimed at improving inter-Korean relations through trust building, part of a larger regional vision that would enable Seoul to pursue balanced diplomacy between the United States and China and build a cooperative regional order in East Asia.[10] To this end, Park established a new Presidential Committee for Unification Preparation.[11] In her New Year's speech in 2014, President Park went even further to call unification "a big bonanza" for the nation.[12] A month later, Park suggested that the unification would be "a new growth engine for both Korea and neighbors in East Asia."[13]

What remained unclear in her new initiative toward Pyongyang, however, was how to parlay it into a larger regional vision and to enhance South Korea's regional role. Park's critics thus dismissed her engagement toward North Korea as far too limited and ambiguous. From their perspective, the rise of China, Japan's perceived militarism, and the U.S. pivot to Asia all point to a region in great strategic flux. Denouncing Park's North Korean policy as a failure similar to her predecessor's insistence on the nuclear question, several opinion leaders called for a new comprehensive plan to engage Pyongyang not just for inter-Korean relations but for South Korea's greater regional leverage in the rapidly changing regional context.[14] The improved ties between the two Koreas, a former unification minister argued, would expand South Korea's regional role and provide Seoul with more policy options in the regional realm.[15] Another columnist for the conservative *Joongang Ilbo* also called on President Park to engage North Korea as a means to overcome dependency on the region's great powers.[16]

Emphasis on the relationship with North Korea continued in China despite the plea from the United States to take greater responsibility in dealing with North Korea. Although Chinese leaders are increasingly sensitive to Beijing's global image, their pursuit of international status would not come at the expense of their equally, if not more, important quest for a greater regional role and autonomy. As the early years of the Xi Jinping presidency demanded greater domestic political legitimacy and an independent foreign policy stance in the region, China largely maintained its regional vision that stressed its strategic ties with Pyongyang.

After the Kim Jong Un regime conducted the third nuclear test, however, China began to put some pressure on North Korea. Chinese Foreign Minister Yang Jiechi remarked that China was "strongly dissatisfied and resolutely opposed" to the test and urged North Korea to "stop any rhetoric or acts that could worsen situations and return to the right course of dialogue and consultation as soon as possible."[17] What followed the unusually strong rebuke was a series of punitive measures against Pyongyang. In September 2013, Beijing announced a rare export ban of a list of items that can be used for North Korea's nuclear and missile programs, including metal alloys and nitric acid.[18]

The seemingly harsh response to the nuclear test betrayed China's continuing emphasis on its ties to the United States and the salience of the U.S.-directed role in China. A *People's Daily* column, for instance, called for strengthening Sino-American cooperation on regional and global issues, including the North Korean and Iranian nuclear issues, in their efforts to create "a new global order with win-win cooperation."[19] China's analysts also expressed greater frustration toward North Korea, one of which, in an op-ed commentary in *The Financial Times*, called for ending Beijing's strategic relations with Pyongyang.[20] Echoing the earlier suspension of a journal critical of the North Korean regime, however, the Chinese Foreign Ministry quickly moved to suspend the author of the op-ed column.[21] Despite the continuing U.S. demand to pressure Pyongyang, Chinese Ambassador to the United States shot back by saying that such a hardline policy would be "a mission impossible."[22]

All in all, its initial rhetoric and policy measures to the contrary, China's overall relations with its communist ally remained largely unchanged. In fact, its trade with North Korea increased to "a record high of $4.69 billon [sic] during January–September 2013, a 4.5 percent increase over the same period last year."[23] Overall, China's response to North Korea's nuclear test was "about maintaining its credibility and saving face after being defied by a client state, rather than changing the regional dynamics in accordance with Washington and Seoul's hopes."[24] This suggests the lingering significance of China's regional role as an independent regional player and its desire to enhance its regional autonomy despite changing external circumstances and the continuing U.S. pressures.

In Japan, the successive governments led by the Democratic Party of Japan (DPJ) tried to reverse the Liberal Democratic Party (LDP)'s government's hardline policies on North Korea. In particular, Prime Minister Hatoyama Yukio's East Asian Community initiative was in line with Japan's earlier efforts to go beyond the U.S.-directed role and play a greater regional role and enhance regional autonomy. In this vein, the

DPJ government, in contrast to LDP Prime Ministers Abe and Aso, did not politicize the abduction issue and even "downplayed" the North Korean threat.[25] However, the 2011 Tsunami and the subsequent Fukushima nuclear disaster catapulted the subsequent Kan Naoto and Noda Yoshihiko governments into a crisis mode, with virtually no chance to pursue the proactive regional initiative laid out by Hatoyama.

After Kim Jong Il's death, however, the Noda government asked former LDP Prime Minister Koizumi to visit Pyongyang to "offer Japan's condolences over the death of Kim Jong Il, hoping to improve bilateral relations."[26] The renewed attempt to engage North Korea culminated in the official meeting in August 2012 when Japan and North Korea held their first talks in four years.[27] The efforts continued with another meeting in November 2012. A Japanese editorial evaluated Noda's efforts positively, calling for "new approaches for moving its ties with North Korea forward, based on the Pyongyang Declaration."[28]

The three years of the DPJ rule was abruptly replaced by the return of hardline Abe Shinzo as prime minister. Given his anti–North Korean position, which centered on the abduction issue, his North Korea policy was predictably hostile. Even before his return to premiership, Abe stressed the U.S.-centered regional role and the importance of working closely with Washington on both the North Korean problem and China's assertive move regarding the Senkaku/Diaoyu Islands.[29] The Kim Jung Un regime made the situation even worse by conducting the third nuclear test in early 2013. Abe called it "a 'grave threat' that could not be tolerated."[30] Latching onto the global frame, Japan's ambassador to the UN Conference on Disarmament, Sano Toshio, condemned it as "totally unacceptable" and "a grave challenge to the international non-proliferation regime."[31]

As the tension subsided later in 2013, however, Abe began to engage North Korea over the abduction issue. In 2014, Abe secretly sent senior Foreign Ministry officials to Hanoi and Hong Kong to contact North Korean officials. To improve the chances of realizing official meetings with Pyongyang, the Abe government made sure not to reveal its behind-the-scenes arrangements to most government officials and members of the abductees' family association.[32] In March 2014, senior Japanese and North Korean officials held a two-day meeting in Beijing.[33] Abe himself embraced the meeting given that "his government has sought to gain its first big diplomatic success."[34] Abe's Chief Cabinet Secretary Suga Yoshihide even declared that Japan would continue to negotiate with North Korea over the abduction issue even after another of North Korea's nuclear or missile tests.[35]

Some suggested that Tokyo's active engagement of Pyongyang was part of its regional strategy to guard against China and South Korea in the midst of its ongoing tensions with them over the history issue.[36] Indeed, the Abe government has taken a series of measures to improve its security, such as the launching of a National Security Council and a revision of the National Defense Program Guidelines (NDPG), and has promoted a "dynamic joint defense force," mainly as an effort to balance and "reinforce deterrence toward China."[37] It is worth mentioning, however, that the Abe government's policy measures were not primarily focused on coping with China's rise. Rather, they were aimed at promoting Japan's greater regional and global role in light of Tokyo's diplomatic isolation vis-à-vis China and South Korea. In March 2015, for instance, the ruling Liberal Democratic Party and its coalition partner Komeito reached an agreement on a new legislative bill aimed at, among other things, allowing the dispatch of the Japan Self-Defense Forces (SDF) overseas and ensuring the right of collective self-defense, all designed to bolster Japan's proactive regional and global role.[38]

The Abe government has also welcomed the U.S. strategic rebalancing toward the Asia Pacific, as it promoted Japan's greater security role. At the same time, however, the conservative government in Tokyo sought to carve out its own regional autonomy by engaging North Korea. It is against this backdrop that Abe in his second term pursued an independent approach toward Pyongyang even in the face of the U.S. concern about prematurely lifting sanctions against North Korea.[39] Paradoxically, in his efforts to enhance Japan's regional role and autonomy, Abe, arguably Japan's most ardent North Korea basher during his first term as prime minister, became the frontrunner in engaging Pyongyang in his second term.

The situation is far more fluid and uncertain in the Middle East as the various effects of the Arab uprisings ricocheted around the region, complicating the local actors' search for a new regional role and foreign policy autonomy. The ongoing civil war in Syria appeared to have dampened Iran's hope for greater regional influence by crippling its major Arab ally and creating new divisions with other regional states. In particular, the Syrian quagmire negatively affected Turkey–Iran relations, as the two countries found themselves on the opposite sides over the fate of the Bashar al-Assad regime. As the findings of this book have demonstrated, however, external circumstances do not always determine regional outcomes. Instead, the Arab uprisings have shown "how external forces can interact with, sharpen and reconfigure internal fault-lines."[40]

For instance, the region-wide political upheavals increased the domestic political need for regional autonomy in many regional countries, causing tension with the U.S. regional priorities. In particular, Egypt and Qatar sought to play a greater regional role in places like Gaza and Syria. The end result was "a far more religiously conservative Middle East that is less beholden to the United States."[41] As of this writing, Iran seems to be preoccupied with addressing various regional challenges and its own economic turmoil, but the changing regional landscape is also fertile ground for Tehran's regional clout over the Arab public and the Gulf monarchies. Under these circumstances, the U.S. policy of seeking a regional alignment of "moderate" states to balance Iran and "conducting an active diplomatic campaign to firm up the anti-Iranian front" is unlikely to succeed.[42]

This is not to suggest, however, that the U.S.-centered regional role and the global rogue frame are no longer valid. In fact, Israel's threat perception of Iran has grown in the post-uprising Middle East. It is important to note, however, that the greater Israeli threat perception had less to do with significant changes in Tehran's behavior than with the increasing relevance of Israel's regional role as a key U.S. ally. This is particularly the case given the changed regional strategic landscape in which "pro-American leaders have been toppled" and the region's "popular feelings, of which a basic trope has been hostility to Israel, have been empowered."[43]

As a consequence, despite positive developments in nuclear diplomacy with Iran, Israel's domestic actors not only latched onto but also magnified the earlier U.S. frame of Iran as a global menace. Hence, when Iran and the P5 + 1 reached an interim deal in 2013 on suspension of Iran's nuclear activities in exchange for a limited lifting of sanctions against Tehran, Israeli Prime Minister Netanyahu made clear that Israel "utterly reject[ed]" the deal.[44] A senior Israeli official even pledged that Israel would work against any deal that would permit Iran to keep the rights to enrich uranium and to develop a plutonium program.[45]

Similar to Israel, Saudi Arabia continued to portray Iran as an existential threat. Riyadh's growing concern about Iran was reflected in most vivid fashion in its call for the U.S. to "cut off the head of the snake" by launching a preemptive strike on Iran.[46] Saudi Arabia's fear of Iran was based on its belief that Iran's nuclear challenge was part of a larger "sectarian proxy war" that would determine the future regional order in the Middle East.[47] For Saudi Arabia, the Syrian civil war "play[ed] into a wider regional struggle against the influence of Shiite Iran."[48] Iran's role in Iraq, Syria, and Lebanon would limit Saudi Arabia's regional role despite the fact that the defense budget of Saudi Arabia is five times bigger than that of Tehran's.[49]

To counter Iran's regional role and recast its role as a leader of the Persian Gulf, in 2011 Saudi Arabia proposed the elevation of the GCC to a "unified military command structure that could combat threats to the region."[50] Given different regional role conceptions and threat perceptions among Gulf states, however, such a regional vision was difficult to put into action.[51] Riyadh also pledged $3 billion to the Lebanese Army in a bold effort to exert its regional role in a nation where Iran played a greater role via Hezbollah.[52] Amid allegations of Iran's backing of the Shiite-led protests, Bahrain also clamped down the political challenges to the Sunni leaders through the military means, mainly with the help of Saudi Arabia, which sent its own troops to the neighboring island kingdom.[53] In the wake of the political uprisings against the ruling Khalifa regime, Bahrain dismissed the opposition as an Iranian proxy and stressed its regional role as an ally of both Saudi Arabia and the United States.[54]

Despite its proactive regional role prior to the Arab uprisings, Turkey lost its regional influence over Arab states, mainly because of its failure to respond to the changing political situations in Egypt and Syria in a timely fashion.[55] Nonetheless, as a sign of the continuing salience of both the U.S.-directed and internally shaped regional roles, Turkey made "an intricate effort to preserve its old relationship with the West while building new ties with its Muslim neighbors."[56] At the same time, however, Turkey resumed efforts to expand its regional role and autonomy by engaging Iran. Hence, Turkish President Abdullah Gul invited the new Iranian president Hassan Rouhani for an official visit to Ankara.[57] Echoing its earlier opposition to join the War in Iraq and signaling its continued emphasis on regional autonomy, Turkey also refused to sign the U.S.-initiated ten-nation communiqué to fight the Islamic State.[58] Prime Minister Recep Tayyip Erdogan's election victory in 2014 as a newly empowered president suggests that his earlier efforts to expand Ankara's regional role and engagement toward Tehran would continue in the years to come.

Among the Gulf states, Oman's continuing engagement with Tehran and its active role in Iran's nuclear deal led to its decision to oppose the upgrading of the Gulf Cooperation Council (GCC) to a security union against Iran.[59] By refusing to "antagonize" Iran with the GCC union and ensuring role congruence between its own regional role and the US-directed role, Oman continued to maintain positive relations with both Iran and the United States, enabling its intermediary role for the nuclear deal.[60] When a U.S. diplomat visited Tehran for a meeting with Iran's new foreign minister Mohammad Javad Zarif, Omani Sultan Qaboos himself held a meeting with Iran's supreme leader Ali Khamenei.[61] Iran's Foreign

Minister Zarif thus expressed Tehran's "appreciation for the very central and positive role that the sultanate had played in facilitating these talks."[62]

With its eyes on a greater regional role, Qatar also improved its relations with Iran. In a February 2014 visit to Tehran, Qatar's Foreign Minister Khalid bin Mohamed al-Attiyah stressed "the significance of talks and co-operation between the two countries on all fronts, pointing to the formation of a joint working committee to boost and activate ties and establish a free zone between both countries."[63] The United Arab Emirates also joined the renewed engagement toward Tehran. Dubai's ruler Sheikh Mohammed Bin Rashid al-Maktoum thus called for ending sanctions against Iran, reaffirming that Iran is "our neighbor [with whom] we don't want any problem, and [i]f there's an opening with Iran, then that opening would have to involve Dubai."[64]

For their part, Iranians restarted their own diplomatic overtures toward Arab neighbors. Signaling a shift in Iran's foreign policy, President Rouhani announced that his foreign ministry, not the more conservative Supreme National Security Council, would be in charge of nuclear talks with the International Atomic Energy Agency (IAEA).[65] In November 2013, Iranian Foreign Minister Zarif also made a series of visit to Gulf states, expressing Iran's hope of improving ties with its Gulf neighbors and reassuring them that "[t]he solution to [the nuclear] issue serves the interests of all countries in the region. It is not at the expense of any state in the region."[66] As the nuclear deal between Iran and P5 + 1 continued, with the subsequent role congruence between the U.S.-directed regional role and internally shaped regional role, Iran's neighbors positively responded to Tehran's diplomatic charm offensive. In 2014, for instance, Turkey and Iran established the High Level Cooperation Council (HLCC) and Iran's President Rouhani visited Turkey in June 2014, the first visit by an Iranian president since 1996. Ankara also "welcome[d] the recent developments" in the nuclear negotiation.[67]

In April 2015, the Rouhani government and the Obama administration, along with five other negotiating partners, reached a political framework to limit Iran's nuclear program for the next fifteen years (i.e., cutting down the number of operating centrifuges and the amount of low-enriched uranium stockpile) in return for sanctions relief for Tehran.[68] Despite the months-long process of finalizing the technical details of the agreement and the much-longer verification procedure that lies ahead, regional responses were immediate and varied. Israeli Prime Minister Netanyahu expressed his strong opposition to the deal, while Saudi Arabia "stopped short of full endorsement," betraying the Gulf monarchy's concern about the impact of the deal on the regional order.[69]

In contrast, Turkey's Foreign Minister Mevlut Cavusoglu enthusiastically endorsed the agreement.[70] Similarly, Oman, with its "unique and potentially crucial relationship with Tehran," embraced the nuclear deal.[71] All in all, regardless of the nature of the final agreement, Iran will remain a key driver behind Middle Eastern states' regional role conceptions and regional order in the Middle East.

More than ten years after the outbreak of the North Korean and Iran nuclear crises, it is far from certain how the decade-long nuclear challenges will unfold in the coming years. Despite positive developments over the Iranian challenge, the restarting of the North Korean nuclear reactor at the Yongbyon complex in 2013 and a series of missile launches revealed the continuing difficulty in resolving the nuclear crisis for President Obama, whose presidency has already witnessed two North Korean nuclear tests.[72] Lacking effective policy options, the Obama administration turned to the decade-long global rogue frame and the urgency of dealing with the nuclear challenge. Using language reminiscent of the harsh rhetoric during the Bush years, in his April 2014 visit to Seoul President Obama reiterated the danger from what he called "a pariah state that would rather starve its people than feed their hopes and dreams."[73] In a similarly dire warning, Henry Kissinger called Iran "the most urgent decision facing [President Obama]" and forecast "uncontrollable military nuclear proliferation throughout a region roiled by revolution and sectarian blood-feuds" and "the near-certainty that several regional powers will go nuclear if Iran does."[74]

As analyzed in this book, however, nuclear crises do not automatically provoke heightened threat perceptions and regional nuclear arms races. In fact, more than ten years after the outbreak of both nuclear crises, such a nuclear chain reaction has not occurred in the Middle East or East Asia. The absence of the nuclear domino was mainly because most regional actors viewed the crises as an opportunity to enhance their regional role and autonomy, rather than an immediate strategic threat to tackle. Instead of assuming a priori actors' preferences over the proliferation challenge, we need to unpack underlying domestic conditions for threat perceptions and policy choices. As argued in this book, regional role conceptions as contested at the domestic level provide a useful lens through which we can understand regional threat perceptions and policy behavior with respect to the two nuclear challenges.

In August 2014, North Korea's Deputy Ambassador to the United Nations Lee Dong-il attributed the Bush administration's axis-of-evil speech to Pyongyang's decision to develop nuclear weapons in 2002. Absent such rhetoric and the U.S. threat of preemption, he argued, the nuclear crisis would have been avoided.[75] No matter how tragic they may be, the nuclear North Korea and Iran's nuclear pursuit, however, are not the only avoidable outcome of the Bush Doctrine. As documented in this book, far more disastrous and consequential is its impact on the larger regional order, especially strained alliance relations and fractured regionalism in the two important regions. These unnecessary yet highly unfortunate regional outcomes ensued despite the U.S. and other external powers' efforts to the contrary. In this sense, paradoxically, it is smaller global rogues, not great powers, that have helped shape the nature and contours of regional order in East Asia and the Middle East.

NOTES

CHAPTER 1

1. The document warns that "there is no greater threat to the American people than weapons of mass destruction, particularly the danger posed by the pursuit of nuclear weapons by violent extremists and their proliferation to additional states." *National Security Strategy*, The White House, Washington, DC, May 2010, p. 4.
2. Suzanne Maloney, *Iran's Long Reach: Iran as a Pivotal State in the Muslim World* (Washington, DC: USIP Press, 2008), p. 58.
3. *Sustaining U.S. Global Leadership: Priorities for 21st Century Defense*, U.S. Department of Defense, January 2012.
4. In various fields of study, scholars have stressed the importance of understanding local contexts in assessing the impact of various global phenomena. In his study of the role of global social media in shaping the conditions for political change around the world, for instance, communication scholar Clay Shirky argues that global actors' success in helping unleash the political power of social media hinges on a better understanding of local conditions, especially the nature of a local public sphere, Clay Shirky, "The Political Power of Social Media," *Foreign Affairs* 90, no. 1 (January/February 2011), p. 35. Similarly, focusing on the contrasting experiences of the East Asian and Latin American trade liberalization, economist Dani Rodrik contends that successful adoption of the liberal economic model depends on the nature of political and social conditions in different regions, Dani Rodrik, "Trading in Illusions," *Foreign Policy* 123 (March/April 2001), pp. 54–62. For a systematic analysis of different regional dynamics in world politics, see Peter J. Katzenstein, *A World of Regions: Asia and Europe in the American Imperium* (Ithaca, NY: Cornell University Press, 2005).
5. Joseph Cirincione, "Can Preventive War Cure Proliferation?" *Foreign Policy* 137 (July/August 2003), p. 66.
6. William R. Polk, *Understanding Iran: Everything You Need to Know from Persia to the Islamic Republic, From Cyrus to Ahmadinejad* (New York: Palgrave MacMillan, 2009), p. 187.
7. Notable exceptions are Etel Solingen, *Nuclear Logics: Contrasting Paths in East Asia and the Middle East* (Princeton, NJ: Princeton University Press, 2007); John S. Park, "Inside Multilateralism: The Six-Party Talks," *The Washington Quarterly* 28, no. 4 (Fall 2005), pp. 75–91; Scott Snyder, "South Korea's Squeeze Play," *The Washington Quarterly* 28, no. 4 (Fall 2005), pp. 91–106;

David C. Kang, "Japan: U.S. Partner or Focused on Abductees?" *The Washington Quarterly* 28, no. 4 (Fall 2005), pp. 107–117; Dalia Dassa Kaye and Frederic Wehrey, "A Nuclear Iran: The Reactions of Neighbours," *Survival* 49, no. 2 (2007), pp. 111–128.

8. *The National Security Strategy of the United States of America*, September 2002, The White House, Washington, DC.

9. Graham Allison, *Nuclear Terrorism: The Ultimate Preventable Catastrophe* (New York: Henry Holt & Company, 2004); Joseph Cirincione, *Deadly Arsenals: Tracking Weapons of Mass Destruction* (Washington, DC: Carnegie Endowment for International Peace, 2002); Alexander T. J. Lennon and Camille Eiss, eds., *Reshaping Rogue States: Preemption, Regime Change, and US Policy toward Iran, Iraq, and North Korea* (Cambridge, MA: MIT Press, 2004). For a useful counterpoint to nuclear alarmism, see John Mueller, *Atomic Obsession: Nuclear Alarmism from Hiroshima to Al-Qaeda* (New York: Oxford University Press, 2010).

10. Michael McDevitt, "Here We Go Again—North Korea and Nuclear Weapons," *PacNet Newsletter*, No. 43A, Pacific Forum, Center for Strategic and International Studies, October 21, 2002. For a detailed account of the second crisis, see Charles L. Pritchard, *Failed Diplomacy: The Tragic Story of How North Korea Got the Bomb* (Washington, DC: The Brookings Institution Press, 2007).

11. In February 2007, the Bush administration agreed to lift financial sanctions against North Korean assets and managed to produce an agreement on North Korea's "nuclear disablement." As discussed later in this chapter and in chapter 5, the welcome development at the Six Party Talks has produced a partial success, such as the halting of the nuclear facilities at Yongbyon in July 2007 and the disabling of the facilities in October 2007.

12. During the second crisis, numerous East Asian heads of state or minister-level officials visited Pyongyang, including Chinese President Hu Jintao in October 2005, Japanese Prime Minister Koizumi in May 2004, former South Korean Prime Minister Lee Haechan in March 2007, China's Defense Minister Cao Gangchuan in April 2006, South Korean Unification Minister Chung Dongyoung in June 2005, Japan's Liberal Democratic Party former Secretary General Yamasaki Taku in January 2007, and South Korean President Roh Moohyun in October 2007.

13. Joseph Kahn, "Chinese Aide Says U.S. Is Obstacle in Korean Talks," *New York Times*, September 2, 2003.

14. Martin Fackler, "North Korean Counterfeiting Complicates Nuclear Crisis," *New York Times*, January 29, 2006.

15. Howard W. French, "North Koreans Sign Agreement with Japanese," *New York Times*, September 18, 2002.

16. Through this agreement, the Bush administration retracted financial sanctions against the Kim Jong Il regime in return for North Korea's gradual disabling of its nuclear programs. "North Korea Agrees to Wind Down Nuclear Program," *The Associated Press*, February 13, 2007; Helene Cooper and Jim Yardley, "Pact With North Korea Draws Fire from a Wide Range of Critics in U.S.," *New York Times*, February 14, 2007; Helene Copper, "In U.S. Overtures to Foes, New Respect for Pragmatism," *New York Times*, March 1, 2007. The agreement seems to have yielded a partial success in July 2007 when North Korea allowed UN inspectors to visit and confirm the halting of operation at the Yongbyon nuclear facilities, followed by the October 2007 agreement in

which North Korea promised to disclose and disable its nuclear programs by the end of 2007.

17. Regionalism in this book is defined as political processes of deepening inter-governmental regional ties. In his study, T. J. Pempel defines regionalism as "the top-down process of government-to-government formation of institutions such as ASEAN, ARF." T. J. Pempel, "Introduction: Emerging Webs of Regional Connectedness," in T. J. Pempel, ed., *Remapping East Asia: The Construction of a Region* (Ithaca, NY: Cornell University Press, 2005), p. 6. For a discussion of such a "complex" regional situation, see Francis Fukuyama, *America at the Crossroads: Democracy, Power, and the Neoconservative Legacy* (New Haven, CT: Yale University Press, 2006), especially pp. 174–175. For a penetrating critique of the Bush administration's Asia policy more broadly, see T. J. Pempel, "How Bush Bungled Asia: Militarism, Economic Indifference and Unilateralism Have Weakened the United States across Asia," *The Pacific Review* 21, no. 5 (2008), pp. 547–581.

18. Amos Yadlin, "Israel's Last Chance to Strike Iran," *New York Times*, February 29, 2012.

19. Majid Al-Khalili, *Oman's Foreign Policy: Foundation and Practice* (Westport, CT: Praeger Security International, 2009), p. 103.

20. Etel Solingen is a notable exception. In a series of pioneering analyses of the East Asian and the Middle Eastern regional orders, Solingen argues that domestic coalition dynamics shape the nuclear decisions of different states and the nature of regional order in the two regions. See her "The Domestic Sources of International Regimes: The Evolution of Nuclear Ambiguity in the Middle East," *International Studies Quarterly* 38, no. 4 (June 1994), pp. 305–337; "The Political Economy of Nuclear Restraint," *International Security* 19, no. 2 (Fall 1994), pp. 126–169; *Regional Orders at Century's Dawn: Global and Domestic Influences on Grand Strategy* (Princeton, NJ: Princeton University Press, 1998); "Pax Asiatica versus Bella Levantina: The Foundations of War and Peace in East Asia and the Middle East," *American Political Science Review* 101, no. 4 (November 2007), pp. 757–780; *Nuclear Logics*; "The Genesis, Design and Effects of Regional Institutions: Lessons from East Asia and the Middle East," *International Studies Quarterly* 52, no. 1 (June 2008), pp. 261–294.

21. Prominent examples include Scott D. Sagan, "Why Do States Build Nuclear Weapons? Three Models in Search of a Bomb," *International Security* 21, no. 3 (Winter 1996/1997), pp. 54–86; Scott D. Sagan and Kenneth N. Waltz, *The Spread of Nuclear Weapons: A Debate Renewed* (New York: W.W. Norton, 2002); Jacques E. C. Hymans, *The Psychology of Nuclear Proliferation: Identity, Emotions, and Foreign Policy* (Cambridge, UK: Cambridge University Press, 2006); Solingen, *Nuclear Logics*; Matthew Kroenig, *Exporting the Bomb: Technology Transfer and the Spread of Nuclear Weapons* (Ithaca, NY: Cornell University Press, 2010); Robert Rauchhaus, Matthew Kroenig, Erik Gartzke, eds., *Causes and Consequences of Nuclear Proliferation* (Routledge, 2011); Jacques E. C. Hymans, *Achieving Nuclear Ambitions: Scientists, Politicians, and Proliferation* (Cambridge, UK: Cambridge University Press, 2012).

22. Kroenig, *Exporting the Bomb*.

23. Kroenig suggests that even major powers with the limited sphere of influence, such as China and Russia, have different, much regionally confined, strategic interests compared to the United States. See his *Exporting the Bomb*, p. 188.

24. While not making a case for region-specific analysis per se, Jacques Hymans similarly highlights the importance of showing "great sensitivity to individual cases and contexts" when he argues that the internal dynamics of proliferators are crucial to understand their nuclear development processes. Hymans, *Achieving Nuclear Ambitions*, p. 272.

25. Solingen, *Nuclear Logics*.

26. Stephen Walt, for instance, views perceived threats as a key driver behind balancing behavior. Stephen M. Walt, "Alliance Formation and the Balance of World Power," *International Security* 9, no. 4 (Spring 1985), pp. 3–43; Stephen M. Walt, *The Origins of Alliances* (Ithaca, NY: Cornell University Press, 1987). Similarly, Barry Buzan points to a high level of mutual threat/fear as key factor defining "security complexes." See his *People, States and Fear: An Agenda for International Security Studies in the Post-Cold War Era* (Boulder, CO: Lynne Rienner, 1991), p. 194.

27. Ok-Nim Chung, "Solving the Security Puzzle in Northeast Asia: A Multilateral Security Regime," *CNAPS Working Paper*, The Brookings Institution, September 1, 2000.

28. Robyn Lim, "Papering Over the Cracks," *Far Eastern Economic Review* 166 (June 5, 2003), p. 21.

29. Ted Hopf thus calls for developing a "theory of threat perception." Ted Hopf, "The Promise of Constructivism in IR Theory," *International Security* 23, no. 1 (Summer 1998), p. 187.

30. Bruce E. Bechtol, Jr., *Defiant Failed State: The North Korean Threat to International Security* (Washington, DC: Potomac Books, 2010); Jonathan Pollack, *No Exit: North Korea, Nuclear Weapons and International Security* (Abingdon, UK: Routledge, 2011); and Alireza Jafarzadeh, *The Iran Threat: President Ahmadinejad and the Coming Nuclear Crisis* (New York: Palgrave Macmillan, 2007). For an opposite narrative, see Gavan McCormack, *Target North Korea* (New York: Nation Books, 2004).

31. Tanya Ogilvie-White, "The Defiant States: The Nuclear Diplomacy of North Korea and Iran," *Nonproliferation Review* 17, no. 1 (March 2010), pp. 120–125.

32. Nicholas D. Kristof, "Hang Up! Tehran Is Calling," *New York Times*, January 21, 2007.

33. Mohamad ElBaradei, *The Age of Deception: Nuclear Diplomacy in Treacherous Times* (New York: Metropolitan Books, 2011); Charles Pritchard, *Failed Diplomacy: The Tragic Story of How North Korea Got the Bomb* (Washington, DC: Brooking Institution Press, 2007); Trita Parsi, *A Single Roll of the Dice: Obama's Diplomacy with Iran* (New Haven, CT: Yale University Press, 2012); and Ali Ansari, *Confronting Iran: The Failure of American Foreign Policy and the Next Great Conflict in the Middle East* (New York: Basic Books, 2007).

34. Gilbert Rozman, *Strategic Thinking about the Korean Nuclear Crisis: Four Parties Caught between North Korea and the United States* (New York: Palgrave Macmillan, 2007); Yoichi Funabashi, *The Peninsula Question: A Chronicle of the Second North Korean Nuclear Crisis* (Washington, DC: Brookings Institution Press, 2007).

35. See, for instance, Kristian Ulrichsen, *Insecure Gulf: The End of Certainty and the Transition to the Post-Oil Era* (New York: Columbia University Press, 2011); Maloney, *Iran's Long Reach*.

36. Gary Samore, "The Korean Nuclear Crisis," *Survival* 45, no. 1 (Spring 2003), p. 14.

37. For a study of such contested national interests at the domestic level and its impact on interstate behavior, see Jonathan Kirshner's study of caution exercised by the financial community on the road to war. *Appeasing Bankers: Financial Caution on the Road to War* (Princeton, NJ: Princeton University Press, 2007). Earlier works, which similarly examined the contested nature of the national interest formation at the domestic level, include Richard Anderson, *Public Politics in an Authoritarian State: Making Foreign Policy During the Brezhnev Years* (Ithaca, NY: Cornell University Press, 1993) and James G. Richter, *Khrushchev's Double Bind: International Pressures and Domestic Coalition Politics* (Baltimore, MD: The Johns Hopkins University Press, 1994).

38. Peter J. Katzenstein, ed., *The Culture of National Security: Norms and Identity in World Politics* (New York: Columbia University Press, 1996); Alastair Iain Johnston, *Cultural Realism: Strategic Culture and Grand Strategy in Chinese History* (Princeton, NJ: Princeton University Press, 1998); Vaughn P. Shannon and Paul A. Kowert, eds., *Psychology and Constructivism in International Relations: An Ideational Alliance* (Ann Arbor, MI: University of Michigan Press, 2011); and Ted Hopf, *Reconstructing the Cold War: The Early Years, 1945–1958* (New York: Oxford University Press, 2012). For a constructivist analysis of arms proliferation, see Dana P. Eyre and Mark C. Suchman, "Status, Norms, and the Proliferation of Conventional Weapons: An Institutional Theory Approach," in Peter J. Katzenstein, ed., *The Culture of National Security: Norms and Identity in World Politics* (New York: Columbia University Press, 1996), pp. 79–113.

39. Hymans, *The Psychology of Nuclear Proliferation*.

40. Andrei P. Tsygankov and Matthew Tarver-Wahlquist, "Dueling Honors: Power, Identity and the Russia–Georgia Divide," *Foreign Policy Analysis* 5 (2009), 307–326; Eyre and Suchman, "Status, Norms, and the Proliferation of Conventional Weapons: An Institutional Theory Approach."

41. Deborah Welch Larson and Alexei Shevchenko, "Status Seekers: Chinese and Russian Responses to U.S. Primacy," *International Security* 34, no. 4 (Spring 2010), p. 93. See also Ted Hopf, *Social Construction of International Politics: Identities and Foreign Policies, Moscow, 1955 and 1999* (Ithaca, NY: Cornell University Press, 2002).

42. Larson and Shevchenko, pp. 82, 85–86.

43. Yong Deng, *China's Struggle for International Status: The Realignment of International Relations* (New York: Cambridge University Press, 2008), p. 209.

44. For a useful review of role theory in the field of sociology, see B. J. Biddle, "Recent Developments in Role Theory," *Annual Review of Sociology* 12 (1986), pp. 67–92. For a discussion of national role conceptions in explaining foreign policy behavior, see K. J. Holsti, "National Role Conceptions in the Study of Foreign Policy," *International Studies Quarterly* 14 (1970), pp. 233–309; Stephen G. Walker, ed., *Role Theory and Foreign Policy Analysis* (Durham, NC: Duke University Press, 1987); Chih-yu Shih, "National Role Conception as Foreign Policy Motivation: The Psychological Bases of Chinese Diplomacy," *Political Psychology* 9, no. 4 (1988), pp. 599–631; Stephen Walker, "Symbolic Interaction and International Politics: Role Theory's Contribution to International Organization," in Martha L. Cottam and Chih-yu Shih, eds., *Contending Dramas, A Cognitive Approach to International Organizations* (New York: Praeger, 1992), pp. 19–38; Michael Barnett, "Institutions, Roles, and Disorder: The

Case of the Arab States System," *International Studies Quarterly* 37, no. 3 (September 1993), pp. 271–296; Glenn Chafez, Hillel Abramson, and Suzette Grillot, "Role Theory and Foreign Policy: Belarusian and Ukrainian Compliance with the Nuclear Nonproliferation Regime," *Political Psychology* 17, no. 4 (1996), pp. 727–757; Philippe G. Le Prestre, ed., *Role Quests in the Post-Cold War Era: Foreign Policies in Transition* (Montreal: McGill-Queen's University Press, 1997); Lisbeth Aggestam, "A Common Foreign and Security Policy: Role Conceptions and the Politics of Identity in EU," in Lisbeth Aggestam and Adrian Hyde-Price, eds., *Security and Identity in Europe: Exploring the New Agenda* (London: MacMillan Press, 2000), pp. 87–115; Katja Weber and Paul A. Kowert, "Language, Rules, and Order: The Westpolitik Debate of Adenauer and Schumacher," in Francois Debrix, ed., *Language, Agency, and Politics in a Constructed World* (Armonk, New York: M.E. Sharpe, 2003), pp. 196–219; Michael Grossman, "Role Theory and Foreign Policy Change: The Transformation of Russian Foreign Policy in the 1990s," *International Politics* 42 (2005), pp. 334–351; Lisbeth Aggestam, "Role Theory and European Foreign Policy: A Framework of Analysis," in Ole Elgstrom and Michael Smith, eds., *The European Union's Roles in International Politics: Concepts and Analysis* (London: Routledge, 2006), pp. 11–29; Yukiko Miyagi, "Foreign Policy Making under Koizumi: Norms and Japan's Role in the 2003 Iraq War," *Foreign Policy Analysis* 5 (2009), pp. 349–366.

45. Holsti, "National Role Conceptions," p. 246.

46. For an analysis of national self-image, see Richard Ned Lebow, *Between Peace and War: The Nature of International Crisis* (Baltimore: Johns Hopkins University Press, 1981). For analyses of elite belief systems see, among others, Alexander George, "The 'Operational Code': A Neglected Approach to the Study of Political Leaders and Decision Making," *International Studies Quarterly* 13 (1969), pp. 190–222; Stephen Walker, "The Interface between Beliefs and Behavior: Henry Kissinger's Operational Code and the Vietnam War," *Journal of Conflict Resolution* 21 (1977), pp. 129–168; Cottam and Shih, *Contending Dramas*; Weber and Kowert, "Language, Rules, and Order."

47. Martha L. Cottam, "Recent Developments in Political Psychology," in Martha L. Cottam and Chih-yu Shih, eds., *Contending Dramas, A Cognitive Approach to International Organizations* (New York: Praeger, 1992), p. 7.

48. Stephen Walker, "Symbolic Interaction and International Politics: Role Theory's Contribution to International Organization," in Martha L. Cottam and Chih-yu Shih, eds., *Contending Dramas, A Cognitive Approach to International Organizations* (New York: Praeger, 1992), p. 24.

49. Rawi Abdelal, Yoshiko M. Herrera, Alastair Iain Johnston, and Rose McDermott, "Identity as a Variable," *Perspectives on Politics* 4, no. 4 (December 2006), p. 697.

50. *Dongbuka-sidae Gusang [The Northeast Asia Cooperation Initiative]*, Presidential Committee on Northeast Asian Cooperation Initiative, Seoul, South Korea, 2004.

51. A case in point is the diplomatic isolation of Japan provoked by Prime Minister Koizumi's repeated visits to Yasukuni Shrine, which worships Japan's war dead, including 14 Class A World War II war criminals. The Shinto shrine also has a war museum, *Yushukan*, which generally downplays Japan's past aggression and praises the spirit of Japanese. Both the Chinese and South Korean

governments vehemently criticized the prime minister's visit. For a detailed analysis of the Yasukuni issue, see Daiki Shibuichi, "The Yasukuni Shrine Dispute and the Politics of Identity in Japan," *Asian Survey* 45, no. 2 (March/April 2005), pp. 197–215.

52. Interview 05–05, Tokyo, March 23, 2005.

53. Kazuhiko Togo, *Japan's Foreign Policy 1945–2003: The Quest for a Proactive Policy* (Boston, MA: Brill, 2005), p. 418.

54. Tsuneo Akaha, "Japan's Multilevel Approach toward the Korean Peninsula after the Cold War," in Charles K. Armstrong, Gilbert Rozman, Samuel S. Kim, and Stephen Kotkin, eds., *Korea at the Center: Dynamics of Regionalism in Northeast Asia* (Armonk, New York: M.E. Sharpe, Inc., 2006), p. 184.

55. One Japanese expert claimed that Japan–North Korean normalization became "the crown jewel" of the Koizumi government. Interview 30–05, Tokyo, July 15, 2005.

56. Xiaoxing Yi, "A Neutralized Korea? The North-South Rapprochement and China's Korea Policy," *Korean Journal of Defense Analysis* XII, no. 2 (Winter 2000), p. 79.

57. To be sure, one could argue that the degree of the salience of North Korea may vary across the region. For instance, the importance of North Korea in the regional vision may be strongest in South Korea due to the two countries' proximity, common history, and the desire of reunification, while North Korea's importance for China may be confined to the Northeast Asian part of its larger regional vision. That said, the potential regional payoffs of the regional visions linked to North Korea for the East Asian countries' regional role and autonomy could be substantial across the region.

58. Interview 07–04, Beijing, November 16, 2004; Interview 04–05, Tokyo, March 22, 2005; Interview 05–05, Tokyo, March 23, 2005; Interview 27–05, Tokyo, June 27, 2005; Interview 33–05, Tokyo, July 27, 2005; Interview 22–05, Seoul, May 12, 2005; Interview 38–05, Seoul, August 4, 2005.

59. Joshua W. Walker, "Introduction: The Sources of Turkish Grand Strategy—'Strategic Depth' and 'Zero-Problems' in Context," in Nicholas Kitchen, ed., *Turkey's Global Strategy*, IDEAS Special Reports, LSE Research Online, London School of Economics and Political Science, available at: http://eprints.lse. ac.uk/43495/, pp. 10–11

60. Graham E. Fuller, *The New Turkish Republic: Turkey as a Pivotal in the Muslim World* (Washington, DC: United States Institute of Peace Press, 2007), p. 79.

61. For a similar point made in the context of grand strategy, see Jeffrey W. Legro, *Rethinking the World: Great Power Strategies and International Order* (Ithaca, NY: Cornell University Press, 2005).

62. Stephen G. Walker and Sheldon W. Simon, "Role Sets and Foreign Policy Analysis in Southeast Asia," in Stephen G. Walker, ed., *Role Theory and Foreign Policy Analysis* (Durham, NC: Duke University Press, 1987), p. 142.

63. Barnett, "Institutions, Roles, and Disorder," pp. 271–296. For an analysis of role conflict from the psychological angle, see Weber and Kowert, "Language, Rules, and Order," pp. 196–219.

64. Barnett, p. 274.

65. Cristian Cantir and Juliet Kaarbo, "Contested Roles and Domestic Politics: Reflections on Role Theory in Foreign Policy Analysis and IR Theory," *Foreign Policy Analysis* 8 (2012), pp. 6–8.

66. Rikard Bengtsson and Ole Elgstrom, "Conflicting Role Conceptions? The European Union in Global Politics," *Foreign Policy Analysis* 8 (2012), pp. 93–108 at 93.

67. Cantir and Kaarbo, "Contested Roles and Domestic Politics," p. 10.

68. A classic work on the agent and structure debate in world politics is Alexander E. Wendt, "The Agent-Structure Problem in International Relations Theory," *International Organization* 41, no. 3 (Summer 1987), pp. 335–370.

69. Vaughn P. Shannon, "Introduction: Ideational Allies—Psychology, Constructivism, and International Relations," in Vaughn P. Shannon and Paul A. Kowert, eds., *Psychology and Constructivism in International Relations: An Ideational Alliance* (Ann Arbor, MI: University of Michigan Press, 2011), p. 3. In a similar vein, a new wave of scholars working on role theory also proposed a dialogue between foreign policy role theory and systemic constructivism. See, for instance, Cameron G. Thies and Marijke Breuning, "Integrating Foreign Policy Analysis and International Relations through Role Theory," *Foreign Policy Analysis* 8, no. 1 (2012), pp. 2–3.

70. Holsti called externally shaped roles "external role prescriptions," while others used the term "role expectations" to capture the roles shaped by outside forces. Holsti, "National Role Conceptions," p. 246; Walker and Simon, "Role Sets," p. 142. Barnett's use of "position roles," as opposed to "preference roles," also refers to the external dimensions. Such external forces include the power structure of the international system, global norms, or alliance commitments. Barnett, "Institutions, Roles, and Disorder," p. 275.

71. Walker and Simon, "Role Sets," p. 159; Stephen G. Walker, "Role Theory and Foreign Policy Analysis: An Evaluation," in Stephen G. Walker, ed., *Role Theory and Foreign Policy Analysis* (Durham, NC: Duke University Press, 1987), p. 242.

72. Deng, *China's Struggle for Status*, p. 34.

73. It is worth noting here that despite the fact that the United States continues to maintain a formidable military presence in East Asia, its regional influence has dramatically decreased in the past few years. As of this writing, the United States still maintains about seventy-eight thousand troops in Japan and South Korea alone, even after some portion of the forces were redeployed to the Middle East due to the ongoing war in Iraq and the Global Posture Review by the Pentagon. The U.S. Pacific Command website, available at http://www.pacom.mil/about/pacom.shtml.

74. Interview 08–04, Beijing, November 18, 2004.

75. Interview 42–05, Seoul, August 5, 2005.

76. Interview 12–04, Beijing, November 24, 2004.

77. It is worth noting in this vein that changes in external circumstances may affect domestic political dynamics, enabling new actors to emerge and reshape domestic debates. For a discussion on the domestic-international linkages, see Matthew Evangelista, "Domestic Structures and International Change," in Michael Doyle and John Ikenberry, eds., *New Thinking in International Relations* (Boulder, CO: Westview Press, 1997); Leonard J. Schoppa, *Bargaining with Japan: What American Pressure Can and Cannot Do* (New York: Columbia University Press, 1997); Richter, *Khrushchev's Double Bind*; Michael J. Hiscox, *International Trade & Political Conflict: Commerce, Coalitions, and Mobility* (Princeton, NJ: Princeton University Press, 2002). The classic manifestation of the link is Robert D. Putnam, "Diplomacy and Domestic Politics: The Logic of Two-Level Games," *International Organization* 42, no. 3 (1988), pp. 427–460.

78. Michael Barnett, "The Israeli Identity and the Peace Process: Re/creating the Un/thinkable," in Shibley Telhami and Michel Barnett, eds., *Identity and Foreign Policy in the Middle East* (Ithaca, NY: Cornell University Press, 2002), p. 69.

79. In a similar vein, Amitav Acharya attributes the demand of regional organizations in Asia in part to efforts to pursue ideologically driven foreign policy goals. For instance, Acharya links Malaysia's pursuit of the East Asian Economic Caucus (EAEC) to "the ideological underpinnings of Mahathirism." See Amitav Acharya, "Regional Institutions and Security in the Asia-Pacific: Evolution, Adaptation, and Prospects," in Amitav Acharya and Evelyn Goh, eds., *Reassessing Security Cooperation in the Asia-Pacific: Competition, Congruence, and Transformation* (Cambridge, MA: The MIT Press, 2007), p. 36.

80. Leonard Schoppa's study of Japan's bargaining with the United States, for instance, shows how external pressure (*Gaiatsu*) can yield different domestic responses. He finds that foreign pressure is successful when "latent support for foreign demands can be found outside the bureaucratic and interest-group circles that ordinarily dominate the policy process." Schoppa, *Bargaining with Japan*, pp. 6–7.

81. This effort is being made primarily to reverse what the Meiji-era intellectual father Fukuzawa Yukichi termed *datsu-a ron* in the late nineteenth century, which was a call for getting out of a backward Asia and joining the advanced West. With economic integration and security consultation on the rise in the region, however, Japanese contemporary intellectuals have recently made a plea for proactively engaging East Asia.

82. Robert Zoellick, "Whither China: From Membership to Responsibility?" Department of State, September 21, 2005, available at http://www.state.gov/s/d/rem/53682.htm.

83. In some cases, notably in Japan and Saudi Arabia, regional actors even use the U.S. approach to advance their distinctive national interests, such as breaking away from the constitutional restraint on defense and becoming a "normal state" or improving the weakened regional status in the wake of the Arab uprisings and "the Shia revival."

84. For a detailed yet succinct account of various Japanese administrations' attempts to engage or demonize North Korea, see T. J. Pempel, "Japan and the Two Koreas: The Foreign-Policy Power of Domestic Politics," in Marie Soderberg, ed., *Changing Power Relations in Northeast Asia: Implications for Relations between Japan and South Korea* (New York: Routledge, 2011), pp. 66–70. On a similar point made in the context of Japan's handling of terrorism and child prostitution, see David Leheny, *Think Global, Fear Local: Sex, Violence, and Anxiety in Contemporary Japan* (Ithaca, NY: Cornell University Press, 2006), p. 6.

85. Here I am not making any definitive claims about the policy preferences of different political groups in China. Given its one-party rule, difference in foreign policy preferences among domestic groups, for instance, the People's Liberation Army and Foreign Ministry, over the North Korean issue is often not clear-cut. That said, a careful look at the way different groups make comments on North Korea reveals discernable contrasts: Foreign Ministry officials tend to highlight the global issues such as nuclear proliferation and China's relations with the United States, while the Communist Party and the military maintain their traditional emphasis on bilateral ties with North Korea. For a recent study of variations in Chinese cooperation with the United States on nonproliferation policies, see Evan S. Medeiros, *Reluctant Restraint: The*

Evolution of China's Nonproliferation Policies and Practices, 1980–2004 (Stanford, CA: Stanford University Press, 2007).

86. Richard Samuels, *Securing Japan: Tokyo's Grand Strategy and the Future of East Asia* (Ithaca, NY: Cornell University Press, 2007).

87. The predominance of North Korea bashers, however, was not uniform across the region. A crucial factor has been political leaders' ability to garner support from the larger society and the degree of domestic resonance of the Bush administration's rogue rhetoric. With the relatively low degree of threat perception vis-à-vis North Korea and the high level of anti-U.S. sentiments among the public, domestic debates in South Korea and China did not result in the collapse of the regional visions anchored to North Korea until the conservative Lee Myung-bak government came to power in 2008. In Japan, as anti–North Korean feelings shaped in part by the abduction scandal involving North Korean special agents spread nationwide, the previous consensus on the merits of a regional approach was weakened. The ensuing rise of new conservatives served to "re-nationalize" the North Korean issue away from a common regional understanding.

88. Aaron L. Friedberg, "Ripe for Rivalry: Prospects for Peace in a Multipolar Asia," *International Security* 18, no. 3 (Winter 1993/1994), pp. 5–33; Richard K. Betts, "Wealth, Power, and Instability: East Asian and the United States after the Cold War," *International Security* 18, no. 3 (Winter 1993/1994), pp. 34–77; Peter J. Katzenstein, *Norms and National Security: Police and Military in Postwar Japan* (Ithaca, NY: Cornell University Press, 1996); Mike Mochizuki and Michael O'Hanlon, "A Liberal Vision for the U.S.-Japanese Alliance," *Survival* 40, no. 2 (Summer 1998), pp. 127–134; Peter J. Katzenstein and Takashi Shirashi, eds., *Network Power: Japan and Asia* (Ithaca, NY: Cornell University Press, 1997); Thomas J. Christensen, "China, the U.S.-Japan Alliance, and the Security Dilemma in East Asia," *International Security* 23, no. 4 (Spring 1999), pp. 49–80; David Shambaugh, "China's Military Views the World: Ambivalent Security," *International Security* 24, no. 3 (Winter 1999/2000), pp. 52–79; Thomas C. Berger, "Set for Stability? Prospects for Conflict and Cooperation in East Asia," *Review of International Studies* 26, no. 3 (July 2000), pp. 405–428; Peter J. Katzenstein and Nobuo Okawara, "Japan, Asia-Pacific Security, and the Case for Analytical Eclecticism," *International Security* 26, no. 3 (Winter 2001/2002), pp. 153–185; Christopher Hemmer and Peter J. Katzenstein, "Why Is There No NATO in Asia? Collective Identity, Regionalism, and the Origins of Multilateralism," with Christopher Hemmer, *International Organization* 56, no. 3 (Summer 2002), pp. 575–607; David C. Kang, "Getting Asia Wrong: The Need for New Analytic Frameworks," *International Security* 27, no. 4 (Spring 2003), pp. 57–85; Muthiah Alagappa, ed., *Asian Security Order: Instrumental and Normative Features* (Stanford, CA: Stanford University Press, 2003); Michael Mastanduno and G. John Ikenberry, eds., *International Relations Theory and the Asia-Pacific* (New York: Columbia University Press, 2003); Ellis S. Krauss and T. J. Pempel, eds., *Beyond Bilateralism: U.S.-Japan Relations in the New Asia-Pacific* (Stanford, CA: Stanford University Press, 2004); J. J. Suh, Peter J. Katzenstein, and Allen Carlson, eds., *Rethinking Security in East Asia: Identity, Power, and Efficiency* (Stanford, CA: Stanford University Press, 2004); T. J. Pempel, ed., *Remapping East Asia: The Construction of a Region* (Ithaca, NY: Cornell University Press, 2005); Allen Carlson, *Unifying China and Integrating with*

the World (Stanford, CA: Stanford University Press, 2005); Avery Goldstein, *Rising to the Challenge: China's Grand Strategy and International Security* (Stanford, CA: Stanford University Press, 2005); Jae-Jung Suh, *Power, Interest, and Identity in Military Alliances* (New York: Palgrave MacMillan, 2007); David C. Kang, *China Rising: Peace, Power, and Order in East Asia* (New York: Columbia University Press, 2009); Aaron L. Friedberg, *A Contest for Supremacy: China, America, and the Struggle for Mastery in Asia* (New York: W. W. Norton, 2011).

89. Friedberg, "Ripe for Rivalry," p. 5.

90. Kang, "Getting Asia Wrong," pp. 57–85.

91. G. John Ikenberry, *After Victory: Institutions, Strategic Restraints, and the Rebuilding of Order* (Princeton, NJ: Princeton University Press, 2001); G. John Ikenberry, *Liberal Leviathan: The Origins, Crisis, and Transformation of the American World Order* (Princeton, NJ: Princeton University Press, 2011).

92. Other domestic factors are elite cohesion/fragmentation, social cohesion/fragmentation, and "the degree of regime or government vulnerability." Randall L. Schweller, *Unanswered Threats: Political Constraints on the Balance of Power* (Princeton, NJ: Princeton University Press, 2006), pp. 11–12.

93. Jeffrey W. Legro, "What China Will Want: The Future Intentions of a Rising Power," *Perspectives on Politics* 5, no. 3 (September 2007), p. 516. See also Legro, *Rethinking the World*.

94. Peter J. Katzenstein, "Regionalism and Asia," *New Political Economy* 5, no. 3 (November 2000), p. 354.

95. Muthiah Alagappa, "Introduction," in Muthiah Alagappa, ed., *Asian Security Order: Instrumental and Normative Features* (Stanford, CA: Stanford University Press, 2003), p. 34.

96. Peter J. Katzenstein, *A World of Regions: Asia and Europe in the American Imperium* (Ithaca, NY: Cornell University Press, 2005), p. 12.

97. In his study of global orders, Andrew Phillips discusses as the main sources of successful orders the legitimacy of the order, "the cultivation of legitimacy and on the maintenance of institutional capacities to suppress subversion, accommodate dissent and mobilize loyalty and support." Andrew Phillips, *War, Religion, and Empires: The Transformation of International Orders* (Cambridge, UK: Cambridge University Press, 2011), p. 45.

98. Ibid.

99. Hideya Kurata, "North Korea's Renewed Nuclear Challenge," *Japan Review of International Affairs* 17, no. 2 (Summer 2003), p. 91.

100. Interview 07–05, Beijing, April 18, 2005.

101. "Kim Jong Il Meets Chinese Vice President," *People's Daily*, June 18, 2008.

102. "Koizumi, Bush Trumpet New Global-Scale Alliance," *Japan Times*, June 30, 2006.

103. The two cases are also different in terms of the significance of transnational dimensions in the Iranian case. Iran's regional influence via its nonstate allies such as Hamas and Hezbollah and the salience of transnational identities, such as Arab, Muslim, Sunni, and Shia, in regional dynamics. See F. Gregory Gause, III, *The International Relations of the Persian Gulf* (Cambridge, UK: Cambridge University Press, 2010), p. 241.

104. A notable exception is a series of cross-regional comparisons on nuclear proliferation by Etel Solingen (cited earlier). But her analytical focus has more to do with decisions about proliferation than regional perceptions and responses.

105. For Japanese sources, I used translated materials available on the websites of the government agencies and other government-related think tanks such as Defense Agency's The National Institute for Strategic Studies, Japan Forum for International Relations, while covering a wide variety of English versions of Japanese news media (Yomiuri, Asahi, Mainichi, Japan Times, Kyodo News) and scholarly journals.

106. Jeffrey T. Checkel, "International Institutions and Socialization in Europe: Introduction and Framework," *International Organization* 59 (Fall 2005), p. 817.

CHAPTER 2

1. According to Joel Wit, Daniel Poneman, and Robert Gallucci, U.S. officials did in fact meet at the White House on June 16, 1994 to "help make a fateful decision on the number of additional troops to send to South Korea, and to deliberate further on the 'Osirak option.'" See Joel S. Wit, Daniel B. Poneman, and Robert L. Gallucci, *Going Critical: The First North Korean Nuclear Crisis* (Washing, DC: Brookings Institution Press, 2005), p. 220.

2. A case can be made that in light of 9/11 and the perceived link between global terrorism and nuclear proliferation, it would be only natural for the Bush administration to use the global frame in coping with the North Korean and Iran nuclear challenges. However, not all proliferation challenges have become a global problem. For instance, while India and Pakistan conducted nuclear tests in 1998 and were punished by a series of sanctions from the United States and other countries, the nuclear challenge in South Asia has since then been portrayed largely as an issue of regional rivalry. Moreover, the Bush administration even went on to sign a civilian nuclear cooperation deal with India.

3. Michael Armacost, "Daunting U.S. Tasks in Asia," *Japan Times*, January 11, 2005.

4. Glenn Kessler, *The Confidante: Condoleezza Rice and the Creation of the Bush Legacy* (New York: St Martin's Press, 2007), pp. 73–74.

5. For a useful conceptual discussion of the role of uncertainty in International Relations Theory, see Brian C. Rathbun, "Uncertain about Uncertainty: Understanding the Multiple Meanings of a Crucial Concept in International Relations Theory," *International Studies Quarterly* 51 (2007), pp. 533–557.

6. Robert Litwak, *Regime Change: U.S. Strategy through the Prism of 9/11* (Washington, DC: Woodrow Wilson Center Press, 2007), p. 8.

7. Michael Klare, *Rogue States and Nuclear Outlaws: America's Search for a New Foreign Policy* (New York: Hill and Wang, 1995), p. 140.

8. Wit, Poneman, Gallucci, *Going Critical*, pp. 32–33.

9. Ibid., p. 196.

10. K. D. Kapur, *Nuclear Diplomacy in East Asia: US and the Korean Nuclear Crisis Management* (New Delhi, India: Lancers Books, 1995), p. 152.

11. Tsuneo Akaha, "Japan's Policy toward North Korea," in Tsuneo Akaha, ed., *The Future of North Korea* (London: Routledge, 2002), p. 82.

12. Ashton B. Carter and William J. Perry *Preventive Defense: A New Security Strategy for America* (Washington, DC: Brookings Institution Press, 1999), p. 129.

13. "US, Japan, ROK Adopt United Front on North Korea," *Japan Times*, June 16, 1994, p. 1, cited in Kapur, *Nuclear Diplomacy in East Asia*, p. 352.

14. Ibid., p. 305.

15. Wit, Poneman, and Gallucci, *Going Critical*, pp. 208–209.
16. "Kakizawa Will Visit Seoul and Beijing," *Japan Times*, June 8 1994, p. 1, cited in K.D. Kapur, *Nuclear Diplomacy in East Asia: US and the Korean Nuclear Crisis Management* (New Delhi, India: Lancers Books, 1995), p. 355.
17. It is worth noting, however, that the Clinton administration's engagement policy toward North Korea was criticized by the Republican-dominated U.S. Congress, which ultimately resulted in the delayed implantation of the 1994 Agreed Framework, especially provision of heavy fuel oil, and the eventual collapse of the agreement in 2003.
18. *Implications of the U.S.-North Korea Nuclear Agreement*, Hearing before the Subcommittee on East Asian and Pacific Affairs of the Committee on Foreign Relations, United States Senate, One Hundred Third Congress, Second Session, December 1, 1994, p. 31.
19. David E. Sanger, "White House Memo; Global Realities Redefine Bush's Agenda," *New York Times*, June 11, 2001.
20. David E. Sanger, "Bush Tells Seoul Talks with North Won't Resume Now," *New York Times*, March 8, 2001.
21. Gary Samore, "The Korean Nuclear Crisis," *Survival* 45, no. 1 (Spring 2003), p. 16.
22. Leon V. Sigal, "Try Engagement for a Change," *Global Asia* 1, no. 1, p. 53.
23. *The National Security Strategy of the United States*, The White House, September 2002.
24. The preemption doctrine itself has been subject to criticism because preemption, as understood in international law, requires "incontrovertible evidence that an enemy attack is imminent." I thank Matthew Evangelista for clarifying this point. On both counts of imminence and degree of certainty, the Bush administration's use of the term as applied to the war in Iraq is problematic. As I elaborate further later in the chapter, the Bush administration deliberately conflated the meanings of preemption and prevention.
25. John Lewis Gaddis, "A Grand Strategy of Transformation," *Foreign Policy* 133 (2002), p. 50, cited in Roxanna Sjostedt, "The Discursive Origins of a Doctrine: Norms, Identity, and Securitization under Harry S. Truman and George W. Bush," *Foreign Policy Analysis* 3 (2007), pp. 233–254.
26. Alejandro Colas and Richard Saull, *The War on Terror and the American Empire after the Cold War* (New York: Routledge, 2006), p. 4.
27. Charles Krauthammer, "The Neoconservative Convergence," *Commentary*, July 5, 2005.
28. Christian Reus-Smit, *American Power and World Order* (Cambridge, UK: Polity, 2004), p. 38.
29. Lou Dubose and Jake Bernstein, *Vice: Dick Cheney and the Hijacking of the American Presidency* (New York: Random House, 2006), p. 94.
30. Ibid., p. 94.
31. Ibid., pp. 94–95.
32. Robert Jervis, "The Compulsive Empire," *Foreign Policy*, no. 137 (July/August 2003), p. 84.
33. *The Quadrennial Defense Review*, The Department of Defense, 2006, p. 30.
34. Michael Barnett defines framing as "conscious strategic efforts by groups of people to fashion shared understandings of the world and of themselves that legitimate collective action." See Michael Barnett, "The Israeli Identity and the Peace Process: Re/creating the Un/thinkable," in Shibley Telhami and Michael

Barnett, eds., *Identity and Foreign Policy in the Middle East* (Ithaca, NY: Cornell University Press, 2002), p. 69.

35. Elizabeth N. Saunders, "Setting Boundaries: Can International Society Exclude 'Rogue States?'" *International Studies Review* 8 (2006), pp. 25, 29.

36. For discussion of the concepts and change in emphasis, see Angus McColl, "Is Counterproliferation Compatible with Nonproliferation? Rethinking the Defense Counterproliferation Initiative," *Airpower Journal* 11 (Spring 1997), pp. 99–109; Jason D. Ellis, "The Best Defense: Counterproliferation and U.S. National Security," *The Washington Quarterly* 26, no. 2 (Spring 2003), pp. 115–133; Jeffrey Record, "Nuclear Deterrence, Preventive War, and Counterproliferation," *Policy Analysis*, No. 519, Cato Institute, July 8, 2004, available at http://object.cato.org/sites/cato.org/files/pubs/pdf/pa519.pdf.

37. Similar military strikes couched in the misguided notion of preemption include the allied attack on German nuclear facilities in Vermok in 1944, Iraqi destruction of the Iranian nuclear facilities in Busher in 1985 and 1987, and of course, the well-known Israeli attack on the Osirak reactor in Iraq in 1981. But these examples are fundamentally different from the Bush administration's drive in that the Bush Doctrine marked the first application of the preemption doctrine and signified a major shift in the global proliferation campaign.

38. George W. Bush, Remarks at 2002 Graduation Ceremony of the United States Military Academy, West Point, New York, June 1, 2002, available at http://www.whitehouse.gov/news/releases/2002/06/20020601-3.html.

39. Another example of violation of the global nonproliferation norm is the case of Israel. However, Israel's de facto nuclear status had been achieved long before the emergence of the nonproliferation regime.

40. Spurgeon M. Keenly, Jr., "South Asia's Nuclear Wake-Up Call," *Arms Control Today* 28, no. 4 (May 1998), p. 2; Nina Tannenwald, "The Nuclear Taboo: The United States and the Normative Basis of Nuclear Non-Use," *International Organization* 53, no. 3 (1999), pp. 433–468.

41. Peter L. Hays, Vincent J. Jodoin, and Alan R. van Tassel, eds., *Countering the Proliferation and Use of Weapons of Mass Destruction* (New York: McGraw-Hill, 1998); Counterproliferation Initiative Presidential Decision Directive PDD/NSC 18, December 1993, available at http://www.fas.org/irp/offdocs/pdd18.htm. Also McColl, "Is Counterproliferation Compatible with Nonproliferation?," p. 100.

42. Ellis, "The Best Defense," p. 116.

43. Robert S. Litwak, "Non-proliferation and the Dilemmas of Regime Change," *Survival* 45, no. 4 (Winter 2003–2004), p. 18. Also, McColl, "Is Counterproliferation Compatible with Nonproliferation?" p. 100; *Counterproliferation and Treaty Activities*, U.S. Department of Defense, available at http://www.defenselink.mil/execsec/adr95/cp.html.

44. Record, "Nuclear Deterrence, Preventive War, and Counterproliferation," p. 8.

45. *The National Security Strategy*, 2002, p. 15.

46. J. Bryan Hehir, "The New National Security Strategy," *America* 188, no. 12 (April 7, 2003), available at http://americamagazine.org/issue/429/article/new-national-security-strategy.

47. Philip C. Bleek, "Nuclear Posture Review Leaks; Outlines Targets, Contingencies," *Arms Control Today*, April 2002, available at http://www.armscontrol.org/act/2002_04/nprapril02.

48. Paul Richter, "U.S. Works Up Plan for Using Nuclear Arms Military," *Los Angeles Times*, March 9, 2002; *Nuclear Posture Review Report*, submitted to U.S. Congress, December 31, 2001, excerpt available at http://www.globalsecurity.org/wmd/library/policy/dod/npr.htm; also Record 2004, p. 8.

49. Seo-Hang Lee, "Global WMD Question: Issues and Policies," Institute for Foreign Affairs and National Security, January 17, 2003, p. 11.

50. *National Strategy to Combat Weapons of Mass Destruction*, December 2002, available at http://www.fas.org/irp/offdocs/nspd/nspd-17.html.

51. John Lewis Gaddis, "Grand Strategy in the Second Term," *Foreign Affairs* 84, no. 1 (Jan/Feb 2005), p. 4. Also see Litwak, "Non-proliferation and the Dilemmas of Regime Change," p. 18.

52. Cited in Litwak, "Non-proliferation and the Dilemmas of Regime Change, p. 17.

53. Joseph Cirincione, "How Will the Iraq War change global nonproliferation strategies?" *Arms Control Today* 33, no. 3 (April 2003), pp. 1–4.

54. Ibid., pp. 3–4.

55. Bill Keller, "The Thinkable," *New York Times*, May 4, 2003.

56. White House, Office of the Press Secretary, "President Bush Outlines Progress in Operation Iraqi Freedom," April 16, 2003, cited in Litwak, *Regime Change*, p. 93.

57. George W. Bush, Remarks at the U.S. Military Academy, West Point, 2002, available at http://www.whitehouse.gov/news/releases/2002/06/20020601-3.html.

58. Litwak, *Regime Change*, p. 266.

59. Ibid., pp. 262–263.

60. Jae-Jung Suh, *Power, Interest, and Identity in Military Alliances* (New York: Palgrave MacMillan, 2007), pp. 158–161.

61. Wit, Poneman, and Gallucci, *Going Critical*, p. 378.

62. Ibid., p. 378.

63. Paul Kerr, "North Korea Extends Missile-Test Moratorium; U.S. to Send Kelly," *Arms Control Today*, October 2002, available at http://www.armscontrol.org/act/2002_10/nkoreaoct02.

64. Michael D. Swaine, "U.S. Security Policy under Clinton and Bush: China and Korea," in Chae-Jin Lee, ed., *U.S. Security Policy Under Clinton and Bush: Continuity and Change*, Monograph Series, Number 17 (The Keck Center for International and Strategic Studies, Claremont McKenna College, 2005), pp. 70–71.

65. Karen DeYoung, *Soldier: The Life of Colin Powell* (New York: Alfred A. Knopf, 2006) p. 475.

66. *Donga Ilbo*, May 26, 2006.

67. Mel Gurtov, "The Bush Doctrine in Asia," in David P. Forsythe, Patrice C. McMahon, and Andrew Wedeman, eds., *American Foreign Policy in a Globalized World* (London: Routledge, 2006), p. 294.

68. Litwak, *Regime Change*, p. 257.

69. Michael J. Mazarr, *North Korea and the Bomb: A Case Study in Nonproliferation* (New York: St. Martin's press, 1995), p. 115.

70. DeYoung, *Soldier*, p. 475.

71. Ibid., p. 499.

72. Dubose and Bernstein, *Vice*, p. 185.

73. Wit, Poneman, and Gallucci, *Going Critical*, p. 400.

74. Litwak, *Regime Change*, p. 329.

75. *The Quadrennial Defense Review*, the Department of Defense, 2006, p. 34.

76. Walter Pincus, "Rumsfeld States Case for Burrowing Weapon," *Washington Post*, February 17, 2005.

77. David E. Sanger, "Dueling Views Pit Baker Against Rice," *New York Times*, December 8, 2006.

78. "Off the Record Interview with U.S. Defense Department Office," *Yomiuri Shimbun*, December 1, 2002, cited in C. Kenneth Quinones, "Dualism in the Bush Administration's North Korea Policy," *Asian Perspective* 27, no. 1 (2003), p. 222.

79. David L. Greene and Mark Matthews, "Bush: U.S. Could Use Force against N. Korea; Military Action Would Be His 'Last Choice,'" *Baltimore Sun*, March 4, 2003.

80. John R. Bolton, Under Secretary for Arms Control and International Security, "The New World After Iraq: The Continuing Threat of Weapons of Mass Destruction," Remarks to the Bruges Group, London, United Kingdom, October 30, 2003, available at http://www.brugesgroup.com/mediacentre/speeches.live?article=191.

81. "Iran Next on W's List," *New York Daily News*, April 1, 2003, cited in Chung-in Moon and Jong-Yun Bae, "The Bush Doctrine and the North Korean Nuclear Crisis," *Asian Perspective* 27, no. 4 (December 2003), p. 31.

82. David E. Sanger, "The World: Over There; A New Front Opens, But It's Still One," *New York Times*, October 20, 2002.

83. Nicholas Kristof, "Secret, Scary Plans," *New York Times*, February 28, 2003.

84. Stephen M. Walt, *Taming American Power: The Global Response to U.S. Primacy* (New York: W.W. Norton & Company, 2005), p. 224.

85. Walt, *Taming American Power*, p. 247.

86. Takeshi Igarashi, "The Evolution of Japan–US Relations," *Japan Review of International Affairs* 18 (Spring 2004), pp. 15–16.

87. Interview 09–05, Beijing, April 22, 2005; Interview 15–05, Beijing, April 29, 2005.

88. Interview 04–04, Beijing, November 10, 2004; Interview 05–04, Beijing, November 11, 2004; Interview 07–04, Beijing, November 16, 2004; Interview 09–04, Beijing, November 22, 2004; Interview 11–04, Beijing, November 23, 2004.

89. A South Korean security expert at a government-affiliated think tank even observed that North Korean provocations have been speeding up Japan's progress toward normal statehood beyond the constitutional constraints to about ten years faster than otherwise would have occurred. Interview 25–05, Seoul, May 13, 2005.

90. Interview 01–04, Tokyo, September 30, 2004.

91. "The Six-Party Talks and 'China Factor,'" *People's Daily*, July 28, 2005.

92. "China Calls for Efforts to End Korean Nuclear Standoff," *People's Daily*, March 5, 2005.

93. Jing-dong Yuan, "The Bush Doctrine: Chinese Perspectives and Responses," *Asian Perspective* 27, no. 4 (2003), p. 126; also Piao Jianyi, "The Six-Party Talks Process & the Role of China and Japan," speech at a lecture luncheon of the 4th "Japan-China Dialogue," hosted by The Tokyo Club, The Council on East Asian Community (CEAC), The Global Forum of Japan (GF), and China Association for International Friendly Contact at International House of Japan, Tokyo, Japan, on September 16–17, 2004, available at http://www.iapscass.cn/english/publications/showcontent.asp?id=98.

94. *Chosun Ilbo*, November 13, 2004.

95. Masao Okonogi, "Dealing with the Threat of a Korean Crisis," *Japan Review of International Affairs* 17, no. 2 (Summer 2003), p. 74; Interview 29–05, July 14, 2004, Tokyo, Japan.

96. "Koizumi seeks normalized ties with DPRK by end of his term," *Yomiuri Shimbun*, July 20, 2005.

97. Fareed Zakaria, "Time for China to Step Up," *Newsweek*, March 3, 2003, U.S. Edition.

98. Thomas L. Friedman, "Brussels Sprouts," *New York Times*, May 11, 2005.

99. Dafna Linzer, "U.S. Says China Should Prod N. Korea on Talks," *Washington Post*, June 24, 2005.

100. Glenn Kessler and Dafna Linzer, "Nuclear Evidence Could Point To Pakistan," *Washington Post*, February 3, 2005.

101. Chung-in Moon and Jong-Yun Bae, "The Bush Doctrine and the North Korean nuclear crisis," in Mel Gurtov and Peter Van Ness, eds., *Confronting the Bush Doctrine: Critical Views from the Asia-Pacific* (London: RoutledgeCurzon, 2005), p. 50.

102. Kongdan Oh and Ralph C. Hassig, "North Korea's Nuclear Politics," *Current History*, September 2004, pp. 278–279.

103. Jae Ho Chung, "China's Korea Policy Under the New Leadership: Stealth Changes in the Making?" *The Journal of East Asian Affairs* XVIII, no. 1 (Spring/ Summer 2004), p. 8.

104. Samuel S. Kim, "China's New Role in the Nuclear Confrontation," *Asian Perspective* 28, no. 4, p. 162; Interview 04–04, November 10, 2005, Beijing, China. Similarly, it is worth noting that among China's three positions on the North Korean nuclear issue the statement that "peace and stability on the Korean Peninsula should be preserved" is the first. The others include "the peninsula should remain nuclear-free," and "the dispute should be resolved through diplomatic and political methods." See Jing-dong Yuan, "China and the North Korean Nuclear Crisis," Center for Nonproliferation Studies, available at http://cns.miis.edu/research/korea/chidprk.htm.

105. Zhenqiang Pan, "Solution for the Nuclear Issue of North Korea, Hopeful But Still Uncertain: On the Conclusion of the Second Round of the Six-Party Talks," *The Journal of East Asian Affairs* XVIII, no. 1 (Spring/Summer 2004), p. 36.

106. Interview 40–05, Seoul, August 5, 2005.

107. Takeshi Igarashi, "The Evolution of Japan-US Relations," *Japan Review of International Affairs*, Spring 2004, p. 15.

108. "Missiles not Welcome in Global Town Square," *Asahi Shimbun*, January 25, 2005.

109. Christopher W. Hughes, *Japan's Re-emergence as a "Normal" Military Power*, *Adelphi Paper* 368–9 (London: The International Institute for Strategic Studies, 2005), p. 43.

110. Yoshihide Soeya, "Democratization in Northeast Asia and Trilateral Cooperation," p. 95.

111. Katsu Furukawa, "Japan's View of the Korea Crisis," Center for Nonproliferation Studies, Monterey Institute of International Studies, February 25, 2003, available at http://cns.miis.edu/research/korea/jpndprk.htm.

112. *Joongang Ilbo*, January 4, 2005.

113. Ching Cheong, "Beijing unwilling to resort to arm-twisting," *Strait Times*, Feb 19, 2005.

114. *Joongang Ilbo*, December 6, 2004.
115. *Donga Ilbo*, December 23, 2004.
116. "The Proliferation Security Initiative (PSI) At a Glance," Arms Control Association, June 2004, available at http://www.armscontrol.org/factsheets/PSI.asp.
117. John Kerin, "Fear US Will Push N Korea into Fight," *The Australian*, July 10, 2003, cited in Rebecca Weiner, "Proliferation Security Initiative to Stem Flow of WMD Matériel," July 16, 2003, Center for Nonproliferation Studies, available at http://cns.miis.edu/pubs/week/030716.htm.
118. "Resolving the North Korean Nuclear Problem: A Regional Approach and the Role of Japan," *JIIA Policy Report*, Project for Northeast Asian Security, The Japan Institute of International Affairs, July 2005, p. 9.
119. Gavan McCormack, "Remilitarizing Japan," *New Left Review* 29 (September/October 2004), p. 43.
120. Dingli Shen, "Accepting a Nuclear North Korea," *Far Eastern Economic Review* 168 (March 2005), pp. 51–54.
121. Interview 07–04, Beijing, November 16, 2004.
122. Doug Struck and Glenn Kessler, "Foes Giving in to N. Korea's Nuclear Aims," *Washington Post*, March 5, 2003.
123. Interview 30–05, Tokyo, July 15, 2005.
124. Interview 07–05, Beijing, April 18, 2005.
125. The view, offered by Hyun-ick Hong of the Sejong Institute in South Korea, was quoted in *Seoul Shinmun*, October 30, 2003.
126. Interview 09–04, Beijing, November 22, 2004.
127. Interview 12–05, Beijing, April 26, 2005; Interview 18–05, Beijing, May 1, 2005; Interview 19–05, Beijing, May 2, 2005; Interview 25–05, Seoul, May 13, 2005; Interview 40–05, Seoul, August 5, 2005.
128. Shen, "Accepting a Nuclear North Korea," p. 54.
129. Interview 25–05, Seoul, May 13, 2005.
130. Michael D. Swaine, "U.S. Security Policy under Clinton and Bush: China and Korea," in Chae-Jin Lee, ed., *U.S. Security Policy Under Clinton and Bush: Continuity and Change*, Monograph Series, Number 17 (The Keck Center for International and Strategic Studies, Claremont McKenna College), 2005, pp. 74–75.
131. Interview 12–05, Beijing, April 26, 2005.
132. Interview 09–05, Beijing, April 22, 2005.
133. Interview 10–05, Beijing, April 23, 2005; Interview 12–05, Beijing, April 26, 2005.
134. Interview 10–04, Beijing, November 22, 2004.
135. *Shindonga*, March 2005.
136. Interview 08–05, Beijing, April 20, 2005.
137. Xun Sun, "Lun yirake zhanzheng dui guoji hekuosan jizhi de yingxiang [The Analysis of the Impact of the Second Iraqi War on International Nonproliferation Mechanism]," *Guoji Luntan [International Forum]* 5, no. 5 (September 2003), pp. 9–15; Interview 08–05, Beijing, April 20, 2005.
138. Piao, "The Six-Party Talks Process & the Role of China and Japan."
139. Evan S. Medeiros, "Strategic Hedging and the Future of Asia-Pacific Stability," *The Washington Quarterly* 29, no. 1 (Winter 2005–2006), p. 158.
140. Interview 07–05, Beijing, April 18, 2005.
141. Interview 41–05, Seoul, August 5, 2005.
142. Yong Deng, "Better Than Power: 'International Status' in Chinese Foreign Policy," in Yong Deng and Fei-Ling Wang, eds., *China Rising: Power and*

Motivation in Chinese Foreign Policy (Lanham, MD: Rowman and Littlefield Publishers, 2005), pp. 61–62.

143. Chu Shulong, "China's Perspectives on the Regional and World Order Since 9/11," in Han Sung-Ju, ed., *Coping with 9–11: Asian Perspectives on Global and Regional Order* (Tokyo: Japan Center for International Exchange, 2003), p. 31.

144. Liu Ming, "Opportunities and Challenges for Sino-American Cooperation on the Korean Peninsula," *The Korean Journal of Defense Analysis* XVI, no. 1 (Spring 2004), p. 138.

145. Howard W. French, "Doubting U.S., China Is Wary of Korea Role," *New York Times*, February 19, 2005.

146. Interview 35–05, Seoul, August 3, 2005.

147. Kong Quan, Foreign Ministry Briefing, Beijing, China, February 5, 2002, cited in Anne Wu, "What China Whispers to North Korea," *The Washington Quarterly* 28, no. 2 (Spring 2005), p. 40.

148. Harvey Stockwin, "The Qian Qichen Op-ed: Official Discontent or Just one Man's Opinion?," Jamestown Foundation, *China Brief* 4, no. 24 (December 7, 2004).

149. "Committing to U.S. strategy," *Japan Times*, May 5, 2006.

150. Daniel M. Kliman, *Japan's Security Strategy in the Post-9/11 World: Embracing a New Realpolitik* (Westport: Praeger, 2006), p. 14.

151. "Committing to U.S. strategy."

152. "Resolving the North Korean Nuclear Problem: A Regional Approach and the Role of Japan," *JIIA Policy Report*, Project for Northeast Asian Security, The Japan Institute of International Affairs, July 2005, p. ix.

153. Mizushima Asaho, "A New Security Framework for Northeast Asia," *Japan Focus*, 2004, available at http://japanfocus.org/article.asp?id=048.

154. Nicholas D. Kristof, "Talking to Evil," *New York Times*, August 13, 2006.

CHAPTER 3

1. At a news conference in July 2005, Prime Minister Koizumi reiterated his hope of finalizing diplomatic normalization with North Korea within his term as prime minister. *Joongang Ilbo*, July 19, 2005.

2. Interview with a South Korean security expert of a Unification Ministry–affiliated research institute, Interview 35–05, Seoul, August 3, 2005.

3. Interview with a senior Chinese regional security expert at Peking University, Interview 16–05, Beijing, April 30, 2005.

4. Heungho Moon, "Dongbuka dajaanbo hyupryukgwa Joonggukui yokhwal [Northeast Asian Multilateral Cooperation and China's Role]," in Hyunik Hong and Daewoo Lee, eds., *Dongbuka Dajaanbo Hyupryukgwa Joobyunsagan [Northeast Asian Multilateral Cooperation and the Neighboring Four Powers]* (Seoul: Sejong Institute, 2001), p. 101.

5. Ibid., p. 117.

6. Youngsun Song, "Dajaanbo hyupruke daehan Ilbonui sigakgwa jeonmang [Japan's view of Multilateral Security Cooperation and Its Prospect]," in Hyunik Hong and Daewoo Lee, eds., *Dongbuka Dajaanbo Hyupryukgwa Joobyunsagan [Northeast Asian Multilateral Cooperation and the Neighboring Four Powers]* (Seoul: Sejong Institute, 2001), p. 85.

7. Tsuneo Akaha, "Japan's Policy toward North Korea," in Tsuneo Akaha, ed., *The Future of North Korea* (London: Routledge, 2002), pp. 82, 84.

8. Tsuneo Akaha, "Japan's Multilevel Approach toward the Korean Peninsula after the Cold War," in Charles K. Armstrong, Gilbert Rozman, Samuel S. Kim, and Stephen Kotkin, eds., *Korea at the Center: Dynamics of Regionalism in Northeast Asia* (Armonk, NY: M.E. Sharpe, Inc., 2006), p. 191.

9. Ibid., p. 188.

10. The text of the statement made by South Korean Foreign Minister Ban Ki-moon at the 59th Session of the United Nations General Assembly, September 24, 2004, Ministry of Foreign Affairs, the Republic of Korea, p. 4.

11. Gilbert Rozman, *Northeast Asia's Stunted Regionalism: Bilateral Distrust in the Shadow of Globalization* (Cambridge, UK: Cambridge University Press, 2004), p. 370.

12. Interview 01–04, Tokyo, September 30, 2004; Interview 01–05, Tokyo, February 3, 2005; Interview 34–05, Tokyo, July 27, 2005.

13. Yongchul Ha et al., *Bukbang Jeongchaek [Nordpolitik]* (Seoul: Seoul National University Press, 2003); Tsuneo Akaha, "Conclusion: Nationalism Versus Regionalism in Northeast Asia," in Tsuneo Akaha, ed., *Politics and Economics in Northeast Asia: Nationalism and Regionalism in Contention* (New York: St. Martin's Press, 1999), p. 372.

14. Akaha, p. 372; Moonseok Ahn, *Bukhani Pilyohan Miguk, Miguki Pilyohan Bukhan [A United States That Needs North Korea, A North Korea That Needs the United States]* (Seoul, Korea: Park Young-Yul Publishing House, 2006), pp. 145–146.

15. Anthony Spaeth, "The American Presence: How Long Can the U.S. Stay?" *Time*, June 12, 2000.

16. Eric V. Larson, Norman D. Levin with Seonhae Baik, Bogdan Savych, *Ambivalent Allies?: A Study of South Korean Attitudes toward the U.S.* (Santa Monica, CA: the Rand Corporation, 2004), p. 24.

17. Cheol Hee Park, "Japanese Strategic Thinking toward Korea," in Gilbert Rozman, Kazuhiko Togo, and Joseph P. Ferguson, eds., *Japanese Strategic Thought toward Asia* (New York: Palgrave Macmillan, 2007), p. 190.

18. Hong Soon-Young, "21segi tongsanjilseowa wooriui tongsang woigyo jeongchaek banghayng [The 21st Century Trade Order and Our Trade and Foreign Policy Prospects]," Speech at the Korean Trade Association, August 27, 1999, p. 143.

19. John Feffer, "Grave Threats and Grand Bargains: The United States and Regional Order in Northeast Asia," in John Feffer, ed., *The Future of US–Korean Relations* (New York: Routledge, 2006), p. 194.

20. Byung-joon Ahn, "The Impact of the U.S.–Japan Defense Cooperation Guidelines," Institute on Global Conflict and Cooperation, *IGCC Policy Papers*, 1998, p. 13.

21. Ibid.

22. Younghee Lee, "Dongbuka jiyokui pyonghwa jilseo guchukul wihan jeon [A Contribution toward the Formation of New International Order in Northeast Asia]," in Bansegiui Shinhwa [*A Myth of the Past Half-Century*] (Seoul: Samin, 1999), pp. 245–246.

23. Hong Soon-Young, "Changing Dynamics in Northeast Asia and the Republic of Korea's Engagement Policy toward North Korea," speech at the 27th Williamsburg Conference, Cheju, May 7, 1999, in Selected Speeches and Strategies by Mr. Hong Soon-Young, Minister of Foreign Affairs and Trade, August 1998–December 1999 (Seoul: Ministry of Foreign Affairs and Trade, 1999), p. 81.

24. Scott Snyder, "South Korea's Squeeze Play," *The Washington Quarterly* 28, no. 4 (Autumn 2005), p. 102.

25. Dongman Seo, "Nambuk jungsang hoidamgwa gukjehyupryuk [Inter-Korean Summit and International Cooperation]," in *Jungsang hoidam yihoo Nambuk gwangye gaesonjollyak [Post-2000 Summit Strategy for Improving Inter-Korean Relations]*, The Sejong Institute (Seoul: Sejong Institute, 2000), p. 40.

26. Ibid., p. 53.

27. *Donga Ilbo*, September 17, 2012.

28. Interview 36–05, Seoul, August 3, 2005.

29. Choong Nam Kim, "The Sunshine Policy and Its Impact on South Korea's Relations with Major Powers," *Korea Observer* 35, no. 4 (Winter 2004), p. 608.

30. Government Information Agency, Seoul, Korea, available at http://www.allim.go.kr/jsp/dataroom/dataroom_news_view.jsp?id=65,055,344.

31. Anthony Faiola and Joohee Cho, "Perils of Investing in N. Korea Become Clear to a Pioneer," *Washington Post*, November 24, 2005.

32. See the official South Korean website of the Kaesung Industrial Complex, http://gaeseong.lplus.or.kr/sales/sub4.php.

33. Interview 37–05, Seoul, August 4, 2005.

34. Others instead use different terms, such as "pan-Korean nationalism," to denote essentially the same meaning of inter-Korean nationalism, see Jiyul Kim, "Pan-Korean Nationalism, Anti-Great Power-ism and U.S.-South Korean Relations," *Japan Focus*, December 13, 2005.

35. Gi-Wook Shin and Paul Y. Chang, "The Politics of Nationalism in U.S.-Korean Relations," *Asian Perspective* 28, no. 4 (2004), p. 139.

36. Sook-Jong Lee, "Allying with the United States: Changing South Korean Attitudes," *Korean Journal of Defense Analysis* XVII/1 (Spring 2005), p. 94.

37. Kim, *Japan Focus*.

38. Larson and Levin, *Ambivalent Allies?* p. 97.

39. Kim, "The Sunshine Policy," p. 596.

40. Interview with former Unification Minister Jung Se Hyun, *Shindonga*, March 2005.

41. Larson and Levin, *Ambivalent Allies?*, p. 35.

42. Kim, "Pan-Korean Nationalism."

43. Kang Choi, "A View on America's Role in Asia and the Future of the ROK-U.S. Alliance," in *The Newly Emerging Asian Order and the Korean Peninsula*, Joint U.S.-Korea Academic Studies, Korea Economic Institute, Washington, DC, 2005, p. 225.

44. Kim, "Pan-Korean Nationalism."

45. Interview 22–05, Seoul, May 12, 2005; Interview 41–05, Seoul, August 5, 2005.

46. Interview 22–05, Seoul, May 12, 2005; Interview 24–05, Seoul, May 13, 2005; Interview 25–05, Seoul, May 13, 2005.

47. Interview 21–05, Seoul, May 11, 2005.

48. Larson and Levin, *Ambivalent Allies?* p. 34.

49. Interview 24–05, Seoul, May 13, 2005.

50. Mel Gurtov, "The Bush Doctrine in Asia," in David P. Forsythe, Patrice C. McMahon, and Andrew Wedeman, eds., *American Foreign Policy in a Globalized World* (London: Routledge, 2006), p. 297.

51. Emanuel Pastreich, "The Balancer: Roh Moo-hyun's Vision of Korean Politics and the Future of Northeast Asia," *Japan Focus*, August 1, 2005.

52. *Yonhap News*, May 10, 2006.
53. Sang-Hun Choe, "South Korea Proposes Meeting with North Korea," *New York Times*, May 11, 2006.
54. *Donga Ilbo*, June 4, 2008.
55. *Chosun Ilbo*, June 4, 2008.
56. "China, ROK Must 'Work Closely' for E. Asian Bloc," *People's Daily*, January 12, 2010.
57. Blaine Harden, "South Korean Voters Opt for Reason over Confrontation' with the North," *Washington Post*, June 5, 2010.
58. *Donga Ilbo*, October 31, 2011.
59. Chico Harlan, "S. Korean President Sees 'Window' to Deal with North," *Washington Post*, January 2, 2012.
60. Chico Harlan, "S. Korea Fails to Block Activists from Dropping Propaganda Leaflets in North," *Washington Post*, October 22, 2012.
61. Russel Ong, *China's Security Interests in the Post-Cold War Era* (London: Curzon Press, 2002), p. 3.
62. Samuel S. Kim, "The Making of China's Korean Policy in the Era of Reform," in David Lampton, ed., *The Making of Chinese Foreign and Security Policy in the Era of Reform* (Stanford, CA: Stanford University Press, 2001), p. 408.
63. Chen Zhimin, "Nationalism, Internationalism, and Chinese Foreign Policy," *Journal of Contemporary China* 14, no. 42 (February 2005), p. 47.
64. Feng Ni, "The Shaping of China's Foreign Policy," in Ryosei Kokubun and Jisi Wang, eds., *The Rise of China and a Changing East Asian Order* (Tokyo: Japan Center for International Exchange, 2004), p. 144. Early signs of such shift emerged in the early 1990s when China's previous emphasis on a Third World identity had to be toned down. For an interesting discussion of China's search for its national identity, see Lowell Dittmer and Samuel S. Kim, eds., *China's Quest for National Identity* (Ithaca, NY: Cornell University Press, 1993).
65. Jianwei Wang, "Adjusting to a 'Strong-Strong Relationship': China's Calculus of Japan's Asian Policy," in Takashi Inoguchi, ed., *Japan's Asian Policy: Revival and Response* (New York: Palgrave MacMillan, 2002), p. 109.
66. "China's Diplomacy Enters Golden Age: Senior Diplomat," *People's Daily*, September 11, 2005.
67. Avery Goldstein points out China's strong support for the international non-proliferation regime as one such effort on display. See his *Rising to the Challenge: China's Grand Strategy and International Security* (Stanford, CA: Stanford University Press, 2005), p. 121.
68. Evan Medeiros, "Agents of Influence: Assessing the Role of Chinese Foreign Policy Research Organizations after the 16th Party Congress," in Andrew Scobell and Larry Wortzel, eds., *Civil-Military Change in China: Elites, Institutes, and Ideas after the 16th Party Congress*, Strategic Studies Institute, Army War College, September 2004, p. 297.
69. Xinbo Wu, "Four Contradictions Constraining China's Foreign Policy Behavior," *Journal of Contemporary China* 10, no. 27 (2001), p. 293.
70. Avery Goldstein, *Rising to the Challenge: China's Grand Strategy and International Security* (Stanford, CA: Stanford University Press, 2005), p. 26, 118.
71. Yong Deng and Fei-Ling Wang, "Introduction," in Yong Deng and Fei-Ling Wang, eds., *China Rising: Power and Motivation in Chinese Foreign Policy* (Lanham, MD: Rowman and Littlefield Publishers, 2005), p. 10.

72. Jin Canrong, "The US Global Strategy in the Post-Cold War Era and Its Implications for China–United States Relations: A Chinese perspective," *Journal of Contemporary China* 10, no. 27) (2001), p. 315.

73. Jia Qingguo, "Learning to Live with the Hegemon: Evolution of China's Policy toward the US Since the End of the Cold War," *Journal of Contemporary China* 14, no. 44 (August 2005), p. 407.

74. Suisheng Zhao, "China's Pragmatic Nationalism: Is It Manageable?" *The Washington Quarterly* 29, no. 1 (Winter 2005–2006), p. 136.

75. Allen Carlson, *Unifying China and Integrating with the World* (Stanford, CA: Stanford University Press, 2005), p. 248.

76. Quansheng Zhao, "China and Major Power Relations in East Asia," *Journal of Contemporary China* 10, no. 29 (2001), p. 668.

77. Yong Deng, "Better Than Power: 'International Status' in Chinese Foreign Policy," in Yong Deng and Fei-Ling Wang, eds., *China Rising: Power and Motivation in Chinese Foreign Policy* (Lanham, MD: Rowman and Littlefield Publishers, 2005), p. 65.

78. "China's Position Paper on the New Security Concept," Ministry of Foreign Affairs, the People's Republic of China, July 31, 2002.

79. David M. Finkelstein, "China's 'New Concept of Security,'" in Stephen J. Flanagan and Michael E. Marti, eds., *The People's Liberation Army and China in Transition* (Washington, DC: National Defense University Press, 2003), pp. 197–198.

80. Sha Zukang, "Some Thoughts on Establishing A New Regional Security Order," Statement by Ambassador Sha Zukang at the East-West Center's Senior Policy Seminar, August 7, 2000, Honolulu, Hawaii, http://www.fmprc.gov.cn/eng/wjb/zzjg/jks/cjjk/2622/t15411.htm.

81. Thomas G. Moore, "Chinese Foreign Policy in the Age of Globalization," in Yong Deng and Fei-Ling Wang, eds., *China Rising: Power and Motivation in Chinese Foreign Policy* (Lanham, MD: Rowman and Littlefield Publishers, 2005), p. 138.

82. Shale Horowitz and Min Ye, "China's Grand Strategy, the Korean Nuclear Crisis, and the Six-Party Talks," paper presented at the International Studies Association annual meeting, Chicago, March 2007, p. 7.

83. Samuel S. Kim, "The Making of China's Korean Policy in the Era of Reform," in David Lampton, ed., *The Making of Chinese Foreign and Security Policy in the Era of Reform* (Stanford, CA: Stanford University Press, 2001), p. 372.

84. Russell Ong, *China's Security Interests in the Post-Cold War Era* (London, UK: Curzon Press, 2002), p. 53.

85. Jisi Wang, "China's Changing Role in Asia," in Ryosei Kokubun and Jisi Wang, eds., *The Rise of China and a Changing East Asian Order* (Tokyo: Japan Center for International Exchange, 2004), p. 9.

86. Samuel S. Kim, "China and the Future of the Korean Peninsula," Tsuneo Akaha, ed., *The Future of North Korea* (London: Routledge, 2002), p. 113.

87. Kay Meller and Markus Tidten, "North Korea and the Bomb: Radicalization in Isolation," *Aussenpolitik* 45, no. 1 (1994), p. 108, cited in Ong, *China's Security Interests in the Post-Cold War Era*, p. 69.

88. Susan L. Shirk, *China: Fragile Superpower* (New York: Oxford University Press, 2007), p. 123.

89. Xiaoxing Yi, "A Neutralized Korea? The North-South Rapprochement and China's Korea Policy," *Korean Journal of Defense Analysis* XII, no. 2 (Winter 2000), p. 79.

90. Jae Ho Chung, "China's Korea Policy under the New Leadership: Stealth Changes in the Making?" *The Journal of East Asian Affairs* XVIII, no. 1 (Spring/ Summer 2004), p. 9; Samuel S. Kim, "China's New Role in the Nuclear Confrontation," *Asian Perspective* 28, no. 4 (2004), p. 151.

91. Interview 09–04, Beijing, November 22, 2004; Interview 11–04, Beijing, November 23, 2004; Interview 09–05, Beijing, April 22, 2005; Interview 23–05, Seoul, May 12, 2005.

92. Interview 09–05, Beijing, April 22, 2005; Interview 38–05, Seoul, August 4, 2005.

93. Andrew Scobell, *China and North Korea: From Comrades-in-Arms to Allies at Arm's Length* (Carlisle, PA: The Strategic Studies Institute, U.S. Army War College, 2004), available at http://www.strategicstudiesinstitute.army.mil/ pdffiles/PUB373.pdf, pp. 19–20.

94. Shi Yinhong's view was cited in Baohui Zhang, "American Hegemony and China's U.S. Policy," *Asian Perspective* 28, no. 3 (2004), p. 101.

95. Shen Jiru, "Weihu dongbeiya anchuan-de dangwu deji—Zhizhi chaohewenti shangde weixian boyi [An Urgent Matter in Order to Maintain Security in Northeast Asia—How to Stop the Dangerous Games in the North Korean Nuclear Crisis]," *Shijie Jingji yu Zhengzhi* [*World Economics and Politics*], no. 9 (September 2003), pp. 57–58.

96. *Joongang Ilbo*, August 20, 2004.

97. Audra Ang, "Experts: China Is Weighing Stronger Measures against North Korea," *Associated Press*, October 21, 2006.

98. Interview 13–04, Beijing, November 24, 2004.

99. Interview 15–05, Beijing, April 29, 2005.

100. Calum MacLeod, "China Supports Punitive Actions against North Korea," *USA Today*, October 10, 2006.

101. "Developing Friendly Ties with DPRK 'unchanged,'" *China Daily*, October 10, 2006.

102. Interview 38–5, Seoul, August 4, 2005. For a useful summary of the liability and buffer zone camps, see You Ji, "Understanding China's North Korea Policy," *China Brief*, The Jamestown Foundation IV, no. 5 (March 3, 2004), pp. 1–3.

103. Interview 04–04, Beijing, November 10, 2004; Interview 07–04, Beijing, November 16, 2004; Interview 10–04, Beijing, November 22, 2004; Interview 07–05, Beijing, April 18, 2005.

104. Interview 04–04, Beijing, November 10, 2004; Interview 07–04, Beijing, November 16, 2004; Interview 10–04, Beijing, November 22, 2004; Interview 09–05, Beijing, April 22, 2005.

105. Interview 08–05, Beijing, April 20, 2005; Interview 09–05, Beijing, April 22, 2005.

106. Interview13–04, Beijing, November 24, 2004.

107. Interview 02–04, Beijing, November 3, 2004; Interview 07–04, Beijing, November 16, 2004; Interview 11–04, Beijing, November 23, 2004; Interview 13–04, Beijing, November 24, 2004; Interview 14–05, Beijing, April 28, 2005.

108. Interview 05–04, Beijing, November 11, 2004; Interview 07–04, Beijing, November 16, 2004; Interview 13–04, Beijing, November 24, 2004; Interview 08–05, Beijing, April 20, 2005.

109. Xu Weidi, "Chaoxianbandu weijide huajie yu bandu zouchu lengzhan [Resolving the Korean Peninsula Nuclear Crisis and Moving the Korean Peninsula out

of the Cold War]," *Shijie Jingji yu Zhengzhi* [*World Economics and Politics*], no. 9 (September 2003), pp. 59–64.

110. Ibid., p. 64.

111. Yu Bin, *Containment by Stealth: Chinese Views of and Policies toward America's Alliances with Japan and Korea after the Cold War*, Asia Pacific Research Center, Stanford University, September 1999, p. 14.

112. Xinfeng Jiang, "US-Japan Military Alliance Reflects Cold War Mentality," *People's Daily*, November 5, 2005; Interview 09–04, Beijing, November 22, 2004; Interview 11–04, Beijing, November 23, 2004; Interview 07–05, Beijing, April 18, 2005.

113. Yu Wanli, "Washington's East Asia Policy Needs Adjustment, Comment," *People's Daily*, November 28, 2005; Minxin Pei, "A Fresh Approach on China," *International Herald Tribune*, September 9, 2005.

114. "China's Diplomacy: Pursuing Balance to Reach Harmony," *People's Daily*, December 27, 2005.

115. "Chinese Gov't 'Resolutely Opposes' DPRK's Nuclear Test," *People's Daily*, May 25, 2009.

116. David Hundt, "China's 'Two Koreas' Policy: Achievements and Contradictions," *Political Science* 62 (2010), p. 136.

117. Blaine Harden, "In North Korea, the Military Now Issues Economic Orders," *Washington Post*, November 3, 2009.

118. Lim Soo-Ho, "China–North Korea Relations and Rajin-Sonbong Special Economic Zone," *SERI Quarterly*, Samsung Economic Research Institute, July 2010, p. 123.

119. "Chinese President Calls for Calm to Avoid Escalating Tension on Korean Peninsula," *People's Daily*, December 6, 2010.

120. Ian Johnson and Helene Cooper, "China Seeks Talks to Ease Korean Tension," *New York Times*, November 28, 2010.

121. Feng Zhu, "Flawed Mediation and a Compelling Mission: Chinese Diplomacy in the Six-Party Talks to Denuclearise North Korea," *East Asia* 28 (2011), p. 192.

122. Robert Sutter, *Chinese Foreign Relations: Power and Policy Since the Cold War*, Third Edition (Lanham, MD: Rowman & Littlefield, 2012), pp. 201–202.

123. "More Top Chinese Leaders Mourn Kim Jong Il as Beijing Seeks to Reassure Pyongyang," *Associated Press*, December 21, 2011.

124. "Top DPRK Leader Meets Senior Chinese Official on Relations," *Xinhua*, August 3, 2012.

125. Choe Sang-Hun, "North Korean Official Cements Status in Beijing Visit," *New York Times*, August 17, 2012.

126. Shan Renping, "South Should Encourage North Korea," *Global Times*, July 11, 2012.

127. Gilbert Rozman, "Japanese Views of the Great Powers in the New World Order," in David Jacobson, ed., *Old Nations, New World: Conceptions of World Order* (Boulder, CO: Westview Press, 1994), p. 17.

128. *Diplomatic Bluebook 1991: Japan's Diplomatic Activities*, Ministry of Foreign Affairs, p. 24, cited in Togo, p. 307.

129. Haruko Satoh, "The Odd Couple: Japan and China—The Politics of History and Identity," *JIIA Commentary*, no. 4, The Japan Institute of International Affairs, August 4, 2006, p. 6, available at http://yaleglobal.yale.edu/content/odd-couple-japan-and-china-politics-history-and-identity.

130. Wolf Mendl, *Japan's Asia Policy: Regional Security and Global Interests* (London: Routledge, 1995), p. 47.

131. See, for example, Kevin J. Cooney, *Japan's Foreign Policy Maturation: A Quest for Normalcy* (New York: Routledge, 2002); Susanne Klien, *Rethinking Japan's Identity and International Role: An Intercultural Perspective* (New York: Routledge, 2002), p. 169; Interview 01–05, Tokyo, February 3, 2005; Interview 31–05, Tokyo, July 21, 2005; Interview 33–05, Tokyo, July 27, 2005.

132. Kazuhiko Togo, *Japan's Foreign Policy 1945–2003: The Quest for a Proactive Policy* (Boston: Brill, 2005), p. 412.

133. Klien, *Rethinking Japan's Identity and International Role*, p. 169.

134. Akio Watanabe, "Has Japan Crossed the Rubicon? Defense Policy Since the Higuchi Report," *Japan Review of International Affairs* 17, no. 4 (Winter 2003), pp. 238–254.

135. Klien, *Rethinking Japan's Identity*, p. 168; Watanabe, "Has Japan Crossed the Rubicon?" pp. 239–241.

136. Tsuyoshi Hasegawa, "Japan's Strategic Thinking toward Asia in the First Half of the 1990s," in Gilbert Rozman, Kazuhiko Togo, and Joseph P. Ferguson, eds., *Japanese Strategic Thought toward Asia* (New York: Palgrave Macmillan, 2007) p. 72.

137. *United States Security Strategy for the East Asia-Pacific Region*, U.S. Department of Defense, Washington, DC, February 1995.

138. Takahara Akio, "Japan's Political Response to the Rise of China," in Ryosei Kokubun and Jisi Wang, eds., *The Rise of China and a Changing East Asian Order* (Tokyo: Japan Center for International Exchange, 2004), p. 169.

139. Tsuneo Akaha, "U.S.-Japan Relations in the Post-Cold War Era: Ambiguous Adjustment to a Changing Strategic Environment," in Takashi Inoguchi, ed., *Japan's Asian Policy: Revival and Response* (New York: Palgrave MacMillan, 2002), p. 181.

140. Hasegawa, "Japan's Strategic Thinking toward Asia in the First Half of the 1990s," p. 58.

141. Alex Macleod, "Japan: A Great Power Despite Itself," Philippe G. Le Prestre, ed., *Role Quests in the Post-Cold War Era: Foreign Policies in Transition* (Montreal: McGill-Queen's University Press, 1997), p. 108.

142. Interview 28–05, Tokyo, July 8, 2005.

143. Toshi Maeda, "Japan Needs Juggling Act to Secure Future in Asia," *Japan Times*, March 6, 2000.

144. "The U.S-Japan Partnership and the Future of an Asian Regional Union," Sakakibara Eisuke interviewed by Hara Manabu, *Asahi Shimbun*, September 6, 2004.

145. Koji Murata, "Japanese Domestic Politics and the U.S.–Japan–ROK Security Relations," pp. 140–149, in Tae-Hyo Kim and Brad Glosserman, eds., *The Future of U.S.–Korea–Japan Relations: Balancing Values and Interests* (Washington, DC: The CSIS Press, 2004), p. 140.

146. Tsuneo Akaha, "Japan's Multilevel Approach toward the Korean Peninsula after the Cold War," in Charles K. Armstrong, Gilbert Rozman, Samuel S. Kim, and Stephen Kotkin, eds., *Korea at the Center: Dynamics of Regionalism in Northeast Asia* (Armonk, NY: M.E. Sharpe, Inc., 2006), p. 184.

147. Brian Bridges, *Japan and Korea in the 1990s: From Antagonism to Adjustment* (Hants, England: Edward Elgar, 1993), pp. 10–11.

148. Togo, *Japan's Foreign Policy 1945–2003*, p. 184.

149. For an overview of Japan's efforts to normalize its ties with North Korea, see Cheol Hee Park, "ROK, US, Japan's Policy Toward North Korea and the Prospect for the Japan–North Korea Relations," *Policy Research Series*, Institute for Foreign Affairs and National Security, July 2003 and Hong Nack Kim, "Japanese-Korean Relations in the 1990s," *Occasional Paper*, No. 59, Asia Program, The Woodrow Wilson Center; Interview 29–05, Tokyo, July 14, 2005.

150. Togo, *Japan's Foreign Policy 1945–2003*, p. 186.

151. Christopher Hughes, "Japan's 'Strategy-less' North Korea Strategy: Shifting Policies of Dialogue and Deterrence and Implications for Japan–U.S.–South Korea Security Cooperation," *Korean Journal of Defense Analysis* XII, no. 2 (Winter 2000), pp. 167–168.

152. C. S. Eliot Kang, "Japan in Inter-Korean Relations," in Samuel S. Kim, ed., *Inter-Korean Relations: Problems and Prospects* (New York: Palgrave MacMillan, 2004), p. 102.

153. Michael J. Green, *Japan's Reluctant Realism: Foreign Policy Challenges in an Era of Uncertain Power* (New York: Palgrave, 2001), pp. 122–123.

154. Togo, *Japan's Foreign Policy 1945–2003*, p.188; Green, *Japan's Reluctant Realism*, p. 129.

155. Prime Minister Yoshihiro Mori's speech, Ministry of Foreign Affairs, April 7, 2000.

156. Prime Minister Yoshihiro Mori's speech, Ministry of Foreign Affairs, July 28, 2000.

157. While there exist various disputes over the scope and validity of Japan's reparation, made largely through economic assistance to the military government in South Korea, the Japanese government addressed this issue of the past with the South Korean government in 1965 when the two countries normalized their diplomatic relations. Togo, *Japan's Foreign Policy 1945–2003*, p. 424.

158. Interview 27–05, Tokyo, June 27, 2005; Masao Okonogi, "Dealing with the Threat of a Korean Crisis," *Japan Review of International Affairs* 17, no. 2 (Summer 2003), p. 74.

159. Interview 02–05, Tokyo, February 10, 2005; "Editorial: One Year after the Pyongyang Summit," *Japan Times*, September 18, 2003.

160. Interview 28–05, Tokyo, July 8, 2005.

161. Togo, *Japan's Foreign Policy 1945–2003*, pp. 189, 424.

162. Gilbert Rozman, "The Geopolitics of the Korean Nuclear Crisis," *Strategic Asia 2003–04*, p. 256.

163. Interview 02–05, Tokyo, February 10, 2005.

164. Selig S. Harrison, "Did North Korea Cheat?" *Foreign Affairs* 84, no. 1 (January/February 2005), pp. 107–110.

165. Park, "ROK, US, Japan's Policy Toward North Korea," p. 14, and Shinju Fujihara, "From Shenyang to Pyongyang: Japan's Diplomatic Trials in Northeast Asia," *Harvard Asia Quarterly* VI, no. 4 (Autumn 2002), p. 31.

166. Fujihara, "From Shenyang to Pyongyang," p. 31.

167. Togo, *Japan's Foreign Policy 1945–2003*, p. 418.

168. Keizo Nabeshima, "A Return to Northern Basics," *Japan Times*, January 24, 2005.

169. Interview 29–05, Tokyo, July 14, 2005.

170. Interview 26–05, Tokyo, June 27, 2005.

171. Masao Okonogi, "Dealing with the Threat of a Korean Crisis," *Japan Review of International Affairs* 17, no. 2 (Summer 2003), p. 75.

172. Makoto Taniguchi, "Without an Independent and Multilateral Foreign Policy, There is No Future for Japan: Some Proposals for Japan's Foreign Policy," [Translated from the July 2002 issue of *Sekai* by Liao Fangfang].

173. Interview 34–05, Tokyo, July 27, 2005; Rozman, "Japan's North Korea Initiative and U.S.-Japanese Relations," p. 536.

174. "Normalizing Pyongyang ties good for all but hurdles remain: Koizumi," *Japan Times*, September 18, 2004.

175. Gavan McCormack, *Client State: Japan in the American Embrace* (London: Verso, 2007), p. 117.

176. Yoshihide Soeya, "Japanese Diplomacy and the North Korean Problem," *Japan Review of International Affairs* 17, no. 1 (Spring 2003), p. 61; Ko Odagawa, "Japan-North Korea Reconciliation Needed for East Asian Stability," *Japan Quarterly* 47 (Oct/Dec 2000), p. 15.

177. Wada Haruki, http://www5d.biglobe.ne.jp/~tosikenn/kyokai1.html, cited in Ryoji Nakagawa, "The Revival of 'Northeast Asia' in Japan," *Ritsumeikan International Affairs* 3 (2005), p. 89.

178. Interview 07–05, Beijing, April 18, 2005; Interview 09–05, Beijing, April 22, 2005.

179. The National Movement for Normalization of Japan-DPRK Relations (Nitcho Kokko Sokushin Kokumin Kyokai), http://www5d.biglobe.ne.jp/~tosikenn/kyokai1.html, cited in Nakagawa, "The Revival of 'Northeast Asia' in Japan," p. 95.

180. Richard Samuels, *Securing Japan: Tokyo's Grand Strategy and the Future of East Asia* (Ithaca, NY: Cornell University Press, 2007), p. 74.

181. Ibid., p. 175.

182. Interview 31–05, Tokyo, July 21, 2005.

183. Interview 27–05, Tokyo, June 27, 2005; Interview 31–05, Tokyo, July 21, 2005; Interview 34–05, Tokyo, July 27, 2005.

184. The Japanese media frenzy about the abduction issue is such that a noted Japanese scholar was banned from appearing on TV for more than a year after he had emphasized the security aspect of the North Korean issue over the abduction issue on a national TV debate. Interview 28–05, Tokyo, July 8, 2005.

185. Norimitsu Onishi, "Japan Rightists Fan Fury over North Korea Abductions," *New York Times*, December 17, 2006.

186. Interview 34–05, Tokyo, July 27, 2005.

187. Glynn Ford and So Young Kwon, "Pyongyang under EU's wing," *Japan Times*, March 17, 2005.

188. "Japan Must Change Constitution to Change Nation: Abe," *Japan Times*, May 3, 2007.

189. *The New National Defense Program Guidelines: East Asian Strategic Review 2005* (Tokyo, Japan: The National Institute for Defense Studies, 2005), p. 36.

190. Samuels, *Securing Japan*, p. 172.

191. Reiji Yoshida, "North Looks to Divide Tokyo and Seoul over Abduction issue," *Japan Times*, July 1, 2006.

192. "Editorial: Committing to U.S. Strategy," *Japan Times*, May 5, 2006.

193. "Editorial: Ozawa's visit to China," *Asahi Shimbun*, July 6, 2006; "Editorial: Mr. Ozawa Makes the Right Moves," *Japan Times*, July 13, 2006.

194. Kaho Shimizu, "Lee Gives Japan Hope for United Front against North," *Japan Times*, February 8, 2008.

195. Blaine Harden, "N. Korea Agrees to Reexamine Abductions," *Washington Post*, June 14, 2008.

196. "Aso Visits Site Tied to Abduction," *Japan Times*, August 2, 2009.
197. "Pyongyang Hopeful of Hatoyama," *Japan Times*, September 12, 2009.
198. "Japan and North Korea to Hold First Government Talks in Four Years," *The Associated Press*, August 14, 2012.

CHAPTER 4

1. Interview: Stephen Bosworth, *Frontline*, The Public Broadcasting System, February 23, 2003, available at http://www.pbs.org/wgbh/pages/frontline/shows/kim/interviews/bosworth.html.
2. Arnold Kanter, "North Korea a Problem to be Managed, Rather Than Solved," *Asia Times*, January 12, 2000.
3. Michael Mastanduno, "Incomplete Hegemony: The United States and Security Order in Asia," in Muthiah Alagappa, ed., *Asian Security Order: Instrumental and Normative Features* (Stanford, CA: Stanford University Press, 2003), p. 151.
4. The first North Korean nuclear crisis began in early 1993 when the North Korean regime refused to allow a special inspection by the International Atomic Energy Agency (IAEA), which suspected a secret nuclear program in Yongbyon.
5. Cited in Michael Klare, *Rogue States and Nuclear Outlaws: America's Search for a New Foreign Policy* (New York: Hill and Wang, 1995), pp. 136–137.
6. For the burgeoning literature on rogue states, see Anthony Lake, "Confronting Backlash States," *Foreign Affairs* 73, no. 2 (March/April 1994), pp. 45–55; Michael Klare, "The Rise and Fall of the 'Rogue Doctrine': The Pentagon's Quest for a Post-Cold War Military Strategy," *Middle East Report* 28 no. 3 (Autumn 1998), pp. 12–13; Michael Klare, *Rogue States and Nuclear Outlaws: America's Search for a New Foreign Policy* (New York: Hill and Wang, 1999); David Mutimer, *The Weapons States: Proliferation and the Framing of Security* (Boulder, CO: Lynne Rienner Publishers, 2000); Paul Hoyt, "Rogue State Image in American Foreign Policy," *Global Society* 14, no. 2 (April 2000), pp. 297–310; and Robert Litwak, *Rogue States and U.S. Foreign Policy: Containment After the Cold War* (Baltimore, MD: Johns Hopkins University Press, 2000); Elizabeth N. Saunders, "Setting Boundaries: Can International Society Exclude 'Rogue States'?" *International Studies Review* 8 (2006), pp. 23–53.
7. Ashton B. Carter and William James Perry, *Preventive Defense: A New Security Strategy for America* (Washington, DC: Brookings Institution Press, 1999); Joel S. Wit, Daniel B. Poneman, and Robert L. Gallucci, *Going Critical: The First North Korean Nuclear Crisis* (Washington, DC: Brookings Institution Press, 2004).
8. As one example of the changing regional security structure, in August 1992 the communist regime in Beijing normalized its diplomatic relations with South Korea, North Korea's archenemy.
9. Chae-Jin Lee, *A Troubled Peace: U.S. Policy and the Two Koreas* (Baltimore, MD: Johns Hopkins University, 2006), p. 188.
10. Warning against Taiwan's growing independence movement led by then President Lee Deng-hui, the People's Republic of China fired a series of missiles in the close vicinity of Taiwan, sparking the so-called Taiwan Strait Crisis. The Clinton administration dispatched two aircraft carrier battle groups to the Taiwan Strait. On the Taiwan Strait Crisis, see James R. Lilley and Chuck Downs, eds., *Crisis in the Taiwan Strait* (Washington DC: National Defense

University Press, 1996); Robert Ross, "The 1996 Taiwan Strait Confrontation: Coercion, Credibility and Use of Force," *International Security* 25, no. 2 (Fall 2000), pp. 87–123; Denny Roy, "Tensions in the Taiwan Strait," *Survival* 42, no. 1 (Spring 2000), pp. 76–96.

11. The sixth and final session of the Four Party Talks was held in Geneva, Switzerland, in August 1999. Tae-Hwan Kwak, "Inter-Korean Relations and Northeast Asian Security," in Christopher M. Dent and David W. F. Huang, eds., *Northeast Asian Regionalism: Learning from the European Experience* (London: RoutledgeCurzon, 2002), pp. 206–225.

12. Chung-in Moon, "Understanding the DJ Doctrine: The Sunshine Policy and the Korean Peninsula," in Chung-in Moon and David I. Steinberg, eds., *Kim Dae-jung Government and Sunshine Policy: Promises and Challenges* (Seoul: Yonsei University Press, 1999), p. 41.

13. Lee, *A Troubled Peace*, p. 194.

14. Ibid., p. 123.

15. Kurt M. Campbell, "Energizing the U.S.–Japan Security Partnership," *The Washington Quarterly* 23, no. 4 (Autumn 2000), p. 130.

16. Oknim Chung, "Solving the Security Puzzle in Northeast Asia: A Multilateral Security Regime," *Korea and World Affairs* 24, no. 3 (Fall 2000), p. 402.

17. Avery Goldstein, *Rising to the Challenge: China's Grand Strategy and International Security* (Stanford, CA: Stanford University Press, 2005), p. 118.

18. G. John Ikenberry and Takashi Inoguchi, "Introduction," in G. John Ikenberry and Takashi Inoguchi, eds., *Reinventing the Alliance: U.S.–Japan Security Partnership in an Era of Change* (New York: Palgrave Macmillan, 2003), p. 3.

19. Interview 05–05, Tokyo, March 23, 2005.

20. Akiko Fukushima, *Japanese Foreign Policy: The Emerging Logic of Multilateralism* (London: MacMillan, 1999), p. 178.

21. Kent E. Calder, "Japanese Foreign Economic Policy Formation: Examining the Reactive State," *World Politics* 40, no. 4 (July 1988), pp. 517–541; Edward J. Lincoln, *Japan's New Global Role* (Washington, DC: The Brookings Institution, 1993). For an alternative view, see Susan Pharr, "Japan's Defensive Foreign Policy and the Politics of Burden Sharing," in Gerald L. Curtis, ed., *Japan's Foreign Policy after the Cold War: Coping with Change* (Armonk, NY: M.E. Sharpe, 1993).

22. Takashi Inoguchi, "Adjusting America's Two Alliances in East Asia: A Japanese View," Working Paper, Asia-Pacific Research Center, Stanford University, July 1999, p. 13.

23. The negotiation for diplomatic normalization began in the early 1990s but the talks were stalled amid the mounting tension on the Korean Peninsula during the first North Korean nuclear crisis. The resumption of the negotiation took place in Beijing in August 1997.

24. Masao Okonogi, "Japan's North Korea Policy: The Long Swing between Dialogue and Deterrence," Paper presented at the conference North Korea Policy After The Perry Report: A Trilateral (Japan, the Republic of Korea, and the United States) Workshop, March 3–4, 2000, p. 2.

25. Paik Haksoon, "Bukmigwangye gaesun-gwa dongbuka pyonghwa: Perry bogoseo goosangul jungsimuiro [The Improvement in U.S.-North Korean relations and Peace in Northeast Asia: With Special Reference to the Vision in the Perry Report]," in Baik Jongchun and Jin Changsoo, eds., *Promoting Peace in*

Northeast Asia and North Korea in the 21st Century (Seoul: Sejong Institute, 2000), p. 62.

26. Executive Summary of the Report of the Commissions to Assess the Ballistic Missile Threat to the United States, July 15, 1998, available at http://www.fas. org/irp/threat/bm-threat.htm.

27. David E. Sanger, "North Korea Site an A-Bomb Plant, US Agencies Say," *New York Times*, August 17, 1998.

28. Madeleine Albright, *Madam Secretary* (New York: Miramax Books, 2003), p. 458.

29. Chung-in Moon and Juchan Kim, "The Perry Report and the Future of the Comprehensive Approach: A South Korean Perspective," in Chung-in Moon, Masao Okonogi, and Mitchell Reiss, eds., *The Perry Report, the Missile Quagmire, and the North Korean Question: The Quest of New Alternatives* (Seoul: Yonsei University Press, 2000), p. 117.

30. Lee, *A Troubled Peace*, p. 195.

31. While participating in the Four Party Talks in January and April 1999, the United States and North Korea held separate bilateral meetings in January and March 1999.

32. Remarks by Wendy R. Sherman, "Past Progress and Next Steps With North Korea," United States Institute of Peace, March 6, 2001.

33. Wit, Poneman, and Gallucci, *Going Critical*, p. 376.

34. Stanley O. Roth, "The United States and Japan—Partnership and Challenges in a New Millennium," Speech to the Japan Society, December 8, 1999.

35. Moonseok Ahn, *Bukhani Pilyohan Miguk, Miguki Pilyohan Bukhan [A United States That Needs North Korea, A North Korea That Needs the United States]* (Seoul: Park Young-Yul Publishing House, 2006), p. 52.

36. Ibid., pp. 51, 119, 121.

37. Eric V. Larson and Norman D. Levin with Seonhae Baik and Bogdan Savych, *Ambivalent Allies?: A Study of South Korean Attitudes toward the U.S.* (Santa Monica, CA: the Rand Corporation, 2004), p. 27.

38. William J. Perry, "Security and Stability in the Asia-Pacific Region," *PacNet*, no. 19, Pacific Forum CSIS, Honolulu, Hawaii, May 12, 2000, available at http://csis.org/files/media/csis/pubs/pac0018.pdf.

39. William J. Perry, The Unclassified Report on North Korea, Testimony before Senate Foreign Relations Committee, October 12, 1999.

40. Ibid.

41. Lee, *A Troubled Peace*, p. 198.

42. "Bilateral Relations," Ministry of Foreign Affairs, Beijing, China, http://www.fmprc.gov.cn/eng/wjb/zzjg/yzs/gjlb/2701/default.htm

43. Jonathan D. Pollack, "The United States, North Korea, and the End of the Agreed Framework," *Naval War College Review* 56, no. 3 (Summer 2003), pp. 24–25.

44. Jin Chang Su, "Bukil Kookgyo Jeongsanghwaui Ilbon Kooknae Jeongchijeok Jeyak [Domestic Constraints on the Japan–North Korean Diplomatic Normalization]" (Seoul: Sejong Institution, 2000), p. 163.

45. "How Japan-North Korea Relations Unfold in the Months Ahead? Preliminary Talks Likely to Occur by the End of the Year toward Holding Diplomatic Normalization Negotiations," *Nihon Keizai Shimbun*, p. S43 (Excerpts), December 13, 1999.

46. Christopher Hughes, "Japan's 'Strategy-less' North Korea Strategy: Shifting Policies of Dialogue and Deterrence and Implications for Japan–U.S.–South Korea Security Cooperation," *Korean Journal of Defense Analysis* XII, no. 2 (Winter 2000), pp. 167–168.

47. Masao Okonogi, "Thoughts on North Korea," *Sankei Shimbun*, December 13, 1999, p. 2.

48. C. S. Eliot Kang, "Japan in Inter-Korean Relations," in Samuel S. Kim, ed., *Inter-Korean Relations: Problems and Prospects* (New York: Palgrave MacMillan, 2004), p. 103.

49. Interview 35–05, Seoul, August 3, 2005.

50. Speaking a few months prior to the 2000 inter-Korean summit, then U.S. Ambassador to South Korea Stephen Bosworth understood South Korea's efforts to encourage the United States and Japan's diplomatic normalization with North Korea in the broader context of ending "the Cold War structures on the Korean Peninsula." See his interview in Linda D. Kozaryn, "Top U.S. Official Updates Korea Situation," *American Forces Press Service*, March 21, 2000.

51. David E. Sanger, "The Korean Breakthrough—News Analysis: Divining the Big Event: A Ray of Hope, at Least," *New York Times*, June 15, 2000.

52. Jim Lobe, "World Smiles, Pentagon Uneasy at Korea Breakthrough," *IPS*, June 16, 2000.

53. John Lancaster, "Albright Reiterates Need for 'Stability'; U.S. Presence Fixed On Korean Peninsula," *Washington Post*, June 24, 2000.

54. Albright, *Madam Secretary*, p. 459.

55. Lee, *A Troubled Peace*, p. 204.

56. "U.S.–D.P.R.K. Joint Communiqué," U.S. Department of State, October 12, 2000.

57. Albright, *Madam Secretary*, p. 459.

58. Alex Wagner, "Albright Visits North Korea; Progress Made on Missile Front," *Arms Control Today* 30, no. 9 (November 2000), available at http://legacy. armscontrol.org/act/2000_11/albrighttalks.

59. "Toast by Secretary of State Madeleine K. Albright at Dinner Hosted by Chairman Kim Jong Il," U.S. Department of State, Pyongyang, Democratic People's Republic of Korea, October 23, 2000.

60. Albright, *Madam Secretary*, p. 469.

61. Ibid., p. 469.

62. William J. Perry, "Proliferation on the Peninsula: Five North Korean Nuclear Crises," in Confronting the Specter of Nuclear Terrorism, Annals of the American Academy of Political and Social Science 607 (September 2006), p. 83.

63. Ibid., p. 470.

64. Bill Clinton, *My Life* (New York: Random House, 2004), p. 938.

65. William Perry's speech at the Asia Society, San Francisco, June 16, 2004, cited in Lee, *A Troubled Peace*, p. 207.

66. Andrew Mack, "The United States and the Asia-Pacific: Bilateralism Plus 'Multilateralism a la Carte,'" in David M. Malone and Yuen Foong Khong, eds., *Unilateralism and U.S. Foreign Policy: International Perspective* (Boulder, CO: Lynne Rienner Publishers, 2003), p. 394.

67. Ibid.

68. Toby Dalton and Scott Snyder, "Ties that Bind? Culture, Values, and Ideation," in Tae-Kyo Kim and Brad Glosserman, eds., *The Future of U.S.–Korea–Japan Relations: Balancing Values and Interests* (Washington, DC: The CSIS Press, 2004), pp. 122–123.

69. Michael Green, *Japan's Reluctant Realism: Foreign Policy Challenges in an Era of Uncertain Power* (New York: Palgrave, 2001), p. 122.
70. Interview 01–04, Tokyo, October 2005.
71. Hughes, "Japan's 'Strategy-less' North Korea Strategy," p. 171.
72. C. S. Eliot Kang and Yoshinori Kaseda, "Korea and the Dynamics of Japan's Post-Cold War Security Policy," *World Affairs* 164, no. 2 (Fall 2001), p. 54.
73. Paik, "Bukmigwangye gaesun-gwa dongbuka pyonghwa," p. 79.
74. Moon and Kim, "The Perry Report and the Future of the Comprehensive Approach," p. 123.
75. Lee, *A Troubled Peace*, p. 202.
76. Interview 36–05, Seoul, August 3, 2005.
77. Lee, *A Troubled Peace*, pp. 4–5.
78. Kang, "Japan in Inter-Korean Relations," p. 103.
79. Moon and Kim, "The Perry Report and the Future of the Comprehensive Approach," p. 117.
80. Ibid., p. 117.
81. James Schoff, "Building on the TCOG: Enhancing Trilateral Policy Coordination Among the United States, Japan, and the Republic of Korea," April 14, 2004, The Center for Global Partnership, available at http://www.cgp.org/index.php?option=article&task=default&articleid=218.
82. Yutaka Kawashima, *Japanese Foreign Policy at the Crossroads: Challenges and Options for the Twenty-First Century* (Washington, DC: Brookings Institution Press, 2003), p. 80.
83. Gilbert Rozman and Shin-wha Lee, "Unraveling the Japan-South Korea 'Virtual Alliance,'" *Asian Survey* XLVI, no. 5 (September/October 2006), p. 762.
84. Jason Manosevitz, "Japan and South Korea: Security Relations Reach Adolescence," *Asian Survey* XLIII, no. 5 (September/October 2003), pp. 807–809.
85. "Korea, Japan to Agree on Regional Body on Security at Ministerial Talks," *The Korea Herald*, October 22, 1999, cited in Chung, "Solving the Security Puzzle in Northeast Asia," p. 405.
86. Press Conference by the Press Secretary, April 7, 2000, Tokyo, Japan, http://www.mofa.go.jp/announce/press/2000/4/407.html.
87. Dalton and Snyder, "Ties that Bind?" p. 125.
88. Kang and Kaseda, "Korea and the Dynamics of Japan's Post-Cold War Security Policy," p. 55.
89. On East Asian regionalism, see Gilbert Rozman, "A Regional Approach in Northeast Asia," *Orbis* 39, no. 1 (Winter 1995), pp. 65–80; Sharine Narine, "ASEAN and ARF," *Asian Survey* XXXVII, no. 10 (October 1997), pp. 961–978; Amitav Acharya, "Ideas, Identity, and Institution-Building: From the 'ASEAN Way' to the 'Asia-Pacific Way?,'" *The Pacific Review* 10, no. 3 (1997), pp. 319–346; Peter J. Katzenstein and Takashi Shiraishi, eds., *Network Power: Japan and Asia* (Ithaca, NY: Cornell University Press, 1997); Peter J. Katzenstein, "Regionalism and Asia," *New Political Economy* 5, no. 3 (2000), pp. 353–368; Peter Katzenstein, Natasha Hamilton-Hart, Kozo Kato, and Ming Yue, *Asian Regionalism* (Ithaca, NY: Cornell University East Asia Program, 2000); Stuart Harris, "Asian Multilateral Institutions and Their Response to the Asian Economic Crisis: The Regional and Global Implications," *The Pacific Review* 13, no. 3 (2000), pp. 495–516; Sheldon W. Simon, "Evaluating Track II approaches to security diplomacy in the Asia-Pacific: the CSCAP experience," *The Pacific Review* 15, no. 2 (2002), pp. 143–173; Richard Stubbs, "ASEAN Plus Three:

Emerging East Asian Regionalism?," *Asian Survey* 42, no. 3 (2002), pp. 440–455; Barry Buzan, "Security Architecture in Asia: The Interplay of Regional and Global Levels," *The Pacific Review* 16, no. 2 (2003), pp. 167–200; Gerald L. Curtis, "East Asia, Regionalism, and U.S. National Interests: How Much Change?," *American Foreign Policy Interests* 26 (2004), pp. 199–208; Gilbert Rozman, *Northeast Asia's Stunted Regionalism: Bilateral Distrust in the Shadow of Globalization* (Cambridge, UK: Cambridge University Press, 2004).

90. Katzenstein and Shiraishi, *Network Power.*

91. The initiative, proposed in 1990 by then Malaysian Prime Minister Mahathir Mohamed, called for an exclusive East Asian free trade zone among the ASEAN members, China, Japan, and South Korea. The proposal eventually failed to materialize due in large part to U.S. opposition.

92. Kim Dae-jung, "Regionalism in the Age of Asia," *Global Asia* 1, no. 1 (2006), p. 11.

93. *Toward an East Asian Community: Region of Peace, Prosperity, and Progress*, The East Asian Vision Group Report, 2001, p. 2.

94. Ibid., pp. 4–5.

95. Rozman, *Northeast Asia's Stunted Regionalism*, p. 286.

96. Kang, "Japan in Inter-Korean Relations," p. 110.

97. David Shambaugh, "Facing Reality in China Policy," *Foreign Affairs* 80, no. 1 (January/February 2001), pp. 52–53.

98. Ibid., p. 53.

99. Yong Deng, "Better Than Power: 'International Status' in Chinese Foreign Policy," in Yong Deng and Fei-Ling Wang, eds., *China Rising: Power and Motivation in Chinese Foreign Policy* (Lanham, MD: Rowman and Littlefield Publishers, 2005), p. 60.

100. Avery Goldstein, "The Future of U.S.–China Relations and the Korean Peninsula," *Asian Perspective* 26, no. 3 (2002), p. 121.

101. Scott Snyder, Testimony before the House Committee on International Relations Hearing on North Korea: Leveraging Uncertainty? March 16, 2000.

102. Sha Zukang, "Some Thoughts on Establishing a New Regional Security Order," Statement by Ambassador Sha Zukang at the East–West Center's Senior Policy Seminar, August 7, 2000, Honolulu, Hawaii, available at http://www.fmprc. gov.cn/eng/wjb/zzjg/jks/cjjk/2622/t15411.htm.

103. Akio Takahara, "Japan's Political Response to the Rise of China," in Ryosei Kokubun and Jisi Wang, eds., *The Rise of China and a Changing East Asian Order* (Tokyo: Japan Center for International Exchange, 2004), p. 169.

104. Jae-Seung Lee, "ASEAN Plus Three and East Asian Cooperation," *IFANS Review* 11, no. 2 (December 2003), pp. 21–41; Victor Cha, "Japan-Korea Relations: Ending 2000 with a Whimper, Not a Bang," *Comparative Connections* (4th Quarter, 2000), available at http://csis.org/files/media/csis/ pubs/0004qjapan_korea.pdf.

105. Chung, "Solving the Security Puzzle in Northeast Asia," p. 401.

106. Kuniko Ashizawa, "Japan's Approach toward Asian Regional Security: from 'Hub-and-Spoke' Bilateralism to 'Multi-Tiered,'" *The Pacific Review* 16, no. 3 (2003), p. 364.

107. Ibid., p. 376.

108. Wu Xinbo, "The End of the Silver Lining: A Chinese View of the U.S.-Japanese Alliance," *The Washington Quarterly* 29, no. 1 (Winter 2005–2006), pp. 126–127.

109. Ibid., p. 128.
110. Chung, "Solving the Security Puzzle in Northeast Asia," p. 410.
111. Interview 04–05, Tokyo, March 22, 2005.
112. *Joongang Ilbo*, September 13, 1999.
113. Muthiah Alagappa, "The Study of International Order: An Analytical Framework," Muthiah Alagappa, ed., *Asian Security Order: Instrumental and Normative Features* (Stanford, CA: Stanford University Press, 2003), p. 76.
114. Interview 12–04, Beijing, November 24, 2004.
115. Ashton B. Carter and William J. Perry, *Preventive Defense: A New Security Strategy for America* (Washington, DC: Brookings Institution Press, 1999), pp. 118, 120.
116. Jin, "Bukil Kookgyo Jeongsanghwaui Ilbon Kooknae Jeongchijeok Jeyak," p. 162.
117. Lee, *A Troubled Peace*, p. 195.
118. Ezra F. Vogel, "Globalization of East Asia: Touring the Horizon," *Modern Asia Series*, Spring 2000, Harvard University Asia Center, May 5, 2000.
119. Perry, The Unclassified Report on North Korea.
120. Albright, *Madam Secretary*, p. 472.
121. Charlie Rose, Interview with Madeleine Albright, March 27, 2007.
122. David E. Sanger and William J. Broad, "U.S. Concedes Uncertainty on North Korean Uranium Effort," *New York Times*, March 1, 2007.
123. All emphases in this table are added.

CHAPTER 5

1. Jonathan D. Pollack, "The United States, North Korea, and the End of the Agreed Framework," *Naval War College Review* 56, no. 3 (Summer 2003), p. 28.
2. The most notable examples of the reversal of policy during the Bush presidency include the Kyoto protocol, the International Criminal Court, and the ABM Treaty. As argued in chapter 2, a policy shift from nonproliferation to counterproliferation is another example.
3. Chae-Jin Lee, *A Troubled Peace: U.S. Policy and the Two Koreas* (Baltimore, MD: Johns Hopkins University Press, 2006), p. 212.
4. Karen DeYoung, *Soldier: The Life of Colin Powell* (New York: Alfred A. Knopf, 2006), p. 325.
5. Hideya Kurata, "North Korea's Renewed Nuclear Challenge," *Japan Review of International Affairs* 17, no. 2 (Summer 2003), pp. 91–92.
6. Lee, *A Troubled Peace*, p. 216.
7. Toby Dalton and Scott Snyder, "Ties That Bind? Culture, Values, and Ideation in U.S.-ROK-Japan Security Cooperation" in Tae-Hyo Kim and Brad Glosserman, eds., *The Future of U.S.-Korea-Japan Relations: Balancing Values and Interests* (Washington, DC: Center for Strategic and International Studies, 2004), p. 126.
8. David E. Sanger, "A Nation Challenged: The Rogue List: Bush Aides Say Tough Tone Put Foes on Notice," *New York Times*, January 31, 2002.
9. Gi-Wook Shin, *Ethnic Nationalism in Korea: Genealogy, Politics, and Legacy* (Stanford, CA: Stanford University Press, 2006), p. 176.
10. Gilbert Rozman, "Regionalism in Northeast Asia," in Charles K. Armstrong, Gilbert Rozman, Samuel S. Kim, and Stephen Kotkin, eds., *Korea at the Center: Dynamics of Regionalism in Northeast Asia* (Armonk, NY: M.E. Sharpe, Inc., 2006), p. 163.

11. Reiko Take, "Searching for Autonomy? Koizumi's 2002 Visit to North Korea," paper presented at the 46th International Studies Association Annual Convention, March 2005, Hawaii, p. 14.
12. Leon V. Sigal, "Try Engagement for a Change," *Global Asia* 1, no. 1 (September 2006), p. 53.
13. Christopher W. Hughes, *Japan's Re-emergence as a "Normal" Military Power*, Adelphi Paper 368–369 (London: Routledge for the International Institute for Strategic Studies, 2005), p. 43.
14. Lee, *A Troubled Peace*, p. 242.
15. Ibid., p. 240.
16. Roh Moo-hyun, "History, Nationalism and Community," Global Asia 2, no. 1 (April 2007), pp. 10–13.
17. Lee, *A Troubled Peace*, p. 228.
18. J. J. Suh, "Bound to Last? The U.S.–Korea Alliance and Analytical Eclecticism," in J. J. Suh, Peter J. Katzenstein, and Allen Carlson, eds., *Rethinking Security in East Asia: Identity, Power, and Efficiency* (Stanford, CA: Stanford University Press, 2004), p. 169.
19. Richard Armitage Interview, *Bungei shunju*, July 2004, cited in Ito Narihiko, "Toward an Independent Japanese Relationship with the United States," *Japan Focus*, http://japanfocus.org/article.asp?id=175.
20. Kenneth B. Pyle, "Abe Shinzo and Japan's Change of Course," *NBR ANALYSIS* 17, no. 4, The National Bureau of Asian Research (October 2006), p. 23.
21. *Gaiko Forum* 2, no.1 (Winter 2002), pp. 29–30, cited in Kenneth B. Pyle, *Japan Rising: The Resurgence of Japanese Power and Purpose* (New York: Public Affairs, 2007), p. 352.
22. Kenneth B. Pyle, *Japan Rising: The Resurgence of Japanese Power and Purpose* (New York: Public Affairs, 2007), p. 352.
23. Jitsuro Terashima in Kiichi Fujiwara, Keiko Sakai, and Jitsuro Terashima, "What Will Result from an Attack on Iraq?" *Japan Echo* 30, no. 2 (April 2003), pp. 10–16, cited in Reiko Take, "Searching for Autonomy? Koizumi's 2002 Visit to North Korea," paper presented at the annual convention of the International Studies Association, March 2005, pp. 19–20.
24. Yoshihide Soeya, "Japanese Diplomacy and the North Korean Problem," *Japan Review of International Affairs* 17, no. 1 (Spring 2003), pp. 53–61.
25. Alastair Iain Johnston and Daniela Stockmann, "Chinese Attitudes toward the United States and Americans," in Peter J. Katzenstein and Robert O. Keohane, eds., *Anti-Americanisms in World Politics* (Ithaca, NY: Cornell University Press, 2007), p. 192.
26. Yang Bo and Jiang Wai, "Dongbeiya anquan jizhi: xianshi yu qianjing [Northeast Asia Security Mechanisms: Reality and Prospects]," *Xiandai Guoji Guanxi [Contemporary International Relations]* 14, no. 4, (2004), pp. 47–48.
27. Chu Shulong, "China's Perspectives on the Regional and World Order Since 9/11," in Han Sung-Ju ed., *Coping with 9–11: Asian Perspectives on Global and Regional Order* (Tokyo: Japan Center for International Exchange, 2003), pp. 31–32.
28. Joseph Kahn, "China, Shy Giant, Shows Signs of Shedding Its False Modesty," *New York Times*, December 9, 2006.
29. Jianwei Wang, "China's Multilateral Diplomacy in the New Millennium," in Yong Deng and Fei-Ling Wang, eds., *China Rising: Power and Motivation in*

Chinese Foreign Policy (Lanham, MD: Rowman and Littlefield Publishers, 2005), p. 163.

30. Cited in Peter Hayes Gries, "China Eyes the Hegemon," *Orbis* 49, no. 3 (Summer 2005), pp. 407–408.

31. "Six-Party Talks Should Become Mechanism: FM Spokeswoman," *People's Daily*, February 23, 2004, cited in Jianwei Wang, "China's Multilateral Diplomacy in the New Millennium," p. 187.

32. Dalton and Snyder, "Ties that Bind?" p. 127.

33. Wu Xinbo, "The End of the Silver Lining: A Chinese View of the U.S.-Japanese Alliance," *Washington Quarterly* 29, no. 1 (Winter 2005–2006), pp. 126–127.

34. Ralph A. Cossa and Alan Oxley, "The U.S.-Korea Alliance," in Robert D. Blackwill and Paul Dibb, eds., *America's Asian Alliances* (Cambridge, MA: The MIT Press, 2000), p. 81.

35. Michael H. Armacost, "The Future of America's Alliances in Northeast Asia," in Michael H. Armacost and Daniel I. Okimoto, eds., *The Future of America's Alliances in Northeast Asia* (Stanford, CA: Asia-Pacific Research Center, 2004), p. 16.

36. Eric V. Larson and Norman D. Levin with Seonhae Baik and Bogdan Savych, *Ambivalent Allies?: A Study of South Korean Attitudes Toward the U.S.* (Santa Monica, CA: the Rand Corporation, 2004), p. 34.

37. Kang Choi, "A View on America's Role in Asia and the Future of the ROK–U.S. Alliance," in *The Newly Emerging Asian Order and the Korean Peninsula*, Joint U.S.–Korea Academic Studies 15 (2005), Korea Economic Institute, Washington, DC, p. 225.

38. Lee, *A Troubled Peace*, p. 242.

39. *New York Times*, October 14, 2003, cited in Lee, *A Troubled Peace*, p. 242.

40. C. S. Eliot Kang, "Japan in Inter-Korean Relations," in Samuel S. Kim, ed., *Inter-Korean Relations: Problems and Prospects* (New York: Palgrave MacMillan, 2004), p. 105.

41. Choong Nam Kim, "The Sunshine Policy and Its Impact on South Korea's Relations with Major Powers," *Korea Observer* 35, no. 4 (Winter 2004), p. 608.

42. Kang, "Japan in Inter-Korean Relations," p. 105.

43. Victor D. Cha, "Multilateral Security in Asia and the U.S.-Japan Alliance," in G. John Ikenberry and Takashi Inoguchi, eds., *Reinventing the Alliance: U.S.–Japan Security Partnership in an Era of Change* (New York: Palgrave Macmillan, 2003), p. 152.

44. For a detailed chronology of the meetings, see *Coordinating Regional Strategies for a Nuclear-Free Korean Peninsula*, Institute for Foreign Policy Analysis Report on the NK Nuclear Crisis, May 2004, pp. 26–27. For a South Korean view of the TCOG, see Jung-Hoon Lee, "Multilateral Security Arrangements: A South Korean Perspective," paper presented at the International Political Studies Association Conference in Quebec, Canada, August 4, 2000. However, few scholarly works have focused specifically on the role of the TCOG. This, in my view, attests to the dwindling role of the group, especially after the outbreak of the second crisis.

45. James L. Schoff, "Building on the TCOG: Enhancing Trilateral Policy Coordination Among the United States, Japan, and the Republic of Korea," The Center for Global Partnership, April 16, 2004, available at http://www.cgp.org/index.php?option=article&task=default&articleid=218.

46. Lee, *A Troubled Peace*, p. 246.
47. *Coordinating Regional Strategies*, IFPA Report, May 2004, p. 18.
48. Ibid., p. 14.
49. Ibid., p. 14.
50. Kurata, "North Korea's Renewed Nuclear Challenge," p. 96.
51. *Coordinating Regional Strategies*, pp. 18–19.
52. Geun Lee, "The Rise of China and Korea's China Policy," in Tae-Hyo Kim and Brad Glosserman, eds., *The Future of U.S.-Korea-Japan Relations: Balancing Values and Interests* (Washington, DC: The CSIS Press, 2004), p. 198.
53. Scott Snyder, "South Korea's Squeeze Play," *The Washington Quarterly* 28, no. 4 (Autumn 2005), p. 94.
54. David C. Kang, "Japan: U.S. Partner or Focused on Abductees?" *The Washington Quarterly* 28, no. 4 (Autumn 2005), p. 114.
55. Jae Ho Chung, *Between Ally and Partner: Korea–China Relations and the United States* (New York: Columbia University Press, 2007), pp. 90–91.
56. Ibid., pp. 90–91.
57. Ibid., p. 86.
58. David Shambaugh, "China and the Korean Peninsula: Playing for the Long Term," *The Washington Quarterly* 26, no. 2 (Spring 2003), p. 50.
59. Chung, *Between Ally and Partner*, p. 90.
60. Interview 02–04, Beijing, November 3, 2004. Interview 04–04, Beijing, November 10, 2004.
61. "Past, Status Quo and Future of China-ROK relations," *People's Daily*, March 30, 2005.
62. Samuel S. Kim, "China's Conflict-Management Approach to the Nuclear Stand-off on the Korean Peninsula," *Asian Perspective* 30, no. 1 (Spring 2006), p. 34.
63. Li Dunqiu, "Sino-ROK Friendship Does N.E Asia a World of Good," *People's Daily*, August 24, 2007.
64. Gi-Wook Shin and Paul Y. Chang, "The Politics of Nationalism in U.S.-Korean Relations," *Asian Perspective* 28, no. 4 (2004), pp. 140–141.
65. Gi-Wook Shin, *Ethnic Nationalism in Korea: Genealogy, Politics, and Legacy* (Stanford, CA: Stanford University Press, 2006), p. 217.
66. Robert Sutter, "The Rise of China and South Korea," in *The Newly Emerging Asian Order and the Korean Peninsula*, Joint U.S.–Korea Academic Studies, vol. 15, Korea Economic Institute, Washington, DC, 2005, p. 32.
67. Andrew Scobell, "China and Inter-Korean Relations: Beijing as Balancer," in Samuel S. Kim, ed., *Inter-Korean Relations: Problems and Prospects* (New York: Palgrave Macmillan, 2004), p. 90.
68. Kim, "The Sunshine Policy and Its Impact on South Korea's Relations with Major Powers," p. 605.
69. Michael D. Swaine, "U.S. Security Policy under Clinton and Bush: China and Korea," in Chae-Jin Lee, ed., *U.S. Security Policy Under Clinton and Bush: Continuity and Change*, Monograph Series, no. 17, The Keck Center for International and Strategic Studies Claremont McKenna College, 2005, pp. 75–76.
70. Michael T. Klare, "Containing China: The US's real objective," *Asia Times*, April 20, 2006.
71. President Roh's address at the 53rd Commencement and Commissioning Ceremony of the Korea Air Force Academy, March 8, 2005, cited in Samuel S. Kim, "China's Conflict-Management Approach to the Nuclear Standoff on the Korean Peninsula," *Asian Perspective* 30, no. 1 (2006), p. 33.

72. Ryu Jin, "Roh Seeks N-E Asian Security Regime," *The Korea Times*, October 21, 2005.
73. Emanuel Pastreich, "The Balancer: Roh Moo-hyun's Vision of Korean Politics and the Future of Northeast Asia," *Japan Focus*, August 1, 2005.
74. *Donga Ilbo*, April 15, 2005.
75. Interview 09–05, Beijing, April 22, 2005.
76. Interview 04–05, Tokyo, March 22, 2005.
77. Aurelia George Mulgan, "Japan and the Bush Agenda: Alignment or divergence?," in Mark Beeson, ed., *Bush and Asia: America's Evolving Relations with East Asia* (Routledge: London and New York, 2005), p. 111.
78. Lee Jongwon, *Hankyoreh Shinmun*, November 3, 2003.
79. McCormack quoted in Jeff Kingston, "Japan, Just a Puppet of America?" Book review of *Client State: Japan in the American Embrace*, by Gavan McCormack," *Japan Times*, July 8, 2007.
80. "Abe Apologizes Anew for Wartime Sex Slavery," *Japan Times*, April 22, 2007.
81. Taro Aso, "Policy Speech by Minister for Foreign Affairs Taro Aso to the 166th Session of the Diet," Ministry of Foreign Affairs, Tokyo, Japan, January 27, 2007.
82. Cynthia Banham, "China Snubbed as Australia, Japan, US Discuss Security," *Sydney Morning Herald*, January 6, 2006.
83. Richard Tanter, "The New American-led Security Architecture in the Asia Pacific: Binding Japan and Australia, Containing China," *Japan Focus*, March 17, 2007.
84. Ibid.
85. Founded in 2002 by Britain's International Institute of Strategic Studies (IISS), the Dialogue is an annual meeting of defense ministers from most of the Asian countries, the United States, and U.S. allies such as Britain, France, Australia, and Canada. See its official website http://www.iiss.org/conferences/the-shangri-la-dialogue. Hughes, "Japan's Re-emergence as a 'Normal' Military Power," p. 122.
86. Akio Takahara, "Japan's Political Response to the Rise of China," in Kokubun Ryosei and Wang Jisi, eds., *The Rise of China and a Changing East Asian Order* (Tokyo: Japan Center for International Exchange, 2004), p. 169.
87. Xia Liping, "North Korea's Nuclear Program and Asian Security Cooperation," in *The Newly Emerging Asian Order and the Korean Peninsula*, Joint U.S.-Korea Academic Studies, vol. 15, Korea Economic Institute, Washington, DC, 2005, p. 118.
88. Gilbert Rozman, "Regionalism in Northeast Asia," in Charles K. Armstrong, Gilbert Rozman, Samuel S. Kim, and Stephen Kotkin, eds., *Korea at the Center: Dynamics of Regionalism in Northeast Asia* (Armonk, NY: M.E. Sharpe, Inc., 2006), p. 166.
89. Lee, *A Troubled Peace*, pp. 242–243.
90. Thomas G. Moore, "Chinese Foreign Policy in the Age of Globalization," in Yong Deng and Fei-Ling Wang, eds., *China Rising: Power and Motivation in Chinese Foreign Policy* (Lanham, MD: Rowman and Littlefield Publishers, 2005), p. 139.
91. ASEAN Plus Three Cooperation, ASEAN Secretariat, available at http://www.aseansec.org/16580.htm.
92. Jae-Seung Lee, "ASEAN Plus Three and East Asian Cooperation," *IFANS Review* 11, no. 2 (December 2003), pp. 21–41; Victor Cha, "Japan-Korea Relations:

Ending 2000 with a Whimper, Not a Bang," *Comparative Connections* (4th Quarter, 2000), available at http://csis.org/files/media/csis/pubs/0004qjapan_korea.pdf.

93. Jianwei Wang, "China's Multilateral Diplomacy in the New Millennium," in Yong Deng and Fei-Ling Wang, eds., *China Rising: Power and Motivation in Chinese Foreign Policy* (Lanham, MD: Rowman and Littlefield Publishers, 2005), p. 176.

94. Xia Liping, "North Korea's Nuclear Program and Asian Security Cooperation," in *The Newly Emerging Asian Order and the Korean Peninsula*, Joint U.S.-Korea Academic Studies, vol. 15, Korea Economic Institute, Washington, DC, 2005, p. 185.

95. "Japan-NK relations," Ministry of Foreign Affairs, Tokyo, Japan, October 2003.

96. Ibid.

97. *Munwha Ilbo*, July 1, 2004.

98. *Japan Times*, November 30, 2004.

99. Kim Dae-jung, "Regionalism in the Age of Asia," *Global Asia*, p. 12.

100. *Segye Ilbo*, June 18, 2003.

101. Overview: The International Situation and Japanese Diplomacy in 2003, Ministry of Foreign Affairs, Japan, May 2004.

102. Ibid.

103. "Koizumi Sends Message to North Korea," *Japan Times*, September 24, 2004.

104. Jisi Wang, "China's Changing Role in Asia," in Ryosei Kokubun and Jisi Wang, eds., *The Rise of China and a Changing East Asian Order* (Tokyo: Japan Center for International Exchange, 2004), p. 14.

105. Zhiqun Zhu, "Japan the Spoiler in Northeast Asia," *Asia Times*, March 23, 2005, available at http://www.atimes.com/atimes/Japan/GC23Dh04.html.

106. Kanako Takahara, "Calls Mount for Sanctions on North Korea," *Japan Times*, November 17, 2004.

107. *Yonhap News*, November 17, 2004.

108. "Defense Strategists Look to China's Attack Threat," *Japan Times*, November 9, 2004.

109. "Japan on Alert as Suspected Chinese Sub Detected in Territorial Waters," *AFP*, November 10, 2004.

110. Reiji Yoshida and Kanako Takahara, "China's Sub Intrusion Sparks Tokyo Protest," *Japan Times*, November 13, 2004.

111. "Japan Plans to Call China, North Korea Key Threats," *Japan Times*, November 27, 2004.

112. James Brooke, "Japan's New Military Focus: China and North Korea Threats," *New York Times*, December 11, 2004.

113. "Bizarre Indication of 'China Threat' in Japanese Defense Program: Commentary," *People's Daily*, December 11, 2004.

114. Jiang Xinfeng, "US–Japan Military Alliance Reflects Cold War Mentality," *People's Daily*, November 5, 2005.

115. "China Rules Out Talks between Premier Wen and Koizumi," *People's Daily*, December 1, 2005.

116. "Japan, China Clash over E. Asia Summit," *The Yomiuri Shimbun*, November 25, 2005.

117. Joel Brinkley, "With Taiwan as Security Issue, Rice Prepares to Meet Japan Leaders," *New York Times*, February 18, 2005.

118. "Aso Says China a Threat; Shrine Overtures Rebuffed," *Japan Times*, April 3, 2006.
119. "Analysis: Japan–US security cooperation breaches bilateral framework," *People's Daily*, February 21, 2005.
120. In February 2005, a prefectural government in Japan inaugurated the Takeshima day, reigniting tension with South Korea over the disputed territory. When Japanese officials dismissed the incident as a local matter, South Korea canceled a scheduled visit by then Foreign Minister Ban Ki-moon to Tokyo. The dispute effectively put an end to the goodwill efforts made earlier by the two neighbors to celebrate 2005 the year of "mutual friendship." Anthony Faiola, "Islands Come Between South Korea and Japan: Ordinance Intensifies Diplomatic Dispute," *Washington Post*, March 17, 2005.
121. Norimitsu Onishi, "Dispute Over Islets Frays Ties Between Tokyo and Seoul," *New York Times*, March 22, 2005.
122. *Donga Ilbo*, April 1, 2005.
123. Natsumi Mizumoto, "Defense Panel Seeks Enhanced Ties with U.S., Flexible Force," *Kyodo News*, October 4, 2004.
124. Hughes, *Japan's Re-emergence as a "Normal" Military Power*, p. 146.
125. Minxin Pei and Michael Swaine, "Simmering Fire in Asia: Averting Sino-Japanese Strategic Conflict," *Policy Brief* 44, Carnegie Endowment for International Peace, November 2005, p. 7.
126. Gavan McCormack, *Client State: Japan in the American Embrace* (London: Verso, 2007), p. 114.
127. Glenn Kessler, "U.S. Open to Bilateral Talks on Ties With N. Korea," *Washington Post*, January 18, 2007.
128. David E. Sanger, "North Koreans Say They've Shut Nuclear Reactor," *New York Times*, July 15, 2007.
129. Despite the positive development, the definitive resolution of the situation remained elusive given the fact that the declaration did not include nuclear weapons, enriched uranium, and the proliferation aspect and that the Bush administration had too little time left to make further progress. Norimitsu Onishi and Edward Wong, "U.S. to Take North Korea Off Terror List," *New York Times*, June 27, 2008.
130. Full text of the declaration is available in Korean in *Chosun Ilbo*, October 4, 2007, http://news.chosun.com/site/data/html_dir/2007/10/04/2007100400774.html.
131. Mitchell B. Reiss, "Hope Over Experience: Denuclearizing the North," *The National Interest*, May/June 2007, p. 22.
132. "Editorial: Sanctions on N. Korea," *Asahi Shimbun*, October 11, 2007.
133. Kaho Shimizu, "Lee Gives Japan Hope for United Front against North," *Japan Times*, February 8, 2008.
134. "Report: N Korea Open to Dialogue with Japan on Abductions, Official Says," *Yomiuri Shimbun*, October 11, 2007.
135. "Chinese Defense Minister to Visit Japan this Month," *Japan Times*, August 11, 2007.
136. Lee won South Korea's presidential election in late 2007 due mainly to unsuccessful economic stewardship during the Roh administration. In Japan, Aso's predecessor, Fukuda, resigned abruptly in September 2008 amid political gridlock in the upper house of the Japanese Diet.
137. Interview 14–05, Beijing, April 28, 2005.

138. Gilbert Rozman, *Northeast Asia's Stunted Regionalism: Bilateral Distrust in the Shadow of Globalization* (Cambridge, UK: Cambridge University Press, 2004), p. 348.

139. Yoichi Funabashi, *Donga Ilbo*, September 19, 2003.

140. Mizushima Asaho, "A New Security Framework for Northeast Asia," *Japan Focus*, 2004, http://japanfocus.org/article.asp?id=048.

141. Amitav Acharya, "The Bush Doctrine and Asian Regional Order," in Mel Gurtov and Peter Van Ness, eds., *Confronting the Bush Doctrine: Critical Views from the Asia-Pacific* (London: RoutledgeCurzon, 2005), p. 221.

142. *Donga Ilbo*, October 28, 2002.

143. "The Coordinator-General's Report of the First Annual Conference of Network of East Asian Think-Tanks," Ministry of Foreign Affairs, China, October 14, 2003, available at http://www.fmprc.gov.cn/eng/topics/zgcydyhz/dqc/t28379.htm.

144. *Hankyoreh Shinmun*, December 16, 2003.

145. *Hanguk Ilbo*, October 11, 2004.

CHAPTER 6

1. James M. Lindsay and Ray Takeyh, "After Iran Gets the Bomb: Containment and Its Complications," *Foreign Affairs* 89, no. 2 (March/April 2010), pp. 33–49 at 38.

2. Kenneth M. Pollack, *The Persian Puzzle: The Conflict between Iran and America* (New York: Random House, 2004), p. 421.

3. A few notable exceptions include Dalia Dassa Kaye and Frederic Wehrey, "A Nuclear Iran: The Reactions of Neighbours," *Survival* 49, no. 2 (2007), pp. 111–128; Suzanne Maloney, *Iran's Long Reach: Iran as a Pivotal State in the Muslim World* (Washington, DC: USIP Press, 2008); Dalia Dassa Kaye and Frederic Wehrey, "Containing Iran? Avoiding a Two-Dimensional Strategy in a Four-Dimensional Region," *Washington Quarterly* 32, no. 3 (July 2009), pp. 37–53; John C. Shenna, "The Case Against the Case Against Iran: Regionalism as the West's Last Frontier," *Middle East Journal* 64, no. 3, (Summer 2010), pp. 341–363.

4. Ray Takeyh, *Guardians of the Revolution: Iran and the World in the Age of the Ayatollahs* (New York: Oxford University Press, 2009), p. 1.

5. Samuel Segev, *The Iranian Triangle: The Untold Story of Israel's Role in the Iran-Contra Affair* (New York: The Free Press, 1988), p. 121.

6. Henry Kissinger, *Years of Upheaval* (Boston: Little Brown, and Company, 1982), p. 669.

7. F. Gregory Gause III, *The International Relations of the Persian Gulf* (Cambridge, UK: Cambridge University Press, 2010), p. 11.

8. Louise Fawcett, "Alliance, Cooperation, and Regionalism in the Middle East," in Louise Fawcett, ed., *International Relations of the Middle East* (Oxford: Oxford University Press, 2009), p. 199.

9. Dana H. Allin and Steven Simon, *The Sixth Crisis: Iran, Israel, America and the Rumors of War* (Oxford: Oxford University Press, 2010), p. 26.

10. Geoffrey Kemp, "The Impact of Iranian Foreign Policy on Regional Security: An External Perspective," in Jamal S. Al-Suwaidi, ed., *Iran and the Gulf: A Search for Stability* (Abu Dhabi: The Emirates Center for Strategic Studies and Research, 1996), pp. 118–135 at 123.

11. Gary Sick, "The United States and Iran: Truth and Consequences," *Contention* 5 (1996), pp. 59–78 at 71, cited in Majid Al-Khalili, *Oman's Foreign Policy: Foundation and Practice* (Westport, CT: Praeger Security International, 2009), p. 103.

12. Richard K. Herrmann and R. Williams Ayres, "The New Geo-Politics of the Gulf: Forces for Change and Stability," in Gary G. Sick and Lawrence G. Porter, eds., *The Persian Gulf at the Millennium: Essays in Politics, Economy, Security, and Religion* (New York: St. Martin's Press, 1997), p. 39.

13. Gary Sick, "Iran's Foreign Policy: A Revolution in Transition," in Nikki R. Keddie and Rudi Matthee, eds., *Iran and the Surrounding World: Interactions in Culture and Cultural Politics* (Seattle, WA: University of Washington Press, 2002), pp. 355–374 at 367–368.

14. Mohamed ElBaradei, *The Age of Deception: nuclear Diplomacy in Treacherous Times* (New York: Metropolitan Books, 2011), p. 131.

15. Flynt Leverett's comment is quoted in Steven Lee Myers and Helene Cooper, "Bush Insists Iran Remains a Threat Despite Arms Data," *New York Times*, December 5, 2007.

16. ElBaradei, *The Age of Deception*, p. 134.

17. William E. Odom, "The Nuclear Option," *Foreign Policy*, no. 160 (May/June 2007), p. 52.

18. Nicholas D. Kristof, "Hang Up! Tehran Is Calling," *New York Times*, January 21, 2007.

19. Ali M. Ansari, *Confronting Iran: The Failure of American Foreign Policy and the Next Great Crisis in the Middle East* (New York: Basic Books, 2006), p. 216.

20. Ibid., p. 223.

21. ElBaradei, *The Age of Deception*, p. 241.

22. Trita Parsi, *A Single Roll of the Dice: Obama's Diplomacy with Iran* (New Haven, CT: Yale University Press, 2012), pp. 5–7.

23. David E. Sanger and Thom Shanker, "Washington Sees an Opportunity on Iran," *New York Times*, September 27, 2007.

24. Thomas L. Friedman, *From Beirut to Jerusalem* (New York: Doubleday, 1990), p. 506.

25. Vali Nasr, *The Shia Revival: How Conflicts within Islam Will Shape the Future* (New York: W.W. Norton, 2006), p. 222.

26. Marc Lynch, *The Arab Uprising: The Unfinished Revolutions of the New Middle East* (New York: PublicAffairs, 2012), p. 205.

27. Takeyh, *Guardians of the Revolution*, p. 6.

28. Roger Cohen, "The U.S.-Iranian Triangle," *New York Times*, September 28, 2009.

29. Nikki R. Keddie, *Modern Iran: Roots and Results of Revolution* (New Haven, CT: Yale University Press, 2006), p. 334.

30. Matthew Kroenig, "Time to Attack Iran: Why a Strike Is the Least Bad Option," *Foreign Affairs* 91, no. 1 (January/February 2012).

31. Brendan O'Reilly, "Egypt Joins China Club," *Asia Times*, August 31, 2012.

32. Robert Baer, *The Devil We Know* (New York: Crown Publishers, 2008), p. 177.

33. John W. Limbert, *Negotiating with Iran: Wrestling the Ghost of History* (Washington, DC: United States Institute of Peace Press, 2009), p. 160.

34. Robert Olson, *Turkey–Iran Relations 1979–2004: Revolution, Ideology, War, Coups and Geopolitics* (Costa Mesa, CA: Mazda Publishers, 2004), p. xxv. In pre-modern history, however, the two countries have endured a long-running rivalry that has its historical roots in the eighteenth century during the Afsharid dynasty, in which the Ottoman and Persian Empires were "in a great ideological and military struggle for hegemony" in the region. See Olson, p. xxii.

35. Olson, *Turkey–Iran Relations 1979–2004*, p. 1.
36. Mustafa Aydin, *Ten Years after: Turkey's Gulf Policy (1990–1991) Revisited*, Ankara Paper no. 3 (London: Frank Cass, 2002), p. 50.
37. Kemal Kirisci, "The Future of Turkish Policy toward the Middle East," in Barry Rubin and Kemal Kirisci, eds., *Turkey in World Politics: An Emerging Multiregional Power* (Boulder, CO: Lynne Rienner, 2001), pp. 93–113 at 99.
38. Olson, *Turkey–Iran Relations 1979–2004*, p. xxxii.
39. Graham E. Fuller, *The New Turkish Republic: Turkey as a Pivotal in the Muslim World* (Washington, DC: United States Institute of Peace Press, 2007), p. 41.
40. Hasan Kosebalaban, *Turkish Foreign Policy: Islam, Nationalism, and Globalization* (New York: Palgrave Macmillan, 2011), p. 117.
41. Burhanettin Duran, "JDP and Foreign Policy as an Agent of Transformation," in M. Hakan Yavuz, ed., *The Emergence of a New Turkey: Democracy and the AP Parti* (Salt Lake City: The University of Utah Press, 2006), pp. 281–305 at 290.
42. Olson, *Turkey–Iran Relations 1979–2004*, pp. 13, 15.
43. Fuller, *The New Turkish Republic*, p. 43
44. William Hale, *Turkish Foreign Policy 1774–2000* (London: Frank Cass, 2000), p. 315.
45. Kirisci, "The Future of Turkish Policy Toward the Middle East," pp. 93–113 at 104.
46. Ersin Kalaycioglu, *Turkish Dynamics: Bridge across Troubled Lands* (New York: Palgrave Macmillan, 2005), p. 200.
47. Joshua W. Walker, *Turkey's Global Strategy: Introduction: The Sources of Turkish Grand Strategy—"Strategic Depth" and "Zero-Problems" in Context*. IDEAS reports—special reports, Nicholas Kitchen, ed., SR007. LSE IDEAS, London School of Economics and Political Science, London, 2011, p. 10
48. Ibid., pp. 10–11.
49. Ibid., pp. 151–152.
50. Kosebalaban, *Turkish Foreign Policy*, p. 152.
51. Fuller, *The New Turkish Republic*, p. 79.
52. Stephen Kinzer, *Reset: Iran, Turkey, and America's Future* (New York: Times Books, 2010), p. 197.
53. Kosebalaban, *Turkish Foreign Policy*, p. 182.
54. Fuller, *The New Turkish Republic*, p. 74.
55. Ibid., p. 183.
56. Parsi, *A Single Roll of the Dice*, pp. 181–182.
57. "Is Turkey Turning?" *The Economist*, June 12, 2010, pp. 55–56.
58. Mustafa Akyol, "An Unlikely Trio: Can Iran, Turkey, and the United States Become Allies?" *Foreign Affairs* 89, no. 5 (September/October 2010), p. 128.
59. James Traub, "Turkey's Rules," *New York Times*, January 20, 2011.
60. Kinzer, *Reset*, pp. 197–198.
61. Mark Landl, "At the U.N., Turkey Asserts Itself in Prominent Ways," *New York Times*, September 22, 2010.
62. One of the top priorities remains the Kurdish issue. See Fuller, *The New Turkish Republic*, p. 113.
63. Ibid., p. 161.
64. Ibid., p. 5.
65. Andrew Finkel, *Turkey: What Everyone Needs to Know* (New York: Oxford University Press, 2012), p. 80.
66. Kosebalaban, *Turkish Foreign Policy*, p. 183.

67. Landl, "At the U.N., Turkey Asserts Itself in Prominent Ways."
68. "Turkey's Crisis over Israel and Iran," *Europe Report,* no. 208, International Crisis Group, September 8, 2010, p. 12.
69. Glenn Kessler, "U.N. Vote on Iran Sanctions Not a Clear-Cut Win for Obama," *Washington Post,* June 9, 2010.
70. Steven Erlanger, "Iran Nuclear Talks in Istanbul Start," *New York Times,* January 21, 2011.
71. Joseph J. St. Marie and Shahdad Naghshpour, *Revolutionary Iran and the United States: Low-Intensity Conflict in the Persian Gulf* (Burlington, VT: Ashgate, 2011), p. 176.
72. Hooshang Amirahmadi and Nader Entessar, "Iranian-Arab Relations in Transition," in Hooshang Amirahmadi, ed., *Iran and the Arab World* (New York: St. Martin's Press, 1993), p. 1.
73. Christin Marschall, *Iran's Persian Gulf Policy: From Khomeini to Khatami* (New York: RoutledgeCurzon, 2003), p. 154.
74. Other regional states with strong strategic relations with Tel Aviv during the Cold War include Ethiopia and Turkey.
75. Trita Parsi, *Treacherous Alliance: The Secret Dealings of Israel, Iran, and the United States* (New Haven, CT: Yale University Press, 2007), p. 104.
76. Parsi, *A Single Roll of the Dice,* p. 23.
77. Ibid., pp. 23–24.
78. Parsi, *A Single Roll of the Dice,* p. 26.
79. David Remnick, "Letter from Tel Aviv: The Vegetarian," *The New Yorker,* September 3, 2012.
80. Parsi, *A Single Roll of the Dice,* p. 25.
81. Itamar Rabinovich, *The Lingering Conflict: Israel, the Arabs, and the Middle East 1948–2011* (Washington, DC: Brookings Institution Press, 2011), p. 276.
82. Ibid., p. 277.
83. Ibid., p. 281.
84. "Netanyahu Begins Election Drive with Tough Talk on Iran," *Gulf Times,* October 16, 2012.
85. Robert Dreyfuss, "Why Israel Won't Attack Iran," *The Diplomat,* August 22, 2012.
86. Ibid.
87. David Remnick, "Letter from Tel Aviv: The Vegetarian," *The New Yorker,* September 3, 2012.
88. Ibid.
89. Barak Ravid, "Shimon Peres Wishes Iranians a Happy New Year," *Haaretz,* March 20, 2014.
90. Marc Lynch, "Upheaval: U.S. Policy toward Iran in a Changing Middle East," Center for a New American Security, June 2011, p. 15.
91. F. Gregory Gause, III, "The International Politics of the Gulf," in Louise Fawcett, ed., *International Relations of the Middle East* (Oxford: Oxford University Press, 2009), pp. 272–289 at 273.
92. Shenna, "The Case against the Case against Iran," pp. 348–349.
93. Mahan Abedin, "Saudi Mull Losses in Lebanon as Bid for Influence Is Shattered," in Joshua Craze and Mark Huband, eds., *The Kingdom: Saudi Arabia and the Challenge of 21st Century* (New York: Columbia University Press, 2009), p. 101.
94. Jamal S. al-Suwaidi, "The Gulf Security Dilemma: The Arab Gulf States, the United States, and Iran," in Jamal S. Al-Suwaidi, ed., *Iran and the Gulf: A Search*

for Stability (Abu Dhabi: The Emirates Center for Strategic Studies and Research, 1996), pp. 327–351 at 339.

95. Mahan Abedin, "Saudi Mull Losses in Lebanon as Bid for Influence Is Shattered," in Joshua Craze and Mark Huband, eds., *The Kingdom: Saudi Arabia and the Challenge of 21st Century* (New York: Columbia University Press, 2009), p. 104.

96. Lawrence G. Potter and Gary G. Sick, "Introduction," in Potter and Sick, eds., *Iran, Iraq, and the Legacies of War*, p. 5.

97. Khalid al-Dakhil, "Lebanon Plays Proxy as Arab States Ponder Iran-Syria Alliance," in Joshua Craze and Mark Huband, eds., *The Kingdom: Saudi Arabia and the Challenge of 21st Century* (New York: Columbia University Press, 2009), p. 114.

98. Mahan Abedin, "Iran Ponders Aims of Saudi Mediation and US Ratchets Up 'Psy-Ops' Against Tehran," in Mark Huband and Joshua Craze, eds., *The Kingdom: Saudi Arabia and the Challenge of 21st Century* (New York: Columbia University Press, 2009), p. 130.

99. During this period, a letter signed by both Ahmadinejad and Khamenei acknowledged "Iran's willingness to work with Saudi Arabia to reduce sectarian and political tensions in the Middle East." Ibid.

100. Ibid., p. 349.

101. Parsi, *A Single Roll of the Dice*, p. 18.

102. Kristian Coates Ulrichsen, *Insecure Gulf: The End of Certainty and the Transition to the Post-Oil Era* (New York: Columbia University Press, 2011), p. 48.

103. Anthony H. Cordesman, *Bahrain, Oman, Qatar, and the UAE: Challenges of Security* (Boulder, CO: Westview Press, 1997), p. 119.

104. Ibid., p. 42.

105. Ibid., p. 117.

106. Henner Furtig, *Iran's Rivalry with Saudi Arabia between the Gulf Wars* (Reading, UK: Ithaca Press, 2002), p. 157.

107. Chris Zambelis, "Saudi Arabia-Bahrain Union Reflects Gulf Rivalry," *Asia Times*, June 20, 2012.

108. Ibid.

109. Lawrence G. Potter, *The Persian Gulf: Tradition and Transformation*, Headline Series, Foreign Policy Association, nos. 333–334 (Fall 2011), p. 12.

110. Gerd Nonneman, "The Gulf States and the Iran-Iraq War: Pattern Shifts and Continuities," in Potter and Sick, eds., *Iran, Iraq, and the Legacies of War*, pp. 167–192 at 168.

111. Ibid., 170.

112. Marschall, *Iran's Persian Gulf Policy*, p. 172.

113. Hooshang Amirahmadi and Nader Entessar, "Iranian-Arab Relations in Transition," in Hooshang Amirahmadi, ed., Iran and the Arab World (New York: St. Martin's Press, 1993), pp. 1–18 at 15.

114. Gause, "The International Politics of the Gulf," p. 274.

115. Richard K. Herrmann and R. Williams Ayres, "The New Geo-Politics of the Gulf: Forces for Change and Stability," in Gary G. Sick and Lawrence G. Porter, eds., *The Persian Gulf at the Millennium: Essays in Politics, Economy, Security, and Religion* (New York: St. Martin's Press, 1997), pp. 45–46.

116. Marschall, *Iran's Persian Gulf Policy*, p. 160.

117. Alireza Jafarzadeh, *The Iran Threat: President Ahmadinejad and the Coming Nuclear Crisis* (New York: Palgrave Macmillan, 2007), p. 208.

118. Maloney, *Iran's Long Reach*, p. 58.
119. Shenna, "The Case against the Case against Iran," p. 350.
120. Allin and Simon, *The Sixth Crisis*, p. 75.
121. Kaye and Wehrey, "A Nuclear Iran," p. 112.
122. Shenna, "The Case against the Case against Iran," pp. 351–352.
123. Marschall, *Iran's Persian Gulf Policy*, pp. 157–158.
124. Kemp, "The Impact of Iranian Foreign Policy on Regional Security," pp. 118–135 at 130.
125. Kaye and Wehrey, "Containing Iran?" p. 41.
126. Ulrichsen, *Insecure Gulf*, p. 79.
127. Parag Khanna, *The Second World: Empires and Influence in the New Global Order* (New York: Random House, 2008), p. 234.
128. Ibid., p. 245.
129. Takeyh, *Guardians of the Revolution*, p. 262.
130. Henner Furtig, *Iran's Rivalry with Saudi Arabia between the Gulf Wars* (Reading, UK: Ithaca Press, 2002), p. 155.
131. Al-Khalili, *Oman's Foreign Policy*, pp. 128–129.
132. Joseph A. Kechician, *Oman and the World: The Emergence of an Independent Foreign Policy* (Santa Monica, CA: RAND, 1995), p. 8.
133. Ibid., p. 10.
134. Ibid., p. 101.
135. Al-Khalili, *Oman's Foreign Policy*, pp. 104–105.
136. Ibid., p. 122.
137. Cordesman, *Bahrain, Oman, Qatar, and the UAE*, pp. 132–133.
138. Ulrichsen, *Insecure Gulf*, p. 48.
139. Ibid., p. 69.
140. Peter Hellyer, "The Evolution of UAE Foreign Policy," in Ibrahim Al Abed and Peter Hellyer, eds., *United Arab Emirates: A New Perspective* (London: Trident Press, 2001), pp. 161–178 at 170.
141. Kambiz Foroohar, "Dubai Helps Iran Evade Sanctions as Smugglers Ignore U.S. Laws," *Bloomberg News*, January 25, 2010.
142. Saban Kardas, "Turkey: Redrawing the Middle East Map or Building Sandcastles?" *Middle East Policy* XVII, no. 1 (Spring 2010), p. 131.
143. Selcan Hacaoglu, "Turkey Joins NATO's Missile Defense Shield," *Associated Press*, September 14, 2011.
144. Sinan Ülgen, "Turkey and the Bomb," *The Carnegie Papers*, The Carnegie Endowment for International Peace, February 2012, p. 10.
145. Tom Shanker, "U.S. Hails Deal With Turkey on Missile Shield," *New York Times*, September 15, 2011.
146. Kechician, *Oman and the World*, p. 61.
147. Ulrichsen, *Insecure Gulf*, p. 46.
148. Lynch, "Upheaval," p. 24
149. Mohsen M. Milani, "Iran's Gulf Policy: From Idealism and Confrontation to Pragmatism and Moderation," in Jamal S. Al-Suwaidi, ed., *Iran and the Gulf: A Search for Stability* (Abu Dhabi: The Emirates Center for Strategic Studies and Research, 1996), pp. 83–98 at 84.
150. Sick, "Iran's Foreign Policy: A Revolution in Transition," p. 365.
151. Ulrichsen, *Insecure Gulf*, p. 70.
152. Ibid., pp. 171–172.
153. Akyol, "An Unlikely Trio," p. 128.

154. Al-Khalili, *Oman's Foreign Policy*, p. 90
155. Ibid., p. 103.
156. Robert Malley and Peter Harling, "Beyond Moderates and Militants: How Obama Can Chart a New Course in the Middle East," *Foreign Affairs* 89, no. 5 (September/October 2010), pp. 18–29 at 19.
157. Vali Nasr, *The Shia Revival: How Conflicts within Islam Will Shape the Future* (New York: W.W. Norton and Company, 2007), p. 222.
158. Parsi, *A Single Roll of the Dice*, p. 234.
159. In the wake of the Arab uprisings and the potential Iranian threat, Saudi King Abdullah called for the unity of the GCC against Iran, and Saudi Foreign Minister Prince Saud al-Faisal went further in April 2012 to urge the GCC to forge common foreign and security policies. However, they not only failed to reach a consensus on the unity plan but also have been unable to agree on a U.S.-led joint missile defense system against Iran. "Gulf FMs say more talks needed on plan for unity," *Gulf Times*, September 3, 2012.
160. Radio Monte Carlo, May 16, 1996, cited in Parsi, *Treacherous Alliance*, p. 173.
161. Takeyh, *Guardians of the Revolution*, p. 265.
162. David. D. Kirkpatrick, "Egyptian Leader Adds Rivals of West to Syria Plan," *New York Times*, August 26, 2012.
163. Lynch, The *Arab Uprising*, p. 206.
164. Nadim N. Rouhana, "Misreading Arab Public Opinion on Iran's Nuclear Program," April 9, 2012, The Middle East Channel, http://mideast.foreignpolicy.com/posts/2012/04/09/risks_of_misreading_arab_public_opinion_on_irans_nuclear_programs.
165. Lynch, The *Arab Uprising*, p. 235.

CHAPTER 7

1. John Feffer, "Grave Threats and Grand Bargains: The United States and Regional Order in Northeast Asia," in John Feffer, ed., *The Future of US-Korean Relations* (New York: Routledge, 2006), p. 190.
2. There are important differences between the two regional cases. First, East Asian states are in general much greater in the size of population and economy vis-à-vis North Korea, while Iran is one of the biggest countries and one of the largest holders of fossil fuels in the Middle East. Hence, the potential payoff from Iran's integration into the regional framework can be much greater than that of North Korea's. However, what Pyongyang lacks in terms of natural resource endowment can be partly compensated by its ideal location among the three East Asian countries and South Korea's desire to jump-start the stalled relationship with the North with the ultimate goal unifying the two Koreas. As such, whether North Korea and Iran can be integrated into larger regional frameworks will remain crucial to each region. Second, unlike East Asian states that are far more ethnically homogenous, most countries in the Middle East are ethnically and religiously divided. This means that their domestic debates over Iran tend to be much more fragmented and more politically vulnerable to transnational challenges associated with Iran's regional role (e.g., its ties to Shia populations and its support for radical Islamists). One could also add different stages of nuclear development (North Korea with confirmed nuclear tests vs. Iran with no weapons capability yet) and difference in the number of countries involved (far more in the Middle East, with a greater difficulty in

regional coordination). That said, a comparative analysis of different regional dynamics concerning proliferation challenges in various parts of the world would not only help us better understand difficulties in nuclear diplomacy but also contribute to our understanding of regional orders in the post-9/11 global context.

3. For instance, Jeffrey Legro argues that countries' responses to external shocks differ significantly, depending on the nature of the prevailing ideas in the domestic setting. Jeffrey W. Legro, *Rethinking the World: Great Power Strategies and International Order* (Ithaca, NY: Cornell University Press, 2005).

4. For an interesting account of how domestic political structures in conjunction with systemic factors shape Latin American countries' participation in peacekeeping missions, see Arturo C. Sotomayor Velazquez, "Why Some States Participate in UN Peace Missions While Others Do Not: An Analysis of Civil-Military Relations and Its Effects on Latin America's Contributions to Peacekeeping Operations," *Security Studies* 19 (2010), pp. 160–195.

5. David A. Lake, "Escape from the State of Nature: Authority and Hierarchy in World Politics," *International Security* 32, no. 1 (Summer 2007), p. 79.

6. Paul K. MacDonald, "Correspondence: The Role of Hierarchy in International Politics," *International Security* 32, no. 4 (Spring 2007), p. 172.

7. Hajime Izumi and Katsuhisa Furukawa, "Not Going Nuclear: Japan's Response to North Korea's Nuclear Test," *Arms Control Today* 37, no. 5 (2007), available at https://www.armscontrol.org/act/2007_06/CoverStory.

8. Interview 01–04, Tokyo, September 30, 2004.

9. Peter J. Katzenstein, "Regionalism and Asia," *New Political Economy* 5, no. 3 (November 2000), p. 354.

10. Bjorn Hettne and Fredrik Soderbaum, "Theorising the Rise of Regionness," *New Political Economy* 5, no. 3 (2000), pp. 457–74.

11. Victor Cha and David Kang, *Nuclear North Korea* (New York: Columbia University Press, 2003), pp. 162–163. For a summary version of the book, see Victor Cha and David Kang, "The Korean Crisis," *Foreign Policy*, no. 136 (May/June 2003), pp. 20–28. Also, Michael Green, *Japan's Reluctant Realism: Foreign Policy Challenges in an Era of Uncertain Power* (New York: Palgrave, 2001), p. 144; Zalmay Khalilzad et al., *The United States and Asia: Toward a New U.S. Strategy and Force Posture* (Santa Monica, CA: RAND, 2001); Nishihara Masashi, ed., *The Japan–U.S. Alliance: New Challenges for the 21st Century* (New York: Japan Center for International Exchange, 2000).

12. G. John Ikenberry and Michael Mastanduno, eds., *International Relations Theory and the Asia-Pacific* (New York: Columbia University Press, 2003); Mike Mochizuki and Michael O'Hanlon, "A Liberal Vision for the U.S.-Japanese Alliance," *Survival* 40, no. 22 (Summer 1998), pp. 127–134.

13. Mochizuki and O'Hanlon, "A Liberal Vision," p. 127.

14. Ibid., pp. 127, 133–134.

15. G. John Ikenberry and Michael Mastanduno, "Conclusion: Images of Order in the Asia-Pacific and the Role of the United States," in Ikenberry and Mastanduno, eds., *International Relations Theory and the Asia-Pacific*, p. 435.

16. Lisbeth Aggestam, "A Common Foreign and Security Policy: Role Conceptions and the Politics of Identity in EU," in Lisbeth Aggestam and Adrian Hyde-Price, eds., *Security and Identity in Europe: Exploring the New Agenda* (London: MacMillan Press, 2000), p. 109.

17. Charles A. Kupchan, *The End of the American Era: U.S. Foreign Policy and the Geopolitics of the Twenty-first Century* (New York: Alfred A. Knopf, 2002), p. 281.

18. Kent E. Calder, "The New Face of Northeast Asia," *Foreign Affairs* 80, no. 1 (January/February 2001), p. 122.

19. Francis Fukuyama, "Re-Envisioning Asia," *Foreign Affairs* 84, no. 1 (January/February 2005), p. 75.

20. Etel Solingen, "The Political Economy of Nuclear Restraint." *International Security* 19, no. 2 (Fall 1994), pp. 126–169; Mitchell Reiss, *Bridled Ambition: Why Countries Constrain Their Nuclear Capabilities* (Baltimore: Johns Hopkins University Press, 1995); Scott D. Sagan, "Why Do States Build Nuclear Weapons?" *International Security* 21, no. 3 (Winter 1996/1997), pp. 54–86; Peter Liberman, "The Rise and Fall of the South African Bomb," *International Security* 26, no. 2 (Fall 2001), pp. 45–86.

21. Scott D. Sagan, *The Limits of Safety: Organizations, Accidents, and Nuclear Weapons* (Princeton, NJ: Princeton University Press, 1993); Scott D. Sagan, "The Perils of Proliferation: Organization Theory, Deterrence Theory, and the Spread of Nuclear Weapons," *International Security* 18, no. 4 (Spring 1994), pp. 66–107; Scott D. Sagan and Kenneth N. Waltz, *The Spread of Nuclear Weapons: A Debate Renewed* (New York: W. W. Norton, 2003).

22. Graham Allison, *Nuclear Terrorism: The Ultimate Preventable Catastrophe* (New York: Henry Holt & Company, 2004); Joseph Cirincione, *Deadly Arsenals: Tracking Weapons of Mass Destruction* (Washington, D.C.: Carnegie Endowment for International Peace, 2002).

23. For a useful discussion on the distinction between supply-side and demand-side measures, see Chaim Braun and Christopher F. Chyba, "Proliferation Rings: New Challenges to the Nuclear Nonproliferation Regime," *International Security* 29, no. 2 (Fall 2004), pp. 5–49.

24. Ibid., p. 47.

25. Francis Fukuyama, "After Neoconservatism," *New York Times*, February 19, 2006; Dueck, "Strategies for Managing Rogue States," p. 240.

26. Charles Kupchan, *No One's World: The West, The Rising Rest, and the Coming Global Turn* (New York: Oxford University Press, 2012), p. 197.

27. Mitchell B. Reiss, "Hope over Experience: Denuclearizing the North," *The National Interest*, May/June 2007, p. 23.

28. Sherle R. Schwenninger, "Beyond Dominance," New America Foundation, February 1, 2004, http://www.newamerica.net/publications/policy/beyond_dominance.

29. Similarly, Michael Mastanduno observes that due to its focus on the war on terror, "the United States may not be prepared to stabilize regional conflicts as consistently and predictably as it did during the 1990s." See his "Hegemonic Order, September 11, and the Consequences of the Bush Revolution," in Mark Beeson, ed., *Bush and Asia: America's Evolving Relations with East Asia* (Routledge: London and New York, 2005), pp. 33–34.

30. Kurt M. Campbell and Celeste Johnson Ward, "New Battle Stations?" *Foreign Affairs* 82, no. 5 (September/October 2003), p. 103.

31. Victor D. Cha, "The U.S. Role in Inter-Korean Relations," in Samuel S. Kim, ed., *Inter-Korean Relations: Problems and Prospects* (New York: Palgrave MacMillan, 2004), p. 143.

32. *Implications of the U.S.–North Korea Nuclear Agreement*, Hearing before the Subcommittee on East Asian and Pacific Affairs of the Committee on Foreign

Relations, United States Senate, One Hundred Third Congress, Second Session, December 1, 1994, p. 12.

33. William E. Odom, "The Nuclear Option," *Foreign Policy*, no. 160 (May/June 2007), p. 51.

34. Parag Khanna, *The Second World: Empires and Influence in the New Global Order* (New York: Random House, 2008), p. 322.

35. In 2011, President Obama pronounced that "as a Pacific nation, the United States will play a larger and long-term role in shaping this region and its future, by upholding core principles and in close partnership with allies and friends." The text of President Barack Obama's address to the Parliament of Australia, The White House, November 17, 2011.

36. Hillary Clinton, "America's Pacific Century," *Foreign Policy*, no. 189 (November 2011), pp. 56–63.

37. Ibid., pp. 1–2.

38. A Chinese column describes the new U.S. regional strategy as "moves against China." "The New US Maritime Strategy Shows Its Two Sides to China," *People's Daily*, March 19, 2015.

39. Robert Wright, "War on Evil," *Foreign Policy*, no. 144 (September/October, 2004), pp. 34–35.

40. "Biden Says China, U.S. Share Global Responsibilities," *Associated Press*, August 21, 2011.

41. To be fair, the Obama administration's policy toward Iran was hamstrung by Congressional pressure to get tough on Iran. While Obama officials emphasized the red line as Iran's weapons capability, the Congress was calling for a position closer to the Israeli red line of not allowing any enrichment capacity, effectively turning Obama's Iran policy into what a State Department official called "a gamble on a single roll of the dice" in Obama's first year in office. See Trita Parsi, "Give Obama Elbow Room on Iran," *New York Times*, June 13, 2012.

42. ElBaradei, *The Age of Deception*, pp. 312–313.

43. Choe Sang-Hun and David E. Sanger, "North Koreans Launch Rocket in Defiant Act," *New York Times*, December 12, 2012.

44. For instance, North Korea not only conducted a second nuclear test but also boasted its second path to nuclear weapons, an enriched uranium program. Also, during the Obama presidency Tehran's rate of enrichment of uranium has tripled. Joby Warrick, "Obama's Policy on Iran Bears Some Fruit, but Nuclear Program Still Advances," *Washington Post*, September 24, 2012.

45. Siegfried S. Hecker, "The Real Threat from North Korea Is the Nuclear Arsenal Built Over the Last Decade," *Bulletin of the Atomic Scientists*, January 7, 2015. In 2012, David Albright and Christina Walrond of the Institute for Science and International Security estimated that North Korea might have about five to twenty-seven nuclear weapons. See David Albright and Christina Walrond, "North Korea's Estimated Stocks of Plutonium and Weapon-Grade Uranium," Institute for Science and International Security, August 16, 2012, p. 36, available at http://isis-online.org/uploads/isis-reports/documents/dprk_fissile_material_production_16Aug2012.pdf.

46. Gary Sick, "The Danger of a Failed Iran Deal," *Politico*, March 8, 2015.

47. Richard L. Armitage and Joseph S. Nye, *The U.S.-Japan Alliance: Getting Asia Right through 2020*, Center for Strategic and International Studies, February 2007, p. 2.

48. Ibid., p. 8.

49. Yoichi Funabashi, "Japan Needs Its Own 'Asian' Vision," *Asahi Shimbun*, December 14, 2004.

50. Ibid.

51. Yoichi Funabashi, *Asia Pacific Fusion* (Washington, DC: Institute for International Economics, 1995) cited in Mike M. Mochizuki, "Japan's Changing International Role" in Thomas U. Berger, Mike M. Mochizuki, and Jitsuo Tsuchiyama, eds., *Japan in International Politics: The Foreign Policies of an Adaptive State* (Boulder, CO: Lynne Rienner Publishers, 2007), p. 17.

52. Jitsuro Terashima, "Shin Bei Nyu A no sogo senryaku o motomete [Aspiring for a Comprehensive Strategy of 'Close to America and Entering Asia']" *Chuo Koron* (March 1996), pp. 20–38, cited in Mochizuki, "Japan's Changing International Role," p. 17.

53. Kazuhiko Togo, "Japan and the Security Structures of Multilateralism," in Kent E. Calder and Francis Fukuyama, eds., *East Asian Multilateralism: Prospects for Regional Stability* (Baltimore: The Johns Hopkins University Press, 2007), p. 188.

54. Scholarly analyses of the rise of China are too many to cite here. Some of the representative recent examples include David C. Kang, China *Rising: Peace, Power, and Order in East Asia* (New York: Columbia University Press, 2009); Aaron L. Friedberg, *A Contest for Supremacy: China, America, and the Struggle for Mastery in Asia* (New York: W. W. Norton, 2011); Henry Kissinger, *On China* (New York: Penguins, 2011); Michael Beckley, "China's Century? Why America's Edge Will Endure," *International Security* 36, no. 3 (Winter 2011/2012), pp. 41–78; Jeffrey A. Bader, *Obama and China's Rise: An Insider's Account of America's Asia Strategy* (Washington, DC: Brookings Institution Press, 2012); and David Shambaugh, *China Goes Global: A Partial Power* (New York: Oxford University Press, 2013).

55. Jeffrey W. Legro, "What China Will Want: The Future Intentions of a Rising Power," *Perspectives on Politics* 5, no. 3 (September 2007), p. 522.

56. Henry Kissinger, "A Nuclear Test for Diplomacy," *Washington Post*, May 16, 2006.

57. Avery Goldstein, "Across the Yalu: China's Interests and the Korean Peninsula in a Changing World," in Alastair Iain Johnston and Robert S. Ross, eds., *New Directions in the Study of China's Foreign Policy* (Stanford, CA: Stanford University Press, 2006), p. 150.

58. Ashton B. Carter and William J. Perry, *Preventive Defense: A New Security Strategy for America* (Washington, DC: Brookings Institution Press, 1999), pp. 118–120.

59. Thomas J. Christensen, "Fostering Stability or Creating a Monster? The Rise of China and U.S. Policy toward East Asia," *International Security* 31, no. 1 (Summer 2006), p. 124.

60. Jonathan D. Pollack, "The Transformation of the Asian Security Order: Assessing China's Impact," in David Shambaugh, ed., *Power Shift* (Stanford, CA: Stanford University Press, 2006), p. 343.

61. Michael D. Swaine, "U.S. Security Policy under Clinton and Bush: China and Korea," in Chae-Jin Lee, ed., *U.S. Security Policy Under Clinton and Bush: Continuity and Change*, Monograph Series, no. 17, The Keck Center for International and Strategic Studies Claremont McKenna College, 2005, pp. 55–57.

62. Michael Mandelbaum, *The Frugal Superpower: America's Global Leadership in a Cash-Strapped Era* (New York: PublicAffairs, 2010); Paul K. MacDonald and

Joseph M. Parent, "Graceful Decline? The Surprising Success of Great Power Retrenchment," *International Security* 35, no. 4 (Spring 2011), pp. 7–44; Christopher Layne, "This Time It's Real: The End of Unipolarity and the Pax Americana," *International Studies Quarterly* 56 (2012), pp. 203–213; Christopher Layne, "The (Almost) Triumph of Offshore Balancing," *The National Interest*, January 27, 2012. For an analysis of the continued preeminence of the United States, see Beckley, "China's Century?"

63. Stephen M. Walt, *Taming American* Power: *The Global Response to U.S. Primacy* (New York: W.W. Norton & Company, 2005), p. 247.

64. G. John Ikenberry, *After Victory*, 2001, G. John Ikenberry, ed., *America Unrivaled*, 2002.

65. Michael Mastanduno, "Hegemonic Order, September 11," pp. 25–26.

66. Fu-Kuo Liu, "East Asian Regionalism: Theoretical Perspectives," Fu-Kuo Liu and Philippe Regnier, eds., *Regionalism in East Asia: Paradigm Shifting?* (London: RoutledgeCurzon, 2003), p. 19.

67. Jitsuo Tsuchiyama, "Ironies in Japanese Defense and Disarmament Policy," in Takashi Inoguchi and Purnendra Jain, eds., *Japanese Foreign Policy Today: A Reader* (New York: Palgrave, 2000), p. 149.

68. This is not to suggest that the presence of a common identity or a common regional vision is the only condition for successful regional cooperation. The existence of common interests, such as dealing with a regional financial crisis, promoted temporary regional cooperation in East Asia. That said, having common, or at least complementary, regional visions would be crucial to achieving more enduring and wide-ranging regional cooperation. Tsuneo Akaha, "Conclusion: Nationalism versus Regionalism in Northeast Asia," in Tsuneo Akaha, ed., *Politics and Economics in Northeast Asia: Nationalism and Regionalism in Contention* (New York: St. Martin's Press, 1999) p. 381.

69. "China, Japan, S Korea Agree to Enhance Systematic Co-op," *Xinhua*, December 13, 2008.

70. Joel Rathus, "China-Japan-Korea Trilateral Cooperation and the East Asian Community," *East Asia Forum*, June 15, 2010, available at http://www.eastasia forum.org/2010/06/15/china-japan-korea-trilateral-cooperation-and-the-east-asian-community. At the Fifth Trilateral Summit in May 2012, leaders from the three Asian states also signed the Trilateral Agreement for the Promotion, Facilitation and Protection of Investment. See Xiaolei Gu, "China-Japan-South Korea Sign Trilateral Agreement and Launch FTA Talks," *China Briefing*, May 14, 2012, available at http://www.china-briefing.com/news/2012/05/14/china-japan-south-korea-sign-trilateral-agreement-and-launch-fta-talks.html.

EPILOGUE

1. Avery Goldstein, "Across the Yalu: National Interests on the Korean Peninsula in a Changing World," in Alastair Iain Johnston and Robert S. Ross, eds., *New Directions in the Study of China's Foreign Policy* (Stanford, CA: Stanford University Press, 2006), p. 152.

2. Rajeev Agarwal, "India and Security in the Gulf," *Asian Times*, December 10, 2013.

3. Trita Parsi, *A Single Roll of the Dice: Obama's Diplomacy with Iran* (New Haven, Yale University Press, 2012), p. 225.

4. Charles K. Armstrong, *Tyranny of the Weak: North Korea and the World, 1950–1992* (Ithaca, NY: Cornell University Press, 2013), p. 289.

5. "Interview with Song Minsoon, Former South Korean Foreign Minister," *Donga Ilbo*, January 21, 2014.

6. *Donga Ilbo*, December 4, 2012.

7. Choe Sang-Hun, "South Korea Is Surprised by Departure of Candidate," *New York Times*, November 23, 2012

8. "Tongil Junbiwiwonhoi, Hwaksilhan Yokhwal-ul Jeonghara [Time to Clarify the Role of the Presidential Unification Committee]," *Donga Ilbo*, December 4, 2012.

9. "Bordering on Comradely," *The Economist*, August 24, 2013.

10. Chung-in Moon, "Washington-ui ddae-annin hanil haekmoojang nonlan [A Debate on Nuclear Proliferation in South Korea and Japan in Washington]," *Joongang Ilbo*, March 10, 2014.

11. *Kyunghyang Shinmun*, March 14, 2014.

12. "Unification Will Become 'Big Bonanza' Only with Thorough Preparation," *Donga Ilbo*, January 7, 2014.

13. *Hankyoreh Shinmun*, January 22, 2014.

14. Giwook Shin, *Donga Ilbo*, August 12, 2014

15. Jaegyu Park, "8·15 Daebuk Message-rul Kidaehanda [Hoping for a New Message to North Korea]," *Hankyoreh Shinmun*, August 12, 2014.

16. Lee Hakyung, "Park Geun-hye, Gangdaeguk-eman Maedalimyon Silpaehanda [Park Geun-hye Will Fail If Relying Solely on Great Powers]," *Joongang Ilbo*, July 16, 2014.

17. David Chance and Jack Kim, "China Joins U.S., Japan in Condemning North Korea Nuclear Test," *Reuters*, February 12, 2013.

18. Jane Perlez, "China Ban on Items for Nuclear Use to North Korea May Stall Arms Bid," *New York Times*, September 29, 2013.

19. "New Vitality in China-US ties," *People's Daily*, February 14, 2014.

20. In 2013, Deng Yuwen, deputy editor of a journal associated with the Central Party School, published an opinion piece in *The Financial Times*, calling for a formal end of strategic relations with North Korea and the unification of the two Koreas. Deng Yuwen, "China Should Abandon North Korea," *Financial Times*, February 27, 2013, cited in Seong-hyon Lee, "Firm Warning, Light Consequences: China's DPRK Policy Upholds Status Quo," *China Brief* 13, no. 23 (November 22, 2013).

21. Yusik Choi, "'Joong, Bukhan Pogi-haeya' Gigo-han Dang Gigwanji Bu-Pyonjipjang Jikwi Haejae Danghae [A Chinese Party Journal Deputy Editor Suspended After His Plea to Abandon North Korea]," *Chosun Ilbo*, April 1, 2013.

22. Ashish Kumar Sen, "Obama Admin Unfairly Pitting China Against North Korea: Diplomat," *Washington Times*, April 10, 2014.

23. *Donga Ilbo*, November 6, 2013, cited in Lee, "Firm Warning, Light Consequences."

24. Lee, "Firm Warning, Light Consequences."

25. T. J. Pempel, "Japan and the Two Koreas: The Foreign-Policy Power of Domestic Politics," in Marie Soderberg, ed., *Changing Power Relations in Northeast Asia: Implications for Relations between Japan and South Korea* (New York: Routledge, 2011), p. 69.

26. "Koizumi Turned down DPJ Offer to Visit North Korea, Pay Condolences After Kim's death," *Japan Times: Sunday*, April 1, 2012.

27. Martin Fackler, "Japanese and North Korean Officials Meet for Their First Talks in 4 Years," *New York Times*, August 29, 2012.

28. "Editorial: Step Forward with North Korea," *Japan Times*, November 23, 2012.
29. "Abe, Obama to Cooperate on N. Korea/2 Leaders Also Discuss Plans for Jan. Summit," *Yomiuri Shimbun*, December 19, 2013.
30. David Chance and Jack Kim, "China Joins U.S., Japan in Condemning North Korea Nuclear Test," *Reuters*, February 12, 2013.
31. "Japan Criticizes N. Korea's Nuclear Testing at U.N. committee," *Kyodo News International*, October 8, 2013.
32. Takashi Nakagawa, "Pyongyang Seeks to Break Deadlock," *Yomiuri Shimbun*, March 17, 2014.
33. "Japan, North Korea Hold First Formal Talks Since 2012," *AFP*, March 30, 2014.
34. Martin Fackler, "Japan and North Korea Said to Agree to Formal Talks," *New York Times*, March 20, 2014.
35. Hyungjoon Park, "Il 'Buk Haeksilhum-haedo Yanggook Gyoseob Jisok' [Japan Would Continue to Negotiate with North Korea Even If North Korea Conducts a Missile Test]," *Donga Ilbo*, June 9, 2014.
36. Geukin Bae, "Abe-ui Wiheom-han Dokju Unjae-kaji [When Will Abe's Dangerous Run End?]," *Donga Ilbo*, June 5, 2014.
37. Tetsuo Kotani, "U.S.-Japan Allied Maritime Strategy: Balancing the Rise of Maritime China," *Strategic Japan*, Center for Strategic and International Studies, April 2014, p. 1. See *National Defense Program Guidelines for FY 2014 and Beyond*, Ministry of Defense, December 17, 2013, http://www.mod.go.jp/j/approach/agenda/guideline/2014/pdf/20131217_e2.pdf.
38. "Coalition Reaches Deal on Security Laws/LDP, Komeito Aim to Submit Bills in May," *Yomiuri Shimbun*, March 19, 2015.
39. During the G7 summit in June 2014, Japanese Prime Minister Abe was seeking to have a summit meeting with President Obama, but the U.S. side refused to hold the summit. The cool reaction from the United States was attributed to Japan's unilateral decision to lift some sanctions against Pyongyang after their bilateral meetings over the abduction issue. *Chosun Ilbo*, June 7, 2014.
40. Kristian Coates Ulrichsen, *Insecure Gulf: The End of Certainty and the Transition to the Post-Oil Era* (New York: Columbia University Press, 2011), p. 181.
41. Neil MacFarquhar, "Sunni Leaders Gaining Clout in Mideast," *New York Times*, November 27, 2012.
42. F. Gregory Gause III, *The International Relations of the Persian Gulf* (Cambridge, UK: Cambridge University Press, 2010), p. 177.
43. Robert Malley, Karim Sadjadpour, and Ömer Taşpınar, "Israel, Turkey and Iran in the Changing Arab World," *Middle East Policy Council* XIX, no. 1 (Spring 2012), available at http://www.mepc.org/journal/middle-east-policy-archives/israel-turkey-and-iran-changing-arab-world.
44. Herb Keinon, "Netanyahu Slams Proposed Deal with Iran in Harshest Words to Date," *Jerusalem Post*, November 8, 2013.
45. Herb Keinon, "Israel to Lobby Against Any Deal That Would Leave Iran with Enrichment Capabilities," *Jerusalem Post*, November 10, 2013.
46. Ross Colvin, "'Cut Off Head of Snake' Saudis told U.S. on Iran," *Reuters*, November 29, 2010.
47. Robert F. Worth, "U.S. and Saudis in Growing Rift as Power Shifts," *New York Times*, November 25, 2013.
48. Loveday Morris, "U.S. Ties in Persian Gulf at Risk as Obama Allows Space for Russian-Syrian Plan," *Washington Post*, September 11, 2013.

49. Nawaf Obaid, "A Saudi Arabian Defense Doctrine." Paper, Belfer Center for Science and International Affairs, Harvard Kennedy School, May 27, 2014.

50. Shounaz Meky and Eman El-Shenawi, "The GCC's Future Military Command a 'Political Signal,' Say Experts," *Al Arabiya*, December 12, 2013.

51. Ibid.

52. Ben Hubbard, Robert F. Worth, and Michael R. Gordon, "Power Vacuum in Middle East Lifts Militants," *New York Times*, January 4, 2014.

53. Ethan Bronner and Michael Slackman, "Saudi Troops Enter Bahrain to Help Put Down Unrest," *New York Times*, March 14, 2011.

54. "Trouble Ahead," *The Economist*, December 14, 2013.

55. "Shifting Sands: A Deal between America and Iran Would Have Big Repercussions," *The Economist*, November 30, 2013.

56. Mohammed Ayoob, "Turkey's Balancing Act between Mideast and West," *Japan Times*, January 12, 2012.

57. Robert F. Worth, "U.S. and Saudis in Growing Rift as Power Shifts," *New York Times*, November 25, 2013.

58. "Kerry in Turkey to Boost Support for Anti-IS Coalition," *BBC*, September 12, 2014.

59. "Oman Opposes Gulf Union Plan," *AFP*, December 9, 2013.

60. Paul Crompton, "Why Is Oman against a Gulf Union?" *Al Arabiya*, December 10, 2013.

61. Robert F. Worth, "Drawing a Line on Syria, U.S. Keeps Eye on Iran Policy," *New York Times*, September 2, 2013.

62. "Tehran 'Looking to Open a New Page in Ties with Gulf,'" *Gulf Times*, December 3, 2013.

63. "Qatar, Iran Discuss Ties on All Fronts," *Gulf Times*, February 27, 2014.

64. "Time to End Iran Sanctions, Dubai Ruler Tells BBC," *Al Arabiya*, January 13, 2014

65. Ramin Mostaghim and Carol J. Williams, "Iran's Rouhani Outmaneuvering Hard-Liners on Syria, Nuclear Talks," *Los Angeles Times*, September 5, 2013.

66. "Iran Reassures Gulf States on Nuclear Deal," *Gulf Times*, December 1, 2013.

67. "Turkey–Iran Relations," Ministry of Foreign Affairs, the Republic of Turkey, http://www.mfa.gov.tr/turkey-iran-relations.en.mfa.

68. Michael R. Gordon and David E. Sanger, "Iran Agrees to Detailed Nuclear Outline, First Step Toward a Wider Deal," *New York Times*, April 2, 2015.

69. Brian Murphy, "Iran Nuclear Pact Stirs Hope—and Fear—of New Political Order in Mideast," *Washington Post*, April 3, 2015.

70. Eline Gordts, "How the World Reacted to the Iran Nuclear Agreement," *Huffington Post*, April 3, 2015.

71. "Riyadh Says Iran Nuclear Deal Must Ensure Arab Security," *AFP*, April 7, 2015.

72. David E. Sanger, William J. Broad, and Choe Sang-Hun, "North Korea Appears to Restart Plutonium Reactor," *New York Times*, September 11, 2013.

73. "Obama Lashes North Korea as Weak 'Pariah State,'" *AFP*, April 26, 2014.

74. Henry A. Kissinger, "Iran Must Be President Obama's Immediate Priority," *Washington* Post, November 16, 2012.

75. *Donga Ilbo*, August 2, 2014.

INDEX

Abbas, Mahmoud, 133
Abdullah II (king of Jordan), 136
Abe Shinzo: abduction of Japanese
    citizens by North Korea and, 73,
    118, 151, 169, 231n39; China and,
    170; constitutional amendment
    debate and, 74; East Asian
    regional order and, 74, 170;
    Japan's regional role conception
    and, 159; Koizumi administration
    and, 71; Liberal Democratic Party
    (LDP) and, 73, 104, 118; North
    Korea and, 18, 71, 73–75, 104,
    113, 118, 121, 151, 169, 231n39;
    United States and, 18, 104, 113,
    159, 169–70
Acharya, Amitav, 123, 185n79
Action Plan for Promoting Trilateral
    Cooperation (2008), 164
Afghanistan: Iran and, 128–29, 144;
    Japan and, 102; Persian Gulf
    states and, 143; Soviet invasion
    of, 126; Taliban regime in, 2, 129,
    144; U.S. war (2001–) in, 102,
    128–29, 143–44
Agarwal, Rajeev, 165
Aggestam, Lisbeth, 154
Agreed Framework (United States and
    North Korea, 1994): Galluci on,
    158; Japan and, 4, 70, 79; Korean
    Peninsula Energy Development
    Organization (KEDO) framework
    and, 79, 88; Negative Security
    Assurance (NSA) in, 44; South
    Korea and, 4, 79; termination
    (2002) of, 38, 108; U.S.-based

opposition to, 82, 189n17; U.S.
    fuel supplies to North Korea
    under, 4, 102; Yongbyon nuclear
    reactor issue addressed by, 4
Ahmadinejad, Mahmoud, 133
Albright, David, 42
Albright, Madeleine, 86–88, 97, 127
alliances and alliance politics: Bush
    Doctrine and, 100, 106–13,
    122–23, 175; common values as
    basis for, 153–54; in East Asia,
    3–6, 8, 16, 20–26, 28–29, 46,
    52–53, 56–58, 62, 64–65, 67–70,
    74–78, 82, 85, 88–95, 97, 99–100,
    104, 106–13, 117–18, 120,
    122–23, 148–50, 153–54, 156,
    160–62, 175; Global Posture
    Review (GPR) on, 157; in the
    Middle East, 3–4, 6, 8, 24, 26,
    126, 129, 142–43, 145, 149–50,
    175; Nye Initiative and, 5–6; Perry
    Process and, 77–78, 85, 88–91, 97,
    106, 149; regionalism and, 92, 94;
    threat perception and, 96; United
    States and, 20–21, 24–26, 28–29,
    46, 52–53, 56–58, 62, 64–65,
    67–70, 74–78, 93–95, 100, 104,
    106, 112–13, 118, 120, 122–23,
    142, 148–50, 153–54, 156,
    160–62
Arab Spring (Arab uprisings) (2011):
    Bahrain and, 138, 146, 172; Egypt
    and, 136, 145, 166, 172; Israel
    and, 135–36; Middle East regional
    order and, 124–25, 160, 164–66,
    170–71; Turkey and, 172

Carter, Ashton, 162
Carter, Jimmy, 155
Cavusoglu, Mevlut, 174
Cha, Victor, 210n104, 213n43,
    215–216n92, 225n11, 226n31
Cheney, Dick, 32–33, 39, 100
Chen Qichen, 46–47
Cheonan sinking (2010), 59, 166
Chiang Mai Initiatives, 164
China: ASEAN Plus Three (APT)
    framework and, 21, 92–94,
    114–15, 119; Bush Doctrine and,
    47; Cold War and, 44; Communist
    Party in, 17, 51, 63–64, 66;
    cooperative security strategy and,
    61–62; domestic political debates
    in, 63–65, 156, 185n85, 186n87;
    "dual national identity" of, 60;
    East Asian regional order and, 2,
    12–13, 15, 17–19, 21–22, 25,
    28–30, 41–44, 46–48, 52–53,
    59–60, 62–65, 70, 78, 80–81,
    93–96, 103, 105–6, 109, 112,
    114–16, 118–19, 123, 156,
    158–63, 165, 168; Four Party
    Talks and, 80–81, 96;
    International Liaison Department
    (Chinese Communist Party) and,
    17, 63–64, 66; Iran and, 159, 168;
    Japan and, 16, 21–22, 41, 47, 51,
    56, 61–62, 65, 74, 78, 93–94,
    113–20, 122–23, 164, 169–70;
    Korean War and, 62; military
    modernization in, 111, 119;
    NATO's accidental bombing of
    embassy in Belgrade (1999) of, 93;
    New Security Concept (NSC) in,
    62; North Korea and, 12–13,
    17–18, 22, 24–25, 28–30, 42–44,
    46, 48–49, 52, 54–55, 60, 62–67,
    79, 81, 84–85, 93, 96, 103–5,
    110–11, 115, 149, 151, 156, 159,
    162, 165, 167–68, 185n85,
    186n87, 193n104; nuclear
    weapons and, 60; "peaceful rise"
    (*heping jueqi*) strategy and, 60–61;
    People's Liberation Army in, 17,
    94; Perry Process and, 78, 83, 93,
    95–96; Proliferation Security
    Initiative (PSI) and, 43–44;

regionalism and, 94, 105–6,
113–17, 160, 164; regional role
conception in, 25, 51, 53, 60–67,
81, 94, 100, 103, 149, 151,
162–63, 167; role conflict in, 162;
Sino-Japanese War (1894) and,
62; Six Party Talks and, 5, 11, 22,
52, 60, 63–64, 81, 103, 105–6,
110, 118, 123; South Korea and, 2,
16, 21, 54–55, 58–59, 66, 78,
93–95, 100, 107, 109–11, 114–18,
123, 160, 164, 166–67; "sunshine
policy" and, 55; Taiwan and, 41,
61–62, 80, 118; Taiwan Straits
Crisis (1995–1996) and, 80;
Tiananmen Square protests
(1989) in, 61; United States and,
5, 15, 17–18, 22, 28–29, 42–43,
46–47, 49, 53–54, 60–65, 74, 93,
95–97, 105, 111, 116, 120,
148–49, 158–63, 167–68;
World War II and, 62; Yeonpyong
Island shelling (2010)
and, 66
China, Japan, South Korea Forum for
    Peaceful Development and
    Security, 117
Cho Sung-tae, 95
Christensen, Thomas, 162
Chung Dong Young, 43, 178n12
Chu Shulong, 105
Cirincione, Joseph, 2
Clinton, Bill: Camp David negotiations
    (2000) and, 88; China and, 28–29,
    54; "dual containment" policy
    regarding Iran and Iraq and, 139;
    Japan and, 28–29; Kim Dae Jung
    and, 88, 90; Middle East regional
    strategic blueprint (1995) and,
    127; nonproliferation doctrine
    and, 25, 27, 34, 36; North Korea
    and, 5, 16, 21, 25–31, 37–39, 45,
    48, 54, 76–79, 82–86, 88–89, 91,
    95, 97, 99–101, 122, 149, 157–58,
    162, 189n17; Perry Process and,
    84–85, 95, 149; regionalism
    approach in East Asia and, 91–92;
    South Korea and, 28–29, 45, 54,
    85, 88, 90, 158
Clinton, Hillary, 158

Kahwaji, Riad, 139
Kakizawa Koji, 30
Kanemaru Shin, 70
Kang, David, 19, 186n88, 225n11
Kan Naoto, 169
Katzenstein, Peter, 153, 177n4, 181n38
Kawaguchi Yoriko, 53, 71, 116
Keeny, Spurgeon, 34
Keller, Bill, 36
Kelly, James, 37–39, 102, 108
Kessler, Glenn, 28
Khalilzad, Zalmay, 32–33
Khamenei, Ali, 172
Khatami, Mohammad, 9, 127–28, 137, 141
Khomeini, Ruhollah, 126
Kim Dae-jung: ASEAN Plus Three framework and, 114; ASEAN Regional Forum and, 94; Bush and, 31, 100–101; Clinton and, 88, 90; East Asian Vision Group and, 92; Japan and, 52, 90–91; Nobel Peace Prize for, 55; North Korea and, 17, 29–30, 44, 49, 52, 55, 80, 84–86, 97, 100–101, 167; Obuchi and, 52, 90–91; Perry Process and, 84–85; regional order and, 12, 17, 21, 52, 95, 97; Six Party Talks and, 115; "sunshine policy" and, 30, 52, 55, 80, 97, 100–101, 167; United States and, 86, 88–89, 100–101
Kim Dalchoong, 117
Kim Hajoong, 58
Kim Jong-il: Albright and, 86–87; China and, 22, 30, 52, 66; death of, 59, 66, 166, 169; Hu Jintao and, 66; Japan and, 55; Pyongyang Declaration (2002) and, 72; second inter-Korean summit (2007) and, 121; Six Party Talks and, 5; United States and, 86–87
Kim Jung Un, 66, 166–67, 169
Kim Samhoon, 120
Kim Young-sam, 29–30, 54, 79–80, 117
Kish gas field, 142
Kissinger, Henry, 2, 162, 174
Koizumi Junichiro: Bush and, 43–44, 47, 102, 107, 118; China and, 114, 118–19; Kim Jong Il and, 72; North Korea and, 12, 17, 41–44, 50–52,

71–72, 74, 102–4, 108, 116, 123, 169, 178n12, 195n1; Pyongyang Declaration and, 72; regional order and, 71–72; Six Party Talks and, 5; South Korea and, 104, 107, 114; United States and, 43–44, 47, 71, 102, 107, 118; World War II shrines and, 182– 83n51
Kong Quan, 43
Kono Yohei, 29
Korea. See North Korea; South Korea
Korea-Japan Millennium Symposium (2002), 117
Korean Peninsula Energy Development Organization (KEDO) framework: Agreed Framework (1994) provision for, 79, 88; Japan and, 70, 81, 88–90; as "minilateralism," 94; regionalism and, 97; role congruence and, 88–89; South Korea and, 88–89
Korean War: Armistice Agreement (1953) and, 80, 87, 89; China and, 62; lingering tensions following, 40–41; origins of, 54
Kristof, Nicholas, 48
Kroenig, Matthew, 7–8
Kumchangri (North Korea), suspected nuclear facility at, 82–83
Kupchan, Charles, 156
Kurds, 131
Kuwait, 137–40

Larson, Deborah, 11
Lebanon: Iran and, 9, 171; Saudi Arabia and, 137, 172; United States and, 9
Lee Dong-il, 174–75
Lee Jong Seok, 58
Lee Myung-bak: China and, 66; departure from regionalism by, 122, 166; election (2007) of, 217n136; North Korea and, 58–59, 75, 122, 166; United States and, 166
Lee Soo Hyuck, 108
Legro, Jeffrey, 161
Leverett, Flynt, 127
Libby, L. Scooter, 32
Liberal Democratic Party (LDP; Japan): abduction of Japanese citizens by

North Korea and, 118; Abe and, 73, 104, 118; collective self-defense legislation and, 170; New Defense Program Outline (2004) and, 118–19; North Korea policy and, 70, 81–82, 85, 104, 168; "Peace Constitution" amendment proposals of, 118

liberal institutionalist analysis in international relations theory, 153

Libya, 42, 129

Lim Dong Won, 55, 84

Lindsay, James, 125

Li Peng, 63

Liu Jianchao, 64

Liu Ming, 46

Li Zhaoxing, 116

Mahathir Mohamad, 114, 185n79

al-Maktoum, Sheikh Mohammed Bin Rashid, 173

Mastanduno, Michael, 154, 163

McCormack, Gavan, 112

McDevitt, Michael, 5

Menashri, David, 135

Middle East regional order: alliances and alliance politics in, 3–4, 6, 8, 24, 26, 126, 129, 142–43, 145, 149–50, 175; Arab Spring uprisings (2011) and, 124–25, 160, 164–66, 170–71; Camp David negotiations (2000) and, 88; Egypt's role in, 137, 145, 171; Gulf Cooperation Council's role in, 24, 26; Iran's role in, 1–4, 6–11, 13–14, 18–19, 22–24, 26, 124–26, 128–30, 134–35, 137–40, 144–53, 156, 161, 166, 170–74, 224n2; nuclear nonproliferation from a regional perspective and, 6–8, 10, 24, 124, 146–49, 151, 156–57, 160, 166, 174; Oman's role in, 13, 144–45; Qatar's role in, 13, 142, 144, 171, 173; role conflict and, 18–19, 22–23, 128, 132, 142, 144, 147–49, 155; role congruence and, 147, 149, 155, 157, 172–73; Saudi Arabia's role in, 4, 19, 137–38, 145, 171, 173; threat perceptions and, 8, 10, 133–35, 139, 150,

152–53, 171–72; Turkey's role in, 11, 13–14, 19, 22, 24, 130–33, 144, 172; United Arab Emirates's role in, 13, 142; United States' role in, 2, 4, 6, 8, 10, 14, 18, 22, 24, 26, 46, 124–30, 132, 139–46, 148–49, 151, 153, 157–58, 160, 171, 175

"minilateralism," 94

Mochizuki, Mike, 153

"The Modality of the Security and Defense Capability of Japan: The Outlook for the 21st Century" (1994 report), 68

Moon Jae-in, 166

Morimoto Satoshi, 104

Mori Yoshiro: ASEAN Plus Three framework and, 114; China and, 114; East Asian regional order and, 70, 114; inter-Korean Summit (2000) and, 85–86; Kim Dae Jung and, 52, 94; North Korea and, 52, 70, 82, 91; Perry Process and, 91; South Korea and, 52, 91, 94, 114, 117; United States and, 70

Mosaddeq, Mohammad, 127

Mount Keumkang (North Korea), 84–85

Mubarak, Hosni, 136

Murayama Tomiichi, 17, 70, 73, 85

Nakasone Yasuhiro, 117

Nakatani Gen, 113

Nasr, Vali, 129

National Association for the Rescue of Japanese Kidnapped by North Korea, 73

National Defense Planning Guidance (NDPG, 1992), 32–33

National Movement for Normalization of Japan-DPRK Relations (Nitcho Kokko Sokushin Kokumin Kyokai), 73

National Security Strategy (United States, 2002), 31–32, 34–35

National Security Strategy (United States, 2010), 1, 177n1

The National Strategy to Combat Weapons of Mass Destruction (United States, 2002), 35, 156 neo-conservatives, 30–32, 123

Netanyahu, Benjamin: election (2012) and, 136; on Iran's nuclear program, 135–36, 171, 173; U.S.-Iran relations and, 18

New Defense Program Outline (NDPO, Japan), 118–19

New Frontier Party (South Korea), 18, 166

New Party Sakigake, 82

New Security Concept (NSC, China), 62

New Zealand, 119

Nippon Kaigi (Japanese nationalist organization), 73

Noda Yoshihiko, 75, 169

Nonaka Hiromu, 85

nonproliferation. *See also* nuclear proliferation: Bush Administration's "counterproliferation" approach and, 16, 32, 34–36, 39–40, 43–44, 47, 99, 105, 122–23, 125, 147, 150, 156, 158–60; Cold War and, 34; demand-side approach to, 155–56; International Atomic Energy Agency and, 128, 141; international regime of, 3–4, 7, 10, 23–24, 29, 31, 34–36, 38, 79, 102, 128–29, 141, 148; Nuclear Nonproliferation Treaty (NPT) and, 4, 23, 29, 34, 38, 79, 102, 129; United States and, 1, 7, 10, 15–16, 19, 27, 29, 31–40, 43–44, 46–47, 57, 71, 76–79, 87, 89, 99, 102–3, 105, 121–25, 128–29, 146–47, 149–50, 155–60, 165, 168, 172–75, 227n41

Nordpolitik (South Korea's foreign policy initiative), 54

North Atlantic Treaty Organization (NATO), 93, 130, 134, 142–43

Northeast Asia. *See also* East Asia: Four Party Talks and, 80; nuclear nonproliferation in, 65; Pyongyang Declaration (2002) and, 72; regionalism in, 69, 72, 117; regional order in, 12, 62, 70, 72–73, 104–5, 110–12, 121, 156, 162

North Korea: abduction of Japanese citizens by, 41, 50, 53, 55, 71, 73–75, 118, 151–52, 169, 231n39; Agreed Framework (1994) with United States and, 4, 38, 44, 70, 79, 82, 88, 102, 108, 158; Basic Agreement (1991) with South Korea and, 54; *Cheonan* sinking (2010) and, 59; China and, 12–13, 17–18, 22, 24–25, 28–30, 42–44, 46, 48–49, 52, 54–55, 60, 62–67, 79, 81, 84–85, 93, 96, 103–5, 110–11, 115, 149, 151, 156, 159, 162, 165, 167–68, 185n85, 186n87, 193n104; East Asian regional order and, 1–19, 21–31, 40–44, 47–53, 55–58, 60, 62, 64–65, 70, 76–80, 87, 90–92, 94–98, 107–9, 114–15, 146–54, 156–58, 161–62, 165–67, 224n2; Four Party Talks and, 80, 87, 207n31; International Atomic and Energy Agency (IAEA) and, 29–30; Japan and, 12–13, 16–18, 22, 24–25, 28–31, 41–44, 48, 50–53, 55, 62, 69–75, 77–82, 85, 88, 91, 93, 96, 99, 102–5, 107–8, 112, 115–16, 119–23, 135–36, 149, 151–52, 168–70, 186n87, 192n89, 195n1, 208n50, 231n39; Kaesung Industrial Zone in, 49, 56, 59, 104, 167; Libya and, 42; missiles and missile tests in, 1, 6, 8, 17, 21, 24, 27, 37, 55, 70–71, 74, 76–77, 82–84, 87–89, 96–97, 159, 168–69, 174; National Defense Policy Guidelines (1992) and, 32; Nuclear Nonproliferation Treaty (NPT) and, 4, 23, 29, 38, 79, 102; nuclear proliferation and, 1–5, 5–117, 7–10, 11, 12, 14–17, 19, 22–31, 36–39, 41–42, 44, 47–50, 53, 57, 60, 62, 64–65, 70–72, 74, 76–79, 81–82, 87–89, 95, 97–98, 100, 102–5, 109–10, 112, 121, 124, 146–52, 157–61, 165–69, 174–75, 193n104, 227n44; nuclear tests in, 1, 5, 22–23, 50, 53, 64–65, 74, 112, 121, 159, 168; Perry Process and, 77–78, 83–84, 86–87, 97; Proliferation Security Initiative and, 44; refugees from,

8; Russia and, 52, 81; sanctions against, 1, 27, 29–30, 65, 74, 82–83, 121, 170, 178n11, 178n16; September 11, 2001 terrorist attacks and, 37; Six Party Talks and, 5, 39, 42, 74, 103, 116; South Korea and, 8, 12–13, 16–18, 21–22, 24–25, 28–31, 37, 41, 43–44, 48, 52–59, 66, 75, 77–81, 84–91, 96, 100–104, 107–10, 115, 117, 121, 133, 148–49, 151, 158, 164, 166–67, 186n87, 208n50, 224n2; United States and, 2, 4–7, 9, 14–17, 21–22, 24–32, 35–40, 42–48, 50, 54–58, 63, 65, 72, 74–89, 92–93, 97–109, 114, 116, 118, 121–22, 147–52, 154–55, 157–59, 162, 165, 167–68, 170, 174–75, 178n16, 186n87, 188n2, 189n17, 207n31, 208n50, 217n129, 231n39; U.S.-DPRK Joint Communiqué (2000) and, 86–87, 89, 97; World War II and, 62; Yeonpyong Island shelling (2010) and, 66; Yongbyon nuclear reactor in, 4, 30, 38, 79, 121–22, 174

Nuclear Nonproliferation Treaty (NPT): Additional Protocol of, 129; Iran and, 23, 129; North Korea and, 4, 23, 29, 38, 79, 102; successes of, 34

Nuclear Posture Review (United States, 1994), 35

Nuclear Posture Review (United States, 2002), 35, 38, 105

nuclear proliferation. *See also* nonproliferation: dominant domestic coalitions' impact on, 7–8; East Asian regional perspectives on, 6–10, 16–17, 19, 24, 41, 44, 76, 79, 147–51, 156–58, 160, 166, 174; ideational factors and, 10, 149; international status factors and, 11, 41, 129; Iran and, 1–4, 6–10, 13–14, 22–24, 28, 124–26, 128–30, 133–36, 139–40, 145–51, 159–61, 165–66, 168, 174–75, 227n41; Middle East regional perspectives on, 6–8, 10, 24, 124,

146–49, 151, 156–57, 160, 166, 174; North Korea and, 1–5, 7–10, 12, 14–17, 19, 22–31, 36–39, 41–42, 44, 47–50, 53, 57, 60, 62, 64–65, 70–72, 74, 76–79, 81–82, 87–89, 95, 97–98, 100, 102–5, 109–10, 112, 115–17, 121, 124, 146–52, 157–61, 165–69, 174–75, 193n104, 227n44; regional order dynamics and, 1–4, 6–7, 9–10, 12, 16–17, 24; terrorism and, 31, 36; United States *National Security Strategy* (2010) on, 1

Nye Initiative, 5–6, 68

Obama, Barack: Iran and, 9, 136, 159–60, 165, 173, 227n41, 227n44; nonproliferation doctrine and, 125, 159–60; North Korea and, 159, 165, 174; "pivot to Asia" strategy and, 2, 158

Obuchi Keizo: Clinton and, 90; East Asian regional balance and, 82; Kim Dae Jung and, 52, 90–91; North Korea and, 70, 84–85, 96; Perry Process and, 84; South Korea and, 90–91; United States and, 90

Odom, William, 158

Ogilvie-White, Tanya, 8

O'Hanlon, Michael, 153

Okonogi, Masao, 72, 117

Oman: civil war in, 134, 141; Egypt and, 141; Gulf Cooperation Council (GCC) and, 141, 144, 172; Iran and, 6, 13, 134, 140–42, 144–45, 172–74; Iraq and, 141; Middle East regional order and, 13, 144–45; role congruence in, 172; Saudi Arabia and, 141; United States and, 142, 172

Omnibus Consolidated and Emergency Supplemental Act (United States), 83

Ozal, Turgut, 131

Ozawa Ichiro, 74

P5+1 Talks on Iran's nuclear program, 124, 171, 173–74

Pahlavi, Reza. *See* Shah of Iran

interest formation and, 10–11, 152; nuclear nonproliferation and, 149–50, 157, 165, 174; Perry Process and, 77, 97; regional order and, 19–20, 23, 25–26, 152–55; role conflict and, 14–22, 25, 99–100, 103–4, 106, 108, 111, 116, 119, 122–23, 128, 132, 142, 144, 147–49, 151, 157, 159, 162, 164; role congruence and, 15, 21–22, 25, 53, 78, 82–83, 85, 88–89, 91, 121, 147, 149, 152, 155, 157–58, 162–63, 165, 172–73; in South Korea, 25, 51, 53–59, 100, 103–4, 107–9, 111–12, 120, 123, 149, 151, 159, 166; threat perception and, 10–11, 17–18, 25, 33, 149–53; in Turkey, 130–34, 143–45, 172

Republican Party (United States), 82, 121

Republic of Korea. *See* South Korea

Reus-Smit, Christian, 32

Rice, Condoleezza: East Asia and, 28, 113; North Korea and, 28, 38, 40, 100

rogues. *See* global rogues; rogue states

rogue states: Bolton on, 40; incentive structures for, 156; Iran as, 1, 35, 148; Iraq as, 31; North Korea as, 1, 35, 148; *Nuclear Posture Review* (1994) on, 35; nuclear proliferation and, 33, 36; Rumsfeld on, 82; September 11, 2001 terrorist attacks and renewed emphasis on, 25, 27, 33–34, 36, 150

Roh Moo-hyun: China and, 59, 110, 112, 114; Hu Jintao and, 110; Japan and, 114; Koizumi and, 107, 114; North Korea and, 17, 41, 43–44, 49, 55–56, 58, 103–4, 107–8, 117, 121; "Peace and Prosperity policy" and, 55; regional order and, 12, 17, 41, 44, 58, 103–4, 108, 111–12, 114, 123; second inter-Korean summit (2007) and, 121; Six Party Talks and, 5; United States and, 111, 114

Roh Tae-woo, 54

role conflict: agency *versus* structure questions in, 14–15; Bush Doctrine and, 23, 99–100, 103, 106, 149, 151, 157, 164; in China, 162; domestic policy elites and, 14, 17–22, 25; in East Asia, 15–18, 21–23, 25, 99–100, 103–4, 106, 108–9, 111, 116, 119, 122–23, 147–49, 151–52, 155, 159, 162, 164; in the European Union, 14; in the Middle East, 18–19, 22–23, 128, 132, 142, 144, 147–49, 155; in pan-Arabism, 14; in the Persian Gulf, 18–19; Six Party Talks and, 16–17; United States and, 157

role congruence: in East Asia, 21–23, 25, 53, 78, 82, 88–89, 97, 121, 147, 149, 152, 155, 157, 162–63; Korean Energy Development Organization (KEDO) and, 88–89; in the Middle East, 147, 149, 155, 157, 172–73; nuclear nonproliferation and, 157, 165; Perry Process and, 21, 23, 78, 83–86, 97, 149, 152; regional order and, 149; Six Party Talks and, 121, 152; Trilateral Coordination and Oversight Group (TCOG) and, 91; United States and, 157–59

Ross, Dennis, 39

Roth, Stanley, 83

Rouhani, Hassan, 160, 172–73

Rozman, Gilbert, 9, 114

Rumsfeld, Donald, 35–36, 38–39, 82

Russia: East Asia regional order and, 65, 70, 81, 95; Iran and, 126, 134; North Korea and, 52, 81; South Korea and, 2, 52; Turkey and, 132; United States and, 112

Ryoo Kihl-jae, 59

Sabah, Muhammad al-, 140

Sakakibara Eisuke, 69

Samore, Gary, 9

Samuels, Richard, 18

Sano Toshio, 169

Saudi Arabia: Bahrain and, 138, 172; Egypt and, 129, 137; Gulf Cooperation Council and, 140–41, 144, 172; Iran and, 6, 19, 129–30, 137–39, 141, 144–46, 171–73; Iraq and, 130, 137, 139; Lebanon and, 137, 172; Middle East regional order and, 4, 19, 137–38, 145, 171, 173; oil production in, 126; Oman and, 141; Shia Muslims in, 6, 137–38, 145; Sunni Islam promoted by, 19, 137, 145; Syria and, 171; United States and, 4, 19, 129, 138, 144–46, 171, 185n83; Wahhabist monarchy in, 137

Schweller, Randall, 20

Security Council. *See* United Nations Security Council

Senkaku Islands, 118, 169

September 11, 2001 terrorist attacks: North Korea's response to, 37; rogue states as policy priority following, 25, 27, 33–34, 36, 150; weapons of mass destruction (WMD) as policy priority following, 25, 27–29, 31–32, 34–36

Sezer, Ahmet Necdet, 132–33

Shah of Iran, 2, 126, 141

Shalikashvili, John, 79

Shangri-La Dialogue (2002), 113

Sha Zhukang, 93

Sherman, Wendy, 83

Shevchenko, Alexei, 11

Shia Muslims: in Bahrain, 6, 137–38, 145, 172; Iran's ties with international communities of, 6, 19, 129, 137, 144–45, 224n2; in Iraq, 137; Israel and, 135; in Kuwait, 138; in Saudi Arabia, 6, 137–38, 145; Sunni Muslims' rivalry with, 125, 129, 145, 172

Sick, Gary, 126–27

Siniora, Fouad, 137

Sino-Japanese War (1894), 62

Six Party Talks: abduction of Japanese citizens by North Korea as issue at, 151–52; alliance politics and, 46, 156; China and, 5, 11, 22, 52, 60, 63–64, 81, 103, 105–6, 110, 118, 123; East Asian regional order and, 12, 16–17, 22, 45–47, 64, 74, 105–6, 115, 118, 123, 147–48, 155–56; Japan and, 5, 12, 72, 74, 103, 151–52; North Korea and, 5, 39, 42, 74, 103, 116; role congruence at, 121, 152; South Korea and, 5, 42, 107; stalemates at, 16–17, 22, 63, 73, 103, 112, 118; Symposium on Northeast Asian Security Cooperation and the Six Party Talks and, 117; Trilateral Coordination and Oversight Group (TCOG) and, 108; United States and, 5, 16, 22, 38–39, 42, 44–46, 103, 107, 121, 147–48, 155; Yongbyon facility closure and, 178n11

Social Democratic Party (Japan), 81–82

Solingen, Etel, 7–8, 177n7, 179n20

Song Minsun, 121–22

South Korea: Agreed Framework (United States and North Korea, 1994) and, 4, 79; ASEAN Plus Three framework and, 12, 21, 92–94, 114–15, 119; Basic Agreement (1991) with North Korea, 54; *Cheonan* sinking (2010) and, 59, 166; China and, 2, 16, 21, 54–55, 58–59, 66, 78, 93–95, 100, 107, 109–11, 114–18, 123, 160, 164, 166–67; domestic political debates in, 57–59, 131–32, 166–67, 186n87; East Asian regional order and, 4, 11–13, 16–18, 21–22, 25, 28–31, 41–44, 48, 52, 54, 56, 58–59, 65, 70, 79–81, 85, 89, 93, 95, 97, 103–4, 106, 108–9, 111–12, 114–17, 160, 165–68; elections (2010–2012) in, 59, 166–67; Four Party Talks and, 80; inter-Korean nationalism *(minjok gongjo)* and, 56–58; Iraq War and, 107; Japan and, 16, 21–22, 30–31, 41, 43, 47, 51–52, 54–55, 62, 69–70, 78, 80, 89–91, 93–94, 102, 107–9, 113–18,

63, 65, 72, 74–89, 92–93, 97–109,
114, 116, 118, 121–22, 147–52,
154–55, 157–59, 162, 165,
167–68, 170, 174–75, 178n16,
186n87, 188n2, 189n17, 207n31,
208n50, 217n129, 231n39;
Nuclear Posture Review (1994) and,
35; *Nuclear Posture Review* (2002)
in, 35, 38, 105; Perry Process and,
77–78, 83–84, 89, 97, 106, 151,
155; role conflict in, 157; role
congruence in, 157–59; Russia
and, 112; Saudi Arabia and, 4, 19,
129, 138, 144–46, 171, 185n83;
South Korea and, 4–5, 16, 18,
21–22, 28–31, 42–46, 51–58, 64,
77–80, 84–91, 93, 95, 100–102,
104, 106–12, 114, 122–23,
148–49, 158–60, 166–67; Taiwan
and, 60–61, 119–20; Taiwan
Strait Crisis (1995–1996) and, 6;
Trilateral Coordination and
Oversight Group (TCOG) and, 21,
78, 90, 97, 100, 107–8, 116, 154;
Turkey and, 13, 19, 22, 130–34,
142–44, 148, 159; U.S.-DPRK
Joint Communiqué (2000) and,
86–87, 89, 97
Uri Party (South Korea), 110
U.S.-DPRK Joint Communiqué (2000),
86–87, 89, 97, 101
U.S.-Japan Defense Cooperation
Guidelines, 6, 68

Vogel, Ezra, 97

Wada Haruki, 72
Walt, Stephen, 40, 163
Wang Jiarui, 66–67
Wang Yi, 5
Ward, Celeste, 157

Watanabe Michio, 70
weapons of mass destruction (WMD).
See also nuclear proliferation: Iraq
and, 34–36; *The National Strategy
to Combat Weapons of Mass
Destruction* (United States, 2002),
35, 156; North Korea and, 84,
86–87, 89; Nuclear
Nonproliferation Treaty and, 34;
Perry Process and, 84; *Quadrennial
Defense Review* (United States,
2006) and, 39; September 11,
2011 terrorist attacks' impact on
U.S. policies regarding, 25, 27–29,
31–32, 34–36; supply-side issues
regarding, 155; U.S.-DPRK Joint
Communiqué (2000) and, 86–87
Wen Jiabao, 66, 114, 119
Wilkerson, Lawrence, 39
Wolfowitz, Paul, 32
World War II, Japanese colonialism in
East Asia during, 62, 67, 69–72

Xi Jinping, 22, 66, 167

Yamagata Aritomo, 69
Yamamoto Ichita, 69
Yang Jiechi, 168
Yang Sung Chul, 101
Yeonpyong Island shelling (2010), 66
Yokota Megumi, 75
Yongbyon nuclear reactor (North
Korea), 4, 30, 38, 79, 121–22, 174,
178n11, 178n16
Yoon Young Kwan, 107, 116
Yu Woo-ik, 59

Zakaria, Fareed, 42
Zarif, Mohammad Javad, 172–73
Zhang Liangui, 63
Zhu Rongji, 93–94, 114–15